MW01000624

The Max Weber Dictionary

The Max Weber Dictionary
Key Words and Central Concepts

Richard Swedberg

With the assistance of Ola Agevall

STANFORD SOCIAL SCIENCES

An imprint of Stanford University Press

Stanford, California

2005

Stanford University Press
Stanford, California
www.sup.org

© 2005 by the Board of Trustees of the Leland Stanford Junior University. All rights reserved.

No part of this book may be reproduced or transmitted in any form or by any means, electronic or mechanical, including photocopying and recording, or in any information storage or retrieval system without the prior written permission of Stanford University Press.

Library of Congress Cataloging-in-Publication Data

Swedberg, Richard.
  The Max Weber dictionary : key words and central concepts / by Richard Swedberg with the assistance of Ola Agevall.
      p.   cm.
  In English with some German.
  Includes bibliographical references.
  ISBN 0-8047-5094-7—ISBN 0-8047-5095-5 (pbk : alk. paper)
    1. Sociology—Dictionaries.   2. Weber, Max, 1864–1920.   I. Agevall, Ola.   II. Title.
HM425.S94 2005
301'.03—dc22   2004008171

Printed in the United States of America on acid-free, archival-quality paper.

Original Printing 2005

Last figure below indicates year of this printing:
14   13   12   11   10   09   08   07   06   05

Designed and typeset at Stanford University Press in 10/12 Sabon.

I have an abundance of new ideas.
—Max Weber, spring of 1920

Contents

Acknowledgments

In putting together this dictionary I have drawn on the insights of many friends and colleagues. The scholarship on Weber has been collective in nature for a long time, and a dictionary of this type is heavily dependent on the scholarship of others. My thanks go to all of the following dear friends and colleagues who have answered my many questions and in other ways supported and inspired this research: Heine Andersen, Patrik Aspers, Filippo Barbera, Margareta Bertilsson, Hinnerk Bruhns, Hans Henrik Bruun, Bruce Carruthers, Frank Dobbin, Nicolás Eilbaum, Sven Eliaeson, Daniel Kinderman, Heino Nau, Victor Nee, Ole Riis, Lawrence Scaff, Alan Sica, Philippe Steiner, Keith Tribe, Stephen Turner, Sam Whimster, and Hans Zetterberg.

I am also very happy that Wendelin Reich kindly read through the whole manuscript with great care and that Ralph Schroeder suggested some new entries as well as criticized others. Two anonymous reviewers made a number of important suggestions for changes and additions. Gavin Lewis did a superb job copy-editing the manuscript. I am also grateful to Kate Wahl, Tony Hicks, and Carmen Borbon-Wu of Stanford University Press.

First and foremost, however, the help of Ola Agevall has been invaluable to me. Ola scrutinized each and every entry, suggesting something like one hundred changes altogether. Ola also wrote some new entries, such as "Deutsche Gesellschaft für Soziologie," "ethnography," "employment regime (*Arbeitsverfassung*)" and "Verein für Sozialpolitik." If Ola had been involved in this project from the beginning, the end result would no doubt have been much better. To compensate a bit for this, I have often referred to Ola's excellent study *A Science of Unique Events: Max Weber's Methodology of the Cultural Sciences* (1999).

This dictionary is dedicated to my beloved Mabel.

Ithaca and Stockholm, June 2004

How to Use This Dictionary

The immediate purpose of this dictionary is to assist the general reader in the study of Max Weber's work—and also the tired teacher who is about to lecture on Weber but does not have the time to reread *Economy and Society* before the next class. It attempts to do this by giving answers to the reader's questions, especially about the many difficult concepts that one can find in Weber's work. Weber's intellectual project can be described as a very bold attempt to lay a new and solid foundation for the cultural sciences (including the social sciences and sociology), as opposed to the natural sciences; and this means that his perspective as well as his terminology are often hard for the reader to penetrate.

The dictionary is intended to be used in the following manner. When the reader comes across some concept or key term in Weber's work that either is unfamiliar or requires further explanation, the dictionary will hopefully supply the answer. It contains information on how Weber defines a specific concept, where he uses it, where it has been discussed in the secondary literature, and which other entries in the dictionary may be of assistance.

A typical entry begins with a short summary of what a concept means in Weber's work. This is followed by Weber's definition (if one exists), some explication, and a few references to secondary literature. The following example will illustrate what has just been said.

> **custom (*Sitte*)**   There exist certain forms of regular behavior, according to Weber, which are important to sociology: custom, self-interest, and usage.
>
> Weber introduces the notion of his three types of "empirical uniformities" in his general sociology in Ch. 1 of *Economy and Society*. A custom is defined as "usage . . . based upon long standing" (ES:29; cf. ES:319). Usage, in its turn, is defined in the following way: "if an orientation toward social action occurs regularly, it will be called 'us-

age' insofar as the probability of its existence within a group is based on nothing but actual practice" (ibid.).

Weber also notes that "adherence to what has as such become customary is . . . a strong component of all conduct and, consequently, of all social action" (ES:320). Custom differs from convention in that it lacks a sanction; the border between the two, however, is fluid (ibid.; cf. SCIS:170).

An important theme in Weber's sociology is that of traditionalism: how it is maintained and how it is broken, through charisma, instrumentally rational action, and otherwise. In *The Protestant Ethic* Weber refers, for example, to "the stone wall of habit" (PE:62).

For a discussion of Weber's concept of habit, including its relationship to disposition (*Eingestelltheit*), see Charles Camic, "The Matter of Habit" (1986), pp. 1057–66. For an argument that *Sitten* should be translated as "mores," see Johannes Raum, "Reflections on Max Weber's Thoughts Concerning Ethnic Groups" (1995), p. 80.

See also habitus, self-interest or self-interested kind of behavior, traditional action, traditionalism, usage

In each entry the concept or key term is given in English, followed by the German equivalent in parentheses. In many cases, the German equivalent also appears as a separate entry, with a cross-reference (Sitte. *See* custom). In choosing definitions from Weber's work priority has been given to his definitions in Ch. 1 of *Economy and Society*, "Basic Sociological Terms." If Weber also discusses the entry in the first version of this text, "Some Categories of Interpretive Sociology" (1913), this has been noted as well. Weber made a huge effort toward the end of his career to develop a new kind of sociology, and I have decided to prioritize this effort in the dictionary.

My own identity as a sociologist has no doubt also played a role in this choice. I also would argue, however, that Weber's sociology represents a formidable intellectual achievement. Weber did not, like say Durkheim or Marx, decide very early in his career that he wanted to construct a new type of sociology, and then steadily work in this direction. Instead Weber tried various approaches till he was in his forties, at which point he decided to pull together a number of different ideas to create a totally new type of sociology that he termed *interpretive sociology*.

When Weber's main works are referred to in the text, abbreviations are used. *Economy and Society*, for example, is referred to as ES, and *The Protestant Ethic and the Spirit of Capitalism* as PE. A full list of abbreviations can be found at the beginning of this dictionary.

I have tried to use the standard translations of Weber's works into English, since these are the most easily available and also the ones that contain formulations with which many readers are likely to be familiar. I have typically used the following works: *Economy and Society* (trans. Ephraim Fischoff et al.), *From Max Weber* (trans. Hans H. Gerth), *The Methodology of the Social Sciences* (ed. and trans. Edward Shils and Henry Finch) and *The Protestant Ethic and the Spirit of Capitalism* (trans. Talcott Parsons).

The reader should be aware, however, that new and usually better translations of many of these works have recently come into being. The crucial first chapter of *Economy and Society* has, for example, just been retranslated by Keith Tribe (EW:311–58). There also exist new translations of *The Protestant Ethic* (by Peter Baehr, Gordon Wells, and Stephen Kalberg) and of many of the texts in *From Max Weber* and *The Methodology of the Social Sciences* (see especially *Political Writings* and *The Essential Weber*, with translations by Ronald Speirs, Keith Tribe, and Sam Whimster). For more information on the translations of Weber, the reader is referred to the entry "translations of Weber's works."

After the definition in an entry, there is typically a sentence or two with material that adds to the understanding of the definition or of how Weber used the concept. In choosing secondary literature, I have in the great majority of cases given preference to references in English. I use references in German only if there does not exist some adequate or equivalent text in English. Since the dictionary is primarily intended to be used by English-speaking readers, it seems natural to concentrate on the secondary literature in that language. A Weber dictionary in German would no doubt look somewhat different, both in terms of entries and in terms of the secondary literature referred to.

In choosing the secondary literature, I have tried to be selective and not to overload the entries. This means that I have drawn heavily on work by well-known experts on Weber, from Alexander von Schelting and Raymond Aron yesterday to their equivalents today. The secondary literature on Weber is enormous and difficult to navigate for a single person, so I would be grateful for comments and corrections, when I have made a mistake or a less than happy choice (rs328@cornell.edu).

The secondary literature is referred to in abbreviated form in the text of the entries. For the full details the reader is referred to the reference list at the end of the dictionary.

I also discuss the difficulties involved in translating Weber's concepts from the original German into English. How to translate Weber is an often discussed issue in the secondary literature (see e.g. Roth, "Interpreting and Translating Max Weber" [1992]; see also the symposium on translating *The Protestant Ethic* in *Max Weber Studies* 1, 2001). By way of summarizing my own position on this issue, I want to emphasize that there is definitely a need to know more about the way in which Weber himself understood various terms, and also about how they were understood by scholars in his academic environment. Where this type of information is available, I have tried to summarize or cite it. No doubt it would be preferable if everyone who read Weber's work were able to do so in the original, but in the meantime readers unfamiliar with German may benefit from discussions about how to translate some of Weber's concepts into English. I should also say that I agree wholeheartedly with my colleague Hans Henrik Bruun that while Weber often supplies definitions of various key terms, his use of a specific concept may vary within one and the same text and can typically not be decided once and for all. Finally, many of Weber's concepts are linked to one another and/or are easier to understand if the reader also is also familiar with other concepts; and for this reason, each entry ends with cross-references.

Besides entries for concepts that are typically associated with Weber's name (such as "charisma" and "domination"), I have also included entries on topics which Weber interpreted and recast in an innovative manner and which the reader may therefore be interested in knowing more about (such as "capitalism" and "salvation"). It is this type of entry that I have designated as key words in the subtitle to this dictionary. To decide which terms of this type to include and which to omit has often been difficult.

Entries have also been added in some cases for terms in Weber's work simply because the average reader may find them useful. I have, for example, included a few entries for uncommon terms that Weber uses (such as "lytric" and "autocephalous"). The reader may also wonder what Weber thought of "norms" and "institutions," two terms that are often used in today's sociology; and entries have therefore been added for these. Since it is my guess that some readers may expect this dictionary to include entries for Weber's life as well as his main works, I have included such entries—as well as a few others that I hope readers may find useful (such as "neo-Kantianism" and "Marxism"). Several entries, finally, give information on the impact of Weber's ideas on today's social science, especially sociology (such as "neo-Weberianism," "secondary literature on Weber's work," and "Weber-inspired scholars and scholarship").

It should finally be emphasized that while much of Weber's work is extremely creative, large parts are still relatively unknown. It is my hope that this dictionary will be of assistance in laying bare some of this creativity and will also make Weber's work better known.

Abbreviations

The following abbreviations of frequently cited works of Max Weber are used throughout the dictionary. Full bibliographical details are given in the reference list.

AJ	*Ancient Judaism* ([1921] 1952).
ASAC	*Agrarian Sociology of Ancient Civilizations* ([1909] 1976)
CS	*Critique of Stammler* ([1907] 1977)
EES	*Essays in Economic Sociology* (1999c)
ES	*Economy and Society* ([1922] 1978)
EW	*The Essential Weber* (2004)
GAR	*Gesammelte Aufsätze zur Religionssoziologie* ([1920–21] 1988)
GASS	*Gesammelte Aufsätze zur Soziologie und Sozialpolitik* ([1924] 1988b)
GASW	*Gesammelte Aufsätze zur Sozial-und Wirtschaftsgeschichte* ([1924] 1988a)
GAW	*Gesammelte Aufsätze zur Wissenschaftslehre* ([1922] 1988)
GEH	*General Economic History* ([1923] 1981)
GM	Hans Gerth and C. Wright Mills (eds.), *From Max Weber* (1946)
GPS	*Gesammelte Politische Schriften* (1921)
GVAN	*Grundriss zu den Vorlesungen über Allgemeine ("theoretische") Nationalökonomie* ([1898] 1990)
HCP	*The History of Commercial Partnerships in the Middle Ages* ([1889] 2003)

MSS	*Essays in the Methodology of the Social Sciences* (1949)
MWG	*Max Weber Gesamtausgabe*
PE	*The Protestant Ethic and the Spirit of Capitalism* ([1904–5] 1930)
PED	David Chalcraft and Austin Harrington (eds.), *The Protestant Ethic Debate* (Chalcraft and Harrington 2001)
PW	*Political Writings* (1994b)
RC	*The Religion of China* ([1920] 1951)
RI	*The Religion of India* ([1921] 1958b)
RK	*Roscher and Knies* ([1903–6] 1975)
RSFM	*The Rational and Social Foundations of Music* (1958)
SCIS	"Some Categories of Interpretive Sociology" ([1913] 1981)
WuG	*Wirtschaft und Gesellschaft* ([1922] 1972)

The Max Weber Dictionary

*A*briss der universalen Sozial-und Wirtschaftsgeschichte (**Outline of Universal Social and Economic History**) This is the title of a course that Weber taught at the University of Munich in the winter semester of 1919–20 and which has been reconstructed (on the basis of student notes) as *General Economic History* (*Wirtschaftsgeschichte*).

See also General Economic History

accounting *See* calculation, capital accounting

acquisitive drive or instinct (*Erwerbstrieb*) This concept was sometimes used in Weber's day to explain the emergence of capitalism—an explanation that Weber was very critical of. The meaning of the term is close to what today is referred to as the profit motive.

In an often cited passage in his sociology of religion Weber emphasizes that "the impulse to acquisition . . . has in itself nothing to do with capitalism" (PE:17). He further states that this impulse has existed in many different groups and countries, but that "it should be taught in the kindergarten of cultural history that this naïve idea of capitalism [as the result of the acquisitive drive] must be given up once and for all."

The reason that it is wrong to identify capitalism with the acquisitive drive is primarily that capitalism is not psychological in nature, but a set of social relations and institutions. To cite from Weber's lecture course in economic history of 1919–20: "if the economic impulse in itself is universal, it is an interesting question as to the relations under which it becomes rationalized and rationally tempered in such a fashion as to produce rational institutions of the character of capitalist production" (GEH:356). In brief, one cannot deduce economic institutions (or a whole economic system) from psychological concepts (cf. MSS:88–9).

In the debate over *The Protestant Ethic* Weber said that "the standard expression 'acquisitive drive' . . . stems from an otherwise long-out-moded school of psychology, but probably cannot be dispensed with al-together"(PED:71–2). Some time later, however, Weber said that the concept of acquisitive drive is "wholly imprecise and better not used at all" (ES:1190–91). It may finally be mentioned that Weber made an early use of the term in his lectures in economics from the 1890s (GVAN:30).

See also capitalism

action (*Handeln*)   The importance of the concept of action to Weber's work derives from the fact that it plays a key role in his interpretive sociology.

According to Weber's well-known definition of sociology, as presented in paragraph 1 in Ch. 1 of *Economy and Society*, "sociology . . . is a science concerning itself with the interpretive understanding of social action and thereby with a causal explanation of its course and consequences" (ES:4; cf. SCIS:152). Action is defined as behavior that is invested with meaning by the actor. Action is social if it is oriented to other actors or to an order. If the element of meaning is absent, action turns into behavior. Reactive behavior may fall into this category, and traditional action may approach it. Action can be internal or external; the actor can do something, avoid doing something or have something done to him or her.

In his 1913 essay on "Some Categories of Interpretive Sociology," Weber writes that "action specially significant for interpretive sociology is, in particular, behavior that: (1) in terms of subjectively intended meaning of the actor, is related to the behavior of others, (2) is co-determined in its course through this relatedness, and thus (3) can be intelligibly explained in terms of this" (SCIS:152).

According to Talcott Parsons, who made the first translation of Ch. 1 of *Economy and Society* into English, "the terms *Handeln* [action] and *Verhalten* [behavior] are directly related." He also notes that while "*Verhalten* [behavior] is the broader term referring to any behavior of human individuals . . . [*Handeln*] refers to the concrete phenomenon of human behavior only in so far as it is capable of 'understanding', in Weber's technical sense, in terms of subjective categories" (Parsons in Weber 1947:89). While social action is usually seen as the main category in Weber's sociology, it deserves to be noted that order (*Ordnung*) is also very important. According to a happy formulation by Stefan Breuer, "Weber's sociology is both a sociology of action and a sociology of order" (Breuer 2001a:125).

In his essay of 1913 "Some Categories of Interpretive Sociology" Weber uses a different German term for "social action" than in Ch. 1 of *Economy and Society* (*Gemeinschaftshandeln* and not *soziales Handeln*).

See also behavior, interpretive sociology, meaning, order, orientation to others, social action, sociology, traditionalism

actual regularities   *See* uniformities

adequacy on the level of meaning (*Sinnadäquanz*)   *See* causality

adequate causality (*Kausaladäquanz*)   *See* causality

administration (*Verwaltung*)   One of the great themes in Weber's sociology is that of administration, that is, organizations and their staffs, including bureaucracy.

In his general sociology, as outlined in Ch. 1 of *Economy and Society*, Weber discusses organizations, including what he terms administrative organizations. An administrative organization is an organization exclusively oriented to the administrative order, that is, to the order that regulates the actions of the staff (*Verwaltungsverband*; ES:51–2).

Weber notes that the character of what constitutes a staff has changed over history, from a few ad hoc individuals to the bureaucratic staff of modern days. The main source of information on administrative staffs in Weber's work can be found in his writings on bureaucracy and domination (see especially ES:212–301, but also ES:941–1211, EES:99–108, GM:295–300). If an organization has an administrative staff, it rests to some extent on domination (ES:54).

The different types of staff that have existed throughout history have typically differed in experience, formal training, how they are paid, and with what they are paid. According to Weber, there has been always a continuous, but latent struggle between chiefs and their staffs. The capacity of a chief to control his or her staff depends partly on whether it is paid in kind, with a salary, through a fief, and so on.

For Weber's relationship to the administrative historian Otto Hintze, see Jürgen Kocka, "Otto Hintze and Max Weber: Attempts at a Comparison" (1987).

See also bureaucracy, domination, means of administration, organization or association, organization theory or organizational sociology

administrative means   *See* means of administration

advantage (*Chance*)   The German term *Chance* is used by Weber in the following two meanings in *Economy and Society*: as "advantage" or "opportunity" and as "probability."

See opportunity (*Chance* as advantage), probability (*Chance* as probability)

adventurers' capitalism (*Abenteurerkapitalismus*)   This type of capitalism has existed in all periods of history, according to Weber. It is typically irrational and speculative in nature; and it often aims at exploiting opportunities opened up by political forces. Adventurers' capitalism is usually immoral as well as traditionalistic in nature, and in many ways it is the opposite of the methodical, ethical and revolutionary type of capitalism that stands at the center of *The Protestant Ethic*.

In this latter work Weber states that "adventurers' capitalism [is] oriented to political opportunities and irrational speculation" (PE:76). He also notes that "this kind of entrepreneur, the capitalist adventurer, has existed everywhere," and that "with the exception of trade and credit and banking transactions, their activities were predominantly of an irrational and speculative character, or directed to acquisition by force, above all the acquisition of booty, whether directly in war or in the form of continuous fiscal booty by exploitation of subjects" (PE:20; cf. PE:58, 69, GEH:289, 350).

Weber notes that many of the types of capitalism that exist in the West of today, especially financial capitalism, bear the mark of adventurers' capitalism (e.g. PE:20). In terms of the typology of capitalism introduced in Ch. 2 of *Economy and Society* (rational, political, and what may be termed commercial-traditional capitalism), adventurers' capitalism is most closely related to political capitalism. Also what Weber calls robber capitalism is closely related to political capitalism and adventurers' capitalism (e.g. PW:89, GPS:322).

The term adventurers' capitalism is inspired by Georg Simmel's essay "The Adventurer" (PED:119).

See also capitalism, economic superman, political capitalism, robber capitalism

affectual action (social action that is *affektuell*)   This represents one of the four major types of social action in Weber's sociology, together with instrumentally rational action, traditional action and value-rational action. It is a type of action that is determined by the actor's emotions.

What primarily characterizes affectual action, according to Weber's general sociology in Ch. 1 of *Economy and Society*, is that it is "determined by the actor's specific affects and feeling states" (ES:25). He adds that "action is affectual if it satisfies a need for revenge, sensual gratification, devotion, contemplative bliss, or for working off emotional tensions (irrespective of the level of sublimation)" (ibid.).

Like value-rational action, affectual action is carried out for its own sake, rather than for some result. Affectual action can have its origin in an uncontrolled reaction, and thereby comes close to lacking the element of meaning (and hence to qualifying as "action" in Weber's sense; cf.

SCIS:152). It may also consist of a controlled release of emotion. Weber often groups together emotional factors with irrationality and error (e.g. ES:6, 9).

Examples of affectual action would be the mother who loses control of herself and slaps her child because of bad behavior, and the soccer player who loses his temper and hits another player (Raymond Aron, "Max Weber," [1970], p. 221).

An increasing amount of attention—and critique—has recently been directed at Weber's concept of affectual action and his view of emotions more generally. See e.g. J. M. Barbalet, "*Beruf*, Rationality and Emotion in Max Weber's Sociology" (2000).

See also body, emotions, social action

affinities   *See* elective affinities

Agrarian Sociology of Ancient Civilizations, The ("**Agrarverhältnisse im Altertum**," trans. 1976)   This book-length study originally appeared as an article in 1909 in *Handwörterbuch der Staatswissenschaften* (for earlier and considerably shorter versions, see Weber 1897, 1898). Its main focus is on the social and economic structure of a series of countries in antiquity. These include not only Greece and Rome, but also Egypt, Israel and Mesopotamia.

The English edition of this work also contains Weber's important essay "The Social Causes of the Decline of Ancient Civilization" (1896).

According to Marianne Weber, *The Agrarian Sociology* can be characterized as "a sort of sociology of antiquity—a historical analysis and conceptual penetration of all important structural forms of the social life of classical antiquity" (Marianne Weber [1926] 1975:329). Weber also addresses the issue of the extent to which the categories of modern economic analysis are applicable to pre-capitalist conditions.

For a general discussion of Weber's study, which is of much interest not only to sociologists but also to historians and economic historians, see e.g. Arnaldo Momigliano, "The Instruments of Decline" (1977); R. I. Frank, "Translator's Introduction," pp. 7–33 in *The Agrarian Sociology of Ancient Civilizations*; and Hinnerk Bruhns, "À propos de l'histoire ancienne et de l'économie politique chez Max Weber" (1998). For the reception of this work during Weber's lifetime, see e.g. Dirk Käsler, *Max Weber* (1988), pp. 199–200.

"Agrarverhältnisse im Altertum"   See *Agrarian Sociology of Ancient Civilizations, The*

aktuelles Verstehen (**direct observational understanding**)   *See* understanding

alienation   *See* depersonalization

Alltag   *See* everyday life

America   *See* United States

Amt   *See* office

Amtscharisma (**charisma of office**)   *See* charisma

Ancient Judaism (*Das antike Judentum*; trans. 1952)   This study by Weber is part of his huge work *The Economic Ethics of the World Religions*, and the German original first appeared in 1917–20. The basic question that Weber attempts to address in this work is the historical importance of ancient Judaism for modern Western culture. The work contains major sections on the following topics: the background of ancient Judaism (Part I); the covenant and confederacy (Part II); priesthood, cult and ethics (Part III); the establishment of the Jewish pariah people (Part IV); and the Pharisees (Part V—Supplement).

   Ancient Judaism has been translated by Hans Gerth and Don Martindale, on the basis of the text in Vol. 3 of Weber's *Gesammelte Aufsätze zur Religionssoziologie*.

   For a summary of the content of *Ancient Judaism*, see e.g. Reinhard Bendix, *Max Weber: An Intellectual Portrait* (1960), pp. 200–56, and Dirk Käsler, *Max Weber* (1988), pp. 127–36.

   For its early reception, see Käsler, *Max Weber*, p. 206. For a discussion, see e.g. Tony Fahey, "Max Weber's *Ancient Judaism*" (1982), Harvey Sacks, "Max Weber's *Ancient Judaism*" (1999) and John Love, "Max Weber's *Ancient Judaism*" (2000). See also Wolfgang Schluchter (ed.), *Max Webers Studie über das antike Judentum* (1981).

   A new edition of *Ancient Judaism*, together with introductory and editorial material, will appear as MWG, Vol. I/21.

   See also *Collected Essays in the Sociology of Religion, Economic Ethics of the World Religions, The; Protestant Ethic and the Spirit of Capitalism, The; Religion of China, The; Religion of India, The*

Anstalt   This term has several meanings in Weber's work: as "compulsory organization or association" and "institution" in his general sociology (ES:52; EW:354) and as the legal concept of "institution" in his sociology of law (e.g. ES:714–15).

   See also compulsory organization

Anstaltsgnade (**institutional grace**)   *See* salvation

anthropology   It is possible to speak of Weber's relationship to anthropology in the old-fashioned sense of the word, and to argue that a special view of human nature underlies his work. "Behind the particular 'action' stands the human being," to cite one of Weber's methodological essays (MSS:38).

Weber does not explicitly propose a view of human nature, but his opinion may nonetheless be distilled from various writings. He appears, for example, to have regarded the capacity to assign values and meaning to things, as well as the capacity to orient oneself to other people, as part of human nature. There are also "the metaphysical needs of the human mind," that is, the existential needs (as we might say today) to understand the world and assign a meaning to it (ES:499).

At one point in his sociology, Weber refers, for example, to the fact that people who are successful in life also want to feel that they deserve this as a "universal phenomenon . . . rooted in certain basic psychological patterns" ("theodicy of good fortune"; cf. ES:491).

Weber occasionally refers explicitly to human nature, as in his Freiburg inaugural lecture of 1895: "we do not want to breed well-being in people, but rather those characteristics which we think of as constituting the human greatness and nobility of our nature (*Natur*)" (PW:15; GPS:13). Elsewhere Weber notes, for example, that among "the most fundamental and universal components" of human behavior are "sexual love," "economic interest" and "the social drives toward power and prestige" (ES:601). Other passages of a similar type may be cited as well.

Talcott Parsons notes in one of his comments on Weber's sociology of religion that "Weber postulates a basic 'drive' toward meaning" (Parsons 1963:xlvii). For an attempt to reconstruct Weber's anthropology, see e.g. Wilhelm Hennis, *Max Weber's Science of Man* (2000).

See also body, ethnography (for Weber's relationship to modern anthropology), human beings, type of human beings

antike Judentum, Das   See *Ancient Judaism*

Antikritiken   This term refers to Weber's articles responding to some of the critics of *The Protestant Ethic* (1904–5), published during 1907–10. For translations of these articles, see PED and Weber [1904–5] 2002a:221–339; and for the original German texts, see e.g. Johannes Winkelmann (ed.), *Die Protestantische Ethik II: Kritiken und Antikritiken* (1978).

Antrieb   See *psychological or religious premium*

appropriation (*Appropriation*)   To appropriate something means essentially to exclude others from it and monopolize it. From a sociological viewpoint, appropriation represents a form of closed social relationship, and it plays a key role in Weber's general sociology as well as in his economic sociology.

Appropriation is discussed in connection with the section on open and closed social relationships in Weber's general sociology in Ch. 1 of *Economy and Society*. Weber here describes appropriation as "ways in which it is possible for a closed social relationship to guarantee its monopolized advantages to the parties" (ES:44).

Weber reserves the term "right" (*Recht*) for the situation where (1) opportunities have become monopolized on a permanent basis, through a closed social relationship, and (2) are more or less alienable (ES:44). To own something, to sell something, and to inherit something, all presuppose different forms of rights in this sense.

Ch. 2 of *Economy and Society*, in which Weber's economic sociology is to be found, contains elaborate typologies of different forms of appropriation (ES:125–38, 144–50; see also GEH:26–50). Status, finally, involves "monopolistic appropriation" of privileged modes of acquisition (ES:306).

See also means of administration, means of production, means of war, open and closed social relationships, opportunity, property

Arbeitsverfassung   See employment regime

Archiv für Sozialwissenschaft und Sozialpolitik   Weber was one of the editors of this journal from 1904 to his death in 1920. Thanks to Weber, as well as to editors such as Werner Sombart and Joseph Schumpeter, the *Archiv* soon became the leading social science journal in Germany.

Many of Weber's own studies appeared in this journal, including *The Protestant Ethic and the Spirit of Capitalism*.

The tasks of the *Archiv* are spelled out in Weber's essay on objectivity of 1904 (MSS:49–112, EW:359–404). Its "prime task" is described as follows: "the scientific investigation of *the general cultural significance of the social-economic structure of human communal life* and its historical forms of organization" (EW:370; emphasis in the original).

For an introduction to the *Archiv*, as well as an index to the articles that appeared in it before its demise in 1933, see Regis Factor, *Guide to the Archiv für Sozialwissenschaft und Sozialpolitik Group 1904–1933* (1988).

See also *Deutsche Gesellschaft für Soziologie* (German Sociological Association)

army   See means of war

art   See sociology of art

ascetic Protestantism (*asketischer Protestantismus*)   According to Weber, some types of Protestantism have an important ascetic component, such as Calvinism, Pietism, Methodism and the Baptist sects. These all played a key role in the formation and spread of the modern capitalist spirit from the sixteenth century onwards (see the chapter "The Religious Foundations of Worldly Asceticism" in *The Protestant Ethic*; PE:95–154).

What made this type of religion so congenial to rational capitalism, Weber famously argues in *The Protestant Ethic*, were the following: the role that it attributed to work as a calling (*Beruf*), its positive attitude to wealth as a sign of God's benevolence, and its ascetic and activist approach not only to the economy but to life in general.

Some additional factors are also important. For example, Protestants, unlike Catholics, could not go to confession but were directly responsible to God for their sins. The Catholic Church also relied much more heavily on priests to mediate between the religious layperson and God, something that made this type of Christianity less independent and more authoritarian than ascetic Protestantism.

That the ascetic Protestants were often gathered together in sects also meant that their religious ideas had more of an impact than they would have had in a church. This argument is especially elaborated upon in "The Protestant Sects and the Spirit of Capitalism" (GM:302–22).

In an often cited letter to Adolf von Harnack of February 5, 1906, Weber notes that "our nation has never in any way experienced the school of hard asceticism. . . . This is the source of all that I find contemptible in it (as in myself)" (Mommsen 1984:94; MWG II/5:32–3).

See Wolfgang Schluchter, "The Role of the Reformation in the Transition to Modernity," pp. 139–74 in *The Rise of Western Rationalism* (1981); and Ernst Troeltsch, *Protestantism and Progress* (1912). For the debate over Weber's argument about the link between ascetic Protestantism and the spirit of modern capitalism, *see* Weber thesis. Weber's writings on "ascetic Protestantism and capitalism" are scheduled to appear as MWG, Vol. I/9.

See also asceticism, Calvinism, Catholicism, Christianity, Protestantism, *The Protestant Ethic and the Spirit of Capitalism*, Weber thesis, Puritanism, sect

asceticism (*Askese*)   Weber devotes much attention in his sociology of religion to asceticism and mysticism as contrasting ways of reaching salvation (e.g. GM:324–26, ES:544–51).

He also singles out asceticism in *The Protestant Ethic* as the main social mechanism that made religious behavior influence economic behavior.

Asceticism can be defined as abstention and restraint, carried out in a systematic manner. While the ascetic, according to Weber, sees himself or herself as *an instrument* for the will of God, the mystic sees himself or herself as *a vessel*. Asceticism in the area of religion may also spread to other areas of society, including the economy—and the way that this happened in the West, via the religious concept of vocation (*Beruf*), constitutes the main theme of *The Protestant Ethic*. In Weber's colorful formulation: "Christian asceticism . . . now strode into the market-place of life, slammed the door of the monastery behind it, and undertook to penetrate [the] daily routine of life" (PE:154; cf. 181).

One may conceptualize asceticism, Weber notes, as "a rational method of living" (RI:220). Asceticism can be *inner-worldly* (*innerweltliche Askese*) or *other-worldly* (*ausserweltliche Askese*). The former means that the believer uses ascetic means and also that he or she aims to change the world according to his or her beliefs. In other-worldly asceticism the believer also uses ascetic means, but does not want to change the world. Calvinism is an example of inner-worldly asceticism and monasticism of other-worldly asceticism.

There exists an affinity between asceticism and discipline—a topic to which Weber paid much attention.

According to Weber, "Indian asceticism was the most rationally developed in the world" (RI:148–49). Yoga is a well-known example of Indian asceticism (RI:163–65). In his sociology of religion Weber also discusses monasticism, which he characterizes as a form of monastic asceticism (ES:1166–73). Monastic asceticism can be of two kinds: individuals can use it to find their own salvation, and hierocratic organizations can use it to train their monks.

Ascetic Protestantism, according to Weber's famous thesis in *The Protestant Ethic*, played a key role in forming and spreading the spirit of modern rational capitalism. It helped to make people work harder, save what they earned ("ascetic saving compulsion") and re-invest the profit (e.g. PED:67, 103–4). See especially in this context the chapter "The Religious Foundations of Worldly Asceticism" in *The Protestant Ethic* (PE:95–154). For a discussion of the role of asceticism in Protestantism as well as in the argument in *The Protestant Ethic*, see Weber's reply to one of his critics on pp. 62–6 in PED.

The translation by Talcott Parsons of *innerweltliche Askese* in *The Protestant Ethic* as "worldly asceticism" has been rejected by later translators of this work, who prefer "inner-worldly asceticism" (Gordon Wells, "Issues of Language and Translation in Max Weber's Protestant

Ethic Writings," [2001], p. 35). For the role of religious asceticism in Weber's work as well as in medieval Christianity, see Lutz Kaelber, *Schools of Asceticism* (1988).

See also ascetic Protestantism, discipline, mysticism, Weber thesis, predestination

association   *See* organization or association

associational action (*Gesellschaftshandeln*)   This term is used in Weber's early general sociology—that is, in the 1913 essay "Some Categories of Interpretive Sociology"—but was later dropped and partly replaced by the concept of instrumentally rational action.

In "Some Categories of Interpretive Sociology," associational action is defined as follows: "social action shall be called 'associational action' when and insofar as (1) it is oriented in meaning toward expectations that are held on the basis of rules (*Ordnungen*), (2) formulation of these rules has resulted purely rationally (*zweckrational*) in view of the expected action of those associated (*Vergesellschaftete*), and (3) the meaning orientation is subjectively rational" (SCIS:160).

The term *Gesellschaftshandeln* is not used in Weber's later general sociology, as outlined in Ch. 1 of *Economy and Society*. Some of its meaning, however, is captured by Weber's concept of instrumentally rational action—that is, social action which is "determined by expectations as to the behavior of objects in the environment and of other human beings; these expectations are used as 'conditions' or 'means' for the attainment of the actor's own rationally pursued and calculated ends" (ES:24; cf. ES:26).

Alternative translations of *Gesellschaftshandeln* are "societal action" (Hiroshi Orihara, "From 'A Torso with a Wrong Head' to 'Five Disjointed Body-Parts Without A Head'" [2003], p. 141); and "rationally regulated action" (Roth and Wittich, in Weber [1922] 1978; ES:1375).

See also community action, instrumentally rational action, social action

associative relationship (*Vergesellschaftung*)   So-called associative relationships play an important role in Weber's general sociology. They are social relationships that are typically based on agreements, especially rational agreements. Markets and organizations based on self-interest are examples of associative relationships.

An associative relationship is defined in Weber's general sociology in Ch. 1 of *Economy and Society* in the following manner: "a social relationship will be called 'associative' if and insofar as the orientation of social action within it rests on rationally motivated adjustment of interests or a similarly motivated agreement, whether the basis of rational judgment be absolute values or reasons of expediency" (ES:40–41).

In connection with his discussion of the associative relationship Weber also brings up the notion of communal relationship (*Vergemeinschaftung*), which is held together by a sense of belonging together. He notes that these two types of relationships should be seen as a continuum, and he explicitly distances himself from Tönnies' sharp distinction between *Gemeinschaft* (community) and *Gesellschaft* (society).

Weber points out that "the great majority" of social relationships have elements of both communal and associative relationships (ES:41). "No matter how calculating and hard-headed the ruling considerations in such a social relationship—as that of a merchant to his customers—may be, it is quite possible for it to involve emotional values which transcend its utilitarian significance" (ES:41).

According to Martin Albrow, "Weber sought to dispel any rigid dichotomy between these two concepts and emphasized process by adding the prefix *Ver-* to create *Vergemeinschaftung* and *Vergesellschaftung*" (Albrow 1990:249). Albrow adds that "both [terms] are difficult to render into English; Parsons [the translator of Ch. 1 of *Economy and Society*] chose communal and associative relationships respectively." David Frisby and Derek Sayer argue that it was Weber's methodological individualism that made him avoid terms such as community and society, and instead use terms such as *Vergemeinschaftung* and *Vergesellschaftung*: "this is why Weber preferred to use verb forms or active nouns in order to delineate the social processes with which he was concerned" (Frisby and Sayer 1986:68).

Frisby and Sayer translate *Vergesellschaftung* in *Economy and Society* as "sociation"—while Roth and Wittich translate it as "association" in Weber's 1913 essay "Some Categories of Interpretive Sociology" (Frisby and Sayer 1986:68; Roth and Wittich in ES:1375). In his new translation of Ch. 1 of *Economy and Society*, Keith Tribe translates *Vergesellschaftung* as "formation of association" (EW:343). When Georg Simmel uses the term *Vergesellschaftung*, it may be added, it is usually translated as "sociation."

The conceptual pair *Vergesellschaftung* and *Vergemeinschaftung* is first found in Weber's general sociology in Ch. 1 of *Economy and Society*. In "Some Categories of Interpretive Sociology" Weber does not use these terms, but rather *Gemeinschaftshandeln* and *Gesellschaftshandeln*. See on this point Hiroshi Orihara, "From 'A Torso with a Wrong Head' to 'Five Disjointed Body-Parts Without A Head'" (2003), 152, 154.

See also communal relationship, social action, social relationship, society

attitude   *See* habitus

ausseralltäglich *See* charisma, everyday life

ausserweltliche Askese (other-worldly asceticism) *See* asceticism

authority *See* domination

"Author's Introduction" This is the title given by Talcott Parsons to the prefatory introduction (*Vorbemerkung*) to Vol. 1 of Weber's three-volume work *Gesammelte Aufsätze zur Religionssoziologie* (*Collected Essays in the Sociology of Religion*, GAR I:1–16). It should not be confused with the introduction ("Einleitung") to the study *The Economic Ethics of the World Religions*, which is known in English as "The Social Psychology of World Religions" (GM:267–301).

The "Author's Introduction" is very important, mainly for its statement about the growth of rationalization in the West. Weber touches, among other things, on art, science, architecture and the economy as part of his discussion of rationalization and "universal history." It was first published in 1920 and is the last text that Weber worked on before his death on June 14 of that year.

Talcott Parsons made the first translation of this text and placed it at the outset of his translation of *The Protestant Ethic and the Spirit of Capitalism*, thereby giving the reader the erroneous impression that it was part of this study (PE:13–31). Two recent translations of the *Vorbemerkung*—both under the title "Prefatory Remarks"—exist: one by Peter Baehr and Gordon Wells, and one by Stephen Kalberg (See Weber [1904–5] 2002a:356–72, [1904–5] 2002a:149–64).

See also *Collected Essays in the Sociology of Religion*, "Einleitung," universal history

autocephalous (*autokephal*) If an organization appoints its own leadership, it is autocephalous; if outsiders do so, it is heterocephalous.

In his discussion of the concept of organization or association in *Economy and Society*, Weber explains what autocephalous means in the following way: "autocephaly means that the chief and his staff are selected according to the autonomous order of the organization itself, not as in the case of heterocephaly, that they are appointed by outsiders" (ES:50). The essence of autocephaly, in other words, is independence of certain outside forces, while the opposite is called heterocephaly.

The term autocephalous comes from the Greek *autokephalos* ("self-headed") and was used in medieval Byzantine law to indicate that a national church organization was independent of the patriarch of Constantinople.

See also organization or association.

Basic sociological terms (*soziologische Grundbegriffe*)   "Basic Sociological Terms" is the title of Ch. 1 of *Economy and Society* which contains the main body of Weber's general sociology (ES:3–62), as originally translated by Talcott Parsons. The reader may want to note that this chapter now also exists in a new translation by Keith Tribe ("Basic Sociological Concepts," EW:311–58).

An early version of some of the material in this chapter can also be found in Weber's 1913 essay "Some Categories of Interpretive Sociology" (SCIS).

See also *Kategorienlehre*

Battle of the Methods (*Methodenstreit*)   For a few decades from the 1880s onwards economists in German-speaking Europe were involved in a heated academic dispute, triggered by an exchange between Austrian economist Carl Menger and Gustav Schmoller, the leader of the German Historical School of economics. The key issue was whether economics should be primarily analytical and abstract in nature or empirical and historical.

The debate ended with a clear victory for the analytical approach of Menger; while the historical-empirical approach was excluded from mainstream economics. Versions of the Battle of the Methods also took place in many other countries, including England, Sweden and the United States; and also here the analytical school won a resounding victory.

Weber argued that both schools of thought had something essential to contribute, and he deplored the fact that economics had split into "two sciences" (MSS:63). He both referred to the "excellent views" of Menger, and complimented Schmoller for having kept alive the historical method in economics "at the time of the most barren economic rationalism" (Swedberg 1998:190).

For discussions of the Battle of the Methods, see e.g. Ola Agevall, *A Science of Unique Events* (1999), pp. 58–69, H. H. Bruun, *Science, Values and Politics in Max Weber's Methodology* (1972), pp. 79–84, and Keith Tribe, *Strategies of Economic Order* (1995), pp. 66–94.

See also economics, Historical School of economics, value-freedom

Battle of Value Judgments (*Werturteilsstreit*)   See value-freedom

Baumgarten family   Several members of the Baumgarten family had an important impact on Weber as a young man. Ida Baumgarten, who was the sister of Weber's mother, influenced him through her intense religious interest; and her husband Hermann through his advocacy of liberalism. Weber discussed theology with the son Otto, and he had a romantic interest in the daughter Emmy (born 1865) when he was in his twenties. See Marianne Weber, *Max Weber* ([1926] 1975). For Weber's relationship to Emmy Baumgarten, see also Arthur Mitzman, *The Iron Cage* (1985), pp. 51–64.

bearer   *See* carrier

behavior (*Verhalten*)   The importance of the concept of behavior derives from the fact that it is part of Weber's well-known definition of sociology, as presented in paragraph 1 of Ch. 1 of *Economy and Society*: "sociology . . . is a science concerning itself with the interpretive understanding of social action (*Handeln*) and thereby with a causal explanation of its course and consequences" (ES:4). Action, in its turn, is defined as behavior (*Verhalten*) that is invested with meaning by the actor.

Behavior can be internal or external; the actor can do something, avoid doing something or have something done to him or her. But only behavior that has *meaning* is of relevance to Weber's type of sociology. Similarly, when the meaning of an action starts to recede, it turns into behavior. Traditional behavior is typically to be found somewhere between behavior and action. "A very considerable part of all sociologically relevant behavior, especially purely traditional behavior, is marginal between the two" (ES:4–5). Finally, reactive behavior often lacks meaning.

According to Talcott Parsons, "the terms *Handeln* [action] and *Verhalten* [behavior] are directly related." He also notes that while "*Verhalten* [behavior] is the broader term referring to any behavior of human individuals . . . [*Handeln* or action] refers to the concrete phenomenon of human behavior only in so far as it is capable of 'understanding', in Weber's technical sense, in terms of subjective categories" (Parsons 1947:89). Parsons adds that *Handeln* may also sometimes be translated as "conduct."

See also action, meaning, understanding

benefice (*Pfründe*)   A benefice, as this term is used in Weber's work, denotes a type of income that can be appropriated by a patrimonial retainer, given in exchange for his support of a ruler. A regime based on benefices is called prebendalism.

In Ch. 3 on domination in *Economy and Society* the following definition of a benefice is given: "we shall speak of *benefices* insofar as the forms of maintenance . . . are always newly granted [the patrimonial retainer] in a traditional fashion which determines amount or locality, and insofar as they can be appropriated by the individual, although not hereditary" (ES:235; cf. ES:222). By the forms of maintenance are meant: "allowances (usually in kind) from the lord's magazines or treasury, . . . by rights of land use in return for services ('service-land'), [and] by the appropriation of property income, fees or taxes" (ES:235).

Different types of benefices exist, some of which are close to fiefs (ES:1032–33; cf. ES:235).
See also fief, prebendalism

Beruf   *See* vocation

Berufsmensch (person who wants to work in his or her calling)   *See* vocation

Betrieb   This term has two different meanings in Weber's work: *enterprise* and *establishment* (*see* these entries).

Bewährung   *See* confirmation

bibliography of Weber's work   *See* Weber, Max—Works

biological factors   *See* body, inheritance, race

Bismarck's legacy   By this expression, which figures prominently in "Politics and Government in a Reconstructed Germany" (ES:1381–1469), Weber denotes the problematic impact that Otto von Bismarck (1815–98) had on Germany's political life during his years as chancellor (1873–90), especially on its prospects for an effective parliamentary system. According to Weber, Bismarck's policies had made the German people less educated in political matters than they had been before Bismarck's coming to power, and also made it "accustomed to fatalistic sufferance of all decisions" (ES:1392; more generally, see "Bismarck's Legacy," ES:1385–92).
For a discussion of Weber's view of Bismarck, see e.g. Wolfgang Mommsen, *Max Weber and German Politics 1890–1920* (1984) and Peter Baehr, "Max Weber as a Critic of Bismarck" (1988).
See also education (for political education)

body   The main emphasis in Weber's sociology is on social action; and the body would therefore seem to disappear from the horizon. This, however, is more apparent than real since, to cite one of Weber's methodological essays, "behind the particular 'action' stands the human being" (MSS:38).
When it comes to both economic behavior and religious behavior it is clear that Weber was deeply interested in the role of the body in these activities. In *The Protestant Ethic*, for example, Weber notes how ascetic Protestantism advocated the control of the spontaneous aspects of human behavior (*status naturalis*) and how this translated into the ethic and discipline of early modern capitalism (PE:127, 166–73). The concept of self-control, more generally, is central to Weber's analysis of the way that ascetic Protestantism affected the individual—including his or her economic behavior (e.g. ES:618–19).

In his sociology of religion Weber also pays careful attention to the use of various forms of intoxicants (alcohol, drugs, sexual orgies) as well as the place allotted to emotions in the various religions (e.g. ES:534–41; cf. RC:232, RI:163–65). "Sexual intoxication," for example, is a way to reach ecstasy (ES:602).

While some religions favor a rational and controlled road to salvation, others emphasize the role of mystical and emotional means. Weber's portrait of the Jewish prophet also deserves special mention in this context because of the close attention Weber pays to the interaction between physical and non-physical factors (AJ:278–86).

Weber's studies of psychophysics, in which he explores the impact of fatigue and the like in the worker's everyday life, are also relevant in this context.

Finally, Weber's notion of the erotic sphere—one of the so-called value-spheres—should be mentioned (GM:343–50). According to Weber, "sexual love" is "the greatest irrational force of life" (GM:343). Erotic love also helps the lover to avoid "the skeleton hands of rational orders" as well as "the banality of everyday routine" (GM:347). Sex ties people to the animal level—but can also be sublimated into eroticism (ES:603, 607). For the role of sexual relationship in the family, see e.g. ES:357–58, 363–65. For comments on the role that the body plays in Weber's work, including the attention that Weber pays to the body in his writings on the military, see Bryan Turner, *Max Weber* (1992), pp. 113–59. For Weber's personal relationship to sex as well as various free love movements, see e.g. Martin Green, *The von Richthofen Sisters* (1974), M. Rainer Lepsius, "Mina Tobler and Max Weber" (2004), Sam Whimster, "Max Weber on the Erotic and Some Comparisons with the Work of Foucault" (1995), and Sam Whimster (ed.), *Max Weber and the Culture of Anarchy* (1999).

See also complexes of meaning, emotions, psychophysics, value-spheres

Brentano, Lujo (1844–1931) Economist and Weber's predecessor at the University of Munich. See e.g. Bertram Schefold, "Brentano, Lujo (Ludwig Josef) (1844–1931)" (1987).

Buddhism Buddhism is one of the religions that Weber terms world-religions. He mainly discusses it in *The Religion of India: The Sociology of Hinduism and Buddhism* and in *Economy and Society* (e.g. ES:627–30, 817–18).

Ancient Buddhism is described by Weber as a religion that advocated a form of asceticism that entails world-rejection. Its goal was to escape from life and arrive at rest; to extinguish "the thirst for life" and to enter "the eternal dreamless sleep of Nirvana" (ES:627–28) The main carrier of Buddhism was the mendicant monk (ES:512).

For a discussion, see Wolfgang Schluchter, *Rationalism, Religion, and Domination* (1989), pp. 117–62. See also Wolfgang Schluchter (ed.), *Max Webers Studie über Hinduismus und Buddhismus* (1984), as well as the introductory and editorial material in *The Religion of India* in MWG I/20.

See also world-religions; *Religion of India, The*; *Collected Essays in the Sociology of Religion*

budgetary management (*Haushalt*)   Following the classical distinction from Aristotle onward between the management of a household and money-making, Weber contrasts what he calls budgetary management (or householding) to profit-making.

According to Weber's definition in his economic sociology in Ch. 2 of *Economy and Society*, "the continual utilization and procurement of goods, whether through production or exchange, by an economic unit for purposes of its own *consumption* will be called 'budgetary management'" (ES:87).

"Wealth" is related to budgetary management (and used to produce "rent"), while "capital" is the equivalent for profit-making (and used to produce "profit"). "Income" is the amount of goods, valued in money, which is available to a household during a particular time period.

In budgetary management calculations are oriented to marginal utility, while in profit-making they are oriented to profitability. Calculations in budgetary management can be rational, in which case they are carried out in accordance with a budget. Units employing budgetary management include the family, the *oikos* and the planned state economy.

Talcott Parsons writes in a note to his translation of *Haushalt* in Ch. 2 of *Economy and Society* that "[Weber] means by it essentially what Aristotle means by 'the management of a household' (Jowett's translation)," and that this management involves "the rational allocation of resources in providing for a given set of needs" (ES:207 n. 14). Parsons also points out that there is no English equivalent of *Vermögen* in the sense that Weber uses it, namely as a form of property which has a certain "function in the management of an economic unit" (ES:207 n. 15). For this reason, Parsons says he will use "wealth" and, when necessary, "budgetary wealth" (ibid.).

See also capital, capital accounting, firm, household, planned economy, profit-making, oikos, rent

bureaucracy (*Bürokratie*)   Weber's theory of bureaucracy constitutes one of the most famous parts of his work. Weber essentially argues that bureaucracy constitutes the most efficient and (formally) rational way in which human activity can be organized, and that it is indispensable to the modern world. Weber also feels that bureaucracy represents a threat to humanity, and that entrepreneurs and politicians may constitute a counter-balance to its power.

No independent place is devoted to the concept of bureaucracy in Weber's general sociology, as this is outlined in Ch. 1 of *Economy and Society*. Weber discusses organizations and associations in this chapter, but not bureaucracy. There do, however, exist two key places in *Economy and Society* where bureaucracy holds center stage. This is Ch. 3 in Part 1, which is devoted to domination, and Ch. 11 in Part 2, which is entitled "Bureaucracy" (ES:216–26, 956–1005). Weber here states that a bureaucracy is "a structure of domination" (ES:219). More precisely, "bureaucratic administration means fundamentally domination through knowledge" (ES:225). The well-known section on bureaucracy in Gerth and Mills' anthology *From Max Weber* is identical to Ch. 11.

This chapter also contains Weber's well-known ideal type or "list" of six features that characterize a bureaucracy: (1) it covers a fixed area of activity, which is governed by rules; (2) it is organized as a hierarchy; (3) action that is undertaken is based on written documents (preserved as files); (4) expert training is needed, especially for some; (5) officials devote their full activity to their work; and (6) the management of the office follows general rules which can be learned (ES:956–58; GM:196–98). Elsewhere in *Economy and Society* Weber gives a shorter description of a bureaucracy: "the combination of written documents and a continuous operation by officials constitutes the 'office' (*Bureau*) which is the central focus of all types of modern organized action" (ES:219, for a longer definition, see ES:223).

Officials are characterized by the importance that *duty* plays for them and their *sense of social esteem* vis-à-vis outsiders (ES:959–63). Weber also notes that that officials typically experience an "abhorrence of the acquisitive drive," and he explains this by referring to the fact that officials have fixed salaries (ES:1108–9). Officials who are elected display less of a tendency toward bureaucracy (e.g. ES:960).

Bureaucracies are portrayed as efficient machines in Weber's sociology: "the fully developed bureaucratic apparatus compares with other organizations exactly as does the machine with the non-mechanical modes of production" (ES:973; cf. ES:223, 973, PW:158). To the argument that the bureaucracy is the most rational form of organization from a technical viewpoint, Weber adds that "the needs of mass administration make it today completely indispensable" (ES:223). Once established, Weber also notes, bureaucratic structures are among "the hardest to destroy" (ES:987).

Weber sometimes touches on the history of bureaucracy. He analyzes, for example, the role of the literati in China and notes that the New Kingdom of Egypt constitutes "the historical model of all later bureaucracies" (RC:107–41, ES:964). Several centuries of bureaucratic growth are summarized as follows: "the Byzantines, later the Italians, then the territorial states of the absolutist age, the French revolutionary centralization and finally, surpassing all of them, the Germans perfected the rational, functional and specialized bureaucratic organization of all forms of domination from the factory to army and public administration" (ES:1400, cf. ES:956–1005).

Weber also points out that the tendency in a bureaucracy to treat everybody without regard to the person goes very well with capitalism. This is also true for the tendency in bureaucracies to separate the means of administration from those who work with them. Bureaucracy means "without regard for persons" (ES:975). Its spirit can be described as *sine ira et studio* (without anger or passion; e.g. ES:225).

In general, rational capitalism can only exist on condition that enterprises and the state are organized as dependable and predictable bureaucracies: "capitalism in its modern stages of development requires the bureaucracy" (ES:224). Modern socialism, Weber also notes, needs it even more (ibid.).

Weber discusses not only what characterizes bureaucracy and its history, but also its future (e.g. PW:149, 158). It is especially in his discussion of the future of bureaucracy that it becomes clear that Weber was not simply an advocate of bureaucracy and its efficiency, but also fundamentally critical and fearful of it. The politician and the entrepreneur, he argues, are needed as counterweights to the bureaucrats inside political and economic organizations, or these will take over and stifle them (e.g. ES:225, PW:159–61).

What is in store in the future is an "inescapable universal bureaucratization," according to Weber, not only of capitalism but also of socialism (e.g. PW:279). If capitalism were to be abolished, there would be only one—and bureaucratized—power center in society.

Finally, for Weber's personal experience of bureaucracy when he managed some hospitals during World War I, see Marianne Weber, *Max Weber: A Biography* (1926; 1975), pp. 537–50 (for the German original of Weber's report, see Weber 1984:23–48).

For an introduction to Weber's theory of bureaucracy, see e.g. Reinhard Bendix, "Bureaucracy" (1968), as well as his summary in *Max Weber: An Intellectual Portrait* (1960), pp. 423–30. Other useful introductory reading can be found in David Beetham, "The Limits of Bureaucratic Rationality" (1985), and in Wolfgang Mommsen, "Max Weber on Bureaucracy and Bureaucratization: Threat to Liberty and Instrument of

Creative Action," pp. 109–20 in *The Political and Social Theory of Max Weber* (1989).

An enormous amount of works have taken Weber's notion of bureaucracy as the point of departure for analyses of organizations in modern society. For a useful discussion of this type of work, by people such as Robert K. Merton, Peter Blau, Alvin Gouldner and many others, see Martin Albrow, *On Bureaucracy* (1970). For an update on the secondary literature that Albrow discusses, the reader may consult the latest edition of Richard Scott, *Organizations* (2002). For Weber and contemporary organization theory, see also e.g. Stewart Clegg, "Max Weber and Contemporary Sociology of Organizations" (1994). For an argument about "the near disappearance of Weber from organization studies," see e.g. Marshall Meyer, "The Weberian Tradition in Organizational Studies" (1990) and Robert Stern and Stephen Barley, "Organizations and Social Systems" (1996). And for an answer to this charge, see Richard Scott, "The Mandate Is Still Being Honored: In Defense of Weber's Disciples" (1996). That organization theory has misunderstood Weber's analysis of bureaucracy is the argument in Hans-Ulrich Derlien, "On the Selective Interpretation of Max Weber's Concept of Bureaucracy in Organization Theory and Administrative Science" (1999).

For the argument that Weber's view of bureaucracy in capitalism was based on some peculiarities of the German situation, see Jürgen Kocka, "The Rise of the Modern Industrial Enterprise in Germany" (1980). For the argument that the prospects for economic development increase if there is a "Weberian" bureaucracy, see Peter Evans and James Rauch, "Bureaucracy and Growth: A Cross-National Analysis of the Effects of 'Weberian' State Structures on Economic Growth" (1999).

See also administration, collegiality, depersonalization, firm, legal domination, means of administration, office, organization or association, organization theory or organizational sociology, socialism

Caesarism (*Cäsarismus*)   This term can be found in Weber's political sociology as well as in his political writings more generally. It essentially denotes a form of political domination or political rule that is built on the masses, say by means of a continual use of referenda.

At one point in *Economy and Society* Weber describes Caesarism as "rest[ing] in general upon the position of the 'caesar' as a free trustee of the masses (of the army or the citizenry), who is unfettered by tradition" (ES:961; cf. ES:962). A detailed discussion of Caesarism, including its role in mass democracy, can be found in "Government and Democracy in a Reconstructed Germany" (e.g. ES:1451–59).

There exists a close relationship between Caesarism and plebiscitary domination.

Weber's attitude to charismatic political leaders is an often discussed topic. See e.g. Stefan Breuer, "The Concept of Democracy in Weber's Political Sociology" (1998), Sven Eliaeson, "Constitutional Caesarism: Weber's Politics in Their German Context" (2000), and Wolfgang Mommsen, *Max Weber and German Politics 1890–1920* (1984), pp. 86–7, 186–88.

See also charisma, charismatic domination, demagogue, plebiscitary domination and leadership

caesaropapism (*Cäsaropapismus*)   This term is part of Weber's political sociology and is used to indicate a distinct kind of rulership, namely that of a secular ruler who has total power over the church.

Weber's formal definition of caesaropapism in *Economy and Society* reads as follows: "a secular, caesaropapist ruler . . . exercises supreme authority in ecclesiastic matters by virtue of his autonomous legitimacy" (ES:1160). Caesaropapism entails "the complete subordination of priests to secular power," and it essentially means that church matters have become part of political administration (ES:1161–62; more generally, see ES:1158–1204).

Caesaropapism differs from hierocracy, which covers the following two cases: either the ruler acquires his legitimacy through religion or the religious leader is the ruler.

According to Guenther Roth, "Weber linked . . . hierocracy and caesaropapism in one historical model," while hierocracy "means the political domination of priests; . . . caesaropapism denotes the secular ruler's control over the priesthood" (Bendix and Roth 1971:124).

See also hierocracy, hierocratic organization

calculation (*Kalkulation, Rechnung*)   Calculation is central to the process of rationalization and holds a prominent role in Weber's analysis, especially of the economy.

Weber, however, typically uses the concept of calculation in a broad sense, and when he says that "the modern capitalist enterprise rests primarily on *calculation*," he refers not only to economic calculation but also to calculation in the areas of political and legal administration (ES:1394). Weber also paid special attention to the role of accounting in rational capitalism.

Economic calculation is very old; and it is intimately connected to the nature as well as the existence of money. It can exhibit different degrees of rationality and accuracy (e.g. GEH:226). "Capital accounting" is central to Weber's economic sociology in *Economy and Society*. It essentially means that the value of a profit-making enterprise is estimated before as well as after its completion. Accounting more generally has played a crucial role in the development of rational capitalism, according to Weber; and this is especially the case with double-entry bookkeeping which constitutes its technically most advanced form. A number of substantive conditions also have to exist for there to be "maximum formal rationality of capital accounting" (ES:161–63). Finally, Weber also refers to something he calls "moral book-keeping," and which consists of an effort to keep very close control of one's actions while trying to improve them (e.g. PE:124, 238 n. 100).

Calculation in kind, which can be found in planned economies, poses special problems. Arthur Stinchcombe argues that Weber's view of accounting is outmoded and needs to be updated ("Max Weber's *Economy and Society*" [1986], p. 282). For Weber's view of accounting as part of a larger analysis, see e.g. Bruce Carruthers and Wendy Nelson Espeland, "Accounting for Rationality: Double-Entry Bookkeeping and the Rhetoric of Economic Rationality" (1991).

See also capital accounting, commenda, money

calling *See* vocation

Calvinism Calvinism is at the center of Weber's famous study *The Protestant Ethic and the Spirit of Capitalism*; it is also discussed in other of his writings, such as *Economy and Society* (PE:98–128; cf. ES:1198–1200). Together with Pietism, Methodism and a few other types of religion, it constitutes what Weber terms *ascetic Protestantism*—a form of religion that can be characterized as an anti-authoritarian and activistic type of Christianity, in which hard and dedicated work (*Beruf*) represents an important way of honoring God. The Calvinist does not think about the meaning of life ("the theodicy problem"—PE:109). While not a sect but a church, Calvinism is nonetheless according to Weber a very special type of church: a sect-like church. Weber refers to "the unique and long-established elective affinity of Calvinism to capitalism" (PED:107).

Weber pays special attention to the doctrine of predestination in Calvinism, which had an "extraordinarily powerful" impact on the believers (PE:128). It put the believers in a constant state of tension ("the fear of damnation"), and made them look for "signs" that they were among the elect (*certitudo salutis*; PE:113–14, 127–29). According to Calvinism (but not according to Calvin himself), the accumulation of riches was one of the signs that the believer was among the elect—"a sign of God's blessing" (PE:172).

But even if believers became rich, they were not allowed to enjoy the fruits of their work, but had to reinvest the profit. Calvinism, according to Weber, is an example of what he terms inner-worldly asceticism. It also commends the rich for their godly behavior, is harsh to the poor and is negative to charity (ES:588–89).

See e.g. Herbert Lüthy, "Once Again: Calvinism and Capitalism" (1968), Malcolm MacKinnon, "Calvinism and the Infallible Assurance of Grace." (1989), and Philip Benedict, "The Historiography of Continental Calvinism," pp. 305–25 in Hartmut Lehmann and Guenther Roth (eds.), *Weber's Protestant Ethic* (1993).

See also ascetic Protestantism, confirmation, predestination, sect, vocation

canon law   *See* sacred law

capital (*Kapital*)   Capital is related to the concept of profit-making in Weber's sociology, just as wealth is related to the concept of householding or budgetary management.

According to Weber's definition in his economic sociology in Ch. 2 of *Economy and Society*, "'capital' is the money value of the means of profit-making available to the enterprise at the balancing of the books" (ES:91).

See also budgetary management, calculation, capital accounting, capitalism, profit-making

capital accounting (*Kapitalrechnung*)   Capital accounting represents a certain type of accounting that is crucial to rational capitalism, according to Weber. It can only exist on certain institutional conditions.

Capital accounting is defined in Weber's economic sociology in Ch. 2 of *Economy and Society* as "the valuation and verification of opportunities for profit and of the success of profit-making activity by means of a valuation of the total assets (goods and money) of the enterprise at the beginning of a profit-making venture, and the comparison of this with a similar valuation of the assets still present and newly acquired, at the end of the process; in the case of a profit-making organization operating continuously, the same is done for an accounting period" (ES:91). The key, in brief, is the valuation before and after.

Capital accounting can be used for market activities but also for economic activities based on political power. Capital accounting has only emerged in the West, and certain institutional conditions are necessary for its existence (see "The Conditions for Maximum Formal Rationality of Capital Accounting"—ES:161–64).

See also calculation, capital, commenda, firm, profit-making

capitalism (*Kapitalismus*)   Weber was fascinated by capitalism all his life, and one may argue that it constitutes *the* central theme of his work. It stands, for example, at the center of *The Protestant Ethic and the Spirit of Capitalism, Economy and Society* and *The Handbook of Social Economics* that Weber edited during his last years. Weber famously described capitalism as "the most fateful force in our modern life" and seems to have been more interested in mapping out different types of capitalism than in defining capitalism in general (PE:17). Of these different types, he was especially interested in *modern rational capitalism* and in its origin. It should also be emphasized that Weber did not only analyze the economic and social dimensions of capitalism, as is common today, but also investigated its cultural dimension.

The one statement in Weber's work that comes the closest to a definition of capitalism in general reads as follows: "where we find property is an object of trade and is utilized by individuals for profit-making enterprise in a market economy, there we have capitalism" (ASAC:51; cf. PE:17–27, GEH:275–78). In another place in his work Weber refers to capitalism an "economic *system*" (PED:75; see also e.g. PED:45, 71, 76). While Weber often emphasized the economic dimension of capitalism, it has to be emphasized that he was also deeply concerned with its "*general cultural significance*" (MSS:67).

In Weber's economic sociology in Ch. 2 of *Economy and Society* one key paragraph is devoted to capitalism (ES:164–66). In this passage Weber does not speak of capitalism in general but of half a dozen qualitatively different forms of "'capitalist' orientation of profit-making activity."

These forms of orientation, he says, can be divided into (a) those that have existed for several thousand years; and (b) those that are unique to the modern West. The former category is divided into "politically oriented capitalism" and profit-making activity that is centered around commodity trade and dealings in money. The latter refer to the modern, specifically Western type of capitalism that is characterized as a "rational, market-oriented form of capitalism." It is described as having the following traits: rational enterprises in a market economy, labor that is formally free, and sophisticated forms of financing.

In *The Protestant Ethic* Weber contrasts modern rational capitalism to traditional capitalism. In traditional capitalism people work to survive, not for the sake of work itself; and profit is used to make life more pleasant, not just to be reinvested (PE:65–9).

Weber also emphasizes that it should be taught in "the kindergarten of cultural history" that modern rational capitalism should not be equated with greed; it is more complex than that (PE:17). Modern rational capitalism also leans heavily on bureaucratic forms of organization; "capitalism in its modern stages of development requires the bureaucracy" (ES:224). This goes not only for the organization of the capitalist firms but also for the modern rational state as well (e.g. GEH:338–51). The legal system of rational capitalism has to be predictable in nature (e.g. ES:847, 1095).

Elsewhere in his work Weber also makes clear that modern capitalism has its irrational elements as well as a distinct dynamic of its own. The prevalence of speculation in modern capitalism, for example, opens it up to charismatic elements (e.g. ES:1118). And as to dynamics, Weber argues that if profit-making is replaced by rent in modern capitalism, the whole economic system will be become stagnant and non-dynamic.

There was, finally, one aspect of capitalism that especially fascinated Weber throughout his scholarly career, namely the origin of modern rational capitalism: "*Why* has a rational capitalism based upon calculation developed *solely* in the Occident?" (Weber in letter to Robert Liefmann, dated March 3, 1920; Swedberg 1994:203). This issue is explored not only in *Economy and Society* but also in *Collected Essays in the Sociology of Religion* and in the *General Economic History*. A useful summary of Weber's view of "The Origin of Modern Capitalism" can be found in the last part in *General Economic History* (GEH:273–96). For Weber's famous lists in this work of the factors that have produced modern, rational capitalism, see GEH:276–77, 312–14, 354. For a similar list of factors essential for "maximum formal rationality of capital accounting," see ES:161–62.

Weber refers in his writings to many other types of capitalism than have been mentioned here, and some of these are discussed in separate entries; *see* e.g. adventurers' capitalism, imperialist capitalism and pariah capitalism. It also deserves to be emphasized that Weber was very interested in the type of capitalism that existed in antiquity (see ASAC).

For discussions of Weber's concept of capitalism, see e.g. Herbert Marcuse, "Industrialization and Capitalism" (1972), Wolfgang Mommsen, "The Alternative to Marx: Dynamic Capitalism instead of Bureaucratic Socialism," pp. 47–71 in *The Age of Bureaucracy* (1974) and Richard Swedberg, "The Economic Sociology of Capitalism: Weber and Schumpeter" (2002). For Weber's analysis of capitalism in antiquity, see e.g. John Love, *Antiquity and Capitalism* (1991), pp. 7–56. For Weber's relationship to Werner Sombart, who popularized the term capitalism in academic discourse through his work *Der moderne Kapitalismus* (1902), see Arthur Mitzman, "Personal Conflict and Ideological Options in Sombart and Weber" (1987).

See also adventurers' capitalism, capital, capital accounting, freedom, market economy, imperialism (for imperialist capitalism), law, pariah capitalism, political capitalism, politics, profit-making, rational capitalism, religion, robber capitalism, science, state, technology

capitalist adventurer   *See* adventurers' capitalism

caritas   *See* charity

carrier (*Träger*)   In his sociology of religion Weber often notes that certain ideas may be associated with certain social groups (ES:468–518). According to *The Protestant Ethic*, for example, ascetic Protestantism has had four major carriers: Calvinism (of a certain type), Pietism, Methodism and certain sects including the Baptists and Quakers (PE:95). Similarly the world religions were all closely related to specific strata, such as Confucianism to prebendaries, and Christianity to itinerant artisan journeymen (e.g. GM:268–69; cf. ES:512).

According to Stephen Kalberg, "ideas are important causal forces of historical change, for Weber, only if they are 'carried' by demarcated and influential groupings, strata, and organizations" (Kalberg 2002: lxxx). For an attempt to present a "typology of carrier strata," see Wolfgang Schluchter, *Rationalism, Religion, and Domination* (1989), pp. 96–99.

See also elective affinities, ideas

caste (*Kaste*)   Weber primarily discusses the concept of caste in his study of Hinduism and Buddhism, known in English as *The Religion of India* (see especially RI:30–54). He here notes that "a caste is . . . a closed status group" (RI:39; similarly ES:933–35).

"Caste," according to Weber, "is the fundamental institution of Hinduism. . . . Without caste, there is no Hindu" (RI:29). Dietary rules and rules of commensality are central to the caste system, which also determines social rank. The "spirit" of Hinduism and the caste system, Weber concludes, constituted a major obstacle to the internal generation of a rational capitalism in India (RI:112).

See e.g. Jan Heesterman, "Kaste und Karma" (1984).
See also Hinduism, pariah people; *Religion of India, The*; status

Catholicism   Weber mainly discusses Catholicism in the opening chapter of *The Protestant Ethic* and in his sociology of religion (e.g. PE:116–17, 119–21, ES:560–63, 828–31, 964).

To Weber Catholicism was traditionalistic in spirit, as exemplified by its relationship to traditional capitalism as described in *The Protestant Ethic*. As opposed to Protestantism, it was split into a religious elite and lay people, and it lacked the concept of vocation (*Beruf*). The emphasis in Catholicism on institutional grace and the fact that it typically is a church (rather than a sect), also made it hard for this type of Christianity to have a methodical impact on its lay members (e.g. PE:116). To this may be added that the possibility of confessing sins also considerably lessened the potential for effectively shaping the lives of the believers (e.g. PE:106, PED:108–9). "The psychological effect of the confessional was everywhere to relieve the individual of responsibility for his own conduct, that is why it was sought, and that weakened the rigorous consistency of the demands of asceticism" (PE:250 n. 149).

While Weber's personal attitude to Protestantism, especially ascetic Protestantism, was positive, he was negative toward Catholicism. According to Paul Honigsheim, Weber was "an unconditional opponent of Catholicism" (Honigsheim [1946–63] 2000:216). Nonetheless, "he was [also] in the habit of using every opportunity to learn more about Catholicism" (ibid., p. 217). For a critique of Weber's view of Catholicism, see e.g. Werner Stark, "The Place of Catholicism in Max Weber's Sociology of Religion" (1968).

See also ascetic Protestantism, Calvinism, Christianity, Weber thesis, Protestantism, religion (for Weber's personal attitude to religion)

causal adequacy (*Kausaladäquanz*)   *See* causality

causality   Weber attempted to develop a theory of causality that answers to the demands of the cultural sciences (including the social sciences) and which consequently differs from the way that causality is perceived in the natural sciences. According to Weber, sociology is a science concerned with causality, and this causality is closely linked to the meaning with which actors invest their behavior. The reason that he takes this stance in relation to meaning, he says, is that sociology belongs to the cultural sciences. Weber's theory of causation, when it comes to sociology, has its roots in the theory of causation that he worked out in his early methodological essays—the so-called theory of adequate causation.

That sociology approaches causality with the help of interpretive understanding is clear from the opening lines of *Economy and Society*, in which Weber presents his well-known definition of sociology:

sociology . . . is a science concerning itself with the *interpretive understanding* of social action and thereby with a causal explanation of its course and consequences (ES:4; emphasis added).

A causal explanation in sociology has several parts to it, according to Weber's explication of this definition. First, the meaning that the actor attaches to his or her action has to make sense, given the action it results in. This is what Weber refers to when he says that an explanation has to be *"adequate on the level of meaning"* (*sinnhaft adäquat*, ES:11). Second, there has to exist a certain probability that a specific type of action will indeed have the intended effect. The explanation, in brief, also has to be *"causally adequate"* (*kausal adäquat*-ES:11; cf. MSS:79).

Weber explains the difference between the two forms of adequacy as follows (ES:11). What is considered the correct solution to a mathematical problem represents adequacy on the level of meaning. Causal adequacy, on the other hand, has to do with the statistical probability of a correct solution to this problem. Weber sums up that "a correct causal interpretation of a concrete course of action is arrived at when the overt action and the motives have both been correctly apprehended and at the same time their relation has become meaningfully comprehensible" (ES:12).

As part of a causal explanation, recourse always has to be had to comparisons between the actual course of events and what would have happened if one or several factors were missing (ES:10). This is where counterfactuals come into the picture as well as comparative sociology. An important theme in Weber's early work is also his neo-Kantian notion that a theory of causation helps the analyst to single out a few features as central to the explanation from an infinite amount of potential candidates.

Talcott Parsons, who made the first translation into English of Ch. 1 of *Economy and Society*, notes that "the expression *sinnhafte Adäquanz* is one of the most difficult of Weber's technical terms to translate" and that "in most places the cumbrous phrase 'adequacy on the level of meaning' has had to be employed" (ES:59 n. 12). Parsons continues that adequacy on the level of meaning only aims at establishing "a satisfying level of knowledge for the particular purposes of the subjective state of mind of the actor" and that for *"causal adequacy,"* one also needs "a satisfactory correspondence between the results of observation from the subjective point of view and from the objective; that is, observations of the overt course of action which can be described without reference to the state of mind of the actor" (ibid.).

Causality in sociology, Weber also notes in *Economy and Society*, primarily aims at "uniformities," while history aims at explaining individual events of a certain type (ES:19). Weber's best-known attempt to work out the causality of an individual event can be found in *The Protestant Ethic*. His later studies of various economic ethics can also be seen as a giant intellectual experiment in working out the same problem, but for areas outside of Europe and the United States. It is by no means easy to see how *The Protestant Ethic* and the later studies on economic ethics are to be understood in relation to the theory of adequate causation.

Weber lays the foundations for his theory of causation in his methodological essays, especially in "Critical Studies in the Logic of the Cultural Sciences" (1906). Drawing heavily on the theories of the physiologist and probability theorist Johannes von Kries, Weber works out a theory for determining what elements should be seen as relevant ("adequate") for causality among the infinite number of aspects that any phenomenon possesses (see e.g. MSS:184; cf. SCIS:161). In Kries' theory of adequate causation, the emphasis is not on developing laws, as in the natural sciences, but on relating phenomena to meaning and values. The social scientist has to proceed in a somewhat similar fashion to legal reasoning: inquire into the motive of the actor, and then try to establish to what extent his or her behavior can reasonably be said to have had the effect that is at issue (cf. Kries 1888). The concepts of counterfactuals and objective possibility also play an important role in this type of inquiry, as part of the attempt to establish a probable link between intention and effect (see especially the second half of Weber's essay on the logic of the cultural sciences, "Objective Possibility and Adequate Causation in Historical Explanation," MSS:164–88).

Weber's theory of causality represents one of the most difficult parts of his work. To this should be added that there appear to exist some important differences between Weber's early theory of causation, as this is to be found in his methodological essays, and what he says about causation in Ch. 1 of *Economy and Society*. It is clearly Weber's early views that have inspired the most discussion, among other reasons because Weber is more explicit about his ideas on causality in his early writings. *See* e.g. Ola Agevall, *A Science of Unique Events: Max Weber's Methodology of the Cultural Sciences* (1999), pp. 148–81, Talcott Parsons, *The Structure of Social Action* (1937), pp. 610–35, Fritz Ringer, *Max Weber's Methodology* (1997), pp. 63–91, Alfred Schutz, *The Phenomenology of the Social World* (1967), pp. 229–36, Alexander von Schelting, *Max Webers Wissenschaftslehre* (1934), pp. 312–25. A special mention should also be made of Stephen Turner and Regis Factor, "Objective Possibility and Adequate Causation in Weber's Methodological Writings" (1981). Turner also describes Weber's early view of adequacy in relation to probability as a "threshold concept rather than a degree concept" (Turner 2003). The reader may also want to consult Gary Goertz and Harvey Starr (eds.), *Necessary Conditions* (2003) in this context.

For the argument that little remains in *Economy and Society* of Weber's original theory of causation, as outlined in his methodological essays, see e.g. Stephen Turner, "Weber on Action" (1983). It may finally be mentioned that Samuel Whimster defines "adequacy of meaning" as "the understanding by an observer of the reasons behind the motive for social behaviour"; and "causal adequacy" as "a sequence of events that is known from experience to recur on a regular basis" (ES:407–8).

See also counterfactuals, comparative sociology, disenchantment of the world, elective affinities, *Evidenz*, explanation, meaning, motive, loaded dice argument, objective possibility, understanding

certainty See *Evidenz*

Chance The German term *Chance* is used by Weber in *Economy and Society* in two different meanings: as "opportunity" (or "advantage") and as "probability."

See opportunity, probability

charisma (*Charisma*) This well-known concept, to which Weber gave its meaning and which he also popularized, describes a person who is truly extraordinary (*ausseralltäglich*). Charisma may also be hereditary or attached to an office. Charisma is adjusted to reality through the process of routinization; and the oscillation between charisma and routinization represents a major theme in Weber's work.

The concept of charisma is not among the concepts that Weber focuses on in his general sociology in Ch. 1 of *Economy and Society*. It does, however, play a central role in his sociology of domination, in his sociology of religion, and in his sociology of law (e.g. ES:241–71, 439–51, 758–75, 1110–57).

Weber defines charisma as follows: "the term 'charisma' will be applied to a certain quality of an individual personality by virtue of which he is considered extraordinary and treated as endowed with supernatural, superhuman, or at least specifically exceptional powers or qualities" (ES:241; cf. e.g. ES:215, 400, GM:295). In early society charisma represented "the great revolutionary force," breaking up traditionalism and ushering in social change (e.g. ES:245; cf. ES:37, 321, 761, 1115–17). In modern society this is much less the case, even if charisma is still part of society. There exists, for example, a link between vocation and charisma (GM:79).

Charismatic figures may appear in situations in which people feel "enthusiasm . . . despair and hope" (ES:242). Typical charismatic figures are heroes, prophets and saviors. Jesus and Napoleon are examples of charismatic individuals. Charisma is unstable, Weber notes, because it is dependent on success.

Charisma in its pure form is deeply hostile to the existing order, especially the economic order. Existing laws and regulations are typically also set aside and replaced with substantive justice, as in Jesus' words, "it is written . . . but I say unto you . . . " (e.g. ES:243, 978, 1115).

Over time an adaptation of charismatic movements to reality will take place—what Weber terms "routinization" (e.g. ES:246–54, 1121–23). This may mean, among other things, that the followers of the original charismatic personality get jobs, and that an administration comes into being. A charismatic movement typically becomes a patrimonial organization. The process of routinization represents a major theme in Weber's sociology as well as a crucial complement to his notion of charisma.

But charisma is not only an individual quality. Together with his or her followers and disciples, the charismatic leader is part of a "charismatic community" (ES:243). There can also be "hereditary charisma" (*Erbcharisma*), "charisma of office" (*Amtscharisma*) and "lineage charisma" (*Gentilcharisma*; ES:248, 1137–41, RI:49). At one point in his work Weber also refers to the "charismatic glorification of 'Reason'" (ES:1209).

Charisma has also played a crucial role in legal development—which begins with charismatic revelation by law prophets and then proceeds to routinized lawmaking and law-finding by legal specialists (ES:882–83). Charismatic elements are attached to subjective justice, as opposed to formal justice, as in kadi justice (e.g. ES:976–78, 1115–16).

While Weber's name is intimately associated with the term charisma, he discovered it in his turn in the work of Rudolf Sohm, especially in the latter's *Kirchenrecht* (1892). Charisma was here used in the sense of "gift of grace" (cf. ES:216, 1112). According to Guenther Roth's formulation, "he [Weber] secularized Rudolf Sohm's notion of charisma" (ES:xcvi). Roth also notes that "Weber [eventually] moved from the nascent usage of 'charisma' in his Sociology of Religion to its systematic usage in the Sociology of Domination" (Roth 1975:151).

For a general introduction to the concept of charisma, see e.g. Charles Lindholm, *Charisma* (1990); and for introductions to Weber's use of this concept, see e.g. Martin Riesebrodt, "Charisma" (2001), S. N. Eisenstadt, "Introduction: Charisma and Institution Building: Max Weber and Modern Sociology" (1968), and Edward Shils, "Charisma, Order and Status" (1965). Talcott Parsons emphasizes the element of "breakthrough" in Weber's comments on charisma (Parsons 1963: xxxii; cf. pp. xxxiii–xlix). It has also been noted that Weber's use of charisma in his early work differs from that in his later work (e.g. Wolfgang Mommsen, "Max Weber's 'Grand Sociology'" [2000], p. 366). For a discussion of "impersonal charisma" (*Versachlichung des Charisma*), see Reinhard Bendix, *Max Weber: An Intellectual Portrait* (1960), pp. 309–14.

Weber's personal advocacy of a kind of charismatic leadership within democracy has been controversial. See, for example, the discussion of Wolfgang Mommsen's assertion that Weber's ideas on this topic served "to make the German people inwardly willing to acclaim Adolf Hitler's leadership position" (Mommsen 1984:410).

See also Caesarism, charismatic domination, demagogue, economic superman, everyday life, irrationality, law, magician, law prophet, plebiscitary domination and leadership, prophet, social change

charismatic domination (*charismatische Herrschaft*)   Domination constitutes one of the major themes in Weber's sociology, and charismatic domination—together with traditional domination and legal domination—constitutes one of its three major forms (ES:241–71).

According to Weber's definition in Ch. 3 on domination in *Economy and Society*, legitimate charismatic domination rests on "devotion to the exceptional sanctity, heroism or exemplary character of an individual person, and of the normative pattern or order revealed or ordained by him (charismatic authority [*Herrschaft*])" (ES:215). Charismatic domination is revolutionary and follows the dictum of Jesus: "it is written . . . , but I say unto you . . . " (ES:1115).

See also charisma, demagogue, domination

charity   The giving of alms is universal in religions and has over the years been rationalized into the enterprise of charity (e.g. ES:581–90; cf. AJ:255–63). Calvinism, however, is an exception here. It eliminated traditional almsgiving and was deeply suspicious of or hostile to those who are able to work but do not work, such as beggars.

Being charitable in a capitalist society presents problems since the relationship between many people is depersonalized. "It is impossible to control a universe of instrumentally rational activities by charitable appeals to particular individuals" (ES:585; cf. ES:1188, 1195; GM:371).

See also depersonalization, state (for the welfare state)

chartal   *See* money

China   See *Religion of China, The*

Christianity   Christianity is one of the world-religions, in Weber's terminology; and it is mainly discussed in Weber's sociology of religion in *Economy and Society* and *The Protestant Ethic and the Spirit of Capital-*

ism. Weber paid most attention to later Christianity and to Protestantism in particular. There exists no single place where he summarizes his opinions on Christianity, and the reader is therefore referred to a number of different places (e.g. ES:828–31, PE, GM:302–22).

Weber's original plan for his *Collected Essays in the Sociology of Religion* was to include studies of "primitive Christianity," "oriental Christianity" and "the Christianity of the Occident," as part of his attempt "to account for the economic and social singularity of the Occident" (see Weber's advertisement in 1919 for the *Collected Essays in the Sociology of Religion*, which is reprinted in the entry for this work).

Jesus is characterized by Weber as a magician (ES:512, 630–34). According to Weber, the main carrier of Christianity was the itinerant journeyman (ES:512). As part of his sociology of law, Weber also discusses canon law (ES:828–31).

For a discussion of Weber's analysis of Christianity, see e.g. Wolfgang Schluchter, "The Emergence of Modernity: Max Weber on Western Christianity," pp. 179–244 in *Paradoxes of Modernity* (1996). See also S. N. Eisenstadt, "Max Weber on Western Christianity and the Weberian Approach to Civilizational Dynamics" (1989) and Wolfgang Schluchter, "Ancient Christianity," pp. 205–48 in *Rationalism, Religion, and Domination* (1989).

See also ascetic Protestantism, Calvinism, Catholicism, *Collected Essays in the Sociology of Religion*, Protestantism, sacred law (for canon law), world-rejection

church (*Kirche*)   A church, according to Weber, is a compulsory religious organization with a staff and a monopoly.

The exact definition, which can be found in Weber's general sociology in Ch. 1 of *Economy and Society*, states: "a compulsory hierocratic organization will be called a 'church' insofar as its administrative staff claims a monopoly of the legitimate use of hierocratic coercion" (ES:54; cf. GM:288, RI:6). The term "hierocratic coercion" refers to the granting or withholding of religious benefits. It is, however, not so much religious benefits that characterize a church as spiritual domination over people with the help of these (ES:56). A hierocratic organization becomes under certain conditions a church (ES:1164).

Churches also base their domination on what Weber terms "office charisma" (e.g. ES:1164–66). The monopolistic character of a church makes it fight virtuoso religions (GM:288).

Weber often contrasts the church to the *sect*. While membership in a church is typically by birth, specific religious qualities are needed to become a member of a sect (e.g. ES:56, GM:314). Churches, in other words, tend to be open, and sects to be closed. While sects have been important in the United States, churches have been central in Europe.

See in this context e.g. Benton Johnson, "A Critical Appraisal of the Church-Sect Typology" (1957) and William Swatos, "Weber or Troeltsch? Methodology, Syndrome, and Development of Church-Sect Theory" (1976). See also Martin Riesebrodt, "Religiöse Vergemeinschaftungen" (2001).

See also charisma, coercion, hierocratic organization, hierocracy, religious benefits, religious communities, sect

citizenship (*Bürgertum, Staatsbürgerschaft* and similar terms) Citizenship represents a major theme in Weber's work and is also part of what has made the West unique. The closest one can come to a definition of what a citizen [*Staatsbürger*] is in Weber's work may be the following: "in the political sense, citizenship signifies membership in the state, with the connotation as the holder of certain political rights" (GEH:315).

Weber touches on the way that the notion of citizenship has developed throughout history in various places in his writings (e.g. ES:1226–31, 1236–65, GEH:315–37). As part of this he discusses the role of the member of the polis, the city state, the medieval city, and the modern nation state. A citizen of the state (*Staatsbürger*) can only be found in the modern state, according to Weber (e.g. PW:103). This type of citizenship "expresses the political unity of the nation" and its purpose is to create "a certain counterbalance" to social inequalities (ibid.).

Jeffrey Alexander points out that "in the German text [of *Economy and Society*] Weber uses the term *Bürger* for citizen, and Roth and Wittich [the two main editors and translators of *Economy and Society*] often translate is simply as 'burgher'" (Alexander 1983:162 n. 162).

See Stephen Kalberg, "Tocqueville and Weber on the Sociological Origins of Citizenship: The Political Culture of American Democracy" (1998).

See also City, The; politics, state

City, The (Die Stadt, trans. 1958) The section entitled "The City (Non-Legitimate Domination)" is included in the current edition of *Economy and Society*, but has also been published as a separate volume in English, translated by Don Martindale and Gertrud Neuwirth (ES:1212–1372; Weber [1921] 1958a). *The City* can be characterized as a historical study in urban sociology and more generally as a study in general and economic history.

Different conceptions of the city are presented and discussed by Weber, who notes that the only thing that these have in common is the view of "the city [as] a relatively closed settlement, and not simply a collection of a number of separate dwellings" (ES:1212). The city is also seen as "a large locality"—and Weber here adds that "sociologically speaking, this would mean: the city is a settlement of closely spaced dwellings which form a colony so extensive that the reciprocal personal acquaintance of the inhabitants, elsewhere characteristic of the neighborhood, is lacking" (ibid.).

The City is divided into sections which discuss different concepts of the city, the city in the West, the patrician city, the plebeian city, and ancient and medieval democracy in the city. Weber touches on such issues as the evolution of the city through history, citizenship, the role of the market for the development of the city, and what differentiates the city in the West from cities in other parts of the world.

The term "non-legitimate domination" (*nichtlegitime Herrschaft*) refers to the special type of domination that developed especially in Western medieval cities: an absence of traditional domination, in combination with new types of legitimacy based on the groups of citizens that ruled the cities (e.g. ES:1234 n. 1, ES:1250ff., GM:84).

The City was published posthumously in 1921 in the *Archiv für Sozialwissenschaft und Sozialpolitik* but was probably written in 1911–13/14. It was also included by the editors in the first (and later) editions of *Economy and Society*.

For a summary of the material in *The City*, see e.g. Reinhard Bendix, *Max Weber: An Intellectual Portrait* (1960), pp. 70–9, and Dirk Käsler, *Max Weber*, pp. 42–8. For the place of *The City* in urban theory, see Don Martindale, "Prefatory Remarks: The Theory of the City" (1958). For its early reception, see Dirk Käsler, *Max Weber* (1988), p. 200. For a discussion, see also Hinnerk Bruhns and Wilfried Nippel (eds.), *Max Weber und die Stadt im Kulturvergleich* (2000) as well as the introductory material by Nippel in the new edition of *The City*, published as MWG I/22–5 (Weber 1999d).

See also domination (for non-legitimate domination), urban sociology

civil society   *See* voluntary organization

civilization (*Kultur* and other terms)   When Weber's "civilizational analysis" is referred to, it is usually his general approach in *The Economic Ethics of the World Religions* that is meant. In this work Weber analyzes various key religions ("world-religions") in their social and political contexts. First and foremost, however, he attempts to capture their *Gestalt* and general cultural significance.

See, for example, "Author's Introduction" (PE:13–31), *Ancient Judaism*, *The Religion of China* or *The Religion of India*. For a discussion and analysis, see e.g. S. N. Eisenstadt, "Max Weber on Western Christianity and the Weberian Approach to Civilizational Dynamics" (1989) and Stephen Kalberg, *Max Weber's Sociology of Civilizations* (forthcoming).

See also *Economic Ethics of the World Religions*

clan   *See* kin group

class (*Klasse*)   The concept of class plays an important role in Weber's sociology, though much less so than in Marx's work. Weber also helped to formulate and introduce the concept of status into the study of sociology.

A shorthand definition of class can be found in *The Religion of India*: "'classes' are groups of people who from the standpoint of specific interests, have the same economic position" (RI:39). What determines a class is first and foremost "economic interest" (ES:928).

Weber discusses the concept of class primarily in two places in *Economy and Society*. The first is in the brief and incomplete Ch. 4, which dates from just before Weber's death in 1920 ("Status Groups and Classes," ES:302–7; for an alternative translation, see Weber 1978:57–61). Just like Marx, in other words, Weber did not find time before his death to complete his theory of class.

Weber's second text on class can be found in Ch. 9 of *Economy and Society*, "Class, Status, Party" (ES:926–40; for an alternative translation, see Weber 1978:43–56). This text was also never finished, and it is not known when it was written. In both of these texts on class and status Weber sees interest as the foundation for "class" or "class situation." Action based on class situation, he also notes, may or may not take place.

One difference between the two texts is that in Ch. 4 Weber speaks of three types of classes, while in Ch. 9 he only talks of one. According to the former section, there are "property classes," "commercial classes," and "social classes" (ES:302–7). For the first type of class, property is decisive, and for the second, marketability of goods and services. The term "social classes" refers to those social formations within which social mobility is typical.

In the latter section Weber emphasizes marketability as characteristic of class, but he also mentions property. He also supplies the following definition of class (in which the term "life chances" famously appears): "we may speak of a 'class' when (1) a number of people have in common a specific causal component of their life chances, insofar as (2) this component is represented exclusively by economic interests in the possession of goods and opportunities for income, and (3) is represented under the conditions of the commodity or labor market" (ES:927). He adds: "this is 'class situation'" (ibid.).

Weber discusses the relationship between class and ideas in his sociology of religion (see e.g. ES:468–80). A class, for example, can be a carrier of certain ideas.

Status or "status situations" differ from classes and class situations primarily in being based on more than just interest, usually also lifestyle as well as esteem or honor.

For an introduction to Weber's concept of class, see e.g. Frank Parkin, "Class, Status, and Party," pp. 90–108 in *Max Weber* (1982). According to Talcott Parsons, who translated Ch. 4 ("Status Groups and Classes") of *Economy and Society*, "Weber uses the term 'class' (*Klasse*) in a special sense, which is defined [in the beginning of this text] and which, in particular, he contrasts with *Stand* [status]" (Weber 1947:424 n. 1). Parsons adds that "there seems no other alternative translation of *Klasse*, but it should be kept in mind that it is being used in a special sense" (ibid.). For a brief discussion of how Weber's class concept has fared in contemporary stratification research, see e.g. David Grusky (ed.), *Social Stratification* (2001), pp. 17–18.

For a recent discussion of Marx versus Weber when it comes to class analysis, see e.g. Erik Olin Wright, "The Shadow of Exploitation in Weber's Class Analysis" (2002) and Frank Parkin, *Marxism and Class Theory: A Bourgeois Critique* (1979). Finally, according to the editors of MWG, "the unfinished fourth chapter ['Status Groups and Classes'] is a new, terminologically sharpened version of the posthumous text ('Classes, Status Groups, Parties')" (Baier, Lepsius, Mommsen and Schluchter 2000:113).

See also carrier, life chances, interest, open and closed social relationships, status

class interest   *See* class

closed social relationships   *See* open and closed social relationships

closure   *See* open and closed social relationships

coercion (*Zwang*)   Coercion is very common in society, Weber says (ES:42). "Coercion, physical or psychic, somehow lies at the root of nearly all social relationships" (SCIS:173)—a term that here includes communal relationships. The two main types of coercion are physical and psychological (e.g. ES:34–5). Violence and coercion are, however, two distinct types in Weber's analysis.

Physical coercion can often be used effectively in the short run, but not in the long run. In some situations status incentives may also be more efficient than physical coercion (ES:967–68). At one point in *Economy and*

Society Weber also says that "whereas the physical whip assures the exertion of the slaves lodged in barracks . . . , the wage whip and threat of joblessness guarantee the effort of the 'free' worker" (ES:1010). Just as there is "legal coercion," the market has "a special kind of coercion" (ES:313, 731).

Psychological coercion can be exemplified by the pressure that may be brought to bear on a member of a religious sect, including the threat of expulsion. In Weber's definition of hierocratic organizations he states that its order is enforced with the help of "hierocratic coercion," which he defines as "psychic coercion [that operates] by distributing or denying religious benefits" (ES:54).

See also economic motivation, interest, means of war, violence

cognitive interest   *See* knowledge

Collected Essays in the Sociology of Religion   Weber planned a four-volume work entitled *Collected Essays in the Sociology of Religion* (*Gesammelte Aufsätze zur Religionssoziologie*), but only three volumes were to appear (1920–21). What the original project looked like is clear from an announcement for this work that Weber published on October 25, 1919:

Almost all the essays collected here have appeared in the *Archiv für Sozialwissenschaft und Sozialpolitik*. However, here they are not only corrected but also supplemented by substantial insertions and by the provision of supporting documentation. Initiating the collection is the much-discussed essay, "The Protestant Ethic and the Spirit of Capitalism." It is followed by the sketch of "The Protestant Sects and the Spirit of Capitalism" (a revision of an essay in the *Christliche Welt* [*Christian World*]), the essays on "The Economic Ethics of the World Religions"—expanded by a short depiction of the Egyptian and Mesopotamian, and the Zoroastrian religious ethics—but especially by a sketch devoted to the rise of the social singularity of the Occident, i.e., an essay on the development of the European bourgeoisie in antiquity and the Middle Ages. The depiction of Judaism covers the period up until the time of the Maccabees. A third volume will contain the depiction of primitive Christianity, Talmudic Judaism, Islam and Oriental Christianity. A concluding volume will treat the Christianity of the Occident. The object of study is in every case the treatment of the question: What is the economic and social singularity of the Occident based upon, how did it arise and especially, how is it connected to the development of the religious ethos? (Schluchter 1989:425)

The three volumes that were published have not been translated into English as such, but their contents have appeared as separate monographs and articles, as follows:

VOLUME 1

Vorbemerkung, pp. 1–16, trans. "Author's Introduction" in PE:13–31.
Die protestantische Ethik und der Geist des Kapitalismus, pp. 17–206, trans. as *The Protestant Ethic and the Spirit of Capitalism* (PE; 2nd ed.).
"Die protestantischen Sekten und der Geist des Kapitalismus," pp. 207–36, trans. as "The Protestant Sects and the Spirit of Capitalism" in GM:302–22.
Die Wirtschaftsethik der Weltreligionen, pp. 237–573: "Einleitung," pp. 237–75, translated as "The Social Psychology of the World Religions" in GM:267–301.
Konfuzianismus und Taoismus, pp. 276–536, trans. as *The Religion of China* (RC).
"Zwischenbetrachtung," pp. 536–73, trans. as "Religious Rejections of the World and Their Directions" in GM:323–59.

VOLUME 2

Die Wirtschaftsethik der Weltreligionen, II: Hinduismus und Buddhismus, pp. 1–378, trans. as *The Religion of India* (RI).

VOLUME 3

Die Wirtschaftsethik der Weltreligionen: Das antike Judentum, pp. 1–400, *Nachtrag: Die Pharisäer*, pp. 401–42, trans. as *Ancient Judaism* (AJ).

The dates when the individual writings first appeared are as follows: *Vorbemerkung* (1920), PE (1904–5, rev. 1920), "The Protestant Sects and the Spirit of Capitalism" (2 versions 1906, rev. 1920), "Einleitung" (1915, rev. 1920), *The Religion of China* (1915, rev. 1920), *Zwischenbetrachtung* (1915, rev. 1920), *The Religion of India* (1916–17, rev. 1920), *Ancient Judaism* (1917–20, rev. 1920).

A useful source for dates and other facts about Weber's various studies in the sociology of religion is Wolfgang Schluchter, "The Sociology of Religion [by Max Weber]: A Reconstruction of Its Development," pp. 411–32, 469–72 in *Rationalism, Religion and Domination* (1989).

See also *Economic Ethics of the World Religions*, sociology of religion

collected works   Various volumes in Max Weber's collected works (*Max Weber Gesamtausgabe*) have been published since 1984 by J. C. B. Mohr in Tübingen, Weber's original publisher.

The plan for the collected works was published in 1981 in a prospectus (*Prospektus der Max Weber Gesamtausgabe* [1981]). Some changes, however, have been made over the years, and the reader is referred to the following Web address for general information about this work as well as continuous news and updates: http://www.mohr.de/mw/mwg.htm. A complete bibliography of Weber's writings has also been included in this Web page.

The editorial committee of the *Gesamtausgabe* consists of Horst Baier, M. Rainer Lepsius, Wolfgang Mommsen, Wolfgang Schluchter and Johannes Winkelmann (deceased). The guidelines of the edition can be found at the end of each volume. The basic idea is to publish Weber's writings and also his letters and lectures.

According to information from 2003, more than forty volumes are planned (twenty-three volumes of Weber's writings, eleven volumes of his letters, and seven volumes of his lectures). Some twenty volumes have already appeared—either in hardcover editions with excellent introductions or (in some cases) in paperback editions without the introductions.

See e.g. Gianfranco Poggi, "Max Weber: A Monumental Edition in the Making" (1986) and Guenther Roth, "The Complete Edition of Max Weber's Work: An Update" (1996).

collective concepts   *See* holism

collegiality (*Kollegialität*)   By collegiality Weber means ways in which the power of an authority is limited. Different types of collegiality exist.

Collegiality is defined in Ch. 3 of *Economy and Society* as the fact that "on either a traditional or a rational basis authority may be limited or controlled by certain specific means" (ES:271). This usually boils down to various ways in which obstacles are raised to "precise, clear, and above all, rapid decision" (ES:277). Collegial bodies, in other words, cannot be bureaucracies since these latter are maximally efficient (e.g. ES:223).

From Weber's discussion in *Economy and Society*, it is clear that collegiality has taken many different expressions in history (ES:271–84, 994–98). The authority of feudal and patrimonial regimes has, for example, often been limited by privileges granted to certain status groups. A bureaucracy may be limited by some outside agency. Weber also speaks of separation of powers as a form of collegiality (ES:282–83, 652–53; for separation of powers in law, see ES:773). If the head of an organization has absolute power, there is monocracy—and by definition no room for collegiality (e.g. ES:220, 222).

While Weber in his last version of *Economy and Society* emphasizes collegiality as a means of limiting authority, in his earlier version the emphasis is on the expert knowledge of collegiate bodies and the ruler's need for this expertise—as well as his need not to lose control over decisions to experts (ES:271–84 versus ES:994–98).

The translators of Weber's political writings say of the term "collegial": "although the English word is fairly rare, referring principally to the sharing by Roman Catholic bishops in the government of the church, it nevertheless conveys the correct sense of co-responsible government" (Lassman and Speirs 1994:376).

For a discussion of Weber's concept of collegiality as well as an attempt to link it to professionalism, see Malcolm Waters, "Collegiality, Bureaucratization, and Professionalization: A Weberian Analysis" (1989). See also Randall Collins, "Democratization in World-Historical Perspective" (1998).

See also domination, monocracy, power

commenda (*Commenda*)   This type of economic organization represents an early form of the modern firm. Weber writes about the commenda in many of his works, from his first dissertation (HCP) to his lecture course of 1919–20, known as *General Economic History*.

Weber describes the commenda in *Economy and Society* as follows: "in the *commenda* relationship various types of goods were entrusted to a traveling merchant to sell in a foreign market. . . . The profit or loss was then divided in a particular proportion between the traveling merchant and the entrepreneur who had advanced the capital" (ES:95; cf. ES:380, 1216).

The fact that the profit was split in pre-determined proportions made it necessary to calculate the value of the venture at the beginning as well as when it was over. This type of calculation constituted an early form of capital accounting, according to Weber (GEH:206–7).

For a discussion of the commenda in Weber's work, see e.g. John Love, *Antiquity and Capitalism* (1991), pp. 165–67.

See also capital accounting, firm

commercial legislation   Weber primarily discusses the relationship of law to the economy in his sociology of law, but also in his sociology of religion. The relationship is of particular importance in this case since, as part of his interest in the relationship of religion to rational capitalism, Weber also investigates the role of commercial legislation. His main finding is that sophisticated commercial legislation has tended to be accompanied by a low level of formal legal rationality.

Weber often points out that the major legal institutions of capitalism were developed as part of the *lex mercatoria* during the Middle Ages and not in Roman law (e.g. ES:977, 1464 n. 14; GEH:341–42).

Weber's first dissertation falls under the topic of commercial legislation, since it deals with the development and origin of the legal forms of the early capitalist firm (HCP). His thesis adviser, Levin Goldschmidt, was the founder of the history of commercial law in Europe. According to Weber, the sophistication of German legal historiography was unsurpassed in the nineteenth century (ES:858).

See e.g. Richard Swedberg, *Max Weber and the Idea of Economic Sociology* (1998), pp. 91–99.

communal relationship (*Vergemeinschaftung*) Communal relationships play an important role in Weber's general sociology. They are social relationships that are held together by a sense of belonging together. Typical examples include families, national communities and religious brotherhoods.

A communal relationship is defined in Weber's general sociology in Ch. 1 of *Economy and Society* in the following manner: "a social relationship will be called 'communal' if and so far as the orientation of social action—whether in the individual case, on the average, or in the pure type—is based on a subjective feeling of the parties, whether affectual or traditional, that they belong together" (ES:40).

In connection with his discussion of a communal relationship Weber also introduces the notion of an associative relationship, which is a social relationship that is held together by an agreement or coordinated interests. He notes that these two types of relationships should be seen as a continuum, and he explicitly distances himself from Tönnies' sharp distinction between *Gemeinschaft* (community) and *Gesellschaft* (society; ES:41, 60 n. 24).

Coercion is common in communal relationships, Weber notes. He also points out that "the great majority" of social relationships have elements of both communal and associative relationships (ES:41).

In his new translation of Ch. 1 of *Economy and Society* Keith Tribe translates *Vergemeinschaftung* as "formation of community" (EW:343).

According to Martin Albrow, "Weber sought to dispel any rigid dichotomy between these two concepts and emphasized process by adding the prefix *Ver-* to create *Vergemeinschaftung* and *Vergesellschaftung*" (Albrow 1990:249). Albrow adds that "both [terms] are difficult to render into English; Parsons [the original translator of Ch. 1 of *Economy and Society*] chose communal and associative relationships respectively." David Frisby and Derek Sayer argue that it was Weber's methodological individualism that made him avoid terms such as community and society, and instead use terms such as *Vergemeinschaftung* and *Vergesellschaftung*: "this is why Weber preferred to use verb forms or active nouns in order to delineate the social processes with which he was concerned" (Frisby and Sayer 1986:68).

The conceptual pair *Vergemeinschaftung* and *Vergesellschaftung* is introduced into Weber's general sociology in Ch. 1 of *Economy and Soci-*

ety. In his essay of 1913 entitled "Some Categories of Interpretive Sociology" Weber does not use these two terms, but *Gemeinschaftshandeln* and *Gesellschaftshandeln*. See on this point Hiroshi Orihara, "From 'A Torso with a Wrong Head' to 'Five Disjointed Body-Parts without a Head'" (2003), pp. 152, 154.

A fifth chapter of *Economy and Society* was presumably planned which would have dealt with "a classificatory account of types of communal relationships [*Vergemeinschaftungen*] and associative relationships [*Vergesellschaftungen*]" (WuG:212 n. 1).

See also associative relationship, community, social relationship, society

communism (*Kommunismus*) Weber uses the term communism in a way that differs from its common usage today. More precisely, he refers to three major forms of communism in his economic sociology in Ch. 2 of *Economy and Society*: household communism (within a family), military communism (among comrades-in-arms), and religious communism (in communities based on love and charity) (ES:153–54). These types of communism are based on non-economic considerations and are indifferent to calculations.

Modern (political) communism represents a new historical phenomenon, especially since it is rational in spirit.

See e.g. Stefan Breuer, "Soviet Communism and Weberian Sociology" (1998).

See also household, socialism

community (*Gemeinde, Gemeinschaft, Vergemeinschaftung*) Weber uses the term community in many of his works, and he was deeply interested in trying to understand the social structure of different types of communities. Weber's terminology for community shifts over the years and is complex. In his general sociology in Ch. 1 of *Economy and Society*, for example, Weber's preferred term is "communal relationship" (*Vergemeinschaftung*), and the reason for this has to do with his attempt to shift sociological terminology in a social action direction. At this stage Weber found Tönnies' famous distinction between *Gemeinschaft* (community) and *Gesellschaft* (society) much too sharp for his own purposes (ES:41, 60 n. 24).

Another term for community that Weber uses in *Economy and Society* is *Gemeinde*. In Weber's sociology of religion a *Gemeinde* denotes a congregation or a congregational community (e.g. ES:452–53, 455). Weber adds that in German, the word *Gemeinde* also means a "neighborhood that has been associated for fiscal or other political purposes" (ES:452; for an example, see e.g. Weber [1895] 1980). Weber's use of *Gemeinde* in the sense of municipality in his sociology of law shows some affinity with this administrative meaning of the term (e.g. ES:715).

In *Economy and Society* Weber also uses *Gemeinde* to denote a local community, for which the neighborhood constitutes the natural basis (e.g. ES:363). In his sociology of domination in the same work Weber, finally, uses *Gemeinde* in still another context or meaning, namely as an organized group subject to charismatic authority; ES:243.

The role that Weber wanted to assign to communities in *Economy and Society* can also be studied in the two plans for that work (1909, 1914). See e.g. Wolfgang Schluchter, *Rationalism, Religion, and Domination* (1989), pp. 466–68, Hiroshi Orihara, "From 'a Torso with a Wrong Head' to 'Five Disjointed Pieces of Carcass'?" (2002), pp. 5–6. One part of the new edition of *Economy and Society* in MWG will be devoted to communities (*Gemeinschaften*—Vol. I/22-1).

According to the editors of MWG, there was "a fifth planned chapter [in the last version of *Economy and Society*] on types of communities [*Gemeinschaften*] ('Forms of Associations' [*Verbände*])" (Baier, Lepsius, Mommsen and Schluchter 2000:114; cf. Weber 1999d:xvii).

According to Jean-Pierre Grossein, the concept of community is "omnipresent" in Weber's work but frequently misunderstood (Grossein 1996:119). Guenther Roth argues that "it is less well understood that he [that is, Weber] also transferred the concept of the congregation or community (*Gemeinde*) from the religious to the political sphere and came to define it as the typical charismatic association (cf. [ES:452, 243, 1119])" (Roth 1975:151).

See also communal relationship, congregation, group, neighborhood, society

comparative sociology (*vergleichende Soziologie*) Much of Weber's work in sociology is comparative in nature, as the reader of *Economy and Society* and other works quickly notices. Comparative sociology, however, also fills an important methodological role in Weber's sociology, among other reasons because comparisons are typically needed to work out the causality involved.

In his general sociology, as outlined in Ch. 1 of *Economy and Society*, Weber refers to what he calls "the fundamental task of comparative sociology" (ES:10). This expression refers to the essential role that comparisons play in verifying the subjective interpretation of an action, by comparing it to the actual course of events—that is, by properly assessing its impact on what happened.

This is something that is very difficult to do, according to Weber, and usually "there remains only the possibility of comparing the largest possible number of historical or contemporary processes which, while otherwise similar, differ in the one decisive point of their relation to the particular motive or factor of their relation to the particular motive or factor the role of which is being investigated" (ibid.). He adds that "often, unfortunately, there is available only the uncertain procedure of the 'imaginary experiment' which consists in thinking away certain elements of the chain of motivation and working out the course of action which would then probably ensue, thus arriving at a causal judgment" (ibid.). The analyst, in other words, has to resort to counterfactuals (rather than to actual comparisons as in John Stuart Mill).

Weber's studies of the different economic ethics of Hinduism, Buddhism and other religions in his sociology of religion can be seen as an illustration of how an imaginary experiment can be carried out—in this case to work out the causality involved in the emergence of the capitalist spirit in the West and its non-emergence elsewhere. Weber himself, it may be added, calls his studies in the economic ethics of the world religions "attempts at comparative studies in the sociology of religion" (GAR, I:237).

Talcott Parsons characterizes Weber's statement about "the fundamental task of comparative sociology" (ES:10) as "an exceedingly compact statement of Weber's theory of the logical conditions of proof of causal relationship" (ES:59 n. 10). For a discussion of Weber's comparative sociology as well as an attempt to relate it to contemporary comparative historical sociology, see Stephen Kalberg, *Max Weber's Comparative-Historical Sociology* (1994) and "Max Weber's Critique of Recent Comparative-Historical Sociology and a Reconstruction of His Analysis of the Rise of Confucianism in China" (1999).

See also causality, history, meaning, objective possibility, verification

competition (*Konkurrenz*, also *Wettbewerb*)   The concept of competition plays an important role in Weber's sociology, especially his economic sociology and his political sociology. Its core meaning is that several actors who all have an interest in getting something will attempt to do so without resorting to force.

The exact definition of competition, as this is to be found in Weber's general sociology in Ch. 1 of *Economy and Society*, reads as follows: "a peaceful conflict is 'competition' insofar as it consists in an attempt to attain control over opportunities and advantages which are also desired by others" (ES:38).

In the market, actors first compete over who will do the buying and the selling; and only after this has been decided, will the exchange take place. Competition on a large scale, Weber states, will lead to a selection of the qualities that are important to success.

If competition is oriented to an order, it is "regulated." Economic actors may also become interested in curbing competition when the number of competitors grows in relation to the profit span (ES:341–42). If competition is curbed in capitalism, a considerably less dynamic form of capitalism will appear.

Competition can exist in many areas of society, not only in the economy. Political competition, as opposed to economic competition, may affect the economy, for example, if the ruler has to compete with other rulers for economic resources (e.g. ES:165).

Finally, Schumpeter's famous theory of democracy as competition for political leadership has according to some scholars been influenced by Weber's ideas on this topic (e.g. Wolfgang Mommsen, *Max Weber and German Politics* [1984], pp. 406–7).

See also capitalism, exchange, market, selection

complex of meaning (*Sinnzusammenhang*)   The meaning that an actor attaches to his or her action is essential to Weber's interpretive sociology. The actor's meaning, however, is typically also part of a larger set of meanings—a complex of meaning, in Weber's terminology. This complex of meaning may consist of some local context or, say, of a whole religion.

In order to understand the meaning of an action, Weber explains in his general sociology in Ch. 1 of *Economy and Society*, the sociologist may need to "place the act in an intelligible and more inclusive context of meaning (*Sinnzusammenhang*)" (ES:8). By doing so, it is possible to decide, for example, if someone who chops wood does this for a living or is just working off a fit of rage (ES:8–9). This makes "complex of meaning" part of what Weber terms "explanatory understanding." Also an order is presumably part of a complex of meaning (or may constitute one).

According to Talcott Parsons, the translator of Ch. 1 of *Economy and Society*, the German term *Sinnzusammenhang* "refers to a plurality of elements which form a coherent whole on the level of meaning." He adds that "there seems to be no single English term that is adequate" and that this is the reason why "'context of meaning', 'complex of meaning', and sometimes 'meaningful system' have been employed" (ES:58 n. 8).

Elsewhere in his writings on Weber, Parsons notes that Weber connects complexes of meaning to interests; and he refers to "[Weber's] concern with systems of meaning (*Sinnzusammenhänge*) which could be interpreted ('understood', in Weber's special sense) and which, as definitions of situations for the actions of individuals, could be linked with individuals' 'interests' (their motives in a psychological sense)" (Parsons, "Introduction," p. xxiii in Max Weber, *The Sociology of Religion* [1963]).

Martin Albrow notes like Parsons that there are many possible translations of *Sinnzusammenhang*, and adds that "the most literal translation is a 'hanging together of meaning'" (Albrow 1990:128). Albrow also emphasizes very strongly that the idea of *Sinnzusammenhang* allows Weber "to develop his analysis beyond the starting point of subjective intentions," and that "one may go so far as saying that social science in the Weberian sense . . . could not proceed without this idea" (ibid.). On this last point he refers to the similar argument that Dirk Käsler makes about the role of "complex of meaning" in Weber's work (Käsler 1988:177). Sam Whimster translates *Sinnzusammenhang* as "context of meaning" and defines it as follows: "the ensemble of meanings in a social situation to which all attribution of motives for actions has to be referred" (EW:408). In his new translation of Ch. 1 of *Economy and Society* Keith Tribe translates *Sinnzusammenhang* as "context of meaning" and "meaningful context" (EW:316, 318).

See also explanation, interpretive sociology, meaning, understanding

comprehension   *See* understanding

compulsory organization (*Anstalt*)   This concept refers in Weber's sociology to an organization in which membership is compulsory.

The exact definition of a compulsory organization in Weber's general sociology in Ch. 1 of *Economy and Society* is as follows: "an organization (*Verband*) which imposes, within a specifiable sphere of operations, its order (with relative success) on all action conforming with certain criteria will be called a *compulsory organization* or *association*" (ES:52; cf. SCIS:174).

A rationally established church or a state are examples of compulsory organizations. The opposite of a compulsory organization is a voluntary organization, in the same way as a sect is the opposite of a church.

See also *Anstalt*, organization or association, coercion, voluntary organization

concept formation   Weber's view of the way that concepts are formed in the social sciences is closely related to his view of the same process in the cultural sciences. Concepts in the social sciences such as history, economics and sociology, he believes, are all related to what people find significant, and this is in turn related to their values. The theory of causality in the cultural sciences is also reflected in the construction of concepts.

Weber's most extensive discussion of this topic can be found in those parts of his work that are devoted to the ideal type and the historical individual (see especially MSS:49–112, EW:359–404).

An ideal type is essentially constructed through the analytical accentuation of certain elements (see the discussion of ideal types in e.g. ES:9, 19–22 and MSS:89–105, EW:387–98). This is a procedure that history, economics and sociology all have in common.

In *The Protestant Ethic*, written at a time when Weber was preoccupied with the issue of the ideal type, he says that his portrait of the capitalist spirit is an example of a "historical individual." The latter is defined as follows: "a complex of elements associated in historical reality which we unite into a conceptual whole from the standpoint of their cultural significance" (PE:47; cf. PE:48).

There is also a link between the cognitive interest of the researcher and how concepts are worked out. According to Raymond Aron, "the choice of facts, the elaboration of concepts, and the delineation of the object, Weber wrote, are marked by the direction of our curiosity" (Aron 1985:337).

See also cognitive interest, culture, historical individual, ideal type, types

conduct of life *See* lifestyle

confession *See* Catholicism

confirmation (*Bewährung*) This concept covers the situation when a religious person checks for signs that he or she has done the right thing (similarly for the charismatic leader; cf. ES:241). When a certain behavior is confirmed in this way, it will typically be repeated by the believer—and the impact of the original religious idea that inspired the action will thereby be strengthened and ensured.

The idea of confirmation is at the very center of *The Protestant Ethic and the Spirit of Capitalism* and to some extent also in Weber's more general concern with how to change one's personality according to one's ideals.

Talcott Parsons translates "the idea of confirmation" (*Bewährungsgedanke*) as "the idea of proof" (PE:126). For Weber's concept of confirmation, see also Jean-Pierre Grossein, "Présentation" (1996), pp. 75, 120.

See also psychological or religious premium, religious benefits, social mechanisms

conflict (*Kampf*) Weber assigns a central role in his sociology to conflicts (or struggles). These are conceptualized as the result of actors trying to carry out their wills against the resistance of other actors.

The definition of a conflict, which can be found in Weber's general sociology in Ch. 1 of *Economy and Society*, reads as follows: "a social relationship will be referred to as 'conflict' (*Kampf*) insofar as action is oriented intentionally to carrying out the actor's own will against the resistance of the other party or parties" (ES:38; cf. SCIS:173).

Conflicts can be peaceful or violent; and they constitute the heart of many different types of phenomena, including competition and selection.

Conflicts are an integral part of society: "conflict cannot be excluded from social life. One can change its means, its objects, even its fundamental direction and its bearers, but it cannot be eliminated" (MSS:26). In the economy there are conflicts within firms as well as in the market. In the latter there are not only conflicts over competition and price (*Preiskampf* and *Konkurrenzkampf*), but also a "struggle of man against man" (*Kampf des Menschen mit dem Menschen;* e.g. ES: 82, 108). Politics is similarly deeply influenced by conflict: "the essence of all politics . . . is *conflict, the recruitment of allies and voluntary following*" (PW:173).

Talcott Parsons notes in a comment to his translation of Ch. 1 in *Economy and Society* that there exists a tendency in the secondary literature on Weber's work to overemphasize his use of the concept of struggle. In Ch. 1, according to Parsons, Weber rather focuses on "the *varieties* of conflict, from the extreme case of violent, unlimited and unregulated struggle to peaceful and regulated competition" (ES:60 n. 23). In his new translation of Ch. 1 in *Economy and Society* Keith Tribe translates *Kampf* as "struggle" (EW:341).

See also competition, power, selection

Confucianism   Confucianism belongs to the category that Weber terms world-religions, and it is mainly discussed in *The Religion of China: Confucianism and Taoism* (see also ES:476–77, 537, 579–81). Weber describes Confucianism as "a religious ethic," which also was "the official ethic of China" (ES:501, 526). It is further characterized by the fact that it does not have a place for salvation or a transcendental ethic. There is no hereafter in Confucianism (RC:206). The main carrier of Confucianism was the world-ordering bureaucrat (ES:512). In the well-known concluding chapter of *The Religion of China* Weber compares Confucianism to Puritanism (RC:226–49). Weber here states that while Confucianism has a strongly rational character, it advocates an accommodation to the world in contrast to ascetic Protestantism.

For discussion, see e.g. Stephen Kalberg, "Max Weber's Critique of Recent Comparative-Historical Sociology and a Reconstruction of His Analysis of the Rise of Confucianism in China" (1999), Wolfgang Schluchter, *Rationalism, Religion, and Domination* (1989), pp. 85–116, and Otto Van Der Sprenkel, "Max Weber on China" (1964). See also Wolfgang Schluchter (ed.), *Max Webers Studie über Konfucianismus und Taoismus* (1983) as well as the introductory and editorial material in

MWG I/19.

See also *Economic Ethics of the World Religions*; *Religion of China, The*

congregation (*Gemeinde*)   By congregation, according to Weber's terminology in his sociology of religion in *Economy and Society*, is primarily meant a specific type of religious community (ES:452–53; more generally, see ES:452–68). An alternative translation of Weber's term *Gemeinde* in this context would be "congregational community" (e.g. ES:455).

According to Weber, "a religious community (*Gemeinde*) arises in connection with a prophetic movement as a result of routinization, i.e., as a result of the process whereby either the prophet himself or his disciples secure the permanence of his preaching and the congregation's distribution of grace" (ES:452). Weber describes "congregational religiosity" (*Gemeindereligiosität*) as "a phenomenon of diverse manifestation and great fluidity," and says that it will only be used in his sociology of religion "when the laity has been organized permanently in such a manner that they can actively participate" (ES:455). A "parish," for example, is an administrative unit and does not in itself qualify as a congregational community (ibid.).

Talcott Parsons explains apropos congregation that "the type of collectivity in which Weber is here interested is one specially organized around religious interests as such, which is thereby distinct from other 'secular' collectivities in the same society" (Parsons 1963:xxxvi). The term *Gemeinde*, it can be added, is used by Weber in different meanings. He points out, for example, that it not only means "congregation" and "community" but also a "neighborhood that has been associated for fiscal or other political purposes" (ES:452). According to Guenther Roth, "it is less well understood that he [that is, Weber] also transferred the concept of the congregation or community (*Gemeinde*) from the religious to the political sphere and came to define it as the typical charismatic association (cf. [ES:452, 243, 1119])" (Roth 1975:151).

See also community, religious communities

consensual action (*Einverständnishandeln*)   This concept from Weber's 1913 essay "Some Categories of Interpretive Sociology" covers those types of social action which are structured in such a way that they evolve as if they were oriented to an order.

Consensual action figures prominently in the essay, where it is defined in the following manner: "there are complexes of social action (*Gemeinschaftshandeln*), which in the absence of a rational agreement on an order, (1) may in effect operate as if such an agreement had occurred, (2) and in which this specific effect is codetermined through the nature of the meaning of the action of the individuals" (SCIS:166; cf. SCIS:168). The concept of consensual action is close in meaning to that of self-interest in Weber's work.

The term consensual action is not used in Weber's general sociology in Ch. 1 of *Economy and Society*. For a discussion of its meaning and role in Weber's sociology, see Hiroshi Orihara, "From 'a Torso with a Wrong Head' to 'Five Disjointed Pieces of Carcass'?," (2000), p. 9.

See also self-interest, social action

constitution (*Verfassung*)   Weber uses the term constitution in a rather special sense in his general sociology in *Economy and Society*. He also uses it elsewhere in his work, in different contexts and meanings.

In his discussion of organizations or associations, which can be found in his general sociology in Ch. 1 of *Economy and Society*, Weber says that "the 'constitution' of an organization is the empirically existing probability, varying in extent, kind and conditions, that rules imposed by the leadership will be acceded to" (ES:50; cf. SCIS:176). Weber adds that this meaning is far from the one that is common in legal contexts (ES:51, 61 n. 29).

In his early work Weber followed the custom in German social science around the turn of the century and used the term "constitution" in a variety of contexts. As part of these writings, the term constitution is hard to translate and means, among other things, "organization," as in "labor organization" or "employment regime." According to some commentators Weber was also innovative in his use of the term "agrarian constitution" in his early work, especially in that he included a social or sociological dimension. For a discussion of the term constitution in Weber's early work, see Lawrence Scaff, "Weber before Weberian Sociology" (1989).

Finally, toward the end of his life Weber got involved in producing the first draft of the constitution for the Weimar Republic. One of his most important texts on constitutional matters is "Suffrage and Democracy in Germany"; another relevant text is "The President of the Reich" (PW:80–129; 304–8). In his work for the Weimar Constitution Weber essentially argued for a president as a counterweight to a parliamentary power; and he felt that "the Reich constitution [that resulted] is . . . very close to my proposals" (Mommsen 1984:368).

For Weber and the Weimar Constitution, see e.g. Sven Eliaeson, "Constitutional Caesarism: Weber's Politics in Their German Contexts" (2000) and Wolfgang Mommsen, "Weber and the Making of the Weimar Constitution," pp. 332–89 in *Max Weber and German Politics 1890–1920* (1984). Weber's relationship to Carl Schmitt (who is infamous for his support of Hitler) is often touched on as part of the discussion of Weber and the Weimar Constitution. According to Jürgen Habermas (who later modified his opinion), Schmitt was a "'legitimate pupil'" of Weber (Habermas 1972:66). For the relationship of Schmitt to Weber, see also Mommsen's *Max Weber and German Politics 1890–1920*, pp. 382–89. Finally, according to commentators Weber "never employed the classical concept of the 'constitutional state' (*Rechtsstaat*)" (e.g. Mommsen 1984:394).

See also constitution, employment regime (*Arbeitsverfassung*), organization or association, politics

context of meaning   *See* complex of meaning

contract (*Kontrakt*)   Contracts are primarily discussed in Weber's sociology of law, and he mainly analyzes contracts of the past.

In the section on the sociology of law in *Economy and Society* a contract is defined as "a voluntary agreement constituting the foundation of claims and obligations" (ES:671). Contracts constitute an example of "empowering" or "enabling law," as opposed to coercive law (ES:730; cf. ES:667).

Weber's sociology of law contains an extensive discussion of different types of contracts and their historical emergence. A key distinction is drawn between "the status contract" (*Status-Kontrakt*) and "the instrumental contract" (*Zweck-Kontrakt*). The former "involves a change in what may be called the total legal situation (the universal position) and the social status of the person involved" (ES:672). The latter, on the other hand, "aims solely . . . at some specific (especially economic) performance or result" (ES:673). When an individual, for example, becomes somebody's slave or master, a status contract is involved; while barter is an early example of an instrumental contract. While the worker is formally free to enter into any contract with his or her employer, in reality he or she is often constrained to do so by circumstances (e.g. ES:729–31).

Formal freedom of contract is crucial to modern capitalism (ES:729–31; cf. ES:869).

See also law

convention (*Konvention*)   Weber's term convention has roughly the same meaning as "norm" in contemporary sociology; and it plays an important role in his sociology.

In Weber's general sociology in Ch. 1 of *Economy and Society* a convention is defined in the following manner: "an order will be called . . . convention so far as its validity is externally guaranteed by the probability that deviation from it within a given social group will result in a relatively general and practically significant reaction of disapproval" (ES:34; cf. ES:319).

A convention differs from what Weber terms "custom" by having a sanction; and it differs from what he terms "law" by lacking a staff to stop behavior that deviates from the convention. "Law, convention, and custom belong to the same continuum with imperceptible transitions leading from one to the other" (ES:319).

Weber points out that a convention is not based on approval or disapproval per se—but always on approval or disapproval in a special social group (ES:324). He also emphasizes that regularities inspired by interest can be much stronger than conventions or norms (ES:30).

Talcott Parsons argues in his comment on his translation of Ch. 1 of *Economy and Society* that Weber's distinction between convention and usage is reminiscent of W. G. Sumner's distinction between "mores" and "folkways." The reason for this is that the concept of mores includes an element of moral obligation to conform, while the concept of folkways does not (ES:60 n. 17). Nonetheless, Parsons concludes, "it has seemed best to retain the English term closest to Weber's own [that is, convention]."

See also custom, law, order

corporation   For the capitalist firm, *see* firm (*Unternehmung*). For Weber's discussion of the legal concept of corporation (*Korporation*), see his sociology of law (e.g. ES:715–16).

corvée state (*Fronstaat*)   *See* state

counterfactual   *See* objective possibility

Critique of Stammler ("R. Stammlers 'Überwindung' der materialistischen Geschichtsauffassung," trans. 1977)   This essay from 1907 (and its postscript) constitute a review of *The Historical Materialist Conception of Law and Economy* (1906) by the legal thinker Rudolf Stammler (1856–1938). Weber vehemently criticizes Stammler's ideas about legal rules also constituting social rules, and in the process outlines some of the tasks of cultural science.

See Guy Oakes, "Introductory Essay," pp. 1–56 in Weber [1907] 1977.

cult   *See* priest

cultural problems of the time (*die grossen Kulturprobleme*)   At any time in history there are certain major problems that people in society are concerned with, including cultural scientists. These are felt to be obvious and are often taken for granted. This means, among other things, that the relationship of problems to values is forgotten in the cultural sciences, and that all energy is focused on collecting facts.

But then "the light of the great cultural problems (*die grossen Kulturprobleme*) moves on, and so do the cultural sciences" (MSS:112). The issue of values now reemerges, and "*the cultural significance of concrete historical events and patterns*" (*die Kulturbedeutung konkreter historischen Zusammenhänge*) reassumes its central place in the cultural sciences (ibid.).

As examples of great cultural problems of today one may mention democracy and equality, and of yesterday, colonies and monarchy.

Weber discusses the issue of the cultural problems of the day toward the end of his famous essay on objectivity from 1904 (MSS:111–12).

See also cultural sciences, culture

cultural sciences (*Kulturwissenschaften*)   The social sciences are part of the "cultural sciences," an expression that Weber uses especially in his methodological essays. The word "cultural" indicates what differentiates the sciences that deal with meaning and significance from the natural sciences (*Kulturwissenschaften* versus *Naturwissenschaften*).

In his essay on objectivity from 1904, Weber provides the following definition of the cultural sciences: "we have designated as 'cultural sciences' those disciplines which analyze the phenomena of life in terms of their cultural significance" (MSS:76). A little later in the same essay he specifies what sets the cultural sciences apart from the natural sciences, namely "the focus of attention on reality under the guidance of values which lend it significance and the selection and ordering of the phenomena which are thus affected in the light of their cultural significance is entirely different from the analysis of reality in terms of laws and general concepts" (ibid., p. 77).

In drawing a sharp line between the cultural and the natural sciences Weber was influenced by the debate on this issue that was going on in his day, and in which a number of philosophers and social scientists participated. Weber's suggestion for how to deal with this difference, however, differed from other proposals in that he insisted on the systematic and scientific nature of the cultural sciences, including sociology. He worked out a theory of causality, for example, that could be used in the social and cultural sciences (as opposed to the natural sciences), and in which counterfactuals, probability and what constitute evidence when it comes to interpretive understanding all play important roles. Weber's views on all of these topics, it should be added, have their roots in his essays on methodology, in which they also were given their first form (see especially MSS, CS, RK, SCIS).

In his essay on objectivity from 1904 Weber notes that "if one wishes to call those disciplines which treat the events of human life with respect to their cultural significance 'cultural sciences', then social science in our sense belongs in that category" (MSS:67). The concept of cultural sciences, in other words, appears to be broader than that of social science. This may mean that it includes sciences that are neither social nor fall into the category of the natural sciences, such as psychology and jurisprudence.

Weber took over the term "cultural sciences" from the work of philosopher Heinrich Rickert, together with the terms "value-relevance" and "historical individual" to which it is closely related (H. H. Bruun, *Science, Values and Politics in Max Weber's Methodology* [1972], p. 95).

For helpful guidance on the discussion of the differences between the cultural and the natural sciences, see e.g. Ola Agevall, *A Science of Unique Events: Max Weber's Methodology of the Cultural Sciences* (1999), Don Martindale, *The Nature and Types of Sociological Theory* (1960), pp. 377–83, and Talcott Parsons, *The Structure of Social Action* (1937), pp. 591–601.

See also causality, cultural problems of the time, culture, explanation, meaning, natural sciences, objectivity

culture (*Kultur*)   Culture is the central category in Weber's view of what characterizes the sciences that do not belong to the natural sciences. In this respect it may well qualify as the single most important concept in Weber's methodology. It is also closely related to Weber's view of values, concept formation, objectivity and causality in the social sciences. In brief, culture should not be seen as one among several concepts in Weber's work, but perhaps as its most fundamental category, to which other concepts are closely related.

Human beings, Weber argues, are evaluative beings, and in singling out certain aspects of reality according to these values, they create culture—which constitutes the object of study for the cultural sciences. The natural sciences, in contrast, do not deal with meaning, significance and value; they focus on the outside.

One place where Weber explicates in detail what he means by culture is in his essay on objectivity from 1904 (MSS:49–112). Weber here supplies what may well be the closest to a definition of culture that can be found in his work:

The concept of culture is a value-concept. Empirical reality becomes "culture" to us because and insofar as we relate it to value ideas. It includes those segments and only those segments of reality which have become significant to us because of this value-relevance. (MSS:76)

In the same essay Weber also notes that "we are cultural beings, endowed with the capacity and the will to take a deliberate attitude toward the world and to lend it significance" (MSS:81). The concept of culture, as Weber uses it, is also closely related to his general view of reality as being infinite in nature: "'culture' is a finite segment of the meaningless infinity of the world process, a segment on which human beings confer meaning and significance" (ibid., p. 81).

Weber emphasizes the need for the social sciences to study capitalism not only as an economic phenomenon but also as a cultural phenomenon (e.g. MSS:67; cf. MSS:112). It should finally be mentioned that Weber was also intensely interested in culture in the sense of the arts. According to his wife, he planned to write "a sociology embracing all the arts"—but only had time to complete a study of music (Marianne Weber [1926] 1975: 500; cf. RSFM).

For secondary literature on Weber's concept of culture, see e.g. H. H. Bruun, *Science, Values and Politics in Max Weber's Methodology* (1972), pp. 25–31, Talcott Parsons, *The Structure of Social Action* (1937), pp. 591–601, Lawrence Scaff, "Culture and Significance: Toward a Weberian Cultural Science" (1991) and "Max Webers Begriff der Kultur" (1994). For the argument that the sociology of culture represents the central theme in Weber's work, see e.g. Ralph Schroeder, *Max Weber and the Sociology of Culture* (1992). For the argument that the word *Kultur* is used much less frequently in Weber's later writings than in his early ones, and discussion of what this may possibly mean, see Francis Emerich, "Kultur und Gesellschaft in der Soziologie Max Webers" (1966).

See also causality, cognitive interest, complex of meaning, cultural problems of the time, cultural sciences, explanation, history, meaning, natural sciences, objectivity, sociology of art, values

custom (*Sitte*)   There exist certain forms of regular behavior, according to Weber, which are important to sociology: custom, self-interest and usage.

Weber introduces the notion of his three types of "empirical uniformities" in his general sociology in Ch. 1 of *Economy and Society*. A custom is defined as "usage . . . based upon long standing" (ES:29; cf. ES:319). Usage, in its turn, is defined in the following way: "if an orientation toward social action occurs regularly, it will be called 'usage' insofar as the probability of its existence within a group is based on nothing but actual practice" (ibid.). Weber also notes that "adherence to what has as such become customary is . . . a strong component of all conduct and, consequently, of all social action" (ES:320). Custom differs from convention in that it lacks a sanction; the border between the two, however, is fluid (ibid., cf. SCIS:170).

An important theme in Weber's sociology is that of traditionalism: how it is maintained and how it is broken, through charisma, instrumentally-rational action and otherwise. In *The Protestant Ethic* Weber refers, for example, to "the stone wall of habit" (PE:62).

For a discussion of Weber's concept of habit, including its relationship to disposition (*Eingestelltheit*), see Charles Camic, "The Matter of Habit" (1986), pp. 1057–66. For an argument that *Sitten* should be translated as "mores," see Johannes Raum, "Reflections on Max Weber's Thoughts Concerning Ethnic Groups" (1995), p. 80.

See also habitus, self-interest or self-interested kind of behavior, traditional action, traditionalism, usage

Darwinism   *See* selection

demagogue (*Demagoge*)   While the word "demagogue" has a negative connotation today, as well as in Weber's time, Weber argues that it also represents a positive quality for a political leader. This is especially the case in a democracy, where the leader has to rely on the support of the masses and not only on the power of small elites.

In a democracy "the typical political leader" is a demagogue, Weber notes in "Politics as a Vocation" (GM:96; EW:331). Political leaders are demagogues not only in their speeches but also in their writings; and Weber refers at this point to the great importance of modern political journalism. Demagogues, he also says, always run the risk of being irresponsible since they will be tempted to make promises that they cannot fulfill and also to simply make an impression on people (GM:116; EW:354).

In *Max Weber and German Politics 1890–1920* (1984) Wolfgang Mommsen refers repeatedly to Weber's attitude to the demagogue. First of all, he credits Weber with having "restored the honor of the figure of the great democratic demagogue in the face of the hierarchical tradition in Germany and for his attempt to restore the concept of demagoguery in its ancient positive sense" (ibid., pp. 407–8). But Mommsen also argues that Weber failed in his sociology to properly distinguish between "good and bad demagogues," and to investigate how "the plebiscitary charismatic leadership of the great demagogue" can result in "a charismatic autocracy" (ibid., p. 408).

See also Caesarism, charisma, charismatic domination, democracy, mystagogue, plebiscitary domination and leadership, politics

democracy   Weber discusses democracy in his writings on politics as well as in his political sociology. He discusses such issues as direct democracy, the role of leaders in a democracy, the relationship between capitalism and democracy, and the possibility of an effective and well-functioning democracy in Germany.

The closest one may come to a definition of democracy, or rather a discussion of such a definition, is the following statement in Weber's essay on socialism: "democracy can mean an infinite variety of things. In itself it simply means that no formal inequality of political rights exists between the individual classes of the population" (PW:275).

Weber also argues that democracy can be seen as a type of competition among leaders for the vote of the citizens, along the lines that Joseph Schumpeter would later popularize in *Capitalism, Socialism, and Democracy* (1942). Weber's approach on this point can be illustrated by the famous anecdote about his meeting with Ludendorff just after World War I, when Weber told the famous commander: "in a democracy the people choose a leader in whom they trust. Then the chosen leader says, 'Now shut up and obey me'" (GM:42).

There is also Weber's statement, in a letter to Robert Michels of August 4, 1908, that "such notions as the 'will of the people', the true will of the people, ceased to exist for me years ago; they are fictions" (Mommsen 1984:395).

While there is an authoritarian dimension to this view, Weber also challenged the right of the German population to be considered a *Kulturvolk* on the ground that it "has never chopped off the head of its monarch" (Honigsheim 1968:13).

It is sometimes noted how little Weber wrote on democracy in his sociology. In this context mention is also often made of Weber's brief reference to democracy as an anti-authoritarian transformation of charismatic domination in the famous Ch. 3 on domination in *Economy and Society* (ES:266–71; cf. ES:1127–30). In this chapter Weber also addresses the issue of direct democracy, mentioning the North American townships and the smaller Swiss cantons as examples of this (ES:289–90; 948–52; cf. ES:290–91). He adds that the element of domination can be minimized through various techniques such as rotation and election by lot, but that a "certain minimum" of domination is nonetheless "unavoidable" (ES:289).

It seems that Weber for a while was thinking of introducing "a fourth form of legitimacy, a domination which (at least officially) derives its legitimacy from the will of the ruled" (Weber 1917). This, however, is only known through a newspaper report of a talk that Weber gave in Vienna in 1917.

Certain social forces lead to a leveling of the governed—and this process prepares to some extent the way for democratization ("*passive'* democratization," ES:983–87). In *Economy and Society* Weber finally also argues that there is a relationship between sects and democracy—"an elective affinity between the sect and political democracy" (ES:1208). The reason for this has to do with two structural features of the sect: its direct democracy type of administration, and the treatment of clerical officials as servants of the sect. Furthermore, "the consistent sect gives rise to an inalienable right of the governed against any power" (ES:1209).

There exists no elective affinity between capitalism and democracy according to Weber (e.g. PW:68–70, ES:1415). Their coexistence in the contemporary West is just the result of a series of historical coincidences. Capitalists are not particularly democratic and prefer to deal with a single authority behind the scenes rather than with a number of elected officials.

For Weber's discussion of the possibilities for democracy in Germany, see especially "Parliament and Government in a Reconstructed Germany" (ES:1381–1469).

Whether Weber was a true democrat or not is a contested issue. For references to the various opinions on this topic, as well as an attempt to reconstruct Weber's ideas on democracy more generally, see Stefan Breuer, "The Concept of Democracy in Weber's Political Sociology" (1998). See also Peter Baehr, "The 'Masses' in Weber's Political Sociology" (1990), and the chapter "Parliament and Democracy" in David Beetham, *Max Weber and the Theory of Modern Politics* (1985).

For the influence of Weber on Schumpeter's theory of democracy, see e.g. Wolfgang Mommsen, *Max Weber and German Politics 1890–1920* (1984), pp. 406–7.

See also Caesarism, demagogue, freedom, living for politics versus living off politics, plebiscitary domination and leadership, political sociology, politics, sect

depersonalization (*Versachlichung, Unpersönlichkeit*) Weber argues that social relationships, especially in the areas of the economy and politics, are becoming increasingly depersonalized in modern capitalist society. This puts pressure on the individual to conform, and makes it hard for the individual to create and maintain what Weber terms a personality. It also makes it hard to intervene in these relationships with some kind of ethical or moral purpose in mind. Depersonalization may be characterized as Weber's equivalent of Marx's alienation.

In *Economy and Society* Weber states that before the birth of modern capitalist society, "power relationships in both the economic and political spheres have a purely personal character" (ES:600). This meant that "one may apply ethical requirements in the same way that one applies them to every other purely personal relationship" (ibid.).

Today, in contrast, key economic and political organizations have an impersonal ethic and operate best if they are run in an impersonal manner. In a rational market or bureaucracy, for example, no special attention should—and can—be paid to specific circumstances in the individual case. Workers, for example, are subjected to "masterless slavery" in capitalism (ES:1186). And in modern political parties with a plebiscitary leader, the followers are "depersonalized" (e.g. Mommsen 1984:401).

Attempts to rectify things by bringing in ethical concerns from the outside will only disturb the operations of markets and bureaucracies (e.g. GEH:357). The religious tradition of *caritas*, in particular, collides with the tendency to depersonalization (e.g. ES:584–85, 1188; GM:371).

For a discussion of depersonalization, see e.g. Rogers Brubaker, *The Limits of Rationality* (1984), pp. 32–3.

See also charity, economic ethic, individual and individualism, personality

determinism Weber was not a determinist. In many of his writings he argues strongly against seeing historical stages as necessary; he is also extremely critical of the notion of historical laws. Weber often emphasized the role of possibilities and choices in history, which may be seen as a sign of a certain anti-determinism. One of Weber's ambitions in *Economy and Society*, it appears, was to try to establish when it was possible to generalize about some social phenomena and when this was not possible because of "historical 'accidents'" (e.g. ES:1177).

See also causality, history, laws in the social sciences, objective possibility

Deutsche Gesellschaft für Soziologie (German Sociological Association)
The German Sociological Association was founded in 1909 and ceased to exist in 1934. Although Weber was not the initiator of the DGS, he took an active part in its formation; he was appointed chairman of its steering committee in 1909; and he declined at one point to become the president of the association (e.g. Dirk Käsler, *Die frühe deutsche Soziologie* [1984], Hans-Inge Rathenow, "Die 'Deutsche Gesellschaft für Soziologie' 1900–1933," [1976]).

Weber took an active part in the meetings of 1910 and 1912, discussing among other things the role of race in sociological analysis (Weber 1973). In various ways he also tried to influence the activities of the DGS, usually without success. For example, he suggested that the *Archiv für Sozialwissenschaft und Sozialpolitik* should become the official journal of the DGS, something that did not happen. He also proposed that the association fund and carry out large empirical research projects—again without success so far as two projects of his own were concerned—one on the press and one on voluntary associations. See Weber [1910] 1998, [1910] 2002.

development *See* evolution

dice *See* loaded dice

dinggenossenschaftliche Rechtsfindung *See* lawmaking and law-finding

direct observational understanding (*aktuelles Verstehen*) *See* understanding

discipline (*Disziplin*) The concept of discipline is closely related to the concepts of power and domination in Weber's sociology. There is also an affinity between discipline and asceticism.

Discipline is defined in Weber's general sociology in Ch. 1 of *Economy and Society* as follows: "'discipline' is the probability that by virtue of habituation a command will receive prompt and automatic obedience in stereotyped forms, on the part of a given group of persons" (ES:53; cf. ES:1149).

Discipline has always played a key role in war ("military discipline"; ES:1150–55). "The *large-scale economic organization* is the second great agency which trains men for discipline" (ES:1155). Weber also notes apropos discipline that bureaucracy is "its most rational offspring" (ES:1149).

See also asceticism, domination, power

disenchantment of the world (*Entzauberung der Welt*) This expression refers to a process through which people no longer explain the world and their cosmos with the help of magical forces, but instead rely on science and rational forms of thinking. Intellectuals have played a key role in the process of disenchantment. According to "Science as a Vocation," where this type of issue is discussed, " . . . there are [today] no mysterious incalculable forces that come into play, but rather . . . one can, in principle, master all things by calculation. This means that the world is disenchanted" (GM:139; cf. GM:155, 350, PE:105).

In an enchanted world, explanations are given in the form of actions of gods and demons, and causality in the modern sense of the word does not exist. In a disenchanted world, on the other hand, the whole world has been "transformed into a causal mechanism" (GM:350).

An alternative translation of *Entzauberung* (which literally means "demagification") would be "demystification." This latter term is, for example, used by S. N. Eisenstadt, who also writes that "*Entzauberung* refers mainly to the 'contents' aspects of culture and describes the de-mystification of the conception of the world connected with growing sec-ularization, with the rise of science, and with growing routinization of education and culture" (Eisenstadt 1968a:xviii, li). Stephen Kalberg ar-gues similarly for using the term "demagification," giving as his reason that "the term 'disenchantment' conjures up many general notions re-garding the decline of the *Gemeinschaft*" (Kalberg 1979:138 n. 10; cf. Kalberg 1980:1146 n. 2). For the role of religion in eliminating magic and, more generally, in the process of disenchantment, see e.g. Lutz Kael-ber, *Schools of Asceticism* (1998), pp. 102–25. Weber's first use of the term "disenchantment of the world" dates to 1913 and his essay "Some Categories of Interpretive Sociology" (Wolfgang Schluchter, *Rationalism, Religion, and Domination* [1989], p. 417; cf. SCIS:155).

See Ralph Schroeder, "Disenchantment and Its Discontent: Weberian Perspectives on Science and Technology" (1995). See also Johannes Winkelmann, "Die Herkunft von Max Webers 'Entzauberungs'-Konzep-tion" (1980).

See also causality, magic, science

disposition *See* habitus

division of labor (*Leistungsverteilung*, also *Arbeitsteilung*) Weber dis-cusses several different types of division of labor in his economic sociol-ogy in Ch. 2 of *Economy and Society*, such as the economic division of labor, the technical division of labor, and social aspects of the division of labor (ES:114–37).

The technical division of labor is centered around the fact that work has to be divided up and then reunited in order to solve technical prob-lems. *The economic division of labor* has to do with the fact that work is carried out within a unit, which is either oriented to profit-making or to household needs (more precisely, to budgetary management). *Social as-pects of the division of labor* include, for example, whether the unit within which the work is carried out is autonomous or not, and whether it is autocephalous or not (the latter meaning that the chief and the staff are appointed from within, rather than from outside the organization).

The concept of division of labor is discussed in close connection with the concept of the combination of labor (*Leistungsverbindung*), as was the custom in German economics in Weber's day.

While Weber pays attention to the division of labor between the sexes in his various writings, this topic is not singled out in a separate section in his economic sociology in Ch. 2 of *Economy and Society*.

See also autocephaly, work

doctrine *See* priest

domination (*Herrschaft*)   The concept of domination plays a central role in Weber's sociology. Its core meaning is that an order will be obeyed. Domination, Weber argues, can be found throughout society.

Domination (*Herrschaft*) is defined in Weber's general sociology in Ch. 1 of *Economy and Society* as "the probability that a command with a given specific content will be obeyed by a given group of persons" (ES:53). An organization or a staff is typically involved in domination but not necessarily so, Weber argues, and points to the example of a household. Those who obey, Weber says, may have an interest in doing so (ES:212; for the relationship of domination to power, see ES:941–48). "Without exception every sphere of social action is profoundly influenced by structures of domination" (ES:941).

While violence or money can be used to make people do something, domination that is seen as *legitimate* is much more stable. According to the famous typology presented in Ch. 3 of *Economy and Society* (and also elsewhere in Weber's work), there exist three forms of legitimate domination: traditional, charismatic, and legal (cf. ES:212–301). Typically there will be a mixture of the three different types.

In the case of traditional domination, there basically is a belief in the sanctity of tradition and of those who exercise power according to tradition. In charismatic domination, there is a belief in some extraordinary individual and the order that that individual stands for. And in legal domination, obedience is not to a person but to the legal system according to which that person holds power. The most common form today is legal domination.

Frank Parkin summarizes Weber's three forms of domination as follows:

Type of domination	Grounds for claiming obedience
Traditional	Obey me because this is what our people have always done.
Charismatic	Obey me because I can transform your life.
Legal-rational	Obey me because I am your lawfully appointed superior.

(Parkin 1982:77)

Parkin also notes, like several commentators, that "in Weber's schema there is no such category as *illegitimate* domination, even though he clearly recognizes it as an empirical probability" (ibid., p. 78).

In *The City* Weber introduces the concept of "non-legitimate domination" (*nichtlegitime Herrschaft*). This refers to the special type of domination that can be found especially in Western medieval cities: an absence of traditional domination, in combination with new types of legitimacy based on the groups of citizens that ruled the cities. Claus Wittich explains as follows in *Economy and Society*: "'non-legitimate domination' (*nichtlegitime Herrschaft*) refers to what was for Weber the decisive feature of the Occidental city, observable already in antiquity: its break with the ruler's traditional legitimacy, and the substitution of authority (*Herrschaft*) based on various types of usurpatory consociations of the ruled (*demos, plebs, comune, popolo, coniuratio,* etc.)" (ES:1234 n. 1; see also ES:1250ff., GM:84).

Weber wrote three major texts (in this order) on the three types of domination (ES:941–1211, EES:99–108 or EW:133–45; ES:212–301; cf. also GM:295–300). These can be dated to 1911–13, about 1918, and 1919–20, with Ch. 3 of *Economy and Society* (from 1919–20) generally being considered as the most authoritative (Wolfgang Mommsen, *The Age of Bureaucracy* [1974], p. 16). Ch. 3 is characterized by the editors of MWG as "a reworked version of the earlier texts for the chapter [in *Economy and Society*] on Domination, compressed to a quarter of its size" (Baier, Lepsius, Mommsen, and Schluchter 2000:113). The texts on domination will appear in MGW, Vol. I/22-4, which is part of *Economy and Society*.

In the fall of 1917 Weber gave a talk in Vienna on the sociology of the state that indicates that at this time he considered introducing a fourth type of domination, in which legitimation was derived from "the will of the ruled" (see e.g. Stefan Breuer, "The Concept of Democracy in Weber's Political Sociology" [1998], p. 2; for the original account of the talk in *Neue Freie Presse*, see Weber 1917).

While Weber in one of his early texts on domination argued that domination could be based either on giving orders ("*domination by virtue of authority*") or on economic power ("*domination by virtue of a constellation of [economic] interests*"), he later changed his mind and stated that domination is *not* the same as economic power (ES:214, 943–44).

There exists a considerable secondary literature on Weber's theory of domination. See e.g. Wolfgang Mommsen, "The Theory of the 'Three Pure Types of Legitimate Domination' and the Concept of Plebiscitarianism," pp. 72–94 in *The Age of Bureaucracy* (1974); Stefan Breuer, *Max Webers Herrschaftssoziologie* (1991); and Edith Hanke and Wolfgang Mommsen (eds.), *Max Webers Herrschaftssoziologie* (2001).

There also exists quite a bit of discussion in the secondary literature on how best to translate *Herrschaft* into English. Among the various candidates are "authority," "domination," "imperative coordination," "leadership," and "rule" (see e.g. ES:61–2 n. 31; for a summary account of the various options, see e.g. Richter 1995:68–77). In his new translation of

Ch. 1 of *Economy and Society* Keith Tribe uses "rulership" (EW:355). Guenther Roth and Claus Wittich, the two editors of *Economy and Society*, alternate between "domination" and "authority" (ibid.; cf. xciv). According to Wolfgang Mommsen, "it is almost impossible to translate the German term *Herrschaft* into English" (Mommsen 1974:72). Mommsen also argues that "domination" is the most appropriate term; and on this point he is in agreement with Raymond Aron and W. G. Runciman. "Rule," Mommsen says, may be preferable to domination in that it is less "austere"; what is problematic about using this term, however, is that it fits governing activity but not the relationship between the one who governs and the one who is governed. He therefore concludes that "the term 'domination' comes closest to the somewhat authoritarian connotation which the word *Herrschaft* has in German, and it is a derivation from the Latin term *dominus* which is a perfect equivalent to the German term *Hastier*" (ibid.). Melvin Richter, finally, argues that the best strategy for dealing with the difficult term *Herrschaft* in *Economy and Society* would be to keep the original German term (Guenther Roth, "Interpreting and Translating Max Weber," [1992], p. 453; cf. Richter 1995:68–77).

See also charisma, collegiality, economic power, legitimacy, power, traditionalism, violence

doppelte Ethik   *See* double ethic

double ethic (*doppelte Ethik* and similar expressions)   During most of history human communities have had one ethic for their own members (an in-group morality) and another for members of other communities (an out-group morality). In economic life there has historically often been an obligation to help members of one's own community who are in distress. Outsiders, in contrast, can be mercilessly cheated (e.g. AJ:343–55, GEH:356, PE:57).

As an example of this type of double ethic or dualism of the economic ethic, as Weber also calls it, one may cite the Bible: "you may exact interest on a loan to a foreigner but not on a loan to a fellow-countryman" (Deuteronomy 23:20; cf. AJ:70, 343).

One of the results of ascetic Protestantism was to introduce a uniform treatment in economic affairs of members of one's own community and people from the outside. In modern capitalism there is as a rule no distinction between in-group morality and out-group morality in economic questions. Prices, for example, are typically fixed at the same level for all buyers, whether members of one's own community or not.

See also economic ethic, usury

dualistic ethic   *See* double ethic

Durkheim, Emile   *See* sociology

Economic action (*Wirtschaften*)   The concept of economic action represents the basic unit in Weber's economic sociology, and it is used to construct more complex structures of the economy. It is the equivalent, in other words, of Weber's concept of social action in his general sociology.

Economic action is defined in Ch. 2 on economic sociology in *Economy and Society* in the following way: "'economic action' is any peaceful exercise of an actor's control over resources which is in its main impulse oriented toward economic ends" (ES:63).

What drives economic action is what Weber terms "a desire for utilities," which includes not only items that can be consumed in some way but also profit-making (ES:64; see ES:68–9 for Weber's concept of utility). An economic action is a form of social action, which means that the actor assigns a meaning to his or her (economic) behavior, and also orients it to some other actor (or order).

An economic action differs from what Weber terms "economically oriented action" in that the latter is either (1) not primarily economic in focus, or (2) uses violence (ES:63–4). Throughout history economically oriented actions have been more important than economic actions (even though the opposite is the case today).

An economic action can be rational, but does not have to be rational by definition. It may, in particular, also be traditional in orientation (ES:69–71). Typical measures of rational economic action include, for example, the systematic allocation of utilities between the present and the future as well as the ranking of utilities according to estimated urgency (ES:71–4).

Weber emphasizes that the concept of economic action, as used in economic sociology, must be constructed in such a manner as to include economic power (ES:67). In this it differs from the concept of economic action as used in theoretical economics (or in mainstream economics, as we would say today).

Economic actions that are oriented to each other constitute economic relationships; these can be communal as well as associative, open as well as closed (e.g. ES:341–43). Economic organizations are, like any organizations, closed social relationships that constitute an order enforced by specific individuals (ES:74–5).

According to Gianfranco Poggi, the term "economizing" is preferable to "economic action" as a translation of *Wirtschaften* (Poggi 1983:14–15). For a discussion of Weber's concept of economic action, see e.g. Richard Swedberg, *Max Weber and the Idea of Economic Sociology* (1998), pp. 22–53.

See also economic organization, rational economic action, utility

economic availability (*ökonomische Abkömmlichkeit*) Someone is economically available who can afford to engage in politics without giving up his or her ordinary job or status position (e.g. PW:109–12). An industrial worker is typically not available in this sense, while a rentier is. Unless some way is found to pay those who are not economically available to participate in politics, political power will tend to drift into the hands of those who are economically available.

See also living for politics versus living off politics

economic ethic (*Wirtschaftsethik*) While the concept of economic ethic plays a key role in Weber's sociological work, it does not figure among the basic concepts in his general sociology in Ch. 1 of *Economy and Society*. No formal definition can be found in Weber's work, even if the meaning of economic ethic is relatively clear. In various social contexts, in brief, economic activities are evaluated negatively or positively; and it is the sum of these evaluations that make up an economic ethic.

To illustrate what an economic ethic is like, one can mention attitudes toward labor or wealth. Manual labor, making profit through trade, and investing in landed property rather than in industry, are activities that are either approved of or looked down on in society. There may also exist one ethic toward people from one's own community and another toward people from the outside (double ethic).

Just as one can speak of the economic ethic of a society, Weber notes, one can also speak of the economic ethic of a religion. What counts in the latter case is not the official religious doctrine but rather "the practical impulses for action which are founded in the psychological and pragmatic contexts of religions" (GM:267). This last quote is the closest that one comes to a definition of economic ethic in Weber's work.

Weber was especially interested in the economic ethics of religions, as evidenced by *The Protestant Ethic* and the individual studies in his *Economic Ethics of the World Religions* (such as *Ancient Judaism*, *The Religion of China* and *The Religion of India*).

Much attention has been devoted to these studies (see e.g. Schluchter 1981b, 1983, 1984, 1985, 1987, and 1988; and for Schluchter's summary view in English, see *Rationalism, Religion, and Domination* [1989]). Little attention, on the other hand, has been devoted to the concept of economic ethic. For an attempt to theorize this concept as a kind of "deeper structure" that is nonetheless concrete, see S. N. Eisenstadt, "Some Reflections on the Significance of Max Weber's Sociology of Religions for the Analysis of Non-European Modernity" (1971), p. 36. See also the discussion in Richard Swedberg, *Max Weber and the Idea of Economic Sociology* (1998), pp. 134–37.

See also double ethic, *Economic Ethics of the World Religions*, vocation

Economic Ethics of the World Religions, The (*Die Wirtschaftsethik der Weltreligionen*)   Several years after completing *The Protestant Ethic* Weber embarked on a huge project of analyzing religions other than Christianity, as part of his general concern with finding out what had made the West, and only the West, produce a rational form of capitalism. *The Economic Ethics of the World Religions* was the title that Weber gave to this project.

In the last lines of *The Protestant Ethic* Weber sketched a program for further study of the cultural significance of ascetic Protestantism (PE:182–83; cf. PE:284 n. 119, PED:45, 49 n. 3). This program from 1905 was picked up again around 1910, and the result was *The Economic Ethics of the World Religions*. Weber has said that he used "the method" of *The Protestant Ethic* also in these studies (letter to Paul Siebeck of June 22, 1915; cf. Grossein, "Présentation" [1996], p. 83).

Weber mainly worked on *The Economic Ethics of the World Religions* between 1911 and 1914 (Dirk Käsler, *Max Weber* [1988], p. 94). He did not complete this project, however, and for an idea of what he had in mind one must consult an advertisement for his *Collected Essays in the Sociology of Religion* that he wrote in 1919 (for the full text, *see* the entry for *Collected Essays in the Sociology of Religion*). Three volumes of these essays were nonetheless published in 1920–21 (*Gesammelte Aufsätze zur Religionssoziologie*, Vols. I-III). These contain studies which are known in English as *Ancient Judaism*, *The Religion of China*, and *The Religion of India* (*see* the entry for *Collected Essays in the Sociology of Religion*).

For a summary of the content of the works that make up *The Economic Ethics of the World Religions*, see e.g. Reinhard Bendix, *Max Weber: An Intellectual Portrait* (1960), pp. 83–284, Dirk Käsler, *Max Weber*, pp. 94–141. For a discussion, see e.g. David Little, "Max Weber and the Comparative Study of Religious Ethics" (1974). For the early reception of *The Economic Ethics of the World Religions*, see Käsler, *Max Weber*, pp. 205–6. The general thesis of *The Economic Ethics of the World Religions*—that civilizations outside the West could not internally generate a spirit of capitalism—is also part of the debate around *The Protestant Ethic*; *see* Weber thesis.

See also Buddhism, Christianity, Confucianism, economic ethic, Hinduism, Islam, Judaism, Weber thesis, Taoism, world-religions

economic geography   *See* geography

economic history (*Wirtschaftsgeschichte*)   Weber had a broad concept

of economics and argued that it should include not only economic theory
but also economic sociology and economic history (social economics or
Sozialökonomik). While sociology (including economic sociology) deals
with type concepts and generalized uniformities, history (including economic history) aims at "the causal explanation of individual actions,
structures, and personalities possessing cultural significance" (ES:29).
The following three works may be considered as Weber's most important
studies in economic history: his dissertation on medieval trading corporations, his book-length study of the economic and social history of antiquity, and *The City* (HCP, ASAC, and ES:1212–1372).

Weber is also known as the author of *General Economic History*
(*Wirtschaftsgeschichte*). This book, however, is not a work from Weber's
hand but a reconstruction based on lectures that he gave in the winter semester of 1919–20 on economic and social history (*Abriss der universalen Sozial- und Wirtschaftsgeschichte*). Drawing on the notes that students took during these lectures, in combination with some imaginative
editing (primarily by Siegmund Hellmann), a manuscript was assembled
after Weber's death and published in the early 1920s as *Wirtschaftsgeschichte*. This work was translated into English by Frank Knight in
1927 as *General Economic History*.

It should also be noted that the conceptual introduction to
Wirtschaftsgeschichte, "The Character of Economic History" (WG:14–
16), is not included in the English translation (but is scheduled to appear
in *Max Weber Studies*, in translation by Keith Tribe). According to this
introduction, the three main questions or problems of economic history
are the following: (1) the division of labor (and related to this, classes);
(2) the orientation of the economy toward profit-making or householding; and (3) the degree to which rationality or irrationality characterizes
economic life.

See in this context e.g. Stanley Engerman, "Max Weber as Economist
and Economic Historian" (2000).

See also *Abriss der universalen Sozial- und Wirtschaftsgeschichte*;
Agrarian Sociology of Ancient Civilizations, The; *City, The*; *Economy and
Society*; *General Economic History*; history; social economics

economic motivation (*Triebfeder des Wirtschaftens*)   In his economic
sociology in Ch. 2 of *Economy and Society* Weber notes that people are
motivated in their economic activities by the need to provide for their
"ideal and material interests" (ES:202). He also points out that "in a
market economy the striving for *income* is necessarily the ultimate driving force of all economic activity" (ibid., p. 203).

Those in a privileged position are primarily motivated by large incomes, ambition, and/or a sense of calling. Those without property, such as workers, are motivated by the fact that they and their families will starve if they do not work; they also view productive work as something positive in itself.

More generally, Weber argues that an individual's inclination to work will be determined either by strong self-interest or by "direct or indirect compulsion" (ES:150). Direct compulsion is not applicable to a market economy, while "indirect compulsion" applies to anyone who is employed.

In a comment on his translation of Ch. 2 of *Economy and Society* Talcott Parsons criticizes Weber's treatment of economic motivation on the ground that it is not sufficiently psychological in nature but only speaks of interests (Weber 1947:319 n. 135; cf. 320 n. 136). To this may be added that what is said in Ch. 2 needs to be complemented by what Weber says in *The Protestant Ethic* and in his writings on the psychophysics of labor.

See also coercion, interests, workers

economic opportunities   *See* opportunity

economic order (*Wirtschaftsordnung*)   An economic order is defined by Weber in *Economy and Society* as "the distribution of the actual control over goods and services, the distribution arising in each case from the particular mode of balancing interests consensually; moreover, the term shall apply to the manner in which goods and services are indeed used by virtue of these powers of disposition, which are based on *de facto* recognition" (ES:312).

The concept of economic order is not singled out in Weber's economic sociology in Ch. 2 of *Economy and Society*, and the definition above is from an early part of this work.

See also economic power, order

economic organization (*wirtschaftlich orientierter Verband*)   An economic organization is defined in Ch. 2 of *Economy and Society* as an organization that is characterized by "*primarily* autocephalous economic action of a given kind" (ES:74). To this should be added that Weber defines an organization as a social relationship, which is closed or limited and where the content of its order will be carried out by a staff ("autocephalous" means that the chief and the staff are appointed from inside the organization, not by outsiders).

There exist several different types of economic organizations (ES:74–5; cf. ES:340–41). There are, first of all, economic organizations such as business corporations, co-ops, and workshops for artisans. There also exist "economically active organizations" and "economically regulative organizations," in Weber's terminology. The former are primarily non-economic in nature but also carry out some economic activity, such as states and churches. The latter regulate economic activity, such as trade unions and employers' associations. The term economic organization is close—but not identical—to a few other terms in Weber's economic sociology, such as establishment and firm.

"It was the Italians," according to Weber, "followed by the English, who developed the modern capitalist form of economic organization" (PW:155).

See also bureaucracy, commenda, establishment, firm, organization or association

economic power (*Verfügungsgewalt, ökonomische Macht*)   The concept of economic power in the sense of "power of control and disposal" over various resources plays an important role in Weber's economic sociology and can also be found in his early work in economics. In Ch. 2 of *Economy and Society* Weber states that it is essential to include the notion of power of control and disposal in the concept of economic action (ES:67).

In the modern capitalist economy the economic power of control and disposal is directly related to law and the legal order, while in other types of economies this does not have to be the case.

While people in a capitalist society have power of disposal over their own bodies (*Eigenverfügung*), slaves do not. Weber also discusses the relationship of economic power to status (ES:926) and to domination (ES:214, 943–44).

According to Talcott Parsons, "the term *Verfügungsgewalt*, of which Weber makes a great deal of use, is of legal origin, implying legally sanctioned powers of control and disposal. This, of course, has no place in a purely economic conceptual scheme but is essential to a sociological treatment of economic systems. It is another way of saying that concretely economic action depends on a system of property relations" (ES:206 n. 5).

Giovanni Poggi notes that "though the expression *Verfuegungsgewalt* is neither as infrequently used nor as execrable-sounding in German as the equivalent 'powers of disposition' is in English, this is in both languages a rather rarefied expression, which unfortunately here and elsewhere Weber uses without further definition" (Poggi 1983:15). Poggi adds that Weber basically means "resources" when he speaks of "powers of disposition," but that he wants to avoid this term since it gives associations to material objects while Weber also has abstract items and social relations in mind.

See also coercion, domination, power

economic sociology (*Wirtschaftssoziologie*)   Weber is one of the founders of economic sociology or the sociological analysis of economic phenomena and their role in society. Many of his works fall into this category, including *The Protestant Ethic* and much of *Economy and Society*. It was, however, only during his very last years (1918–20) that Weber developed a theoretical economic sociology, namely the text that can be found in Ch. 2 of *Economy and Society* ("Sociological Categories of Economic Action," ES:63–301, cf. WG:1–16). The basic idea in this theoretical economic sociology is that the focus in economic sociology should be on economic actions that are oriented to the behavior of others, not on economic actions per se, as in economic theory.

On a more general level, Weber's economic sociology can be described as an attempt to unite an interest-driven type of analysis with a social one. Like all sociology, economic sociology "seeks to formulate type concepts and generalized uniformities of empirical process" (ES:19). It also falls under Weber's general definition of sociology: "sociology . . . is a science concerning itself with the interpretive understanding of social action and thereby with a causal explanation of its course and consequences"(ES:4). Economic sociology is finally also part of the much broader science of economics or social economics (*Sozialökonomik*), as Weber called it.

Weber's economic sociology deals with "economic phenomena," "economically relevant phenomena" and "economically conditioned phenomena," to use the terminology from his 1904 essay on objectivity (MSS:64–5). The first of these covers straightforward economic phenomena, e.g. banks. Economically relevant phenomena are non-economic phenomena that are relevant for economic phenomena, e.g. ascetic Protestantism. Economically conditioned phenomena are non-economic phenomena that are partly conditioned by economic phenomena, e.g. the religious beliefs of social classes.

For an introduction to Weber's economic sociology, see Richard Swedberg, *Max Weber and the Idea of Economic Sociology* (1998).

See also accounting, budgetary management, capitalism, class, economic action, economic ethic, economic organization, economic power, *Economy and Society*, entrepreneur, firm, *Handbook of Social Economics*, money, opportunity, political capitalism, social economics, vocation, workers

economic superman (*ökonomischer Übermensch*)   This term, which has obvious Nietzschean overtones and which occasionally appears in Weber's work, covers extremely successful businessmen who have existed in all times and who consider themselves "beyond good and evil" (e.g. PE:258 n. 187, PED:102–3). Examples include American captains of industry such as Pierpont Morgan, John D. Rockefeller, and Jay Gould (e.g. GM:308–9).

See also adventurers' capitalism, charisma, entrepreneur, political capitalism

economic theory   Weber drew heavily on (analytical) economic theory in his sociology, especially for his concepts of ideal type and rationality. His own contribution to economic theory, as conventionally defined, was on the other hand limited and essentially consists in his essay on marginal utility theory. Weber's argument in this essay is that psychology does not represent the foundation of economics, and that economics is consequently not dependent on psychology but is sufficient in itself (EES:249–60).

During the years that he worked as an economist Weber's lectures were characterized by a mixture of material from analytical economic theory and the more empirically oriented Historical School. For example, Weber found the fiction of *homo economicus* useful for certain purposes; and he was one of the first (after John Stuart Mill) to give this idea a succinct formulation. "Abstract [economic] theory," as Weber wrote in what was probably intended to be a textbook in economics:

a. *ignores*, treats as if *not present* all those motives which have an influence on real men which are specifically *non-economic*, i.e. all those motives not arising from the satisfaction of material needs;

b. *imputes* as actually present in men particular qualities which are either *not* present or incompletely, namely

   (a) complete insight into the given *situation*—perfect economic knowledge;

   (b) exclusive selection of the *most appropriate means* for a given end—absolute "economic rationality";

   (c) exclusive devotion of one's own powers to the attainment of economic goods—tireless economic endeavor.

It therefore argues on the basis of *unrealistic* men, analogous to a mathematical ideal. (GVAN:30 as translated in Tribe 1989b:6)

It may be added parenthetically that Weber also discusses *homo economicus* in a somewhat broader sense in *The Protestant Ethic and the Spirit of Capitalism*, this time in a comment on the coming into being of this theoretical construct. The Puritan way of life, Weber here says, "stood at the cradle of modern economic man" (PE:174).

For methodological reasons Weber was deeply impressed by the use of what he termed ideal types in economic theory; and he strongly advocated their use also in sociology (e.g. ES:9). The insights of economic theory, he adds, provide "the basis" for economic sociology (ES:68). Weber did not explicate this last statement. It is nonetheless clear that Weber, on a number of points, advocated a type of sociology (and economic sociology) that differed on important points from analytical economic theory. For one thing, Weber does not make the assumption in his sociology that economic behavior is rational. Sociology also has a different relationship to empirical reality and does not, along the lines of economic theory, engage in "conceptual analysis" (CS:111). On this last point, Weber noted in another context that "the explanatory methods of *pure* economics are as tempting as they are misleading" (ES:115). Finally, sociology does not only take economic factors into account but also non-economic ones.

Weber's lectures on economics are scheduled to appear as MWG, Vols. III/1–3. For a discussion of Weber's view of economics, see e.g. Heino Nau, *Max Weber als Ökonom* (forthcoming), and Richard Swedberg, *Max Weber and The Idea of Economic Sociology* (1998), pp. 173–206. The reader may also want to consult Weber's "Economic Theory and Ancient Society," in which the relevance of modern economic categories for an understanding of pre-capitalist economies is discussed (ASAC:37–79). For Weber's relationship to Carl Menger, see e.g. Wilhelm Hennis, "The Pitiless 'Sobriety of Judgment': Max Weber between Carl Menger and Gustav von Schmoller. The Academic Politics of Value Freedom" (2000).

See also Battle of the Methods, economics, *Handbook of Social Economics*, Historical School of economics, ideal type, marginal utility, social economics, utility

economically conditioned phenomena   These are non-economic phenomena, according to Weber's 1904 essay on objectivity, which are influenced to an important extent by economic phenomena (MSS:64).
See economic sociology

economically relevant phenomena   These are non-economic phenomena, according to Weber's 1904 essay on objectivity, which influence economic phenomena (MSS:64).
See economic sociology

economics   Though Weber was primarily trained in law; his major academic appointments were in economics; and during most of his life as a scholar he presented himself officially as an economist. Guenther Roth writes that "in his methodological essays between 1903 and 1906 Weber has in mind economics whenever he writes 'our science'. As late as 1919, he spoke of 'we economists' in 'Science as a Vocation'" (Roth in Bendix and Roth 1971:37). Weber, it may be added, had a very high opinion of economics and thought that it had much to teach sociology.

Weber worked as an economist in the 1890s, and from his notes and publications from these years we can reconstruct his views of economics (see especially GVAN). Weber drew both on analytical economics and the more empirically oriented works of the members of the Historical School of economics. He essentially argued that analytical economic theory was indispensable for the conceptualization of economic problems—but also that its usefulness declined at the stage when empirical material had to be brought into the picture.

Weber was also very interested in the role of institutions in economic life and noted at one point that "the fundamental substantive and methodological problem of economics is constituted by the question: how are the origin and the persistence of the institutions of economic life to be explained, institutions which were not purposefully created by collective means, but which nevertheless—from our point of view—function purposefully. This is the basic problem of economics" (RK:80).

Weber was unhappy over the polarization in economics which had been caused by the Battle of the Methods in the late nineteenth century, and advocated in response to this development a broad concept of economics. Under the umbrella of what he termed social economics (*Sozialökonomik*), Weber included not only economic theory but also economic history and economic sociology. This broad approach is reflected, in particular, in the *Handbook of Social Economics* (*Grundriss der Sozialökonomik*) which Weber edited during the last ten or so years of his life, and to which representatives of both analytical economics and the Historical School contributed.

In his famous inaugural lecture of 1895 Weber points out that the economic way of looking at things has increased enormously in popularity in his time (Weber [1895] 1980). Economic ideals, in particular, tend to be accepted in an uncritical manner as natural and objective values that society should strive for. In reality, however, values can never be justified through science, and this also goes for economics. Values, in brief, should be consciously chosen.

Weber's work has not been much appreciated in mainstream economics, save for a few casual references to *The Protestant Ethic* and his essay on marginal utility theory (EES:249–60). For a general discussion of Weber's work in economics, including his *Handbook of Social Economics*, see e.g. Richard Swedberg, *Max Weber and the Idea of Economic Sociology* (1998). See in this context also Hinnerk Bruhns, "Max Weber, l'économie et l'histoire" (1996); Heino Nau, Eine "Wissenschaft von Menschen": *Max Weber und die Begründung der Sozialökonomik in der deutschsprachigen Ökonomie* (1997). For Weber's relationship to individual economists, including Schmoller and Schumpeter, see Wolfgang

Mommsen and Jürgen Osterhammel (eds.), *Max Weber and His Contemporaries* (1987).

For economics in nineteenth-century Germany, see e.g. the history of the so-called *Staatswissenschaften* (economics, politics, statistics, and so on) during the nineteenth century in David Lindenfeld, *The Practical Imagination* (1997).

See also commercial legislation, economic history, economic sociology, economic theory, economy, *Economy and Society*, *Handbook of Social Economics*, marginal utility, social economics, utility, Verein für Sozialpolitik

economy (*Wirtschaft, Ökonomie*) The economy represents one of the main institutional arenas in society, according to Weber. In modern society the economy is set off more sharply from the rest of society than in early societies.

In his economic sociology in Ch. 2 of *Economy and Society* Weber defines "economy" by referring to the concept of economic action: "we will call autocephalous economic action an 'economy'" (*Wirtschaft*; ES:63; cf. ES:339). (Autocephalous means in this context that the economy is independent and not directed from the outside.)

In his essay on objectivity of 1904 Weber approaches the concept of the economy from a somewhat different angle, and argues that social economics should deal with the following three categories: "economic phenomena" (economic events or institutions), "economically relevant phenomena" (non-economic phenomena whose consequences are of importance from the economic point of view), and "economically conditioned phenomena" (non-economic phenomena which are to some degree influenced by economic factors; MSS:64–65).

For the term "economy" in Weber, see Pertti Ahonen, "'Wirtschaft' in Max Weber" (1999).

See also autocephalous, economic action, *Handbook of Social Economics*, market economy, planned economy

Economy and Society (*Wirtschaft und Gesellschaft*; trans. 1968) This study, which is seen by many scholars as Weber's most important work, is part of the huge *Handbook of Social Economics* (*Grundriss der Sozialökonomik*) that Weber edited in the last decade of his life.

Economy and Society is a giant work—nearly fifteen hundred pages in its current English edition. It opens with a famous chapter on general sociology, in which Weber presents his interpretive sociology and its major concepts. This is followed by a chapter on theoretical economic sociology and a famous chapter on domination. *Economy and Society* also contains a full-fledged sociology of law, a sociology of religion and a historical sociology. There are, finally, also a book-length section on cities and a major analysis of the political situation in Germany at the time.

Weber did not have the time to finish *Economy and Society* before his death in 1920, and the various editions that exist are all seen as problematic. This includes the first and trend-setting edition that appeared after Weber's death in 1921–22 (edited by Marianne Weber, assisted by Melchior Palyi, a Hungarian-born economist); as well as the current German edition, the fifth, edited by Johannes Winkelmann. A new edition is planned as part of MWG, but there is by now no way of knowing how Weber himself would have organized his work.

The existing translation into English of *Wirtschaft und Gesellschaft* was made over a number of years by many people, including Talcott Parsons, Edward Shils, and Ephraim Fischoff. It is based on the fourth German edition of 1956, as revised in 1964. The two main editors are Guenther Roth and Claus Wittich. The initiative of putting together a full English translation of *Wirtschaft und Gesellschaft* into English came from Swedish sociologist Hans Zetterberg. Chapter 1 is also available in a new translation by Keith Tribe (EW:311–58).

Economy and Society has, to repeat, a difficult and complex history. In all brevity, only the four first chapters were sent by Weber to the printer and had their galley proofs corrected by him (ES:1–307). The rest of the English (and German) edition consists of various writings that the different editors of this work have on their own decided should belong to *Economy and Society* (ES:309–1469).

Weber's own plans for *Economy and Society* changed quite a bit over the years. Two plans from Weber's hand are in existence, and according to both of these his contribution was to be part of Book 1 of *The Handbook of Social Economics*. The focus of Book 1 was on the basic conditions of the economy: nature, technology, and society. Weber's original plan—dating from 1910—is as follows:

a. Economy and Law (1. Principal Relations. 2. Periods of Development until the Present)

b. Economy and Social groups (Family and Community [*Gemeindeverband*], Status Groups [*Stände*], Classes, the State)

c. Economy and Culture (Critique of Historical Materialism) (Baier, Lepsius, Mommsen, and Schluchter 2000:105; for the German original, see Weber 1999d:ix)

The second plan dates from 1914, and by this time Weber had changed his ideas for his contribution quite a bit. In a famous letter to his publisher of December 30, 1913, Weber says that in the new and expanded version of his manuscript he has "propounded a well-knit sociological theory and presentation that places all major forms of community in relation to economic life: from the family and household to the 'enterprise', the sib, ethnic community, religion (encompassing *all* major religions of the globe: sociology of the doctrines of redemption and religious ethics,—what Troeltsch has done, but now for *all* religions, only much more concise), and finally a comprehensive sociological theory of the state and domination. I venture to assert that there has been nothing like it yet, not even a 'precedent' for it" (Baier, Lepsius, Mommsen, and Schluchter 2000:106; for the German original, see Weber 1999d:x).

Weber's plan of 1914 is as follows:

1. Categories of Social Orders. Economy and Law and the Principles of their Relationship. Economic Relationships of Associations in General.

2. Household, *Oikos* and Enterprise,

3. Neighbourhood, Sib, Community.

4. Ethnic Communities.

5. Religious Communities. Class Conditioning of Religions; Cultural Religions and Religious Mentality.

6. Formation of Community through the Market (*Marktvergemeinschaftung*).

7. The Political Association. Developmental Conditions of Law. Status Groups, Classes, Parties. The Nation.

8. Domination: (a) The Three Types of Legitimate Domination, (b) Political and Hierocratic Domination, (c) Non-Legitimate Domination. Typology of Cities, (d) Development of the Modern State, (e) Modern Political Parties. (Baier, Lepsius, Mommsen, and Schluchter 2000:106; for the German original see Weber 1999d:ix–x)

Thus, all that we know for sure about the final version of *Economy and Society*, is what Weber intended the first four chapters to look like. The rest—as well as the idea of dividing up the whole work into two parts—comes from Marianne Weber and Melchior Palyi. What follows is the table of contents in the current English translation of *Economy and Society*:

Part One: Conceptual Exposition
    I.   Basic Sociological Terms
    II. Sociological Categories of Economic Action
    III. The Types of Legitimate Domination
    IV. Status Groups and Classes

There exist different opinions on when Weber worked on the various
parts of the manuscripts that make up *Economy and Society*, and on how
they fit together. According to the editors of MWG, Weber's work on
Economy and Society went through three phases: (1) 1909–12, (2) end
of 1912 to mid-1914, and (3) 1919–20 (Baier, Lepsius, Mommsen, and
Schluchter 2000:109). During 1909–12 Weber produced a first version
of *Economy and Society*, which was then rewritten during a creative
phase in 1912–13. It appears that the volume was close to being ready at
this stage, and that Weber was planning to let it go into print in 1915—
but World War I intervened and put a stop to these plans. When the war
began in August 1914, Weber set aside his work on *The Handbook of
Social Economics*. Once the war was over he wanted to slim it down and
make it more textbook-like, and during 1919–20 he therefore wrote the
three first chapters in Part 1 of *Economy and Society* but left Chapter 4
unchanged (ibid., pp. 105–10).

For a summary of the contents of *Economy and Society*, see e.g. Dirk
Käsler, *Max Weber* (1988), pp. 142–73; and for a critical analysis, see
e.g. Randall Collins, "Weber's Sociological Encyclopaedia," pp. 125–41

in *Max Weber* (1986) and Arthur Stinchcombe, "Review of Max Weber's *Economy and Society*" (1986). See also Otto Hintze, "Max Webers Soziologie" ([1926] 1964).

For the standard view of the history and the general structure of *Economy and Society*, see Horst Baier, M. Rainer Lepsius, Wolfgang Mommsen, and Wolfgang Schluchter, "Overview of the Text of *Economy and Society* by the Editors of the Max Weber *Gesamtausgabe*" (2000), Wolfgang Mommsen, "Max Weber's 'Grand Sociology': The Origins and Composition of *Wirtschaft und Gesellschaft: Soziologie*" (2000), and Wolfgang Schluchter, "*Economy and Society*: The End of a Myth," pp. 433–63 in *Rationalism, Religion and Domination* (1989). For the view that the first version of *Economy and Society* constitutes a distinct work of its own, rather than a fragmentary manuscript (as the editors of the *Gesamtausgabe* argue), see Hiroshi Orihara, "From 'A Torso with a Wrong Head' to 'Five Disjointed Body-Parts without a Head'" (2003). For the reception of *Economy and Society* in Weber's days, see Käsler, *Max Weber*, pp. 206–9. For the role of *Economy and Society* in *The Handbook of Social Economics*, *see* the entry for the latter work. It may finally be mentioned that the majority of the manuscripts that make up *Economy and Society* no longer exist.

For a long time *Economy and Society* was automatically seen as Weber's major work, but this opinion has now been challenged (see especially Friedrich Tenbruck, "The Problem of Thematic Unity in the Works of Max Weber" [1980]). Alternative candidates include *The Economic Ethics of the World Religions*, Weber's theory of rationalization, and his sociology of religion in combination with *Economy and Society* (see e.g. Stephen Kalberg, "The Search for Thematic Orientations in a Fragmented Oeuvre: The Discussion of Max Weber in Recent German Sociological Literature" [1979] and Wilhelm Hennis, "Max Weber's 'Central Question'" [1988]).

According to the plans, six volumes of MGW will be devoted to *Economy and Society* (Vol. 1: "Communities" ["*Gemeinschaften*"]; Vol. 2: "Religious Communities" ["*Religiöse Gemeinschaften*"]; Vol. 3: "Law" ["*Recht*"]; Vol. 4: "Domination" ["*Herrschaft*"]; Vol. 5: "The City" ["*Die Stadt*"]; and Vol. 6: "Materials and Index" ["*Materialien und Register*"]).

See also *Handbook of Social Economics, The*; "Some Categories of Interpretive Sociology"

education   While it is not possible to find a full-fledged sociology of education in Weber's work, he nonetheless discusses education in several of his writings and he also participated in the debate about education that was under way in his lifetime. According to Weber, education is central in modern society, and has increasingly come to divide up the population into different status groups (as opposed to different classes, which are related to the distribution of economic means; e.g. PW:83, 103). Certificates of education, in brief, are used to establish status vis-à-vis other people (e.g. ES:1000).

In *Economy and Society* there is, for example, a section on bureaucracy and education (ES:998–1002). Weber also devotes an important part of his sociology of law to the issue of legal education and how "law as a craft" (as in England) versus "law as taught in special schools" (as in Germany) has affected legal thought (ES:784–802). In his sociology of religion Weber similarly notes how education has helped to differentiate priests from magicians (e.g. ES:425–26; cf. RC:115–19). Charisma, Weber argues, cannot be "learned" or "taught," only "awakened" and "tested" (ES:249). "Science as a Vocation" contains a discussion of academic careers, including the problem of coming up with creative ideas (GM:129–38). Finally, one can find a thorough discussion of the literati and their education in *The Religion of China* (RC:17–41).

In his political writings Weber uses the notion of "political education" to indicate the level of maturity in political matters of a group or a class (e.g. PW:27, 144). As a result of Bismarck's authoritarian politics, for example, the political maturity of the German middle classes had severely suffered. See e.g. Lawrence Scaff, "Max Weber's Politics and Political Education" (1973).

For Weber's writings on the universities (and on the policy aspects of science), see the forthcoming volume I/13 of MGW. For a sample in English of Weber's writings on universities, see Max Weber, *On Universities: The Power of the State and the Dignity of the Academic Calling in Imperial Germany* (Weber 1974); see also Dirk Käsler, *Max Weber* (1988), pp. 16–17. For the general context of higher education in Germany, see Fritz Ringer, *The Decline of the German Mandarins: The German Academic Community, 1890–1933* (1969). Finally, see also Wilhelm Hennis, "Max Weber as Teacher" (2000).

See also Bismarck's legacy

Eigengesetzlichkeit (limited autonomy)   *See* value-spheres

Eingestelltheit (disposition)   *See* habitus

einfühlend evident (empathetically evident)   See *Evidenz*

"Einleitung"   This is the title of an article that was first published in 1915, and then appeared in revised form in 1920 in Vol. 1 of Weber's

Collected Essays in the Sociology of Religion (*Gesammelte Aufsätze zur Religionssoziologie*; GAR, I:237–75). It is known to most English readers as "The Social Psychology of the World Religions" (GM:267–391), which today also exists in a new and fuller translation by Sam Whimster ("Introduction to the Economic Ethics of the World Religions," EW:55–80). The title of this essay ("Introduction") derives from the fact that it represents the introduction to Weber's work *The Economic Ethics of World Religions* (which is part of his *Collected Essays in the Sociology of Religion*).

The "Introduction" is one of Weber's most famous and spectacular essays. Its main focus is on the relationship between religion and society, but it also contains passages on theodicy, the relationship of ideas to society, and much more.

This essay should be distinguished from the introduction to Vol. 1 of *Collected Essays in the Sociology of Religion*, which is entitled "Vorbemerkung" and is known in English as the "Author's Introduction" (PE:13–31).

See Sam Whimster, "Notes and Queries: Translator's Note on Weber's 'Introduction to the Economic Ethics of the World Religions'" (2002).

See also *Collected Essays in the Sociology of Religion*

Einverständnishandeln   *See* consensual action

elective affinities (*Wahlverwandschaften*)   The exact meaning of this term, which Weber often uses, is contested. The most common interpretation, however, is that "elective affinity" is used by Weber to express the fact that two sets of social facts or mentalities are related to each other or gravitate to each other—even though no direct and simple causality between the two can be established.

At one place in *Economy and Society* Weber notes, for example, that there exists "an elective affinity between the sect and political democracy" (ES:1208). He also uses this expression to characterize the relationship of ideas to interests, say between Protestant ideas and capitalism (e.g. PE:91–2, PED:107).

Stephen Kalberg points out that in situations of elective or inner affinity "the causal relationship is not strong enough to be designated 'determining'" (Kalberg in Weber [1904–5] 2002b:lxxvii). Jean-Pierre Grossein argues that elective affinity is closely related to Weber's concept of causality (Grossein, "Présentation" [2003], pp. xxxix–xlv). According to Hans Gerth and C. Wright Mills, elective affinity is "the decisive conception by which Weber relates ideas and interests" (GM:62). The term "elective affinities," it is often noted, has its origin in eighteenth-century chemistry and was popularized through Goethe's novel of 1809 with that name. See e.g. Richard Herbert Howe, "Max Weber's Elective Affinities: Sociology Within the Bounds of Pure Reason" (1978). It may finally be suggested that the term "compatibility" may also capture some of the meaning of Weber's *Wahlverwandschaft*.

See also carrier, causality, ideas

emotions   One can often find references to the role of emotions in Weber's work, especially in his sociology of religion (e.g. ES:432–37, 402–99, 602–4, PE:105, 166–71, RI:201). Emotions are also central to one of his four main types of social action (affectual action), to his concept of legitimacy, and to his concept of (emotional) empathy (ES:5, 25, 33–8).

Weber occasionally refers to "emotional values" and "emotional interests" (ES:41; cf. WuG:22). This may indicate that Weber did not see emotions as either positive or negative. It is rather up to the individual to evaluate things—including emotions.

An increasing amount of attention—and critique—has recently been directed at Weber's view of emotions and how he handles these. See e.g. J. M. Barbalet, "*Beruf*, Rationality and Emotion in Max Weber's Sociology" (2000) and Mustafa Emirbayer, "Beyond Action Theory" (forthcoming). According to Jon Elster, "there is nothing to indicate that Weber had thought much or deeply about the role of emotion (the most important aspect of affect) in behavior, an exception being his analysis of shame and guilt in religious and secular life" (Elster 2000:34).

See also affectual action, body, empathy, legitimacy

empathy (*Einfühlung*)   Weber uses this and related terms in somewhat different meanings in his sociology. In his general sociology in Ch. 1 of *Economy and Society*, for example, Weber refers to empathetic *Evidenz* (verifiable certainty) as part of his discussion of how to establish the view of the actor (ES:5; cf. ES:6). The basis for such certainty, he says, can be either "rational" or of "an emotionally empathetic or artistically appreciative quality" (ES:5). The former is logical or mathematical, while "empathetic or appreciative understanding is attained when through sympathetic participation, we can adequately grasp the emotional context in which the action took place" (ibid.). Weber also notes that "one need not have been Caesar in order to understand Caesar" (ES:5; cf. SCIS:151–52).

In the older parts of *Economy and Society*, on the other hand, Weber addresses the issue of what role empathy can play in generating new behavior (ES:321–22).

For a critique of "empathy theory," see Alfred Schutz, *The Phenomenology of the Social World* ([1932] 1967), pp. 114–15.

See also emotions, *Evidenz*

empirical justice *See* justice

empirical uniformities *See* uniformities

empiricism Weber argued for the importance of taking empirical facts into account in his interpretive sociology which he explicitly labels a form of "empirical sociology" (ES:3). His studies from the 1890s of agrarian conditions in Germany are part of the early history of empirical social science research more generally.

It is also possible to trace Weber's view of empiricism as a philosophy as well as his personal attitude toward empirical facts and the methods to use in collecting data.

In his philosophy of science Weber emphasizes the role that researchers and their values play in the selection of what to study. More generally Weber also highlights the active conceptual role that the researcher in his opinion should play in carrying out an analysis (*see* in particular the entries for ideal type and causality). "In Goethe's words, 'theory' is involved in the 'fact'" (MSS:173). But even if facts are infused by theory, theory itself must be grounded in facts. "Theory must follow the facts, not vice versa" (PED:36–7).

According to *The Protestant Ethic*, there exists a connection between empiricism and Protestant asceticism, especially Calvinism ("it was hoped from the empirical knowledge of the divine laws of nature to ascend to a grasp of the essence of the divine revelation"; PE:249 n. 145).

For Weber's use of empirical data and the methods he used to collect these, see e.g. Paul Lazarsfeld and Anthony Oberschall, "Max Weber and Empirical Research" (1965) and Anthony Oberschall, *Empirical Social Research in Germany 1848–1914* (1965). For Weber's positive attitude to religious activist Paul Göhre's book based on three months in a factory, see Weber [1892] 1993.

See also facts, interpretive sociology, sociological theory, sociology

employment regime (*Arbeitsverfassung*) This concept figures prominently in Weber's study of the situation of agrarian workers east of the Elbe and related early writings.

Arbeitsverfassung is usually translated as "organization of labor" or "labor organization" (e.g. Martin Riesebrodt, "From Patriarchalism to Capitalism" [1989]), but may also be translated as "employment regime"

(Ola Agevall, "Science, Values, and the Empirical Argument in Max We-ber's *Freiburger Antrittsrede*" [forthcoming]).

No formal definition of *Arbeitsverfassung* appears to exist in Weber's work. The closest that we get to a definition is the following statement in one of Weber's early writings: "[*Arbeitsverfassung* means] the principles according to which the agriculturalist uses his labor force" (Weber [1892–99] 1993:127).

An employment regime can also be described as the ways in which em-ployers organize and select their labor force. These ways or principles may or may not be laid down in a formal contract, and *Arbeitsverfassung* is therefore not a legal concept but an analytical concept. What the con-crete employment regime will look like depends on questions such as the following. Are the workers employed during the whole year or only dur-ing certain seasons? Are they paid in money or in kind? What categories of workers are employed (special ethnic groups? family members or sin-gle men or women?).

See e.g. Ola Agevall, "Science, Values, and the Empirical Argument in Max Weber's Freiburger Antrittsrede" (forthcoming) and Martin Riese-brodt, "From Patriarchalism to Capitalism" (1989).

See also constitution, patriarchy, rural sociology

England Problem   According to a popular interpretation of Weber's so-ciology of law, there exists a contradiction between Weber's argument that rational capitalism demands the existence of formal-rational law and the fact that England did not have such a law at the time when capitalism had its breakthrough in this country. This is what constitutes the so-called England Problem.

It can, however, also be argued on good grounds that Weber was well aware of this "problem"—as indicated by many passages to this effect in his work (e.g. ES:814, 889–92, 977).

For the pioneer article on the England Problem, see David Trubek, "Max Weber on Law and the Rise of Capitalism" (1972). For other con-tributions to the debate, see e.g. Sally Ewing, "Formal Justice and the Spirit of Capitalism: Max Weber's Sociology of Law" (1987), Anthony Kronman, *Max Weber* (1993), pp. 120–24, and Richard Swedberg, *Max Weber and the Idea of Economic Sociology* (1998), pp. 105–7.

enterprise (*Betrieb*)   This term—which should not be confused with that of the firm (*see* that entry)—denotes *continuous instrumental action*, which can be of an economic, religious, or some other type. An enterprise first becomes an organization or an association when it has a special staff. In this latter case, it becomes a formal enterprise, or what the current translation of *Economy and Society* calls a formal organization—that is, a modern organization (*see* organization or association).

The exact definition of an enterprise, which is given in Weber's general sociology in Ch. 1 of *Economy and Society*, reads as follows: "continuous instrumental activity of a specified kind (*Zweckhandeln*) will be called an *enterprise (Betrieb)*" (ES:52; my trans.). A formal enterprise or organization is defined as follows: "an organization with a continuously and rationally operating staff will be called a *formal organization (Betriebsverband)*" (ES:52).

The German term *Betrieb* is also used in another sense by Weber, namely to denote a firm in the sense of an "establishment" rather than of a profit-making entity (ES:116). "Establishment," in brief, is primarily a technical term, while "firm" is an economic one.

See also economic organization, establishment, firm

entrepreneur (*Unternehmer*)   While Weber is usually not credited with having a theory of entrepreneurship, he clearly does. According to Weber, the entrepreneur plays a crucial role in the capitalist economy by being the one who makes the central decisions in the firm and who directs its bureaucracy. The modern entrepreneur brings dynamism to capitalism and counters the negative impact of the bureaucracy.

The concept of entrepreneurship is not defined in Weber's economic sociology in Ch. 2 of *Economy and Society*. Nonetheless, Weber discusses entrepreneurship at various points in his economic sociology as well as in his writings on the economy more generally (e.g. GVAN:57). In contrast to Joseph Schumpeter (whose theory of entrepreneurship Weber was thoroughly familiar with), Weber however does not focus on the creativity of the individual entrepreneur but rather on the capitalist enterprise as directed by the entrepreneur, and on the general mentality ("spirit") that the entrepreneur brings to it.

According to Weber, the average entrepreneur hopes to make a profit higher than the existing rate of interest and draws in this effort on "business imagination" (GM:136). The entrepreneur is "the 'directing mind' [and] the 'moving spirit'" of the enterprise in modern capitalism (ES:1403). He or she knows more than the bureaucrats when it comes to the direction of the enterprise, and is a counter-balance to their power (e.g. ES:225).

In his various writings Weber often points out that entrepreneurship has been looked down upon by certain groups and in certain societies (e.g. ES:1295–96). In *The Protestant Ethic* Weber also importantly contrasts "the new entrepreneur," who saw money-making as a calling and who wanted to reform things, with the traditional kind of entrepreneur who was satisfied with the way things were (PE:69, 75).

Weber mentions the existence of "political 'entrepreneurs'," and it may be argued that his work points in the direction of public choice theory (e.g. PW:216, 320).

For managerial work, as opposed to entrepreneurship, *see* work.

Weber was personally an advocate of a dynamic form of capitalism and wrote in 1920 that Germany did not need socialization: "we need *the entrepreneur*" (Mommsen 1984:310 n. 105). He also criticized socialism for its "stupid hatred of the entrepreneur" (Beetham 1985:173).

For Weber's relationship to Schumpeter, see Jürgen Osterhammel, "Varieties of Social Economics: Joseph A. Schumpeter and Max Weber" (1987) and Richard Swedberg, *Joseph Schumpeter: His Life and Work* (1991), pp. 88–93.

See also bureaucracy, capitalism, firm, profit-making, spirit of capitalism

Entzauberung   *See* disenchantment

epistemology   *See* knowledge

Erbscharisma (hereditary charisma)   *See* charisma

erklärendes Verstehen (explanatory understanding)   *See* understanding

Erlösung   *See* salvation

Erlösungsreligion   *See* salvation

eroticism   *See* body, value-spheres

Erwartungen   *See* expectations

Erwerbsspielraum (scope of economic resources in relation to acquisition)   *See* open and closed social relationships

Erwerbstrieb   *See* acquisitive drive or instinct

establishment (*Betrieb*)   Weber makes a distinction between an "establishment" (*Betrieb*) and a "firm" (*Unternehmung*). While "establishment" is primarily a technical term, "firm" is primarily an economic one.

Weber describes an establishment in the following way in his economic sociology in Ch. 2 of *Economy and Society*: "'establishment' is a *technical* category which designates the continuity of the combination of certain types of services with each other and with material means of production" (ES:116).

The antithesis of a technical establishment is action that is discontinuous, such as in a household; while the antithesis of a firm is a budgetary unit where economic maintenance is what counts.

In *Economy and Society* the term *Betrieb* is also translated as "(non-economic) enterprise" when the contrast to the firm is not at issue; and in this case *Betrieb* simply means "continuous rational activity" (ES:52; *see* enterprise). When this continuous action is entrepreneurial in nature, Weber uses the term "profit-making enterprise" (*Erwerbsbetrieb*).

For the difficulties involved in translating Weber's use of the term *Betrieb*, see Claus Wittich's comment in a note to Ch. 2 of *Economy and Society* (ES:208 n. 27).

See also enterprise, firm

estate (*Stand*) *See* status

estate state (*Ständestaat*) *See* state

estate-type domination *See* patrimonialism

esthetic sphere *See* value-spheres

ethic See entries starting with the word "ethic"; *Protestant Ethic and the Spirit of Capitalism, The*

ethic of conviction *See* ethic of ultimate ends

ethic of responsibility (*Verantwortungsethik*) According to Weber, action can be oriented to an ethic of responsibility or to an ethic of ultimate ends (e.g. GM:120–28). In the latter type of ethic good intentions are what count, while in the former actors always have to take into account what impact their actions will have when they decide on what action to take.

If actors follow an ethic of responsibility in political matters they must face the fact that violence ultimately has to be used—and "diabolic forces lurk in all violence" (GM:125–26).

Weber himself sides with the ethic of responsibility in "Politics as a Vocation"—but also makes clear that this is an issue that cannot be decided on scientific grounds. He also states that anyone who wants to be involved in politics has to understand "ethical paradoxes," and that anyone who fails to realize that good may come from evil, and that evil may come from good, is a "political infant" (GM:123).

While there is a sharp and decisive difference between the ethic of responsibility and the ethic of ultimate ends, the two may also supplement each other. Someone who adheres to an ethic of responsibility may come to a stage where he or she decides that the only right thing to do is to take a stance, come what may ("here I stand; I can do no other"; GM:127).

For a discussion of the ethic of responsibility, see e.g. Wolfgang Schluchter, "Value-Neutrality and the Ethic of Responsibility," pp. 65–118 in Guenther Roth and Wolfgang Schluchter, *Max Weber's Vision of History* (1979). For a discussion of the relationship between Weber's methodology and his notion of an ethic of responsibility, see e.g. Alexander von Schelting, *Max Webers Wissenschaftslehre* (1934), pp. 8–11.

See in this context also Talcott Parsons, *The Structure of Social Action* (1937), Vol. 2, pp. 642–45, where the link between the ethic of responsibility and Weber's concept of instrumentally rational action is discussed. More generally, see e.g. Wolfgang Schluchter, "Conviction and Responsibility: Max Weber on Ethics," pp. 48–101 in *Paradoxes of Modernity* (1996).

See also ethic of ultimate ends, instrumentally rational action, paradoxical results of people's actions, unintended consequences

ethic of ultimate ends (*Gesinnungsethik*) According to Weber, action can be oriented to an ethic of responsibility or to an ethic of ultimate ends (e.g. GM:120–28). In the latter type of ethic good intentions are what counts, while in the former actors always have to take into account what effects their actions will have when they decide on what action to take.

An ethic of ultimate ends is common in Christianity, and according to a well-known formula that Weber sometimes cites (and which probably should be ascribed to Luther), "the Christian does what is right and places the outcome in God's hands" (PW:359, RI:184). Another example would be the syndicalist who argues for a strike, regardless of its results (e.g. PW:125).

According to Weber, who himself sides with the ethic of responsibility, adherents of an ethic of ultimate ends do not assume responsibility for the results of their actions. Neither do they face the difficult question of whether one can use dubious moral means when this would lead to good results ("dirty hands").

According to Guenther Roth, "'ethic of responsibility' is a literal rendering of *Verantwortungsethik*, but there is no equally easy translation for *Gesinnungsethik*" (Roth in Roth and Schluchter 1979:66 n. 1). Alternatives to the usual translation *Gesinnungsethik* as "ethic of ultimate ends" include "ethic of conviction" (Bruun), "ethic of single-minded conviction" (Roth), and "ethic of principled conviction" (Lassman and Speirs; see Bruun 1972:255–60, Roth and Schluchter 1979:66 n. 1, Lassman and Speirs in PW:359).

For the link between the ethic of ultimate ends and Weber's concept of value-rational action, see e.g. Talcott Parsons, *The Structure of Social Action* (1937), Vol. 2, pp. 642–45. More generally, see e.g. Wolfgang Schluchter, "Conviction and Responsibility: Max Weber on Ethics," pp.

48–101 in *Paradoxes of Modernity* (1996).

See also ethic of responsibility, paradoxical results of people's actions, unintended consequences, value-rational action

ethics   Since values play a key role in Weber's general worldview as well as in his view of the cultural sciences, ethics is of great importance to him. The emphasis in Weber's work is not on ethics or values from a theoretical viewpoint, but on the way they are expressed in people's lives—in their actions and lifestyles (*Lebensführung*). In brief, what matters is what Weber terms "practical ethics" or "practical impulses for action" (e.g. RI:177, GM:267).

Another important theme in Weber's approach to ethics is his distinction, as expressed in a letter of 1907, between what constitutes desirable behavior of the select few ("ethics of heroes") and of common people ("ethics of the average"; Weber 1990: 399).

See also double ethic, economic ethic, ethic of ultimate ends, ethic of responsibility, religious ethic, teacher of ethics, value spheres, values, vocation

ethnic groups (*ethnische Gruppen*)   The concept of ethnic group is not included in Weber's general sociology in Ch. 1 of *Economy and Society*. It does, however, play an important role in another section of this work where Weber also discusses race and nationality (ES:385–98; cf. ES:933–34).

The closest to a definition of ethnic groups that may be found in Weber's work reads as follows: "we shall call 'ethnic groups' those human groups that entertain a subjective belief in their common descent because of similarities of physical type or of customs or both, or because of memories of colonization and migration; this belief must be important for the propagation of group formation; conversely, it does not matter whether or not an objective blood relationship exists" (ES:389). To be a member of a certain ethnicity does not necessarily mean that an ethnic group exists; simply that the formation of such a group is facilitated. The notion that one belongs to some ethnic group is primarily inspired by the political community.

It appears that Weber had difficulty in nailing down the exact meaning of ethnicity. For example, he ends his major section on this topic with the statement that "the concept of 'ethnic group' . . . dissolves if we define our terms closely" (ES:395).

Ethnicity can be centered around many different phenomena, such as a common language, a common religion, a memory of once having belonged to the same community, "conspicuous differences of physical appearance," and "perceptible differences in the conduct of everyday life" (ES:390). There is typically a distinct preference when it comes to food, division of labor between the sexes, and many other things, including what is proper or not, and what is honorable or not ("ethnic honor"; ES:391). Weber also notes that all ethnic groups think that they are "the chosen people," and that one can often find "repulsion" between different ethnic groups (ibid.).

While Weber took a stance against anti-Semitism and racial prejudices in general, it is common to find ethnic slurs in his early social science writings on the role of the Poles in Germany. See on this last point e.g. Guenther Roth, "Between Cosmopolitanism and Ethnocentrism: Max Weber in the Nineties" (1993). See also Maurice Jackson, "An Analysis of Max Weber's Theory of Ethnicity" (1983) and Johannes Raum, "Reflections on Max Weber's Thoughts Concerning Ethnic Groups" (1995).

See also nature, race

ethnicity (*Ethnizität*)   The term "ethnicity" did not exist in Weber's time, but one can nonetheless find a discussion of the term "ethnic groups" in his work (Johannes Raum, "Reflections on Max Weber's Thoughts Concerning Ethnic Groups" [1995], p. 79); *see* that entry.

See also ethnography

ethnography   The science of ethnography or (modern) anthropology was little developed in Weber's days, and he now and then complains about the lack of relevant ethnographic material, especially in his sociology of religion (e.g. ES:320–21, 370, 420 n. 1, 909).

In the beginning of his lecture course of 1919–20 that was later reconstructed and published as *General Economic History*, Weber nonetheless takes as his point of departure the early anthropological theories of agrarian communism, matriarchy, and the like. These theories were first formulated in J. J. Bachofen's *Das Mutterrecht* ([1861] 2003), L. M. Morgan's *Ancient Society* ([1877] 2001), and H. S. Maine's *Ancient Law* ([1861] 2001), but were embraced above all by socialist scholars. Weber confronts these theories with historical empirical material on agrarian organization and forms of appropriation, and finds that they contain interesting hypotheses but are untenable on points of detail.

For Weber's relationship to the ethnography of his time and related topics, see e.g. Paul Honigsheim, *On Max Weber* (1968), pp. 55–61 as well as "Max Weber as Applied Anthropologist" (1948). For the use of Weber's work and terminology in modern anthropology, see e.g. Johannes Raum, "Reflections on Max Weber's Thoughts Concerning Ethnic Groups" (1995).

See also anthropology (for anthropology in its old-fashioned, philosophical sense), body, race

ethos (*Ethos*)   The term "ethos" is sometimes used in Weber's work, but it is not included among the key concepts in Weber's general sociology in Ch. I of *Economy and Society*. It can roughly be described as the collective self-representation of a style of life that is characteristic for a group of individuals.

In a central passage in *The Protestant Ethic*, Weber describes, for example, what characterizes the lifestyle of textile manufacturers in continental Europe in the nineteenth century, and then adds that this is what was "at the basis, one may say, of the ethos (*Ethos*) of this group of business men" (PE:67; cf. e.g. PE:51–2). Weber is also careful to point out that the ethos of a religion is not the same as its doctrine (GM:321).

The term "ethos" is close to several other terms in Weber's work. *Gesinnung*, which is usually translated as "mentality," is also sometimes translated as "ethos" (e.g. ES:1200–1201). Jean-Pierre Grossein states that ethos is closely related to concepts such as disposition (*Gesinnung*), spirit (*Geist*), and habitus in Weber's work (Grossein, "Présentation" [1996]. p. 61 n. 1).

See also habitus, lifestyle, mentality, spirit of capitalism

everyday life (*Alltag*) The notion of everyday life or everyday activities plays an important role in Weber's various concepts. Charisma, for example, is defined as something which is *not* part of everyday life and is therefore truly extraordinary (*ausseralltäglich*). Weber terms the process whereby charisma wears off and becomes more like everyday life "routinization" or "becoming like every day" (*Veralltäglichung*). The term "mundane" also captures something of the meaning of *Alltag*.

According to Parsons, "Weber uses the term *Alltag* in a technical sense, which is contrasted with charisma" (ES:210 n. 50; cf. Weber 1947:361 n. 41). Parsons also argues that there is an ambiguity to Weber's use of this term since it sometimes is used to indicate what is routine (the opposite being extraordinary and temporary), and at other times what is profane (the opposite being sacred). According to Jean-Pierre Grossein, to translate Weber's use of *alltäglich* as "routine" and *Veralltäglichung* as "routinization" gives the English-speaking reader the erroneous impression that these terms denote something inferior or negative. Weber's intention in using these terms was instead to point to everyday life and ordinary activities without any pejorative intent (Grossein, "Présentation." [1996], pp. 123–24).

See also charisma, routinization

***Evidenz* (verifiable certainty)** When the sociologist uses the concept of meaning, which is central to Weber's sociology, it is imperative that this be done in accordance with normal scientific standards and that proper evidence be produced. *Evidenz* roughly means "verifiable certainty," and especially refers to two interrelated qualities that the use of the concept of meaning has to live up to: clarity and verifiability.

According to Parsons, "there is no good rendering [in English] of the German term *Evidenz*" (ES:58 n. 6). The truth of this statement can be illustrated by the fact that he needs several words (italicized in the following quote) in order to translate the term *Evidenz* in paragraph 1 of Ch. 1 of *Economy and Society*, "all interpretation of meaning, like all scientific observations, strives for *clarity and verifiable accuracy of insight and comprehension (Evidenz)*" (ES:5). An alternative translation of the German original of the same sentence reads as follows: "each interpretation, like all science in general, strives for 'certainty'" (Burger 1987:113).

Verifiable certainty can be achieved in two ways: one that is primarily rational and another that is primarily empathetic. In the former case the basis for the certainty is "rational," and in the latter "emotionally empathetic or artistically appreciative" (*rational evident* and *einfühlend evident*; ES:5). An example of rationally based certainty would be the proposition that two times two equals four; and of the emotionally empathetic when we try to understand Caesar by taking the view of Caesar.

For a discussion of Weber's concept of *Evidenz* see e.g. Thomas Burger, *Max Weber's Theory of Concept Formation* (1987), pp. 113–14. See also Weber's early formulation of his ideas on certainty in sociology in SCIS:151, 152; cf. RK:174–76.

See also causality, explanation, meaning

evolution   Weber was deeply interested in the general evolution or development of human history; how to conceptualize it; and how to explain it. However, he firmly rejected the idea that history follows certain laws, be it in the form of necessary stages or otherwise.

The notion that there exist certain stages that society goes through was very popular in Weber's days, especially in economic history. Gustav Schmoller, for example, argued that the economy goes through the following stages: "domestic economy," "village economy," "seigneurial and princely patrimonial household economy," "town economy," "territorial economy," and "national economy" (ES:117–18, 208–9, 1218–19). Karl Bücher also had a stage theory of his own.

Weber's response to this was that stages should be seen as "guiding threads for the discovery and ordering of facts"—but that is all (MSS:131; for Weber's devastating critique of the theory of cultural stages [*Kulturstufen*], see GAW:517). There are no laws involved in history or necessary stages.

During his last decade Weber became interested in the fact that the West had come to lead the development of human culture in a number of areas. While he did not himself formulate this in terms of laws, the reader may nonetheless get the impression that Weber thought that this development was, if not inevitable, still extremely hard to change.

For the complexities involved in Weber's early acceptance and later rejection of stage theory, see e.g. Lawrence Scaff, *Fleeing the Iron Cage* (1989), pp. 39–43. See also H. Kellenbenz, "Wirtschaftsstufen" (1965). For Weber's acceptance of stage theory in the field of religion, see e.g. Martin Riesebrodt, "Ethische und exemplarische Prophetie" (2001), pp. 194–95.

For an attempt to relate Weber's ideas to the sociology of development, see Bryan Turner, "Weber and the Sociology of Development," pp. 234–56 in *For Weber* (1981).

See also laws in the social sciences, race, selection, universal history; West, the

exchange (*Tausch*)   Exchange is a form of economic action in Weber's sociology and not a universal form of social action as in exchange theory in contemporary sociology. Exchange is in all brevity characterized by Weber as a compromise reached by two actors in relation to something of value that passes between them.

Exchange is defined in Weber's economic sociology in Ch. 2 of *Economy and Society* as "a compromise of interests on the part of the parties in the course of which goods or other advantages are passed as reciprocal compensation" (ES:72). A supplementary definition is given as part of the explication of the earlier cited definition: "[exchange is] a formally voluntary agreement involving the offer of any sort of present, continuing, or future utility in exchange for utility of any sort offered in return" (ES:73; cf. CS:113).

Exchange is an economic means par excellence and does not involve violence. It can be traditional, conventional or rational; it can also be regulated or formally free. You can enter into exchange for consumption as well as for acquisition.

Conflict is inherent in the notion of exchange, as Weber uses it (*Tauschkampf*). More precisely two types of conflicts are typically involved in an exchange. First there is a conflict over who will do the exchange ("competitive bidding"; *Konkurrenzkampf*); and then there is a conflict between the parties involved in the actual exchange ("bargaining"; *Preiskampf*). Repeated forms of exchange constitute the core of a market.

See also competition, gift, market

existentialism   *See* philosophy

expectations (*Erwartungen*)   The concept of expectations plays an important general role in Weber's sociology, inasmuch as social structures only exist as expectations—in the sense of a probability (*Chance*) that they will come into being also in the future. Weber also uses the concept of expectations (*Erwartungen*) in reference to individuals' directing their actions to their expectations of what others will do. This is, for example, the way that Weber defines his early concept of social action (*Gemeinschaftshandeln*), in his 1913 essay "Some Categories of Interpretive Sociology" (SCIS:159–60). Weber also uses expectations in this sense in the concept that replaces his early concept of social action in *Economy and Society*, namely the concept of instrumentally rational action. "An important (though not indispensable) normal component of social action (*Gemeinschaftshandeln*)," he states, "is its meaningful orientation to the expectations of certain behavior on the part of others and, in accordance with that, orientation to the (subjectively) assessed probabilities for the success of one's action" (SCIS:159).

The concept of expectations is also important to Weber's concept of instrumentally rational action, as presented in his general sociology in Ch. 1 of *Economy and Society*. This concept is defined as "determined by expectations (*Erwartungen*) as to the behavior of objects in the environment and of other human beings; these expectations are used as 'conditions' or 'means' for the attainment of the actor's own rationally pursued and calculated ends" (ES:24; cf. ES:26). Expectations is also part of what guarantees the legitimacy of an order (ES:33).

That expectations figure prominently in Weber's analysis in *Economy and Society* is contested. According to Stephen Turner, the concept of expectations, "which figured so heavily in the *Logos* essay [that is, in SCIS], both in the discussion of action and in the discussion of various social relations, . . . drops out [in Ch. 1 on general sociology in *Economy and Society*]" (Turner 1983:513).

See also probability, orientation to others

explanation (*Erklären*)   Weber attempted to develop a theory of explanation that answers to the demands of the cultural sciences (including the social sciences) and which consequently differs from the way that explanation is perceived in the natural sciences. Sociology, according to Weber, seeks to explain social behavior, and in the process of doing so, draws heavily on the actors' own view of their actions and motives.

Sociology is defined by Weber in his general sociology in Ch. 1 of *Economy and Society* as a science concerned with "a causal explanation" of the "course and consequences" of social action (ES:4). The concept of explanation is also closely tied to the concept of meaning: "for a science which is concerned with the subjective meaning of action [as sociology is], explanation requires a grasp of the complex of meaning in which an actual course of understandable action thus interpreted belongs" (ES:9).

For a discussion of the different steps in a sociological explanation, *see* causality. For a more detailed discussion of the role that the subjective understanding of the actor plays in explaining something, *see* meaning.

In Weber's time it was common to set "explanation" against "understanding" (*Verstehen*) and to argue that the former was characteristic of the natural sciences, and the latter of the social or cultural sciences (see e.g. Fritz Ringer, *Max Weber's Methodology* [1997]). Weber himself strongly opposed this type of argument and insisted that one could and should unite explanation and understanding. In one of his methodological essays Weber refers, for example, to "understanding explanation" (*verstehende Erklärung*; MSS:41).

Talcott Parsons has argued that there is "a brilliant ad hocness to Weber's analysis," which has had a negative impact on the further development of his thought. "Weber's enormous historical erudition, as well as his high level of empirical insight and judgment, served to cover over whatever theoretical deficiencies were inherent in his conceptual framework" (Parsons 1963:lxi–lxv).

See also causality, motive

explanatory understanding (*erklärendes Verstehen*)   *See* understanding

exploitation   While Weber never developed a theory of exploitation along the lines of Marx, he was well aware of the brutality of life for the great majority of the population. In one of his political writings, for example, he refers to the fact that "hundreds of millions of people, year after year, waste away in body and soul" (PW:78).

expropriation (*Expropriation*)   The fact that the workers have been expropriated from the means of production plays an important role in Weber's economic sociology in Ch. 2 of *Economy and Society* (ES:137–40). As in the work of Marx, it is one of the preconditions for modern rational capitalism or, in Weber's words, for the "maximum formal rationality of capital accounting" (ES:161–63).

As opposed to Marx, however, Weber distinguishes between technical and economic reasons for the expropriation. The former are important for the separation of the individual worker from the means of production, while the latter are central for the expropriation of *all* of the workers.

Weber also, again in contrast to Marx, discusses the expropriation not only of the workers from the means of production, but also the expropriation or separation of various actors from the means of administration, from the means of war, and so on.

See also accounting, firm, means of administration, means of production, means of war, workers

Facts

Facts   There is in principle always a subjective dimension to the type of facts that the social sciences are concerned with, according to Weber, and this means that interpretation has to be used. What type of facts social scientists deal with also has to do with the values of the society in which they live (so-called value-relevance). "'To let the facts speak for themselves' is the most unfair way of putting over a political position to the student" (GM:146).

The social scientist must always look at alternative ways of acting and what their consequences would have been, as part of figuring out the causality involved in social action.

At one point Weber notes: "in Goethe's words, 'theory' is involved in the 'fact'" (MSS:173). This, however, must not detract from the general maxim in sociological research that "theory must follow the facts, not vice versa" (PED:36–7). See in this context also Paul Lazarsfeld and Anthony Oberschall, "Max Weber and Empirical Research" (1965) and Anthony Oberschall, *Empirical Social Research in Germany 1848–1914* (1965).

See also cognitive interest, empiricism, historical individual, meaning, value-relevance

family (*Familie*)   Weber discusses the role of the family in various parts of his work. His analysis of the family can often be found in connection with his analysis of the household, and the two terms are sometimes used interchangeably (e.g. ES:356–69). According to Weber, a family needs to be a household to be stable (ES:357).

Drawing on the terminology of Weber's general sociology in Ch. 1 in *Economy and Society*, a family can be characterized as a closed social relationship of a communal character, that is, a family is strongly characterized by a sense of belonging together (e.g. ES:41).

The modern family is centered around a father, a mother, and their children, but other people can also be included such as grandparents and cousins. Marriage essentially means that special relationships are created with groups and people outside the father-mother-children relationship (ES:357–58, 368).

The family constitutes the first important trading group, and the modern firm also has its origins in the family (e.g. HCP, GEH:225–29, ES:378–80, 1009). So does the *oikos* and economic units which are centered around autarchy rather than profit-making (e.g. ES:381–83).

In 1905 Weber announced a work on "Family and Prostitution," but only the preparatory notes for this item remain (Weber 2001a:282–327).

See e.g. Randall Collins, "Weber's Theory of the Family," pp. 267–96 in *Weberian Sociological Theory* (1986) and Bryan Turner, "Family, Property and Ideology," pp. 289–317 in *For Weber* (1981).

See also household, kin group, males, *oikos*, patriarchalism, women

feminism   Marianne Weber was active in the women's movement, and Max Weber was supportive of her efforts. See Patricia Madoo Lengermann and Jill Niebrugge-Brantley, *The Women Founders: Sociology and Social Theory, 1830–1930* (1998); see also e.g. Guenther Roth, "Introduction to the New Edition," pp. xv–lx in Marianne Weber, *Max Weber* ([1926] 1975) and Christa Krüger, *Max und Marianne Weber* (2001).

There are also feminist analyses of Weber's work; see e.g. Roslyn Wallach Bologh, "Marx, Weber, and Masculine Theorizing: A Feminist Analysis" (1987) and *Love or Greatness: Max Weber and Masculine Thinking—A Feminist Inquiry* (1990). Bologh analyzes Weber's male and patriarchal vision of the world, including his ideas on politics, religion, love, and eroticism. She especially points to Weber's tendency to set "masculine greatness" against "feminine love."

See also males, women, patriarchalism

feudalism (*Feudalismus*)   Weber discusses feudalism primarily in his sociology of domination and in his historical sociology.

At one point in *Economy and Society* Weber gives the following shorthand description of feudalism: "the rule of a landed military aristocracy" (ES:1070). In Ch. 3 on domination in *Economy and Society* Weber discusses feudalism in some detail and notes that it differs from charismatic domination as well as patrimonial domination (ES:255–66, 1071–1110). It primarily takes the following two forms: "feudalism based on fiefs" (*Lehensfeudalismus*) and "prebendal feudalism" or "feudalism based on benefices" (*Pfründen-Feudalismus*). Feudalism based on fiefs is sometimes also translated in *Economy and Society* as "occidental feudalism" (e.g. ES:1072; for additional forms of feudalism, including "urban feudalism" [*Stadtfeudalismu*], see e.g. GASW:3, ES:1072).

A fief is described in *Economy and Society* as "any grant of rights, especially of land use or of political territorial rights, in exchange for military or administrative service" (ES:1071). A fief is also a type of contract; it is personal; and it lasts for a person's lifetime. If a fief is also hereditary, the only thing that makes the vassal obey his lord is loyalty—something that makes this type of feudalism chronically unstable.

Prebendal feudalism rests on benefices, as opposed to fiefs, and benefices are lifelong assignments of rent payments or allowances. While feudalism based on fiefs typically emerged in situations where members of communities could not afford to equip themselves as knights, prebendal feudalism emerged in situations when there was a reversal from monetary financing to financing in kind.

In a discussion of the iron cage(-)like future, Weber at one point characterized the United States as "benevolent feudalism" (PW:68).

For a presentation of Weber's views on feudalism, see e.g. Reinhard Bendix, *Max Weber: An Intellectual Portrait* (1960), pp. 360–80. See also Gianfranco Poggi, "Max Weber's Conceptual Portrait of Feudalism" (1988), Wolfgang Schluchter, *Paradoxes of Modernity* (1996), p. 146–55, and Bryan Turner, "Feudalism and Prebendalism," pp. 203–33 in *For Weber* (1981).

See also benefices, domination, fief, means of administration

fief (*Lehen*)   A fief is a type of income for a patrimonial retainer, often a land grant in exchange for military services. It is also a type of contract. A regime based on fiefs is called feudalism.

In Ch. 3 on domination in *Economy and Society* the following definition of a fief is given: "appropriated seigneurial powers will be called a *fief* if they are granted primarily to particular qualified individuals by a contract and if the reciprocal rights and duties involved are primarily oriented to conventional standards of status honor, particularly in a military sense" (ES:235). Elsewhere in *Economy and Society* another definition of a fief is given: "any grant of rights, especially of land use or of political territorial rights, in exchange for military or administrative service" (ES:1071).

Feudalism can be described as "the rule of a landed military aristocracy" (ES:1070). Different types of feudalism exist, including "feudalism based on fiefs" (*Lehensfeudalismus*) and "prebendal feudalism" or "feudalism based on benefices" (*Pfründen-Feudalismus*; ES:1072). Western feudalism is a form of feudalism based on fiefs.

See also benefice, feudalism

field   *See* value-spheres

firm (*Unternehmung*)   The firm and its evolution play a key role in Weber's analysis of modern rational capitalism and in his economic sociology more generally.

According to Ch. 2 of *Economy and Society*, which contains Weber's economic sociology, the firm falls in the generic category of economically oriented organizations (*wirtschaftlich orientierter Verband*). An economic organization (*Wirtschaftsverband*) becomes an economically oriented organization "if its organized action, as governed by the order, is *primarily* autocephalous economic action of a given kind" (ES:74; autocephalous means that the organization appoints its own leadership). A firm, Weber further specifies, is an economic organization that is oriented to profit-making (*Unternehmung*; ES:116; cf. ES:208 n. 27).

The historical origin of the firm is to be found in the family (e.g. HCP, GEH:225–29, ES:378–80). The family itself, however, is centered around householding and not profit-making. The antithesis of a firm is a budgetary unit (*Haushalt*).

The firm is mainly discussed in Weber's economic sociology but important information can also be found in Weber's historical studies and in his legal studies, such as his agrarian sociology of antiquity and his dissertation on the early forms of the firm in medieval times (ASAC, HCP). "It was the Italians," Weber says, "followed by the English, who developed the modern capitalist form of economic organization" (PW:155).

In *The Protestant Ethic* Weber makes the distinction between the "form" of a firm and its "spirit." The two usually coincide, but do not have to do so, as the phenomenon of traditional firms operated in a non-traditional manner or spirit indicates (e.g. PE:64–5, 67). Several examples are given in *The Protestant Ethic* (e.g. PE:65–8).

In a capitalist firm the workers are separated from the means of production, something which increases the formal rationality of the firm. A modern capitalist firm is led by an entrepreneur, but can also be controlled either by the owners, the managers, or by outside interests (ES:139–40; *see* outside interests). Bureaucracies can primarily be found in the huge firms of modern capitalism.

In his sociology of law Weber discusses, among other things, the emergence of the concept of legal personality which is central to the modern firm (ES:705–29). A comparison is also made between the law of the firm in the West and in other parts of the world.

The term "firm" is primarily an economic one for Weber, who uses "establishment" (*Betrieb*) for the technical side of a firm (ES:116).

While there exists a huge secondary literature on Weber's concept of bureaucracy and its role in modern firms, there exist next to no literature on Weber's concept of the firm (see, however, Søren Jagd, "Max Weber's Last Theory of the Modern Business Enterprise" [2002]). According to an authority on Weber's sociology of law, "more of the *Rechtssoziologie* is devoted to the subject of contractual association than to any other single topic" (Kronman 1983:96).

See also accounting, bureaucracy, capitalism, commenda, economic organization, enterprise, entrepreneur, establishment, organization or association

force   *See* coercion

formal organization (*Betriebsverband*)   This type of organization is defined in Weber's general sociology in Ch. 1 of *Economy and Society* in the following manner: "an association (*Betrieb*) with a continuously and rationally operating staff will be called a *formal organization*" (ES:52).

Continuous instrumental activity constitutes the core of a formal organization—which may be economic or non-economic.

See also enterprise (*Betrieb*), organization or association

freedom (*Freiheit*)   The notion of freedom plays an important part in Weber's political thinking as well as in his personal vision of life. In his early writings Weber refers, for example, to "the magic of freedom" that many of the rural workers east of Elbe felt (PW:8). This magic of freedom made them leave the countryside for the city, even if they "objectively" had a better economic future in the former.

Freedom in the West, Weber notes, was due to a series of "never-to-be-repeated historical constellations" (PW:69–70). He did not accept that there exists an affinity between capitalism and freedom (e.g. PW:69; cf. similarly for the affinity of tolerance and economic development, PED:66, 78, 98–100). He also argued that the growth of bureaucracy led to a loss of freedom.

For Weber on freedom, see e.g. Jürgen Habermas, "From Lukacs to Adorno: Rationalization as Reification," pp. 339–99 in Vol. 1 of *The Theory of Communicative Action* (1984); and Karl Löwith, *Max Weber and Karl Marx*, pp. 43–47.

See also democracy, politics, value-freedom

Freiheitsrechte   *See* privileges, rights

Freud, Sigmund   *See* psychology

functionalism   This type of approach may be characterized as an explanation of a certain phenomenon in a way that differs from ordinary causality by relying heavily on analogies to organic wholes. The emphasis is typically on the "function" that something has in the operation of such a whole.

In his general sociology in Ch. 1 of *Economy and Society* Weber discusses the extent to which a functional approach can be used in sociology (ES:14–18). He argues that functional analysis is not only helpful but even "indispensable," when it is used for illustration or at an early stage of the research process (ES:15). Going beyond these two uses, however, can be "highly dangerous" (ibid.). He also points out that sociology is concerned with the subjective dimension of the phenomena it studies, as opposed to the natural sciences-which are concerned with functional relationships and similar phenomena that lack a subjective dimension.

See also holism

Games and game theory   In the *Critique of Stammler* one can find a lengthy analysis of skat, a card game that Weber was fond of playing as a young man (CS:98–143; for Weber's view of games more generally, see ES:1105–6).

The main point that Weber makes in his discussion of the work of legal thinker Rudolf Stammler is that while jurisprudence is primarily interested in issues that have to do with the following of rules, one may also look at the extent to which the rules are indeed followed in reality. While the former approach is not social (or sociological), the second is.

It is sometimes argued that Weber's approach in sociology accords well with game theory. In this case Weber's definition of social action is often cited—that an action is social if it is oriented to the behavior of another actor. It has, however, also been argued that Weber only takes "paradigmatic rationality" into account (or opportunities that are given), not "strategic rationality" (or opportunities that depend on what the other actor does—as in game theory; see e.g. Jon Elster, "Rationality, Economy and Society" [2000], pp. 38–39; and for a passage in Weber that contradicts Elster's argument, see e.g. CS:114).

Gebilde   Weber uses this term in multiple meanings, including "formation," "construction" and "structure."
See also social structure

Geist   Weber uses the term *Geist* in several meanings, most famously as "spirit" in *The Protestant Ethic and the Spirit of Capitalism*. But he also uses it, for example, in the sense of mentality (e.g. AJ:61).
See spirit of capitalism

Geltung   *See* legitimacy, validity

Gemeinde   *See* community, congregation

Gemeinschaft   *See* community

Gemeinschaftshandeln   *See* social action

gender   *See* feminism, males, women

General Economic History (***Wirtschaftsgeschichte*, trans. 1927**)   This work is based on notes that students took during a lecture course that Weber gave in the winter semester of 1919–20 at the University of Munich, entitled "Outline of Universal Social and Economic History" (*Abriss der universalen Sozial-und Wirtschaftsgeschichte*). The German edition was published in 1932, a few years after Weber's death. For a number of reasons, including the fact that the original student notes on which the 1923 edition is based have disappeared, it is not possible to decide how closely this work answers to Weber's actual lectures.

Weber's course started with a conceptual introduction, which was followed by four parts running from agriculture in early history to capitalism in the nineteenth century (I. "Household, Clan, Village and Manor"; II. "Industry and Mining Down to the Beginning of the Capitalistic Development"; III. "Commerce and Exchange in the Pre-Capitalistic Age"; IV. "The Origin of Modern Capitalism").

The *Wirtschaftsgeschichte* was edited or rather reconstructed by Siegmund Hellmann (1872–1942), professor of history in Munich, who was assisted by Melchior Palyi (1892–1970), a Hungarian-born economist, and Marianne Weber. Among Weber's papers all that was found from the course was "a bundle of sheets with notes little more than catchwords" (Hellmann and Palyi in Weber 1927:xix).

The English translation was made in 1927 by economist Frank Knight. For various reasons the introductory pages were not included in the translation (but will appear in *Max Weber Studies* in a translation by Keith Tribe). These pages are similar to Ch. 2 on economic sociology in *Economy and Society* ("Conceptual Preliminary Comment," pp. 1–16). According to Guenther Roth, the *General Economic History* is nonetheless "inferior in terminological and systematic respects" when compared to *Economy and Society* (ES:lxiv).

For the reception of *General Economic History* in Weber's time, see e.g. Dirk Käsler, *Max Weber* (1988), p. 200; See also Richard Swedberg, *Max Weber and the Idea of Economic Sociology* (1998), pp. 205–6. Robert Merton famously questions one passage in *General Economic History* which has to do with the relationship of Protestantism to science, and suggests that it may not reflect Weber's opinion but instead may be the result of an error by the editors or in the student notes on which the book is based (Robert Merton, *The Sociology of Science* [1973], p. 245 n. 52). The definitive edition of this work is scheduled to appear as MWG, Vol. III/7.

See also economic history

general sociology   See *Kategorienlehre*

Gentilcharisma (**lineage charisma**)   *See* charisma

geography   That Weber paid much attention to the role of geographical factors in his work is as clear from his study of rural workers in the 1890s as from his course of 1919–20 on which the *General Economic History* is based. Weber repeatedly referred to Europe's varied geographical situation as being one of many factors that favored the emergence of modern rational capitalism, just as he often noted the role of the centralized control of water as being one of the factors that favored unitary empires. He also commissioned a study of the geographical conditions of the economy for the *Handbook of Social Economics*.

From a theoretical perspective, geographical factors fall into a special category in Weber's interpretive type of sociology. It is to these and similar facts that he refers when he writes in his general sociology in Ch. 1 of *Economy and Society* that "account must be taken of processes and stimuli which are devoid of subjective meaning, in the role of stimuli, results, favoring or hindering circumstances" (ES:7; cf. ES:13).

Weber points out that bureaucracy and control of water supply go together since the former typically implies a centralized power (e.g. ES:971–72, 1054). It should also be noted that the concept of territory plays a key role in Weber's definition of the state (e.g. ES:54).

Weber reportedly regarded the discipline of geography "with some skepticism" (Honigsheim 2000:155). For his attitude to economic geography as well as the relationship of his ideas to Karl A. Wittfogel's theory of hydraulic despotism, see e.g. Richard Swedberg, *Max Weber and the Idea of Economic Sociology* (1998), pp. 152–53. According to Reinhard Bendix, "Weber's emphasis on centralization is much more qualified than Wittfogel's" (Bendix 1960:101). For Wittfogel's ideas, see especially his *Oriental Despotism* (1957). See, finally, Stefan Breuer, "Stromuferkultur und Küstenkultur. Geographische und ökologische Faktoren in Max Webers 'ökonomischer Theorie der antiken Staatenwelt'" (1985).

German Historical School   *See* Historical School of economics

German Sociological Association   *See* Deutsche Gesellschaft für Soziologie

Germany   Weber wrote continually on German politics, and these writings also give a good picture of German social structure and its major groups. Weber's views of German culture and social life are somewhat less accessible. Weber was a strong nationalist and is reputed to have said

"I thank God that I am a German" (Jaspers 1989:16).

For the young Weber's view of German politics and social structure, see e.g. "The Nation State and Economic Policy" (PW:1–28), and for the mature Weber's view, "Parliament and Government in a Reconstructed Germany" (ES:1381–1469). For a standard work on Germany during Weber's lifetime, see Hans-Ulrich Wehler, *The German Empire 1871–1918* (1985); see also the historical literature discussed in Gordon Martel (ed.), *Modern Germany Reconsidered 1870–1975* (1992). For the German universities and academic life, see e.g. Fritz Ringer, *The Decline of the German Mandarins: The German Academic Community, 1890–1933* (1969). For a history of the so-called *Staatswissenschaften* (economics, politics, statistics and allied fields) during the nineteenth century, see David Lindenfeld, *The Practical Imagination* (1997). For the general culture of late nineteenth- and early twentieth-century Germany, see e.g. Norbert Elias, *The Germans* (1996).

For some glimpses of Weber's view of German culture and social life, the reader is recommended to read Marianne Weber, *Max Weber: A Biography* ([1926] 1975). Weber's letters also give much information on this score. See also in this context e.g. Sam Whimster (ed.), *Max Weber and the Culture of Anarchy* (1999).

See also letters

gerontocracy (*Gerontokratie*)   This represents a form of traditional domination, which is discussed in Ch. 3 on domination in *Economy and Society*.

Gerontocracy is defined as a situation in which (1) the traditional ruler has no staff, and (2) the power is in the hands of elders (ES:231). Very important is also that those in power are supposed to administer things so that they benefit the members.

See also traditional domination

Gesammelte Aufsätze zur Religionssoziologie (1920–21)   See *Collected Essays in the Sociology of Religion*

Gesammelte Aufsätze zur Sozial- und Wirtschaftsgeschichte (1924)
This work, edited by Marianne Weber, has been only partially translated into English. The following studies exist in translation: *The Agrarian Sociology of Ancient Civilizations*, *The History of Commercial Partnerships in the Middle Ages*, and "Developmental Tendencies in the Situation of East Elbian Rural Labourers" (Weber [1909] 1976, [1889] 2003, [1894] 1989).

See also *Agrarian Sociology of Ancient Civilizations*, economic history, history

Gesammelte Aufsätze zur Soziologie und Sozialpolitik (1924)   This work, edited by Marianne Weber, has been only partially translated into English. The following studies exist in translation: "The Stock Exchange," "A Research Strategy for the Study of Occupational Careers and Mobility Patterns," and "Socialism" (Weber [1894, 1896] 2000, [1908] 1980, [1918] 1994). For some of Weber's interventions on topics such as religion and race, see Weber [1910] 1971, [1910] 1973 (cf. Weber 1973a).
   See also industrial sociology, socialism, state (for social policy)

Gesammelte Aufsätze zur Wissenschaftslehre (1922)   Some of the individual articles that make up this volume, which was originally put together by Marianne Weber, can be found in English translation in *The Methodology of the Social Sciences*. This work contains three famous essays: on objectivity (1904), cultural science (1906), and value-freedom (1917). For most of the others—including *Critique of Stammler* and *Roscher and Knies*—see Weber [1903–6] 1975, [1907] 1977, [1908] 1999, [1909] 1984, [1913] 1981, [1919] 1946, [1922] 1999. The current German edition of this work (1988) is slightly different from the original edition (1922).
   See also methodology, *Wissenschaftslehre*

Gesammelte Politische Schriften (1921)   Some of these writings, originally edited by Marianne Weber (and later by Johannes Winkelmann who added some texts), can be found in English translation in Max Weber, *Political Writings* (1980). This collection includes texts such as "On the Situation of Constitutional Democracy in Germany," "Parliament and Government in Germany under a New Political Order" (also in ES:1381–1469), and "Socialism."
   See also politics, political sociology

Gesamtausgabe (*Max Weber Gesamtausgabe*)   *See* collected works

Gesellschaft   *See* community, society

Gesellschaftshandeln   *See* associational action

Gesinnung   *See* mentality

Gesinnungsethik   *See* ethic of ultimate ends

Gewalt   Weber uses this term in multiple meanings, including "power," "use of power," and "violence."
   See also violence

Goldschmidt, Levin (1829–1897)   Jurist and famous historian of commercial law at the University of Berlin Levin Goldschmidt was also the thesis adviser for Weber's first dissertation (Weber [1889] 2003). See e.g. Ernest Heymann, "Goldschmidt, Levin (1829–1897)" (1931) and Lothar Weyhe, *Levin Goldschmidt: Ein Gelehrterleben in Deutschland* (1996).

greed   *See* acquisitive drive or impulse

group (*Gruppe* and other terms)   Weber was much concerned with groups and their structures, not least in his sociological works. He did not, however, use the term "group" very often but usually preferred some other concept of his own.

Weber does not use the concept of group in his general sociology in Ch. 1 of *Economy and Society*, even if the term can occasionally be found elsewhere in this work (e.g. ES:141, 389, WuG:196, 442). The reason may have to do with Weber's hostility to holism and his related attempt to shift the sociological terminology in a more social action–oriented direction. In his general sociology Weber uses such terms as "communal and associative relationships" and "organizations" to capture the type of social formation constituting a group (ES:40–3, 48–50).

The centrality of the idea of group in *Economy and Society* (if not the use of the term *Gruppe*), is reflected, among other things, in the fact that the section of this work on the sociology of religion has been translated as "Religious Groups (The Sociology of Religion)" (*Religionssoziologie* [*Typen religiöser Vergemeinschaftung*]; ES:399–634).

In his important letter of 1913 to his publisher in which Weber summarizes how far the manuscript for *Economy and Society* has proceeded at this stage, he similarly says that he has "propounded a well-knit sociological theory and presentation that places all major forms of community in relation to economic life: from the family and household to the 'enterprise', the sib, ethnic community, religion" (letter of December 30, 1913 to Paul Siebeck; cf. Baier, Lepsius, Mommsen, and Schluchter 2000:16). Additional information on the centrality of the idea of group in *Economy and Society* can be had by inspecting the two plans for this work (1910, 1914) as well as its first edition (1921–22). Weber essentially uses the term *Gruppe* in the first plan but then lets it go; *see* the entry for *Economy and Society*.

Martin Albrow notes that "only those who do not read beyond Weber's definition of action, that is beyond Section 2 of Chapter 1 in *Economy and Society*, could possibly imagine that he was not concerned with the structure of groups" (Albrow 1990:248; cf. 248–51).

See also community, ethnic groups, methodological individualism, society

Grundbegriffe   *See* basic sociological terms

Grundherrschaft   *See* manorial domination

Grundriss der Sozialökonomik   See *Handbook of Social Economics*

H abit   *See* custom, traditional action

habitus   This term has become popular in contemporary sociology, thanks to Bourdieu, and is also used by Weber (and many earlier thinkers). It does not, however, figure among Weber's key concepts in the chapter on general sociology in Ch. 1 of *Economy and Society* (but see e.g. GAW:391, 532).

The meaning of habitus in today's sociology, following Bourdieu, is often given as a system of dispositions. This meaning can be found in Weber as well, although he also speaks of "outer habitus," roughly meaning "bearing," "deportment," or "outward appearance" (Raum 1995:77).

Sam Whimster notes that Weber uses the term habitus in the sense of "a disposition to behave and view the world in a particular and distinctive manner" (EW:408). As to the term "disposition," Charles Camic has noted that Weber's term *Eingestelltheit* (which Weber borrowed from psychology) also means "disposition" (Camic 1986:1057). Jean-Pierre Grossein, finally, argues that habitus in Weber's work is closely related to such concepts as ethos (*Ethos*), disposition (*Gesinnung*), and spirit (*Geist*; Grossein 1996:61 n. 1, 120). For a discussion of the concept of attitude in Weber, and of how attitudes are related to disposition in his thought, see Paul Lazarsfeld and Anthony Oberschall, "Max Weber and Empirical Social Research" (1965), pp. 191–93.

See also ethos, custom, lifestyle, mentality, spirit of capitalism

Handbook of Social Economics (*Grundriss der Sozialökonomik*)   In 1909 Weber accepted his publisher's offer to become the main editor of a giant *Handbook of Social Economics*, to replace Gustav Schönberg's *Handbook of Political Economy* (*Handbuch der politischen Oekonomie*) which had become outmoded. Weber died long before his *Handbook* was completed, but nonetheless drew up its overall structure and oversaw the production of a few volumes, which started to appear from 1914 onwards. *Economy and Society* (*Wirtschaft und Gesellschaft*) appeared in 1921–22 as part of the *Handbook*.

Weber invited many well-known economists, sociologists, and political economists to contribute to the *Handbook*, including Karl Bücher,

Friedrich von Wieser, Robert Michels, and Joseph Schumpeter. He also assigned a number of topics to himself, either because he was interested in them or because he had difficulty in finding an author.

The *Handbook* was divided into five books, usually with a number of parts and subparts. The books were the following:

    I. The Foundations of the Economy

    II. Specific Elements of the Modern Capitalist Economy

    III. Single Economic Branches of the Capitalistic Economy and Domestic Economic Policy in the Modern State

    IV. Relations in the Capitalist World Economy and Foreign Economic and Social Policy in the Modern State

    V. Social Relations of Capitalism and Domestic Social Policy in the Modern State

Economy and Society was included in Book I, "The Foundations of the Economy," which was divided as follows in the plan for the whole *Handbook* of 1914:

    A. Economy and the Science of Economics

    B. Natural and Technical Conditions of the Economy

    C. *Economy and Society* 1. The Economy and the Societal Orders and Powers; 2. The Course of Development of the Systems and Ideals of Economic and Social Policy. [Weber's work was set in bold type; cf. Johannes Winkelmann, *Max Webers hinterlassenes Hauptwerk* (1986), pp. 168–71; Wolfgang Schluchter, *Rationalism, Religion, and Domination* (1989), p. 467]

There also exists a plan dating from 1910, which looks somewhat different (see Winkelmann, *Max Webers hinterlassenes Hauptwerk*, pp. 150–55 for the plan, with Weber's notes).

After Weber's death a new main editor was appointed, and volumes kept coming out till 1930. According to Schumpeter, the *Handbook* represents "an important landmark in the world of German economics" (Schumpeter 1954:891).

While the literature on the complex coming into being of *Economy and Society* is growing, little has been written on the *Handbook of Social Economics*. No-one, for example, has made use of the letters on the *Handbook* between Weber and his publisher (which have not been published). Still, the various plans for the *Handbook* (1910, 1914) are often included and commented upon in the course of discussions of *Economy and Society*. See on this point Wolfgang Schluchter, "*Economy and Society*: The End of A Myth," pp. 433–64 in *Rationalism, Religion and*

Domination. For more details about the plans, see Winkelmann, *Max Webers hinterlassenes Hauptwerk*, pp. 149–209; cf. Weber 1994a:766–74. Similarly, some material relevant to the *Handbook* is scheduled to appear in the new edition of *Economy and Society* that is planned as part of MWG (see Vol. I/22–6: *Materialien und Register* [Materials and index]). For the *Handbook* itself, see Richard Swedberg, *Max Weber and the Idea of Economic Sociology* (1998), pp. 153–62.

  See also economics, *Economy and Society*, social economics

Hausgemeinschaft   *See* household

Haushalt   *See* budgetary management

Heilsgüter   *See* religious benefits

Heilsprämie   *See* psychological or religious premium

Hellmann, Siegmund   See *General Economic History*

hereditary charisma   *See* charisma

heredity   *See* inheritance, race

Herrenvolk   This term is used by Weber in his political writings when he describes the central place that some nations hold in world politics and that others aspire to hold, especially Germany. It can be translated as "a nation of masters" or alternatively as "master race" (e.g. PW:129, 269; Otto Stammer, ed., *Max Weber and Sociology Today* [1971], p. 85).

  According to the translators of the anthology of Max Weber's *Political Writings*, "Weber's use of the term *Herrenvolk* ought not to be confused with the National Socialists' later misappropriation of Nietzschean vocabulary. Weber's usage does not have imperialist implications but rather conceives of a nation in which each individual is master of his own life and responsible for his own political fate" (PW:129). According to another commentator, "it should be pointed out that the terms *Pariavolk* and *Herrenvolk* used by Weber are for him scientific concepts and in no way pejorative" (Raphaël 1973:55 n. 2). Wolfgang Mommsen, finally, notes that a *Herrenvolk* "is linked with the concept of the exercise of political power abroad in a way that we justifiably view as questionable today" (Mommsen 1984:172).

  See also pariah people

Herrschaft   This term is generally considered very difficult to translate into English, with "domination" currently being the favored candidate. Other translations include "authority," "rule," "leadership," and "imperative coordination." See the discussion of *Herrschaft* in e.g. Melvin

Richter, *The History of Political and Social Concepts: A Critical Introduction* (1995), pp. 68–77.
See also domination

heterocephalous   *See* autocephalous

heteronomous organization   *See* organization or association

hierocracy (*Hierokratie*)   This term is used by Weber to indicate a distinct kind of religious rulership—either the ruler gets his or her legitimacy through religion or the religious leader is also the political ruler.

According to a more formal definition in *Economy and Society*, hierocracy covers the following two cases: "(1) a ruler who is legitimated by priests, either as an incarnation or in the name of God, (2) a high priest is also king" (ES:1159; for a discussion, see ES:1158–1204).

The importance that Weber assigned to the term hierocracy in his general sociology is clear from the fact that Ch. 1 of *Economy and Society* contains a section on "Political and Hierocratic Organizations" (ES:54–6).

There typically is a tension between hierocratic and political organizations; and this can be worked out in different ways, depending on various factors.

According to Guenther Roth, "Weber linked . . . hierocracy and caesaropapism in one historical model" (Bendix and Roth 1971:124). While hierocracy "means the political domination of priests; . . . caesaropapism denotes the secular ruler's control over the priesthood" (ibid.). See also Vatro Murvar, "Max Weber's Concept of Hierocracy: A Study in the Typology of Church-State Relationships" (1967).
See also caesaropapism, hierocratic organization

hierocratic organization (*hierokratischer Verband*)   This type of organization relies for the exercise of its power on the use of various religious sanctions.

A hierocratic organization is defined in Weber's general sociology in Ch. 1 of *Economy and Society* as "an organization which enforces its order through psychic coercion by distributing or denying religious benefits ('hierocratic coercion')" (ES:54).

A church is an example of a hierocratic organization. For Weber's analysis of the role of hierocracy throughout history, see especially Ch. 15, "Political and Hierocratic Domination," of *Economy and Society* (ES:1158–1211). There is typically a tension between hierocratic and political organizations; and this can be worked out in different ways, depending on various factors.
See also church, coercion, hierocracy, organization or association, re-

ligious benefits

Hinduism   Hinduism is one of the religions that Weber terms world-religions. He mainly discusses it in *The Religion of India: The Sociology of Hinduism and Buddhism* and in *Economy and Society* (e.g. ES:435–37, 493–99, 816–18).

According to Weber, the world was seen as "a great enchanted garden" in Hinduism (ES:630). In this type of religion, he also notes, the existing world was provided with "absolutely unconditional justification," thanks to the idea that people's existence was the result of their behavior in earlier lives (ES:629). Hinduism, and especially the caste system, helped block the possible emergence of a rational type of capitalism in India. The main carrier of Hinduism was the world-ordering magician (ES:512).

As part of his sociology of law, Weber touches on Indian law (ES:816–18).

For a discussion of Weber's analysis of Hinduism, see e.g. Wolfgang Schluchter, *Rationalism, Religion, and Domination* (1989), pp. 117–62. See also Wolfgang Schluchter (ed.), *Max Webers Studie über Hinduismus und Buddhismus* (1984) as well as the introductory and editorial material in the volume including *The Religion of India* in MWG (I/20).

See also Buddhism, caste, *Economic Ethics of the World Religions; Religion of India, The*

Hinduismus und Buddhismus (*The Religion of India*, trans. 1958)   This work is part of Weber's *The Economic Ethics of the World Religions*.

See also Buddhism, *Economic Ethics of the World Religions*, Hinduism; *Religion of India, The*

Hintze, Otto (1861–1940)   Administrative historian who worked with and further developed some of Max Weber's ideas. See e.g. Jürgen Kocka, "Otto Hintze and Max Weber: Attempts at a Comparison" (1987).

historical individual (*historisches Individuum*)   This term is used by Weber to refer to an individual object of study in the cultural or social sciences. The most famous example of a historical individual in Weber's work is his concept of the capitalist spirit in *The Protestant Ethic*. While the term itself is not present in Weber's later work in *Economy and Society*, the idea presumably is.

In *The Protestant Ethic* Weber describes a historical individual as follows: "a complex of elements associated in historical reality which we unite into a conceptual whole from their standpoint of cultural significance" (PE:47–8). Weber is also very insistent that a historical individual cannot be presented already at the beginning of a study, but has to be the end result of the research: "anything like a *definition* is not possible at the start but only at the conclusion as the result of a step-by-step synthesis" (e.g. PED:75, 106). A historical individual mainly differs from an ideal type in not being a means of ordering several phenomena; "it refers in its content to a phenomenon significant for its unique individuality" (PE:47).

In Weber's methodological writings it is also stressed that any historical fact that is to be explained represents a historical individual since it is related to the values of the society in which the researcher lives. The facts themselves that are used to explain the object of study, however, do not constitute historical individuals (e.g. MSS:79, 81, 155–56, 159). Another important point that Weber makes in all of these writings—and which is also reflected in his use of the term "historical individual"—is that the analysis must take into account the unique and individual character of historical facts.

Weber borrowed the term "historical individual" from the work of philosopher Heinrich Rickert, just as he borrowed the term "value-relevance" to which it is closely related (see MSS:79 n. 2, 149–50; see also Thomas Burger, *Max Weber's Theory of Concept Formation* [1987], pp. 46, 83 and H. H. Bruun, *Science, Values and Politics in Max Weber's Methodology* [1972], p. 95). Parsons describes a historical individual as "the immediate object of scientific study" and "the thing to be explained" (Parsons 1937:594, 610). See also Guy Oakes, "Weber and the Southwest German School: The Genesis of the Concept of the Historical Individual" (1987).

See also concept formation, ideal type, value-relevance

Historical School of economics   During the nineteenth century German scholars developed a type of economics that differed substantially from the analytical type of economics that was popular in England, primarily by being more historical and empirical in nature. For an introduction to various key figures in the Historical School, including Gustav Schmoller, see e.g. the essays in Part 1 of Wolfgang Mommsen and Jürgen Osterhammel (eds.), *Max Weber and His Contemporaries* (1987).

Weber essentially took a mediating position between historical and analytical economics. In his inaugural lecture of 1895, however, he referred to himself as a "disciple of the German Historical School" (PW:19). See also e.g. Richard Swedberg, *Max Weber and the Idea of Economic Sociology* (1998), pp. 174–77, 186–87.

See also Battle of the Methods, marginal utility, *Verein für Sozialpolitik*

historical sociology   If one defines historical sociology as sociology that draws on historical (rather than contemporary) material, then most of Weber's sociology falls into this category.

Three outstanding examples of historical sociology are Weber's study of antiquity, *The Protestant Ethic and the Spirit of Capitalism* and *Economy and Society* (ASAC, PE, ES).

For an introduction to Weber's historical sociology, see e.g. Reinhard Bendix, *Max Weber: An Intellectual Portrait* (1960). See also Guenther Roth, "History and Sociology in the Work of Max Weber" (1976), Bryan Turner, "Max Weber's Historical Sociology: A Bibliographical Essay," pp. 22–37 in *Max Weber* (1992), Stephen Kalberg, *Max Weber's Comparative Historical Sociology* (1994) and "Max Weber's Critique of Recent Comparative-Historical Sociology and a Reconstruction of His Analysis of the Rise of Confucianism in China" (1999), and Arnold Zingerle, *Max Webers Historische Soziologie* (1981).

See also comparative sociology, history, universal history

history Weber was deeply interested in history his whole life and made important contributions to that field as well as to historical sociology. Several of his historical studies are of relevance to historians as well as sociologists, such as his writings on the social and economic history of antiquity, *The City*, and his methodological essay on Eduard Meyer (ASA, Weber [1896] 1999, ES:1212–1372, MSS:131–88).

In his statements on sociological methodology Weber was concerned with distinguishing history from sociology. In his general sociology in Ch. 1 of *Economy and Society*, for example, he outlines the similarities as well as the differences between sociology and history. Both sociology and history deal with "the subjective meaning-complexes of action" (ES:13). But while sociology focuses on "type concepts and generalized uniformities of empirical process," history is centered around "individual actions, structures, and personalities possessing cultural significance" (ES:19; cf. ES:29). Weber argued strongly against the existence of specific stages and laws in history. This means that sociology has a tendency to produce "a greater precision of concepts" than history—but also that the sociological analysis is less rich in "concrete content" than a historical analysis (ES:20).

In a famous letter to historian Georg von Below Weber states that while the task of history is "to establish what is specific," the role of sociology is to do "modest preparatory work" for history in this respect (Roth 1976:307). Whether this means that sociology should always be subordinate to history is not clear.

Weber also made contributions to economic history, such as his studies of antiquity, *The City*, and the reconstructed lecture course from

1919–20 that is known in English as *General Economic History* (e.g. ASAC, ES:1212–1372, GEH).

In Weber's later work he refers to a "universal history of culture" (*Universalgeschichte der Kultur*), by which is meant a broader type of history than ordinary history (PE:23, cf. SCIS:150). For a discussion of the theme of universal history in Weber, see e.g. Wolfgang Mommsen, "Max Weber's Political Sociology and His Philosophy of World History" (1965) and "Max Webers Begriff der Universalgeschichte" (1986).

Weber's ideas on the process of rationalization are often seen as constituting the core of his philosophy of history. *See* rationalization as well as works such as Gabriel Kolko, "A Critique of Max Weber's Philosophy of History" (1959) and Wolfgang Schluchter, *The Rise of Western Rationalism* (1981).

For an introduction to Weber and history, see e.g. Guenther Roth, "History and Sociology in the Work of Max Weber" (1976) and Schluchter, *The Rise of Western Rationalism*. For Weber's view of the history of antiquity, see e.g. Wilfried Nippel, "From Agrarian History to Cross-Cultural Comparisons: Weber on Greco-Roman Antiquity" (2000) and Hinnerk Bruhns, "À propos de l'histoire ancienne et de l'économie politique chez Max Weber" (1998).

For an introduction to the various historical schools in Weber's day as well as Weber's relationship to these, see Paul Honigsheim, *On Max Weber* (1968), pp. 43–54. It is often said that Weber started as a historian and then became a sociologist (e.g. Raymond Aron, *German Sociology* [1964], p. 69, Roth 1976:306; cf. Carlo Antoni, *From History to Sociology* [1959]). For an attempt to assess Weber as a historian and also to trace his relationship to the discipline of history, see e.g. Jürgen Kocka (ed.), *Max Weber, der Historiker* (1986). Kocka's own assessment is that "Max Weber was not a historian by profession," but that "the close link of his work to the science of history is obvious" (ibid., p. 8)—mainly through its focus on certain historical material and its concern with methodological questions in historical research. For Weber's relationship to specific historians, such as Eduard Meyer and Karl Lamprecht, see Part 2 of Wolfgang Mommsen and Jürgen Osterhammel (eds.), *Max Weber and His Contemporaries* (1987).

See also historical sociology, rationalization (for philosophy of history), universal history

History of Commercial Partnerships in the Middle Ages, The (*Zur Geschichte der Handelsgesellschaften im Mittelalter*, trans. 2003) Weber's first dissertation is part of this work, which was recently translated into English (Weber [1889] 2003:85–125).

holism   Weber was very critical of holism or the idea that sociology should be centered on the whole, which was opposed to his own view that sociology should start with the individual (methodological individualism). He writes in his general sociology in Ch. 1 of *Economy and Society* that "for sociological purposes there is no such thing as a collective personality which 'acts'," and that "when reference is made in a sociological context to a state, a nation, a corporation, a family, or an army corps, or to similar collectivities, what is meant is . . . *only* a certain kind of development of actual or possible social actions of individual persons" (ES:14).

In the first version of his theoretical sociology of 1913, Weber similarly noted that while the sociologist may use holistic concepts for terminological reasons, "all analogies to the 'organism' and to similar biological concepts are doomed to sterility" (SCIS:167).

See the discussion of holism in Martin Albrow, *Max Weber's Construction of Social Theory* (1990), pp. 251–54.

Despite the arguments that can be found in Weber's general statements about sociology in favor of methodological individualism, there are also those who argue that in his actual analyses Weber does assign an independent existence to social structures and groups. See e.g. Bryan Turner, *For Weber* (1981); and for an answer, see e.g. Lawrence Scaff, "Weber before Weberian Sociology" (1989).

See also functionalism, methodological individualism

homo economicus   *See* economic theory

homo politicus   *See* politics

Honoratioren, *honoratiores*   *See* legal *Honoratioren*, notables

household (*Hausgemeinschaft*)   The English word "household" covers two concepts in Weber's sociology: *Haushalt*, or a way of managing resources (the opposite of profit-making), and *Hausgemeinschaft*, or a form of socio-economic organization that includes the family and is sometimes identical to it. For the former meaning, *see* budgetary management.

A household is described by Weber as "a unit of economic maintenance" which constitutes "the most 'natural' of the externally closed types of social action" and whose members typically have a common residence (ES:357, 359, 363; for the household in general, see ES:356–60, 363–69, GEH:26–7, 46–50).

The household did not automatically emerge with the appearance of human beings, but developed at a certain stage in history. Its size and membership have varied over time. Authority and loyalty characterize its mental structure; and there is a common use of resources, especially early in its history (what Weber terms "household communism"; e.g. ES:359). As time goes on, however, the authority of the household over its members typically decreases—because of the emergence of other sources of protection, education outside the household, employment outside the household, and so on (e.g. ES:375).

Weber's discussion of the family often takes place in connection with his discussion of the household, and the two terms are sometimes used interchangeably (e.g. ES:356–69). Weber also argues that a family needs to be a household to acquire the necessary social stability (ES:357).

See e.g. Randall Collins, "Weber's Theory of the Family," pp. 267–96 in *Weberian Sociological Theory* (1986) and Bryan Turner, "Family, Property and Ideology," pp. 289–317 in *For Weber* (1981).

See also family, males, *oikos*, patriarchalism, women

human beings, type of human beings (*Menschentum, Menschentyp*) Weber refers to many different types of human beings in his various studies, such as the specialist (*Fachmensch*), the cultivated person (*Kulturmensch*), the sensualist (*Genussmensch*), and so on (e.g. ES:1001–2, PE:163, 182).

Weber was extremely interested both in what characterized these different types and in what made one type rather than another come into being and take precedence over the others. Depending on the way that salvation is approached, for example, different types of people will emerge. Of great importance for the development of the West, Weber says, is that ascetic Protestantism helped to create the vocational and/or professional person (*Berufsmensch*). Similarly, religious sects help to breed a certain type of human being—and so may political regimes.

In his inaugural lecture of 1895 Weber states, for example, that "we do not want to breed well-being in people, but rather those characteristics which we think of as constituting the human greatness and nobility of our nature" (PW:15). Similarly, he argues that "every type of social order . . . must, if one wishes to *evaluate* it, be examined with reference to the opportunities which it affords to *certain types of persons* to rise to positions of superiority" (MSS:27).

According to Jean-Pierre Grossein, Weber was always interested in the actor, not only in social action; and this is what led to his analysis of different types of human beings ("Présentation" [1996], pp. 62, 122).

See also anthropology

human nature   *See* anthropology

human rights   *See* rights

humor   While it is hard to find any jokes in Weber's writings, one can nonetheless find some interesting ideas about humor in his work. In his speech in memory of his friend Georg Jellinek Weber made a distinction between wit and humor, and also suggested that "genuine humor in its finest sense presents us with hearty, healthy, good, liberating laughter, which is far removed from any mockery" (Marianne Weber [1926] 1975:477). This type of humor, Weber added, makes it easier to put up with the "paralyzing power" of "humdrum existence [*Alltag*]" (ibid., p. 478).

According to his wife, Weber had a "superior sense of humor" (ibid., p. 78).

hydraulic bureaucracy *See* geography

I deal and material interests   *See* interests

ideal type (*Idealtypus*)   This is one of Weber's most celebrated concepts, and it can in all brevity be described as an attempt to capture what is essential about a social phenomenon through an analytical exaggeration of some of its aspects. What is at the heart of an ideal type, according to Weber's famous formulation, is an "analytical accentuation (*Steigerung*) of certain elements of reality" (MSS:90). The concept of ideal type is mainly developed in Weber's early writings on methodology but is also mentioned in the methodological part of *Economy and Society*. Ideal types are especially used in economic theory, according to Weber—but they can also be very useful in the other social sciences. There are close links between Weber's concept of ideal type and his methodology in general.

The fullest discussion of the ideal type in Weber's work is to be found in his essays on methodology (see especially MSS:89–105, EW:387–98, but also e.g. ASAC:77–9, 371–72, CS:111–14, GM:323–24, MSS:41–45, RK:188–91). Weber also touches on the ideal type in his general sociology in Ch. 1 of *Economy and Society*, where he mentions the need for sociology to make use of "a scientifically formulated pure type (ideal type)" (ES:9; cf. 19–22). He also refers the reader to the discussion of ideal types in the 1904 essay on objectivity.

An ideal type, Weber adds, must not be confused with an average type. Neither does the word "ideal" mean that only phenomena one somehow approves of can be captured with the help of ideal types; there are ideal types of brothels as well as churches. There can also be ideal types of unique individual phenomena (say "Christianity") as well as of general phenomena (say, "exchange"). An ideal type differs from a historical individual mainly in being intended to order several phenomena; whereas the latter "refers in its content to a phenomenon significant for its unique individuality" (PE:47).

An ideal type is a conceptual tool with which to approach reality; and in this sense it is a "conceptual construct" (*Gedankenbild*; MSS:93). When confronted with an empirical situation, it is often helpful to introduce a series of ideal types. In doing so, Weber argues, it is more important to capture what is essential about a phenomenon than to merely reproduce the often confusing empirical situation: "sharp differentiation in concrete fact is often impossible, but this makes clarity in the analytical distinction all the more important" (ES:214). In this sense, the introduction of an ideal type serves as a first step in analysis. The ideal type "serves as a harbor until one has learned to navigate safely in the vast sea of empirical facts" (MSS:104). Once some order has been brought into an analysis through the introduction of ideal types, however, it may be important for the sociologist to decide why and how empirical reality deviates from these. On this account the sociologist differs from the economist. "Pure economic theory [in contrast to sociology] utilizes ideal types exclusively" (MSS:43–44; cf. e.g. ES:9).

In the secondary literature on the ideal type it is sometimes argued that this concept plays an important role in Weber's general approach to social science, especially his theory of adequate causation, and that this theory cannot be understood without explicit reference to the ideal type. Fritz Ringer, for example, argues along these lines: "one cannot understand Weber's doctrine of ideal types apart from his broader vision of causal analysis and interpretation" (Ringer 1997:5). Sam Whimster describes the ideal type as "a methodological instrument created by Weber to analyze cultural meanings into their logically pure components" (EW:409). He also adds that the ideal type is "essential for clarity of *understanding* and the operations of causality."

Weber got the expression "ideal type" from his friend and colleague Georg Jellinek, but invested it with his own distinct meaning (cf. Weber's letter to Rickert from June 14, 1904; H. H. Bruun, *Science, Values and Politics in Max Weber's Methodology* [1972], p. 209).

For a general introduction to the concept of ideal type, see e.g. Martin Albrow, *Max Weber's Construction of Social Theory* (1990), pp. 149–57 and Dirk Käsler, *Max Weber* (1988), pp. 180–83. See also the questions raised in relation to the concept of the ideal type by e.g. H. H. Bruun, "Weber on Rickert: From Value Relations to Ideal Type" (2001), Thomas Burger, *Max Weber's Theory of Concept Formation* (1987), pp. 115–79, Alfred Schutz, *The Phenomenology of the Social World* (1967), pp. 176–

250, Dieter Henrich, *Die Einheit der Wissenschaftslehre Max Webers* (1952), pp. 83–103, and Talcott Parsons, *The Structure of Social Action* (1937), pp. 601–10.

See also concept formation, economic theory, historical individual, *Kategorienlehre*, methodology, types

idealism   *See* materialism/idealism

ideas   The role of ideas in society represents a major theme in Weber's work. While his position on this issue is complex, some points nonetheless stand out.

There is first of all the fact, according to Weber, that "ideas [can] become effective forces in history" (PE:90; cf. e.g. MSS:54). The ideas that tend to influence people's behavior the most, Weber argues, are those that somehow speak to their interests (*see* interest). In a famous statement Weber notes that ideal and material interests drive human behavior—but that certain "'ideas'" in the form of "'world images'" ("*Weltbilder*") may steer people's actions onto different "tracks" and thereby direct them in novel directions (GM:280). *The Protestant Ethic* can be seen as paradigmatic in the way that it shows how ideas become connected to people's interests and thereby tend to affect their behavior in fundamental ways.

Weber also argues that one may sometimes find a distinct relationship between certain ideas and certain groups, even if no direct causality is involved. Some groups, for example, may act as "carriers" for certain ideas (*see* carrier). There also exists a tendency for certain ideas and groups to gravitate toward one another (*see* elective affinities).

Weber was also much interested in the unintended consequences of ideas. When one attempts to realize certain ideas, something else may happen, as *The Protestant Ethic* shows. At one point Weber even speaks of "a universal 'Tragedy' . . . that dooms every attempt to realize ideas in reality" (Weber [1910] 2002:204). What this tragedy consists of, it turns out, is that an organization usually comes into being as a result of an attempt to realize ideas; and this organization soon develops its own interests and becomes ruled by careerists. Weber sees this process as a necessary part of the "objectification" of ideas (ibid., p. 205).

It may finally be mentioned that "Science as a Vocation" contains some famous passages about the circumstances under which scientists, including social scientists, get their ideas. According to Weber, "ideas occur to us when they please, not when it pleases us" (GM:136).

Talcott Parsons refers to "Weber's general theory of the relations between interests and ideas," and notes that this is particularly developed in his sociology of religion (ES:211 n. 59). The main point of this theory is that an action is not motivated by either ideas or by interests, but by both ideas and interests. While ideas "define the situation," interests "motivate actors to implement implications of this definition of the situation" (Parsons 1975:668). Hans Gerth and C. Wright Mills, however, have a different view of the way that Weber handles the relationship between ideas and interests; they claim that *elective affinity* is "the decisive conception by which Weber relates ideas and interests" (GM:62). Finally, Stephen Kalberg cautions the reader apropos the use of the term "ideas" in Weber's work: "despite its centrality in the secondary literature, Weber employs it only sparingly and less so in his writings after *The Protestant Ethic and the Spirit of Capitalism*" (Kalberg 1985:62 n. 3). See also in this context Kalberg's "Should the 'Dynamic Autonomy' of Ideas Matter to Sociologists?" (2001).

In the spring of 1920, a few months before his death, Marianne Weber quotes her husband as saying, "I have an abundance of new ideas [*es strömt mir zu*]" (Marianne Weber [1926] 1975:687; my trans.).

See also carrier, elective affinities, intellectuals, interests, materialism/idealism, mentality, paradoxical results of actions

ideographic sciences   *See* neo-Kantianism, natural sciences, value-freedom

imitation (*Nachahmung*)   Imitation can be either social or non-social, according to the important paragraph 1 on sociology in Ch. 1 of *Economy and Society* (ES:23–4). An example of non-social imitation would be behavior that is purely reactive. An example of imitation that is social would be when an actor imitates behavior that is fashionable or traditional.

According to "Some Categories of Interpretive Sociology," "'imitation' can be simply 'mass-conditioned' behavior or it can be more an action oriented toward the behavior of the imitated one, in the sense of emulation" (SCIS:168).

While imitation, according to *Economy and Society*, is of "extraordinary importance," it is "secondary" in relation to charisma when it comes to social change (ES:322; cf. ES:388). The reason for this is that imitation by itself does not produce change.

See also mass-conditioned behavior

imperative coordination   *See* domination

imperialism (*Imperialismus*)   Even though Weber does not provide a definition of imperialism, it is clear that he (in contrast to, say, some Marxists) regards imperialism primarily as a political phenomenon.

Weber nonetheless discusses the economic foundations of imperialism at some length in *Economy and Society* (ES:913–21). This discussion contains, among other things, some reflections on the relationship between politics and economic interests. Weber also argues that trade is not the decisive factor in political expansion. It is the general economic structure of a society that determines imperialism—but only to some extent. If the state provides capitalist opportunities, as was the case in Rome in antiquity, there will be a tendency toward "imperialist capitalism" (ES:917–19). But just as there are industries that profit from war, there also are industries that profit from peace. In terms of the terminology that Weber presents in his economic sociology in Ch. 2 of *Economy and Society*, imperialist capitalism would fall under the heading of political capitalism (ES:164–66).

According to Wolfgang Mommsen in *Theories of Imperialism*, "he [Weber] did not develop a consistent theory of imperialism [but] he did assemble important elements of such a theory from a sociological point of view" (Mommsen 1980:19). For Weber's attitude to German imperialism before World War I, see especially Ch. 4 in Wolfgang Mommsen, *Max Weber and German Politics 1890–1920* (1984).

See also nation, political capitalism, political communities, power prestige

imperialist capitalism *See* imperialism

imperium This Latin term (meaning "power," "empire") is often used by Weber to denote authoritarian power, such as that of the prince or the master of a household. Weber, for example, draws heavily on this term in his sociology of law (e.g. ES:651–52, 839–48).

impersonality *See* depersonalization

imposition (*Oktroyierung*) This concept, which is used at several points in Weber's work, essentially means to force something upon someone. Actors may, for example, ascribe legitimacy to an order that is imposed by an authority which is seen as legitimate (ES:36; cf. SCIS:175). In an organization the enacted order may either be entered into voluntarily—or it may be imposed (ES:50–1). Law may also develop in different ways, including imposition from above (ES:760–65).

imputation (*Zurechnung*) *See* mutual responsibility

incentives *See* economic motivation, willingness to work

income *See* budgetary management, economic motivation

India See *Religion of India, The*

individual and individualism The individual holds a very special place in Weber's work in social science (including his methodology) as well as in his political writings. In methodological questions Weber firmly embraced the idea that only an individual can be an actor (*see* methodological individualism). In politics, one of Weber's goals was to safeguard the freedom of the individual in the spirit of liberalism (*see* politics).

In his social science work Weber also pays much attention to the charismatic individual and the single ruler, whether patrimonial, feudal, or legal. Modern society, mainly through the growth of bureaucracy and rational capitalism, creates pressure on the individual to conform and behave in a disciplined and uniform manner. Capitalism also leads to what Weber terms depersonalization (*see* that entry). Weber uses the term "personality" for the kind of individual who takes a stance on the world and rejects just being a product of it.

In ascetic Protestantism, Weber notes in *The Protestant Ethic*, the emphasis is on the lone individual; and modern individualism has one of its roots here (PE:105). Otherwise, he also says, the concept of individualism covers rather different phenomena (PE:222 n. 21).

See e.g. Ralph Schroeder, "'Personality' and 'Inner Distance': The Conception of the Individual in Max Weber's Sociology" (1991).

See also depersonalization, methodological individualism, personality, politics (for liberalism), tension

industrial sociology   This branch of sociology, which did not exist in Weber's time, mainly studies the conditions of work in industry and how these are related to social structure. Some of Weber's findings would later play an important role in industrial sociology, such as the fact that workers create norms to restrict production (Weber [1908] 1971:133).

The following texts by Weber are usually cited as falling in the category of industrial sociology: "A Research Strategy for the Study of Occupational Careers and Mobility Patterns" and "Zur Psychophysik der industriellen Arbeit" ("On the Psychophysics of Industrial Work"; Weber [1908] 1980, [1908–9] 1988, or 1995b).

According to Ralf Dahrendorf, Weber should be considered the founder of industrial sociology (*Industrie-und Betriebssoziologie* [1956], p. 24). See e.g. Dirk Käsler, *Max Weber* (1988), pp. 66–73 and Gert Schmidt, "Max Weber and Modern Industrial Sociology: A Comment on Some Recent Anglo-Saxon Interpretations" (1976).

See also economic sociology, inheritance, psychophysics, work, workers

inheritance (*Vererbung*)   The term inheritance has an economic and legal meaning as well as a biological one, and only the latter will be discussed in this entry (for the role of inheritance in the economic sense, *see* property).

According to Weber, sociology only deals with behavior to which significance can be attached, and inherited biological factors definitely fall outside of this category. Explanations based on inheritance should only be made as a last resort, Weber argues, once all social factors have been thoroughly explored.

If at some time in the future it becomes possible to link "non-interpretable uniformities" to differences in inherited characteristics, Weber argues, these will have to be treated just as any physiological data (ES:7–8, SCIS:153). This means that they should be treated as "stimuli which are devoid of subjective meaning . . . favoring or hindering circumstances" (ES:7; cf. ES:13).

In his work on industrial workers and psychophysics Weber explicitly addresses the issue of the role of inherited factors in social science research. He argues strongly that only after having exhausted the impact of cultural and social factors can the notion of inheritance be introduced (e.g. Weber [1908] 1980:126–32). In practical terms, this means that at the current stage of knowledge, inheritance should be kept out of the picture. For a discussion of Weber's position, see e.g. Dirk Käsler, *Max Weber* (1988), pp. 66–73.

See also property, race, selection

inner distance   *See* personality

inner-worldly asceticism   *See* asceticism

innerweltliche Askese (inner-worldly asceticism)   *See* asceticism

innovation   *See* charisma, entrepreneur, prophet

institution (*Institution*)   The closest equivalent to the concept of institution in Weber's general sociology in Ch. 1 of *Economy and Society* is probably that of "order" (which however also covers phenomena that do not constitute institutions, according to Weber's usage of this term). By order Weber essentially means a set of prescriptions for how to behave that exist outside of the individual, and which he or she sees as obligatory or binding (*see* order).

The term institution can also be found in many of Weber's works, including the early part of *Economy and Society* (see e.g. ES:364, 907, PE:152). In one of his methodological essays, for example, Weber writes that "the fundamental substantive and methodological problem of economics is constituted by the question: how are the origin and the persistence of the institutions (*Institutionen*) of economic life to be explained, institutions which were not purposefully created by collective means, but which nevertheless—from our point of view—function purposefully. This is the basic problem of economics" (RK:80).

In his essay on objectivity of 1904 Weber notes that while psychology may be of help, "we will not . . . deduce institutions from psychological laws or explain them by elementary psychological phenomena" (MSS:89, EW:386–87). In *The Protestant Ethic* Weber makes an important distinction between the organizational structure of the capitalist firm (its "form") and the mental attitude of the people who work in it (its "spirit") that is absolutely central to the argument of this work. When the "spirit" of a "social institution" changes, he explains, its meaning seems different to us (PED:94).

The legal concept of institution (*Anstalt*) is discussed in Weber's sociology of law (ES:714–15). Weber's term *Anstalt* in his general sociology is sometimes translated as "compulsory organization or association" and sometimes as "institution" (ES:52 vs. EW:354; cf. SCIS:173–76).

For an attempt to outline the various institutions that Weber saw as essential to the emergence of capitalism, see e.g. Randall Collins, "Weber's Last Theory of Capitalism" (1980). For the argument that Weber "never formulated a General Theory of Institutions" but only "fragments" of one, see L. M. Lachmann, *The Legacy of Max Weber* (1970), pp. 49–91.

See also order, orientation to others

instrumentally rational action (social action that is *zweckrational*)   This is one of Weber's four major types of social action, together with affectual action, traditional action, and value-rational action. It is a type of action that is centered around attaining some end by the conscious and calculated use of certain means.

What primarily characterizes instrumentally rational action, according to Weber's general sociology in Ch. 1 of *Economy and Society*, is that it is "determined by expectations as to the behavior of objects in the environment and of other human beings; these expectations are used as 'conditions' or 'means' for the attainment of the actor's own rationally pursued and calculated ends" (ES:24).

In instrumentally rational action an actor takes the following three factors into account and considers them in relation to possible alternatives: the end, the means, and the secondary results. It is possible to choose between different possible ends in a value-rational manner but to use instrumental rationality in deciding upon the means.

Weber's associational action (*Gesellschaftshandeln*), as presented in "Some Categories of Interpretive Action" (1913), is considered an early version of instrumentally rational action (*see* the entry for this term).

Raymond Aron describes instrumentally rational action as "rational action in relation to a goal," and value-rational action as "rational action in relation to a value" (Aron 1970:220). Martin Albrow has suggested "purposively rational" as a translation of *zweckrational* (Albrow

1990:141). Examples include the engineer who builds a bridge and the speculator on the stock exchange trying to make money. Instrumentally rational action is also at the center of the process of rationalization (e.g. Wolfgang Schluchter, *The Rise of Western Rationalism* [1981]). See also Talcott Parsons, *The Structure of Social Action* (1937), Vol. 2, pp. 642–45, where the link between instrumentally rational action and Weber's concept of ethic of responsibility is discussed.

See also affectual action, associational action, ethic of responsibility, rationality, rationalization, social action, traditional action, value-rational action

intellectual sacrifice (*Opfer des Intellekts*) The person who takes an unconditional stance for religion comes up against reason and science and must make what Weber (and others) refers to as an intellectual sacrifice (e.g. GM:154–55).

intellectual sphere *See* value-spheres

intellectualism *See* intellectuals

intellectuals (*Intellektuelle*) Weber discusses intellectuals in various parts of his work, such as his political writings and his sociology of religion (for the latter, see especially ES:500–18). Most of his scholarly attention was on religious intellectuals; most of his political, on modern intellectuals.

The closest that one can come to a definition of intellectuals in Weber's writings may well be the following statement: "intellectuals . . . we shall tentatively call those who usurp leadership in a *Kulturgemeinschaft* (that is, within a group of people who by virtue of their peculiarity have access to certain products that are considered 'culture goods')" (ES:926).

The tendency to focus strongly on the understanding of the world Weber terms "intellectualism" (*Intellektualismus*), and he refers to such types of intellectualism as "proletarian intellectualism," "aristocratic intellectualism" and "pariah intellectualism" (e.g. ES:499–501).

In his analysis of the attitude of intellectuals to the problem of salvation, Weber emphasizes the great importance that intellectuals attach to the element of meaning. "The intellectual seeks in various ways . . . to endow his life with a pervasive meaning, and thus to find unity with himself, with his fellow men, and with the cosmos" (ES:506). "It is the intellectual who conceives of the 'world' as a problem of meaning" (ibid.). Weber adds that "the conflict of this requirement of meaningfulness with the empirical realities of the world and its institutions, and with the possibilities of conducting one's life in the empirical world, are responsible for the intellectual's characteristic flight from the world" (ibid.).

The great Asian religions were created by intellectuals (ES:502; cf. ES:517). The ideal in Judaism was the scholar or the intellectual who immersed himself in interpreting the law, while Jesus was hostile to Jewish legalism and praised those who were "poor in spirit" (ES:617, 631).

At times Weber also refers to the evolution of modern intellectuals and notes their role in e.g. revolutionary movements (e.g. ES:515–17, PW:88–9, 298). More generally, Western intellectuals have played a key role in bringing about the disenchantment of the world.

In his political writings Weber also often scorns the intellectuals for their naivete, ignorance, and immaturity. They are "infantile littérateurs," "coffee-house intellectuals," "well-fed prebendaries," and so on (e.g. PW:95, 124, 270).

See e.g. Ahmad Sadri, *Max Weber's Sociology of Intellectuals* (1992). For a general discussion of Weber's view of intellectuals and intellectualism, see e.g. Gangolf Hübinger, "Intellektuelle, Intellektualismus" (2001).

See also disenchantment of the world, intellectual sacrifice, value-spheres

intention (*Meinen*)   Weber uses the concept of intention in his very own special way in his sociology. In explicating the definition of sociology in the first paragraph in Ch. 1 of *Economy and Society*, Weber refers to "intended meaning." He states that while it is common only to use the term "intention" when it comes to rationally pursued goals, he will also use it for affectual action.

In Talcott Parsons' comment on Ch. 1 of *Economy and Society*, he writes that Weber "does not restrict the use of this concept to cases where a clear self-conscious awareness of such meaning can be reasonably attributed to each actor." Parsons adds that "the question is not whether in a sense obvious to the ordinary person such an intended meaning 'really exists', but whether the concept is capable of providing a logical framework within which scientifically important observations can be made" (ES:58 n. 9). See also Peter Munch, "'Sense' and 'Intention' in Max Weber's Theory of Action" (1975).

See also affectual action, meaning, motive, paradoxical results of people's actions, unintended consequences

interaction   *See* social interaction

interessenbedingt   *See* self-interest or self-interested kind of behavior

Interessenlage   *See* self-interest or self-interested kind of behavior

interest (*Interesse*)   This term, which plays a central role in Weber's analysis, roughly indicates the primary motivation of the actor. Weber often refers to different types of interest, such as "market interests," "emotional interests," "sexual interests," and so on. He also repeatedly uses some version of the phrase "material and ideal interests" in his sociological writings (e.g. ES:202, 224, 1129, GM:280). What Weber calls "religious benefits" (*Heilsgüter*) may also be translated as religious interests.

The concept of interest is referred to a few times in Weber's general sociology in Ch. 1 of *Economy and Society*. In one of his most important statements about interests and social action, he argues that some regularities of social action that are driven by "interest" may be far more stable than actions oriented to norms (*interessenbedingt*—ES:29; *see* self-interest or self-interested kind of behavior).

A legitimate order can be guaranteed by "interest"; associative relationships are often centered around "interests"; and so on (ES:33, 40–1).

Weber, however, does not single out the term "interest" in his general sociology in Ch. 1 of *Economy and Society*, nor does he define it anywhere else in his work. On the other hand, he does define the term "motive," which is closely related to the notion of interest. Talcott Parsons, for example, has suggested that while ideas "define the situation" for Weber, interest is what "motivate[s] actors to implement implications of this definition of the situation" (Parsons 1975:668; cf. ES:211 n. 59). Elsewhere in his writings on Weber, Parsons similarly notes that Weber connects so-called complexes of meaning to interests; and he refers to Weber's "concern with systems of meaning (*Sinnzusammenhänge*) . . . which, as definitions of situations for the actions of individuals, could be linked with individuals' 'interests' (their motives in a psychological sense)" (Parsons 1963:xxiii).

Weber notes at one point that "economic interests" are among "the most fundamental and universal components" of human behavior (ES:601). While this may seem to indicate a biological foundation of interest, and rule out a subjective approach to the concept of interest, Weber occasionally does stress the importance of how interests are perceived by the actor (e.g. ES:30).

The concept of economic interest is also absolutely central to Weber's concept of class. We read, for example, that "the factor that creates 'class' is unambiguously economic interest" (ES:928; cf. ES:302). Weber was, on the other hand, skeptical of the notion of class interest, arguing that the "direction" of individual interests is very difficult to determine a priori (ES:928–30).

There exists an important "elective affinity," according to Weber, between ideas and interests, say between Protestantism and a certain work ethic (PE:91–2). In one of his most cited and discussed formulations, which can be found in his sociology of religion, Weber expresses the relationship between different systems of religion and interests in the following manner:

Not ideas, but material and ideal interests, directly govern men's conduct. Yet very frequently the "world images" that have been created by "ideas" have, like switchmen, determined the tracks along which action has been pushed by the dynamic of interest. (GM:280)

In German:

Interessen (materielle und ideelle), nicht Ideen, beherrschen unmittelbar das Handeln des Menschen. Aber: die "Weltbilder," welche durch "Ideen" geschaffen wurden, haben sehr oft als Weichensteller die Bahnen bestimmt, in denen die Dynamik der Interessen das Handeln fortbewegte. (GAR, I:252).

The new translation by Sam Whimster reads as follows:

It is interests (material and ideal), and not ideas which have directly governed the actions of human beings. But the "worldviews" that have been created by ideas have very often, like switches, decided the lines on which the dynamic of interests has propelled behaviour. (EW:69)

Stephen Kalberg, in discussing this passage, points out that "Weber generally uses the term 'ideas' (*Ideen*) in the nineteenth century usage to refer to coherent views of the cosmos and man's place within it" (Kalberg 1979:137 n. 6). According to Wolfgang Schluchter, the passage dates from 1919/1920 when Weber was revising his introduction to "The Economic Ethic of the World Religions" (*The Rise of Western Rationalism* [1981], p. 25). Schluchter also argues that "the term 'directly' [in 'interests *directly* govern men's conduct'] must not be misunderstood. Interests are direct insofar as they constitute motivations. However, motives are always mediated historically; they are interpreted and institutionalized" (ibid.). Marianne Weber, finally, simply says in her comment on this passage that "the causal sequences [between interests and ideas] run back and forth" (Marianne Weber [1926] 1975:332).

With the term "ideal interests" in this particular passage, Parsons argues, Weber meant such things as "interests in religious salvation, the interest in the growth of knowledge through scientific research and many others" (Parsons 1975:668). Whimster states that it is easy to misunderstand Weber's use of the term "ideal interests" in this passage and not realize that "the emphasis has to be placed on 'interests' not 'ideal'" (Whimster 2002:97). Weber, in brief, equates ideal and material interests; and what makes them similar is precisely that both are interests.

Weber's general concept of interest has been neglected in the secondary literature. For exceptions, see e.g. Pierre Bourdieu, "Legitimation and Structured Interests in Weber's Sociology of Religion" ([1971] 1987),

Stephen Kalberg, "The Role of Ideal Interests in Max Weber's Comparative Historical Sociology" (1985), Michael Peillon, *The Concept of Interest in Social Theory* (1990), and Richard Swedberg, *Principles of Economic Sociology* (2003), pp. 1–5, 15–16.

See also class, ideas, motive, economic motivation, knowledge (for cognitive and scientific interest), outside interests, interest groups, opportunity, religious benefits, self-interest or self-interested kind of behavior

interest groups (*Interessenverbände*)   Weber discusses interest groups in his political writings as well as in his political sociology. As part of his sociological analysis of representation, for example, Weber also discusses representation of interest groups by agents (e.g. ES:297–99). Weber's focus is on groups where representatives are chosen because of their profession, class or social membership; and he notes that this type of group represents a competitor to political parties.

One can also find scattered remarks about interest groups throughout Weber's work (e.g. PW:95, 98). He notes, for example, that certain economic interest groups (like entrepreneurs) may have superior knowledge to bureaucrats (ES:994, cf. ES:997).

See also interests, representation

"Intermediate Reflection"   *See* "Zwischenbetrachtung"

interpretation   *See* interpretive sociology, interpretive understanding, meaning, understanding

interpretive sociology (*verstehende Soziologie*)   This is the name that Weber gave to his sociology. It can be found in the subtitle of *Economy and Society* and it captures well the type of sociology that Weber tried to create—one centered around the meaning that actors attach to their behavior, and which the sociologist has to interpret in order to understand this behavior.

The place where Weber's ideas about interpretive sociology come to their most concentrated and fullest expression is in Ch. 1 of *Economy and Society*. This chapter currently exists in two English versions—by Talcott Parsons and by Keith Tribe (ES:1–62, EW:311–58). The term "interpretive sociology" also figures prominently in Weber's first attempt to formulate his sociology in theoretical terms, "Some Categories of Interpretive Sociology" (SCIS:151–53).

Alfred Schutz describes "the goal" of his book *The Phenomenology of the Social World* to be "the clarification of Weber's basic concept of interpretive sociology" (Schutz [1932] 1967:13). For an argument that strongly emphasizes that Weber wanted to unite understanding and explanation, see Fritz Ringer, *Max Weber's Methodology* (1997).

See also explanation, interpretive understanding, meaning, neo-Kantianism, sociology, "Some Categories of Interpretive Sociology," understanding

interpretive understanding (*deutendes Verstehen*)   According to Weber's well-known definition of sociology, which can be found in paragraph 1 in Ch. 1 of *Economy and Society*, "sociology . . . is a science concerning itself with the *interpretive understanding* of social action and thereby with a causal explanation of its course and consequences" (ES:4; emphasis added). In order to access the meaning that an actor invests his or her behavior with, it has to be interpreted; and it is this process that Weber has in mind when he speaks of interpretive understanding.

See also interpretive sociology, meaning, neo-Kantianism, understanding

intersubjectivity   According to an important argument by Alfred Schutz in *The Phenomenology of the Social World*, Weber failed to develop a theory of intersubjectivity in his sociology, that is, a theory of how actors are able to understand what other persons mean (Schutz [1932] 1967:97–138; for a summary of Schutz on Weber, see e.g. Helmut Wagner, *Alfred Schutz: An Intellectual Biography* [1983], pp. 13–16, 122–25).

See also meaning

"Introduction to the Economic Ethics of the World Religions" (**"Einleitung"**)   *See* "Einleitung"

iron cage (*stahlhartes Gehäuse*)   This term, which can be found in *The Protestant Ethic and the Spirit of Capitalism*, represents Weber's most famous metaphor and has taken on a life of its own in contemporary social theory (PE:181; for similar expressions, see e.g. ES:1401–2, PW:158). As a metaphor, the term refers to the harsh capitalist order that the individual is forced to live in, with its unrelenting demand that he or she work hard and methodically. The term itself also suggests a prison that is impossible to break out of.

The term "iron cage" was chosen by Talcott Parsons, the first translator of *The Protestant Ethic*. The general context in Weber's text is that the Puritan saint was supposed to wear his worldly goods "like a light cloak which can be thrown aside at any moment"—but . . . this light cloak has today become 'an iron cage'" (PE:181).

Later translators have preferred other versions of *stahlhartes Gehäuse*, such as "a shell as hard as steel" and "a steel-hard casing" (Weber [1904–5] 2002a:121; [1904–5] 2002b:123). *Stahlhartes* literally means "hard as steel," and *Gehäuse* means "shell," "casing," "housing," or "carapace," so these translations are considerably closer to the German original than Parsons' term (cf. PW:68 n. 57, 374).

Talcott Parsons would later recall that the reason for his choice of "iron cage" was not that it had been used by John Bunyan but probably that "I thought it [the term 'iron cage'] appropriate to the Puritan background of Weber's own personal engagement in the Puritan Ethic problem" (letter of 1975 to Benjamin Nelson; cf. Swedberg 1998:262n.34).

For discussions of the term "iron cage," see e.g. David Chalcraft, "Bringing the Text Back In: On Ways of Rendering the Iron Cage Metaphor in the Two Editions of 'The Protestant Ethic'" (1994) and Peter Baehr, "The 'Iron Cage' and the 'Shell as Hard as Steel': Parsons, Weber, and the *stahlhartes Gehäuse* Metaphor in *The Protestant Ethic and the Spirit of Capitalism*" (2000).

irrationality (*Irrationalität*) Weber often refers to irrational forces or structures in his sociology. It is, for example, at the heart of his concept of affectual social action as well as those of charisma and kadi justice.

In his general sociology in Ch. 1 of *Economy and Society* Weber writes that even if sociology starts out from rational social action for methodological reasons, "sociological investigation attempts to include in its scope various irrational phenomena, such as prophetic, mystic and affectual modes of action, formulated in terms of theoretical concepts which are adequate on the level of meaning" (ES:20).

In one of his essays on the sociology of religion Weber refers to "the greatest irrational force of life: sexual love" (GM:343). He also says that "the world of the Indian remained a garden of irrational charm" (AJ:222). In his sociology of law Weber counterposes formal irrationality to substantive irrationality—with the former meaning that the legal decision cannot be controlled by the intellect, and the latter that the case is decided on the basis of the concrete details of the case, as opposed to general norms (ES:656).

For a discussion of irrationality in Weber's work, see e.g. Martin Albrow, *Max Weber's Construction of Social Theory* (1990), pp. 129–31. Albrow notes that for Weber irrationality was not defined as the negative mirror image of rationality, but "had its own shape and complexity" (ibid., p. 129).

See also charisma, instrumentally rational action, kadi justice, rationality, value-rational action

Islam Islam is one of the religions that Weber terms world-religions. Before his death Weber planned a study of "Islam" as part of his broader attempt to "account for the economic and social *singularity* of the Occident," according to his 1919 advertisement for the *Collected Essays in the Sociology of Religion* (which is reprinted in the entry for this work). This study, however, was never carried out, and all that Weber wrote on Islam is fragments (e.g. ES:472–77, 623–27, 818–23, 1232–34).

Islam, in Weber's interpretation, is mainly a warrior religion, and its ideal personality type is the warrior. An important part of Islam is its advocacy of political unity in the face of outside enemies. The main carrier of Islam was also the warrior (ES:512).

Islam, Weber says, has a distinctly feudal dimension, as illustrated by its acceptance of slavery, polygamy, the subjection of women, and serfdom. Its attitude to the economy is traditionalistic, due to its hostility to risk and rate of interest. The brand of predestination that can be found in Islam leads to utter abandon in battle, but not to a methodical and rational everyday life as in Puritanism. This is because Islam does not make believers all the time look for signs and adjust their behavior accordingly—and this, in its turn, is related to Islam's being more about "predetermination" than about "predestination," and more about fate in this life than in the beyond (PE:227 n. 36; cf. 240 n. 106).

What prevented rational capitalism from emerging spontaneously in Islamic societies, however, was not so much the type of individual produced by Islam as "the religiously determined structure of the Islamic states, their officialdom and their jurisprudence" (ES:1095). As part of his sociology of law, Weber also discusses Islamic law (ES:818–23).

For an attempt to reconstruct Weber's projected study of Islam and assess the academic response to Weber's analysis of Islam, see Wolfgang Schluchter, "Hindrances to Modernity: Max Weber on Islam," pp. 105–78 in *Paradoxes of Modernity* (1996). See also Toby Huff and Wolfgang Schluchter (eds.), *Max Weber and Islam* (1999), and Bryan Turner, *Weber and Islam* (1974) and "Islam, Capitalism and the Weber Thesis" (1974).

See also *Collected Essays in the Sociology of Religion*

Jaffé, Edgar (1866–1921)   Economist and friend of Max Weber. Married to Else von Richthofen.

Japan   There exists an important section on Japan in *The Religion of India* (RI:270–82). It is here argued, among other things, that "while . . . Japan was able to take over capitalism as an artifact from the outside, . . . it could not create capitalism out of its own spirit" (RI:275).

For the reception of Weber in Japan, see Wolfgang Schwentker, *Weber in Japan* (1998).

Jaspers, Karl (1883–1969) Philosopher of the existentialist school and an acquaintance of Max Weber. See e.g. Karl Jaspers, *On Max Weber* (1989). See also Dieter Henrich, "Karl Jaspers: Thinking with Weber in Mind" (1987).

Jellinek, Georg (1851–1911) Legal and constitutional scholar as well as a friend of Max Weber. For Max Weber on Jellinek, see Marianne Weber, *Max Weber*, pp. 473–78. See also Alexander Hollerbach, "Jellinek, Georg" (1968) and Stefan Breuer, *Georg Jellinek und Max Weber* (1999).

Judaism Weber mainly discusses Judaism in *Ancient Judaism* and in the section on sociology of religion in *Economy and Society* (e.g. ES:493–99, 611–23, 823–28, 1200–1204).

Judaism is characterized by the central place that the covenant (*berith*) or mutual contract between God and the people of Israel plays in this type of religion. The Jews, Weber also argues, constitute a pariah people, in the sense that they are ritually segregated and socially disadvantaged (e.g. ES:492–99).

Ancient Judaism helped to break the hold of magic and thereby contributed to the world-historical process of rationalization. Its economic ethic, however, was traditionalistic in spirit and furthermore it did not develop a systematic asceticism. Its impact on the emergence of rational, industrial capitalism was minor—contrary to what people like Werner Sombart have argued (e.g. ES:1203–4). Instead, under the impact of ritualism and attacks from the outside, it developed a kind of pariah capitalism (ES:611–23).

The ideal personality type of Judaism is the scholarly scribe and Judaism's main carrier is the wandering trader (ES:512, 626).

Before his death Weber planned a study of "Talmudic Judaism," as part of his broader attempt to "account for the economic and social *singularity* of the Occident," to cite his advertisement of 1919 for the *Collected Essays in the Sociology of Religion* (*see* the entry for that work).

As part of his sociology of law, Weber discusses Jewish law (ES:823–28).

For a discussion of Weber and Judaism, see e.g. Gary Abraham, *Max Weber and the Jewish Question* (1992), Freddy Raphaël, "Max Weber and Ancient Judaism" (1973), and Wolfgang Schluchter, "Ancient Judaism," pp. 163–204, in *Rationalism, Religion, and Domination* (1989). For Weber's view of Zionism, see his letter of 1913 to E. J. Lesser, as reproduced in Marianne Weber, *Max Weber* ([1926] 1975), pp. 469–70;

and for his view of his relationship to Jewish friends and acquaintances, see e.g. Wolfgang Mommsen, *Max Weber and German Politics 1890–1920* (1984), p. 310. See also Guenther Roth, "Max Weber's Views on Jewish Integration and Zionism: Some American, English and German Contexts" (2002).

See also pariah, pariah capitalism, prophet

jurisprudence   *See* law

justice   Weber distinguishes between many different types of justice in his sociology of law, including formal and substantive justice. Formal justice (legal formalism) is centered around the procedures of the law, as opposed to the ideals of justice (substantive justice; e.g. ES:809–15). Authoritarian powers typically rely on substantive justice, while market forces profit from predictable, formal justice. At one point in his sociology of law Weber refers to "the insoluble conflict between the formal and substantive principles of justice" (ES:893).

The sense of justice is basically unstable and emotional, according to Weber, unless it is guided by interests (e.g. ES:759). The sense of justice is also one of the sources of kadi justice, which represents an irrational type of justice focused on the single case. Empirical justice, on the other hand, is characterized by a legal situation in which analogies are used and precedents interpreted (e.g. ES:976).

The structure of the administration of justice is critical to the legal system—and also decides if this is to be theocratic, patrimonial, or of other types (e.g. ES:816–31).

For a discussion of Weber on formal versus substantive justice, see e.g. Anthony Kronman, *Max Weber* (1983), pp. 93–5.

See also kadi justice, law

Kadi justice (*Kadijustiz*)   Kadi justice essentially means a type of justice that is individualistic in nature as well as substantive—that is, (formally) irrational. It is a concept that is central to Weber's sociology of law with its preoccupation with rational versus irrational types of law.

At one point Weber defines kadi justice as "informal [legal] judgments rendered in terms of concrete ethical or practical valuations" (ES:976). The prophet's attitude to law, Weber notes, is "pure kadi justice" since he follows the dictum (of Jesus), "it is written . . . but I say unto you" (ES:978). Rational capitalism, Weber also notes, cannot live with a legal system based on kadi justice (e.g. ES:1395).

While commentators often note Weber's use of the expression kadi justice in connection with Islamic law, it may be noted that he frequently also uses it to refer to various aspects of English and ancient law (e.g. ES:814, 891–92, 1115).

Weber borrowed the term kadi justice from Richard Schmidt, his colleague at the University of Freiburg (ES:1003 n. 2).

According to Reinhard Bendix, "the *khadi* was a Mohammedan judge, but Weber used 'khadi-justice' quite generally" to describe an administration of justice that is oriented to substantive justice and not to formally rational law (Bendix 1960:400 n. 36).

See also irrationality, justice

Kantianism   *See* neo-Kantianism

Kategorienlehre   This term is mainly used to describe Part I of *Economy and Society* ("Conceptual Exposition" or Chs. 1–4), but sometimes also its first chapter ("Basic Sociological Terms"; see ES:1–307 [or EW:312–58] and ES:1–62, respectively). Whether one has Part 1 or Ch. 1 in mind, it is clear that this material mainly contains a large number of sociological concepts or "categories" and that these are presented in such a dry and difficult manner that they deserve the label of casuistry. "People are going to shake their heads," Weber reportedly said, anticipating the reactions of his readers (Marianne Weber [1926] 1975:676).

Part 1 of *Economy and Society* is entitled "Soziologische Kategorienlehre" (translated as "Conceptual Exposition"). The term *Kategorienlehre* allegedly comes from Marianne Weber; Weber himself would have preferred "general sociology" (*Allgemeine Soziologie*) for part 1 of *Economy and Society* (Dirk Käsler, *Max Weber* [1988], p. 149). Part 1 consists of the following four chapters: "Basic Sociological Terms," "Sociological Categories of Economic Action," "The Types of Legitimate Domination," and "Status Groups and Classes." A fifth chapter was planned, which would have dealt with "types of communities ('Forms of Associations [*Verbände*]')" (Horst Baier, M. Rainer Lepsius, Wolfgang Mommsen, and Wolfgang Schluchter, "Overview of the Text of *Economy and Society*" [2000], p. 114).

Ch. 1 contains what can be called Weber's general sociology. His essay of 1913 "Some Categories of Interpretive Sociology" represents an early version of parts of Chap. 1 (SCIS; for an excerpt, see ES:1375–80). It may be added that Weber himself rarely uses the term "general sociology" (*allgemeine Soziologie*) in his work (for an exception, see ES:356).

See also *Economy and Society*, interpretive sociology, sociology

Kaulsaladäquanz (adequate causality)   *See* causality

khadi justice   *See* kadi justice

kin group (*Sippe*)   According to *Economy and Society*, a kin group or a kinship group is a protective group; it has sexual rules similar to that of the household; and its members may expect to inherit from each other (ES:365; for kin groups in general, see e.g. ES:365–69, GEH:43–6).

In the West the power of the kin or kinship group has been broken, while this is not the case in many other countries, especially China (e.g. GEH:44–5; cf. RC:86–100, RI:49–54, ES:1243–44). Certain religions and sects have been instrumental in eliminating the hold of the kin group (e.g. RC:237). Weber also notes that the power of kin groups is one of the factors that have helped to block the emergence of rational capitalism.

A certain type of charisma may attach to the kin group: "'lineage charisma' (*Gentilcharisma*) means that this extraordinary quality [of charisma] adheres to kinship group members per se and not, as originally, to a single person" (RI:49; my trans.).

According to a statement in *General Economic History* Weber preferred the German term *Sippe* to the Gaelic term "clan" (GEH:43; cf. RI:53). Reinhard Bendix notes that "Weber used the term 'sib' when I shall use the term 'kinship group' or 'extended kinship group'" (Bendix 1960:73). Hans Gerth writes in the preface to *The Religion of China* that "with great hesitancy we have felt obliged to use the term sib rather than clan for *Sippe* as Weber rejected [the term clan]" (RC:x).

See also charisma, family

kinship   *See* kin group

Klasse   *See* class

Klinger, Max (1857–1920)   One of Germany's foremost artists in his day, Max Klinger excelled as a sculptor, painter, and engraver. It was especially Klinger's engravings that fascinated Max Weber, and in 1894 he presented his wife, on the first anniversary of their wedding, with nearly two hundred of these. What is characteristic about the engravings that Weber bought, and which soon decorated the home of the Webers as well as Max Weber's own office at the University of Freiburg, is their strong Freudian and surrealistic themes. See David Chalcraft, "Love and Death: Weber, Wagner and Klinger" (1999).

Knies, Karl (1821–1898)   One of the leading members and founders of the German Historical School of economics and an important influence on Weber. Knies was also Weber's predecessor at the University of Heidelberg. Knies is at the center of *Roscher and Knies* (Weber [1903–6]

1975). See e.g. Bertram Schefold, "Knies, Karl Gustav Adolf (1821–1898)" (1987) and Wilhelm Hennis, "A Science of Man: Max Weber and the Political Economy of the German Historical School" (1987).

knowledge   Weber addresses the issue of knowledge at different levels and from different angles in his work. One may, for example, speak of his views on epistemology and how this is reflected in his sociology. One may also try to establish how Weber looked at the generation of knowledge through science—in the natural sciences as well as in the social sciences.

In his comments on various paragraphs in Ch. 1 of *Economy and Society* Weber broaches a number of epistemological questions. How does the observer know what an actor means by some social action? And when does the meaning of some action vanish, because the action is part of an unthinking habit?

Alfred Schutz notes that Weber "was interested in epistemological problems only insofar as they bore directly on specialized research or provided tools for its pursuit. Once they were at his disposal, he lost interest in the more fundamental problems" (Schutz [1932] 1967:7).

But Weber was also very concerned with the issue of how knowledge is generated by the natural scientist and the social scientist. As to the natural sciences, these have changed considerably over time and so has the kind of knowledge they are interested in (*see* science). In his discussion of the social sciences Weber starts out from the position that the researcher faces an infinitely rich reality and has to make a choice. And the choice that the researcher makes—what he or she finds interesting—depends squarely on what the major (cultural) problems are at the time. Depending on how this, the researcher may have different "cognitive interests" or "scientific interests" (e.g. MS:45, 64).

Weber specifies: "just as without the investigator's conviction regarding the significance of particular cultural facts, every attempt to analyze concrete reality is absolutely meaningless, so the direction of his personal belief, the refraction of values in the prism of his mind, gives direction to his work" (MSS:82).

According to Raymond Aron, "the choice of facts, the elaboration of concepts, and the delineation of the object, Weber wrote, are marked by the direction of our curiosity" (Aron 1985:337).

See also cultural problems of the time, cultural sciences, interest, intersubjectivity, meaning, objectivity, value-relevance

Konfuzianismus und Taoismus (*The Religion of China*, trans. 1951) This work is part of Weber's *The Economic Ethics of the World Religions*.

See also Confucianism, *Economic Ethics of the World Religions*; *Religion of China, The*; Taoism

Korporation   *See* corporation

Kultur   *See* culture

Kulturbedeutung   *See* cultural problems of the time

Kulturprobleme   *See* cultural problems of the time

Kulturwissenschaften   *See* cultural sciences

L

abor   *See* work, workers

law (*Recht*)   Weber had a lifelong interest in legal matters and was primarily trained in law and as a legal historian. He often wrote on legal subjects and is one of the founders of the sociology of law. His major writings on this topic can be found in *Economy and Society*; they have also been collected in a volume entitled *On Law in Economy and Society*.

Sociology of law and jurisprudence, Weber argues, look at law from very different perspectives. While the jurist primarily focuses on the internal logic of legal rules, the sociologist studies the impact of these rules on social behavior (ES:32–33; cf. e.g. ES:311–12, CS:115–43, SCIS:158–59).

From a legal perspective, Weber says, modern law consists of legal propositions or norms which are either prescriptive, prohibitory, or permissive (ES:667). In sociological terms, the former two constitute "claims," and the latter a "privilege"; law of the contractual type Weber also terms "enabling law" (e.g. ES:730).

More generally, Weber presents his well-known definition of law in his general sociology in Ch. 1 of *Economy and Society*: "an order (*Ordnung*) will be called . . . law if it is externally guaranteed by the probability that physical or psychological coercion will be applied by a staff of people in order to bring about compliance or avenge violation" (ES:34; see also ES:34–6).

A convention (or norm) is also an order, according to Weber. It differs, however, from a law in that it does not have a staff to enforce it. The concept of order (*Ordnung*) is very important to Weber's sociology; *see* the entry for this term.

The current version of *Economy and Society* includes a huge section known as Weber's sociology of law (ES:641–900). Weber here discusses topics such as legal norms, legal right, types of legal thought, and codifications. At the center of his interest is the rationalization of law, in formal as well as in substantive terms (ES:656–57).

According to an often cited passage, law has gone through the following stages: (1) charismatic legal revelation through "law prophets"; (2) the making and application of law by legal *Honoratioren*; (3) the imposition of law by secular or theocratic powers; and (4) the systematic elaboration and administration of law through people specially trained in law (ES:882; see also ES:776 for the rationalization of law). Given the speed of technological and economic development, Weber predicts that in the future the average person's knowledge of law will decrease (ES:895).

Certain types of law have only developed in the West, such as natural law and Roman law with its high degree of legal formalism (e.g. ES:883). An important discussion of early Israelite law can also be found in *Ancient Judaism* (AJ:61–89).

Much of Weber's work on law is centered around the economy. In his early career, for example, he took part in the discussion of attempts to regulate the stock exchange (Weber 1999a). In *Economy and Society*, which Weber mainly worked on in the 1910s, he also often discusses the relationship of law and the economy. Modern rational capitalism needs a legal system that it is predictable; there also has to exist a certain amount of enabling or empowering law, such as contract law.

In 1882 Weber started his studies of law at the University of Heidelberg and later continued at the University of Berlin (see e.g. Dirk Käsler, *Max Weber* [1988], pp. 3–8, who also enumerates the professors of law whose lectures Weber attended). Several of Germany's foremost legal minds were also Weber's teachers, such as Otto von Gierke and Levin Goldschmidt. In 1886 Weber passed the examination for junior barrister (*Referendar*) and served in this capacity at a court in Berlin till he had completed his studies in law. He received his doctorate in 1889 and his *Habilitation* in 1892, both in law. During 1892–93 Weber taught Roman law, German law, and commercial law at the University of Berlin. In 1894 Weber moved to the University of Freiburg, where he took a chair in economics.

The main section on sociology of law in *Economy and Society* was probably written in 1913–14 and was by 1919–20 still considered ready for publication, despite Weber's new design for *Economy and Society* (Wolfgang Mommsen, "Max Weber's 'Grand Sociology'" [2000], pp. 377, 381). Weber's manuscript for his sociology of law still exists, as well as his corrections of the typescript (Horst Baier, M. Rainer Lepsius, Wolfgang Mommsen, and Wolfgang Schluchter, "Overview of the Text of

Economy and Society" [2000], p. 110). Weber also contributed to the Weimar Constitution and had a certain influence on its final form.

According to one authority on Weber's work in law, his "lifelong interest is law is reflected in nearly everything he wrote" (Kronman 1983:1). For general introductions to Weber and the role that law plays in his work, see e.g. Reinhard Bendix, *Max Weber: An Intellectual Portrait* (1960), pp. 385–457, Anthony Kronman, *Max Weber* (1983), Max Rheinstein, "Introduction," pp. xvii–lxiv in Max Weber, *On Law in Economy and Society* (1954), and Stephen Turner and Regis Factor, *Max Weber: The Lawyer as Social Thinker* (1994). For the general context of the discussion of law in Weber's day, see e.g. Michael John, "The Politics of Legal Unity in Germany, 1870–1896" (1985).

For Weber's work on the history of law, see e.g. Harold Berman and Charles Reid, "Max Weber as Legal Historian" (2000); and for his writings on the law of the stock exchange, see Knut Borchardt, "Max Weber's Writings on the Bourse: Figuring out a Forgotten Corpus" (2002). For introductions to Weber's sociology of law, see e.g. Sally Ewing, "Formal Justice and the Spirit of Capitalism: Max Weber's Sociology of Law" (1987) and Alan Hunt, "Max Weber's Sociology of Law" (1978). For Weber and the so-called England Problem, see David Trubek, "Max Weber on Law and Capitalism" (1972); and, for Weber's view of criminology, see Paul Honigsheim, *On Max Weber* (1968), pp. 68–75. For Weber's work on the Weimar Constitution, see Wolfgang Mommsen, *Max Weber and German Politics 1890–1920* (1984), pp. 332–89. Finally, for Weber's relationship to law and economics as well as more generally on Weber and law, see Richard Posner, "Weber, Max (1864–1920)" (1998).

See also commercial legislation, constitution, contract, convention, education (for legal education), England Problem, firm (for legal personality), jurisprudence, justice, kadi justice, law prophet, law specialist, lawmaking and law-finding, legal domination, legal *Honoratioren*, legal norm, legal order, order, rights (also for natural law), sacred law, sociology of law

law prophet (*Rechtsprophet*)   The law prophet has access to the principles of law through his or her charismatic qualities and was particularly common in the early stages of history (e.g. ES:768–72, 882). According to a famous passage, law has gone through the following stages: (1) charismatic legal revelation through law prophets; (2) the making and application of law by legal *Honoratioren*; (3) the imposition of law by secular or theocratic powers; and (4) the systematic elaboration and administration of law through people specially trained in it (ES:882).

The legal oracle and the legal sage are examples of legal prophets. Independent bearers of charisma sometimes constituted a threat to the prince and his officials.

See also charisma, kadi justice, law, prophet

law specialist (*Rechtskundiger*)   A formally elaborate law can only come into being through the help of trained specialists such as attorneys and lawyers (ES:775–76). These assist in what Weber terms "legal invention," that is, the discovery of new legal categories and ways of reasoning in legal matters (e.g. ES:775).

See also law prophet, legal *Honoratioren*

law-finding   *See* lawmaking and law-finding

law-finding by the folk assembly (*dinggenosssenschaftliche Rechtsfindung*)   *See* lawmaking and law-finding

lawmaking and law-finding (*Rechtsschöpfung, Rechtsfindung*)   In modern legal thought, Weber explains in his sociology of law, lawmaking refers to the "creation of general [legal] norms" (ES:653). Lawmaking is complemented by law-finding or the "application of these norms to particular cases" (ES:653–54).

Lawmaking as well as law-finding can be rational or irrational. They can also be formal or substantive. Kadi justice falls into the category of lawmaking and law-finding that is substantive as well as irrational. The work of legal oracles is formal and irrational. Certain theocratic legal systems are examples of law that is substantive and rational, while modern law is formal and rational (cf. Anthony Kronman, *Max Weber* [1983], pp. 76–77).

Weber terms "law-finding by the folk assembly" situations in which "the folk assembly . . . can accept or reject the decision recommended by the charismatic or official possessor of legal knowledge and can influence the decision in some way" (ES:774). One example of this is the Germanic military community.

According to Reinhard Bendix, "Weber used the term 'lawfinding' (*Rechtsfindung*) to express the idea that the law that is declared is believed to exist—for example, as part of the divine order" (Bendix 1960:393 n. 21).

See also law, sociology of law

laws in social science   According to Weber's general sociology in Ch. 1 of *Economy and Society*, sociology approaches its objects of study very differently from the natural sciences, and it also has a different goal than establishing general laws. Like the natural sciences, it observes its objects of study from the outside, but it also observes them from the inside, in the sense of interpretive understanding. It cannot produce general laws, only typical probabilities.

In explicating the first paragraph in *Economy and Society*, where the nature and goal of sociology is stated, Weber says that "the natural sciences [are] limited to the formulation of causal uniformities in objects and events and the explanation of individual facts by applying them" (ES:15). In this type of approach, the behavior of, say, a cell is not "understood"; instead functional relationships are established, and generalizations based on these are made. By adding the interpretive dimension, and not only relying on "external observation," sociology also adds to the difficulty involved (ibid.).

One of the prices that sociology pays for this is that it cannot develop general laws of the type that can be found in the natural sciences, but at the most generalizations in the form of "typical probabilities confirmed by observation" (ES:18). In confirming these generalizations, Weber stresses, observations have to be made that analyze actions in terms of understandable motives and intentions.

What has just been said about sociology can also be applied to history, with one important qualification. This is that history looks primarily at individual actions and structures, while sociology is more interested in formulating types and uniformities (ES:19–20). Economic theory differs from sociology and history through its focus on purely rational action oriented to economic ends, but it nonetheless deals with human actions which are explained by reference to the motives of the actors (ES:20–1). Some types of psychology, Weber notes, follow the procedures of the natural sciences, while others do not (ES:19).

Weber's ideas about the differences between the social sciences (which are part of the cultural sciences) and the natural sciences, both when it comes to their general approach (external versus internal) and their intended goals (general laws versus typical probabilities), are primarily discussed in his methodological essays (see especially MSS, RK, CS, and SCIS). In these essays, which are difficult to penetrate (especially in translation), Weber addresses the debate in his own time about the differences between the natural sciences and the social sciences. Philosopher Wilhelm Windelband, for example, had suggested a sharp theoretical distinction between the natural sciences and their search for abstract laws on the one hand, and the cultural sciences with their interest in concrete and unique events on the other ("nomothetic sciences" versus "ideographic sciences"). According to philosopher Wilhelm Dilthey, the natural sciences with their concern for outer events differ from the sciences which deal with the inner experiences of the human mind (*Naturwissenschaften* versus *Geisteswissenschaften*).

Weber's response to this type of argument was that the social or cultural sciences are scientific just like the natural sciences—but they go about their systematic search for regularities (not laws) differently from the natural sciences. They not only rely on external observation, but also try to establish the motives and intentions of the actor. By proceeding in this manner, Weber argues, a whole new type of causality has to be worked out, one that is centered around meaning and values rather than around those aspects of (external) reality that lend themselves to being formulated in terms of general laws.

Reality is infinite in its richness, and it is through the values of people that certain aspects of it become meaningful to them, according to Weber (and philosopher Heinrich Rickert; cf. the latter's *The Limits of Concept Formation in Natural Science* ([1902] 1986). In analyzing the causality involved, Weber says (following physiologist and probability thinker Johannes von Kries), the social scientist has to ask questions that are similar to those of legal science: Under what conditions can a motive be said to have typically caused some action to be carried out?

In his methodological essays Weber argues that the laws that can be found in Marxism should simply be regarded as hypotheses and ideal types (MSS:103). Weber was similarly critical of the idea that human society goes through certain stages and that there are equivalent evolutionary laws (MSS:101–2).

For discussions of the concept of law in the social and natural sciences, see e.g. Ola Agevall, *A Science of Unique Events: Max Weber's Methodology of the Cultural Sciences* (1999), Don Martindale, *The Nature and Types of Sociological Theory* (1960), pp. 377–83, and Talcott Parsons, *The Structure of Social Action* (1937), pp. 591–601.

Lebenschancen   *See* life chances

Lebensführung   *See* lifestyle

Lebensstil   *See* lifestyle

lectures   Max Weber's lectures are scheduled to appear in seven volumes as part of MWG. These are to include volumes on, for example, economics, agrarian policy, and the sociology of the state. For more information on these volumes, see the Web page for the *Max Weber Gesamtausgabe*: http//:www.mohr.de/mw/mwg.htm.

In Weber's days reporters were often present at public lectures, and good summaries of his talks can many times be found in daily newspapers. This way a number of Weber's lectures have become known, such as his important lecture on "The Problems of the Sociology of the State" in Vienna in 1917 (Weber 1917).

Some of Weber's lectures on economics from the 1890s have been published but are only available in German (see GVAN). His most famous lectures, however, may well be the ones that he gave in 1919–20 and which are known today as *Wirtschaftsgeschichte*. These are available in English as *General Economic History*.

Weber was a brilliant lecturer as a young man, until his nervous illness put an end to this type of activity. In the 1910s Weber resumed the task of lecturing, often spellbinding his audience.

For Weber as a lecturer, see e.g. Marianne Weber, *Max Weber* ([1926] 1975), pp. 202, 234–37, 604–5, 611–15.

See also *General Economic History*, personality

legal domination (*legale Herrschaft*)   Domination constitutes one of the major themes in Weber's sociology, and legal domination—together with traditional domination and charismatic domination—constitutes one of its three major forms (ES:217–26).

According to Weber's definition in Ch. 3 on domination in *Economy and Society*, legal domination rests on "a belief in the legality of enacted rules and the right of those elevated to authority under such rules to issue commands (legal authority [*Herrschaft*])" (ES:215; cf. EES:99).

Legal domination can be found in economic, political, religious, and other organizations. In each of these versions of legal domination the staff is organized in the form of a bureaucracy. How central bureaucracy is to legal domination is clear from the fact that most of the text on this type of domination in Ch. 3 of *Economy and Society* is devoted to a discussion of bureaucracy.

For discussion of whether Weber's concept of legitimacy based on legality is purely formalistic and therefore untenable (Mommsen), or if it is related to substantive values (Winkelmann), see Johannes Winkelmann, *Max Webers Herrschaftssoziologie* (1952) and Wolfgang Mommsen, *Max Weber and German Politics 1890–1920* (1984), pp. 402–5, 448–53.

See also domination, law, politics, sociology of law

legal education   *See* education

legal formalism   *See* justice

legal *Honoratioren* (*Rechtshonoratioren*)   By this term Weber essentially means legal experts of high status and prestige. He makes frequent use of it in his sociology of law and devotes a full section to "legal *Honoratioren* and the types of legal thought" (ES:784–808).

In a note to Weber's sociology of law Max Rheinstein points out that the Latin word *honoratiores* means "those of higher honor" and adds that "in German the word *Honoratioren* is used, often with a slight implication of friendly ridicule, to mean the more respectable citizens of a town" (ES:664 n. 18). Rheinstein also says that "in the present context [that is, Weber's sociology of law] Weber means by 'legal *Honoratioren*' (*Rechtshonoratioren*), those classes of persons who have (1) in some way made the occupation with legal problems a kind of specialized expert knowledge, and (2) enjoy among their group such a prestige that they are able to impress some peculiar characteristics upon the legal system of their respective societies" (ibid.).

According to Talcott Parsons, "there is no good English equivalent" for the term *Honoratioren*. Parsons' own definition reads as follows: "persons performing functions and exercising authority who do not depend on the position as a major source of income and generally enjoy an independent status in the social structure" (ibid.).

For a summary of Weber's view of legal *Honoratioren*, see e.g. Reinhard Bendix, *Max Weber: An Intellectual Portrait* (1960), pp. 407–16.

See also notables

legal maxim *See* maxim

legal norm (*Rechtsnorm*) A legal norm can be described as a consensual understanding of how to behave, which is guaranteed by coercive enforcement (ES:754).

A large part of Weber's sociology of law is devoted to the role of legal norms (see especially "The Emergence and Creation of Legal Norms," ES:753–84).

legal order (*Rechtsordnung*) Depending on the context in Weber's work, this term refers either to the legal order, as viewed in jurisprudence, or to the legal order in a sociological type of analysis. In the former case, it refers to "a set of norms of logically determinable correctness"; and in the latter case, it refers to "a complex of actual determinants of human conduct" (ES:312; cf. e.g. ES:317).

See also law, order

legal personality *See* firm

legal profession *See* profession

legal science *See* law

legitimacy (*Legitimität*) The concept of legitimacy represents one of the key elements in Weber's sociology and it is used most famously in his analysis of political regimes. Its range, however, extends in principle well beyond the political order, and includes, for example, the religious and economic orders. To exclusively base a political regime on interests or violence tends to create instability, while the regime becomes stable if it is seen as valid or binding. Weber's typology of legitimacy mirrors his well-known typology of domination (traditional, charismatic, and legal).

Three different types of actors may experience domination as legitimate: the ruler, the staff, and the subjects. While the legitimacy of the staff and the subjects is similar in Weber's work—they simply come to see domination as valid or binding—the ruler is primarily driven by a need for justification. Weber's ideas on "the generally observable need of any power . . . to justify itself" are close to what he elsewhere terms the "theodicy of good fortune" (ES:953; cf. GM:271). It should finally also be emphasized that according to Weber it is under certain circumstances possible for the ruler "to drop even the pretense of a claim of legitimacy" (ES:214).

Weber discusses legitimacy in his general sociology in Ch. 1 of *Economy and Society*, in his analysis of domination (*Herrschaft*) in Ch. 2 of that work, and elsewhere. He writes in Ch. 1 of *Economy and Society* that "action, especially social action which involves a social relationship, may be guided by the belief in the existence of a legitimate order" (ES:31). Weber adds that "the probability that action will actually be so governed will be called the 'validity' (*Geltung*) of the order in question" (ibid.).

Weber goes on to say that convention and law constitute two types of such a legitimate order (ES:33–6). He notes that individual actors may ascribe legitimacy to a social order on certain subjective grounds (affectual, traditional, and value-rational beliefs, or beliefs that refer to enactments that are thought to be legal; ES:36–38). He also points out that what guarantees the legitimacy of the order itself are such subjective beliefs or self-interest (*Interessenlage*; ES:33–6).

In Ch. 2 of *Economy and Society* (and in his other discussions of domination), Weber introduces his three types of domination or authority (ES:941–1211, ES:212–301, EES:99–108, or EW:133–45; see also GM:295–300). He also discusses their claim to legitimacy, and how this legitimacy is based respectively on rational, traditional, and charismatic grounds.

In legal domination, legitimacy rests on "a belief in the legality of enacted rules and the right of those elevated to authority under such rules to issue commands" (ES:215). Traditional domination rests on "an established belief in the sanctity of immemorial traditions and the legitimacy of those exercising authority under them" (ibid.). And charismatic domination rests on "devotion to the exceptional sanctity, heroism or exemplary character of an individual person, and of the normative patterns or order revealed by him" (ibid.).

Weber notes that "as a rule both rulers and ruled uphold the internalized structure as 'legitimate' by right, and usually the shattering of this belief has far-reaching ramifications" (EES:99). Weber also emphasizes that "experience shows that in no instance does domination voluntarily limit itself to the appeal to material or affectual or ideal motives . . . in addition every such system attempts to establish and to cultivate the belief in its legitimacy" (ES:213).

Sam Whimster defines legitimacy as "the belief of the ruled in the validity of rulership" (EW:409). Talcott Parsons notes in a comment on Ch. 1 of *Economy and Society* that the reader may easily be confused by Weber's distinction between, on the one hand, motives for guaranteeing a legitimate order and, on the other hand, motives for attributing legitimacy to an order (ES:33–6 and ES:36–38, respectively; for Parsons' comment, see ES:60 n. 20). Parsons points out that self-interest is part of the motives for guaranteeing an order (but not for attributing legitimacy to it), and uses as an illustration the example of a person who is not religious but nonetheless supports a religious regime out of fear that anarchy may otherwise ensue.

For the argument that Weber's concept of legitimacy lacks a reference to truth, see Jürgen Habermas, "Max Weber's Concept of Legitimation" (1975). For a discussion whether Weber's concept of legitimacy based on legality is purely formalistic and therefore untenable (Mommsen), or if it is related to substantive values (Winkelmann), see Wolfgang Mommsen, *Max Weber and German Politics 1890–1920* (1984), pp. 402–5, 448–53. More generally on the concept of legitimacy, see e.g. Stefan Breuer, *Max Webers Herrschaftssoziologie* (1991), pp. 19–23 and Martin Albrow, *Max Weber's Construction of Social Theory* (1990), pp. 161–65.

See also democracy, domination, emotions, order, politics, self-interest or self-interested behavior

Lehen See fief

Lehensfeudalismus (feudalism based on fiefs) *See* feudalism

letters Weber's letters are a rich source for a variety of topics—his views on everyday political questions, his personal relationships, among many others. The letters are scheduled to appear in eleven volumes as part of MWG. By 2003 four of these volumes had appeared. For more information on these, see the Web page of *Max Weber Gesamtausgabe*: http//: www.mohr.de/mw/mwg.htm. See also the letters in Max Weber, *Jugendbriefe* (1936) and "Political Letters (1906–19)," pp. 451–88 in *Gesammelte Politische Schriften*.

lex mercatoria *See* commercial legislation

liberalism   *See* politics

life   *See* Weber, Max—Life

life-chances (*Lebenschancen*)   This concept can be found in Weber's best-known definition of class: "we may speak of a 'class' when (1) a number of people have in common a specific causal component of their *life chances*, insofar as (2) this component is represented exclusively by economic interests in the possession of goods and opportunities for income, and (3) is represented under conditions of the commodity or labor markets" (ES:927; emphasis added).

Many decades after Weber's introduction of the concept of life-chances, Robert K. Merton was to refer to the "still loosely utilized but important concept of what Weber called 'life-chances'" (Merton 1968:230). Merton has also argued that "the concept of differential access to opportunities . . . could be taken to correspond to Weber's concept-and-term of *life chances*" (Merton 1995:33). See also in this context the discussion in Ralf Dahrendorf, *Life Chances* (1979).

See also class, opportunity

life orders   *See* value-spheres

lifestyle (*Lebensführung, Lebensstil,* and similar terms)   It is often noted that the concept of *Lebensführung* is absolutely central to Weber's work, especially *The Protestant Ethic*. Many other translations of this term than "lifestyle" have been suggested, such as "conduct of life," "way of life," "manner of conducting one's life," and the like. According to some scholars, "lifestyle" is a serious mistranslation and *Lebensführung* represents something quite different.

Lebensführung does not seem to be defined anywhere in Weber's work. It is not part of the key concepts in the general sociology that Weber presents in Ch. 1 of *Economy and Society*. It does, however, appear in Ch. 4 of the same work, in Weber's discussion of status. He notes here that status is typically founded, among other things, on "style of life" (*Lebensführungsart*; ES:305). The link between status and lifestyle is also clear from other passages in *Economy and Society* (e.g. ES:529, 538, 1296, 1304).

A provisional definition of lifestyle in the Weberian sense might be that it represents the actual conduct of a group of people, as valorized by them.

In *The Protestant Ethic* the focus is on how one economic lifestyle (typical for traditional capitalism) is replaced by another (typical for modern rational capitalism; e.g. PE:55, 58, 59). Weber is careful to emphasize the ethical dimension of lifestyles as well as their group dimension.

There also exists a close relationship between the concept of lifestyle and what Weber terms the spirit of capitalism, even if the two are by no means identical. The spirit of capitalism represents more precisely "a particular constitutive component of the lifestyle that stood at the cradle of modern capitalism" (e.g. PED:74).

According to Jean-Pierre Grossein, *Lebensführung* "is never defined by Weber, but designates a structured whole of behavior and practices" (Grossein 1996:120). Peter Ghosh, who has recently retranslated the first edition of *The Protestant Ethic* (1904–5) together with Gordon Wells, criticizes Talcott Parsons' translation of *Lebensführung* as "lifestyle" and "conduct," and argues that "conduct of life" is preferable (Ghosh 1994:108–9). Gordon Wells argues similarly for "conduct of life" or "manner of conducting one's life," referring to the "pro-active quality of the concept" of *Lebensführung* (Wells 2001:35). In his translation of Wilhelm Hennis' *Max Weber: Essays in Reconstruction* (1998) Keith Tribe leaves *Lebensführung* and *Lebensstil* in German.

Elsewhere Tribe notes that translating *Lebensführung* as "conduct of life" does not adequately capture the active element in Weber's term since this term denotes "a way of consciously conducting one's life" (Tribe 2000:210; similarly Kalberg 1996:56 n. 17). Tribe adds that the term *Lebensstil* is less critical than *Lebensführung* and can in principle be translated as "lifestyle," but that this may still be a less than happy solution since "'lifestyle' today entails a consumerist orientation to life" (Tribe 2000:210). For the argument that *Lebensstil* ("lifestyle") encompasses *Lebensführung* ("life conduct"), see Thomas Abel and William Cockerham, "Life Style or *Lebensfuehrung*? Critical Remarks on the Mistranslation of Weber's Class, Status, Party" (1993).

See also status, vocation

limited autonomy (*Eigengesetzlichkeit*)   *See* value-spheres

lineage charisma   *See* charisma

liturgical state   *See* state

liturgy (*Leiturgie*)   In his discussion of topics such as how wants are satisfied and how domination is financed Weber often uses the term liturgy, which he defines as follows: "want satisfaction through negative privileges is called *liturgy*" (ES:350).

Examples of liturgy would include, for example, a village which is collectively liable for taxes, and an aristocracy which is liable for supplying armed men to the king. Liturgies as a way of financing a ruler was most highly developed in the patrimonial state (e.g. ES:1022–25).

See also state (for the liturgical state)

living for politics versus living off politics (*leben für die Politik, leben von der Politik*)   Due to what Weber calls "economic availability," certain categories of people can afford to devote themselves full-time to politics (e.g. GM:85–6, PW:109–12). One example of this is notables (ES:290–92). Industrial workers and modern entrepreneurs, on the other hand, are handicapped in this respect.

If politicians are not paid, political power will gravitate toward those who are economically available—and for this reason democracy needs to have paid politicians. "Democracy has only the choice of being run cheaply by the rich who hold honorary office, or of being run expensively by paid professional politicians" (PW:276).

See also economic availability, notables

loaded dice argument   Weber refers to a loaded dice as part of his argument about probability and objective possibility in his essay "Critical Studies in the Logic of the Cultural Sciences" (MSS:182–85). When a dice is repeatedly thrown, there is a one-in-six probability that any particular side will come up. When the dice is loaded there is still a definite probability that any particular side will come up, but the probability is different. Historical reality is similar to the second situation, with the crucial difference that no absolute probability can be assigned to the occurrence of any particular historical event.

This, however, does not mean that all attempts to analyze historical reality in terms of probability are futile. "We can . . . well enough estimate the relative 'degree' to which the outcome is 'favored' by the general rule by a comparison involving the consideration of how other conditions operating differently 'would' have favored it" (MSS:183). In this way we may be able to estimate "the 'degree' of objective possibility" (ibid.).

For references to Weber's loaded dice argument, see e.g. Seymour Martin Lipset, *The First New Nation* (1963), p. 7.

See also causation, objective possibility, probability

Lukács, Georg   *See* Marxism

Lutheranism   *See* Protestantism

lytric policy (*lytrische Politik*)   This term, which is used in Weber's economic sociology in Ch 2 of *Economy and Society*, roughly means rational monetary policy. Weber says at one point in this chapter that "[the] type of monetary policy which attempts to control the factors of irrationality in the monetary field, will, following G. F. Knapp, be called 'lytric' policy" (ES:160).

Lytron is Greek for "means of payment" and was introduced as a social scientific term by economist and economic historian G. F. Knapp. See also the comment on the term lytric by Claus Wittich (ES:210 n. 57). Weber was very positive about Knapp's tendency to create new social science terms (PED:77 n. 5).

See also money

M_{acht}　*See* power

Machtprestige　*See* power prestige

magic (*Magie, Zauberei*)　In the beginning of human history, according to Weber, magic ruled. The modern world, in contrast, is characterized by disenchantment or the lack of a belief in magic, spirits, and the like. The concept of magic plays a central role in Weber's sociology of religion. It is at the heart of his analysis of primitive religion; he also uses it in his sociology of law and in his analysis of charisma.

While prayer, sacrifice and worship are used in relation to gods, in magic (or sorcery) magical coercion is used in relation to demons (ES:424). The line between religion and magic is fluid. Peasants often believe in magic, due to their work with nature. In general, magic has a conservative impact on society.

While what Weber calls the disenchantment of the world has eliminated much magic from the modern world, there are still religions that qualify as "magical gardens" and where people live in "magical bondage" (e.g. RI:255, 336, 342, RC:227; cf. RI:196–203). Ascetic Protestantism, in contrast, was deeply hostile to magic and tried to eliminate it (e.g. RC:226). For Weber's discussion of the relationship of magic to law, including magical ritualism, see e.g. ES:815–16.

For an overview of Weber's use of magic as well as an attempt to relate his use of magic to that of his contemporaries, see Stefan Breuer, "Magie, Zauberer, Entzauberung" (2001).

See also disenchantment of the world, magician

magician (*Zauberer*)　Together with the priest and the prophet, the magician is one of the key figures in Weber's sociology of religion. A magician, according to *Economy and Society*, is a person with personal gifts (charisma) who uses magical coercion to charm and force demons to do what he wants them to do (ES:424–25).

As opposed to the priest, the magician works individually and not permanently. He is self-employed and not part of an organization. He draws on his personal gifts rather than on some special knowledge developed into a doctrine. Also his education differs from that of the priest. Finally, as opposed to the prophet, the magician is paid and has a clientele.

For an overview of Weber's use of the concept of magic as well as an attempt to relate his use of the concept of magician to that of his contemporaries, see Stefan Breuer, "Magie, Zauberer, Entzauberung" (2001).

See also disenchantment of the world, magic, magician, mysticism, priest, prophet

males   While Weber does not single out males (or females) in his general sociology, he sometimes comments on them or touches on topics that exclusively involve males. This is, for example, the case with his discussion of men's houses (e.g. ES:906–8, GEH:39ff.; cf. e.g. RI:171–72). In his study of Chinese religions Weber also comments on the ideal of the gentleman in Confucianism (RC:161–63).

In one of his writings Weber refers to "the cultivation of manliness [in Germany], which the fraternities doubtless did much to nurture" (Mommsen 1984:312). As a student, Weber himself belonged precisely to one of these fraternities. Nationalism and World War I also brought out the masculine side of Weber. During the war he wrote, for example, to his mother that, "of all your sons, I have the greatest natural 'warrior' instinct" (ibid., p. 195).

See also body, feminism, household, patriarchalism, women

manorial domination (*Grundherrschaft*)   The historical importance of this type of agrarian estate was much debated in Weber's time. Its impact on German history as well as its origin were especially at issue. For Weber's position, see especially *General Economic History* (e.g. GEH:65–73, 79–111). For the debate, see e.g. Guenther Roth, "Introduction," ES:xlii–xlvi.

marginal utility (*Grenznutzen*)   This concept, which plays a key role in analytical economics, is often used by Weber in his economics as well as in his sociology (e.g. GVAN:48–9, ES:26, 71, 927, PE:277). Weber also wrote an essay in which he argued against the idea that marginal utility theory, and economic theory more generally, are based on psychology ("Marginal Utility Theory and 'The Fundamental Law of Psychophysics,'" EES:249–60). Different opinions exist about the role that Weber attached to the notion of marginal utility in his sociology as well as in his economics.

The notion of marginal utility, as used in economic theory, Weber explains in "Marginal Utility Theory," is based on common experiences in everyday life of the following three kinds: (1) people are motivated by needs which can only be satisfied through scarce material means; (2) the more that is consumed, the more a need is usually satisfied; and (3) people allocate scarce goods according to the importance that they attach to different needs. Weber also notes that in capitalist society "the approximation of reality to the theoretical propositions of economics has been a *constantly increasing* one" (EES:257).

It has been argued that for Weber marginal utility "epitomizes instrumental action, which, in its most rationalized version or form, follows the principle of marginal utility" (Schluchter 1989:454). It has also been argued that Weber's whole sociology is based on marginal utility theory (e.g. Simon Clarke, *Marx, Marginalism and Modern Sociology* [1982], pp. 204–12). However claims of this type are adjudicated, the many references to marginal utility in Weber's sociological work clearly show that he was positive about it—and also that he found a sociological use for it. It should also be pointed out that Weber's interpretive sociology is based, just like marginal utility theory, on the subjective perception of the actor.

Nonetheless, Weber was well aware of the limits of marginal utility theory. "Even the 'theory of marginal utility'," as he once put it ironically, "is subsumable under a 'law of marginal utility'" (MSS:89).

See also budgetary management, economic theory, rational choice, utility

market (*Markt*)   The core of a market, according to Weber, consists of two sets of interactions: competition and exchange. Buyers and sellers first compete among themselves to establish who will be the actual buyer and seller; these two then negotiate the price and do the exchange. In addition to this interactional element, a market typically also has specific rules, norms, regulations, and the like—an "order" in Weber's terminology and "institutional elements" in that of modern sociology.

A definition of the market can be found in an early fragment, written for *Economy and Society*: "A market may be said to exist wherever there is competition, even if only unilateral, for opportunities of exchange among a plurality of potential parties. Their physical assemblage in one place, as in the local market square, the fair (the 'long distance market'), or the exchange (the merchants' market), only constitutes the most consistent kind of market formation. It is, however, only this physical assemblage which allows the full emergence of the market's most distinctive feature, viz. dickering" (Weber [1922] 1978:635).

In the rest of this fragment (which is five pages long) Weber addresses a number of issues that are central to an understanding of the market, including its impersonality, its antagonism to status groups, and the ways in which market freedom can be restricted. Two often cited statements in this section are that exchange in a market represents "the archetype of all rational social action" (ES:635) and that a free market is "an abomination to every system of fraternal ethics" (ES:637). In "Some Categories of Interpretive Sociology," Weber also refers to "the amorphous structure of the market" (SCIS:166).

There is no definition of the market in the theoretical chapter on economic sociology in *Economy and Society* (Ch. 2). There does, however, exist a paragraph in this chapter that is centered around the following terms: "market situation," "marketability," "market freedom," and "regulation of the market." The first of these terms is defined as follows: "by the market situation (*Marktlage*) of any object of exchange is meant all the opportunities of exchanging it for money which are known to the participants in exchange relationships and aid their orientation in the competitive price struggle" (ES:82).

In his sociology of the market Weber emphasizes the element of struggle or conflict. He refers, for example, to the "market struggle" and "the battle of man against man in the market" (ES:93, 108). This emphasis on struggle in the market can also be found in Weber's lectures on economics in the 1890s and in his writings from this decade on the stock exchange in Germany (e.g. Weber [1894, 1896] 2000:369, GVAN:45).

While Weber did not devote much attention in his economic sociology to the problem of how prices are formed, one may nonetheless find some suggestive statements on this topic in his work. In an often cited formulation Weber writes, for example, that "prices are expressions of the struggle [of man against man]; they are instruments of calculation only as estimated quantifications of relative chances in this struggle of interests" (ES:108). Weber had also on his own come to the same conclusion as Ludwig von Mises about socialism and prices, namely that socialism would be unable to formulate realistic prices since it did not rely on the market (cf. ES:106–7). For Weber's view of just prices and the fixed price, see e.g. ES:636–37, 1188.

An economy dominated by the market is referred to as a market economy by Weber (ES:109–13). For the evolution of markets over time, see e.g. GEH:195–271.

See also capitalism, competition, contract, depersonalization, exchange, market economy, status

market economy (*Verkehrswirtschaft*)   What characterizes a market economy, according to Weber, is that needs are satisfied through exchange.

According to Weber's more precise explanation in his economic sociology in Ch. 2 of *Economy and Society*, "want satisfaction will be said to take place through a 'market economy' so far as it results from [economic] action oriented to advantages in exchange on the basis of self-interest and where co-operation takes place only through the exchange process" (ES:109).

This definition, Weber points out, does not address the issue if, and to what extent, an economy is capitalistic. In a market economy individual economic units are independent, and calculations are made in money. As a contrast to this type of economy Weber points to the "planned economy," where economic action is oriented to a substantive order, where individual economic units are not independent, and where a budget is used and calculations are made in kind.

The incentive to work is stronger in a market economy than in a planned economy since no substantive order is involved in the former.

See also exchange, market, planned economy, socialism

marriage   *See* household

Marxism   Weber had studied Marx and was both influenced by his writings and critical of these. He was very negative about what is known as Marxism and also saw socialism as a threat to mankind.

Weber is reported to have summed up his attitude to Marx (as well as Nietzsche) in the following way: "The honesty of a present-day scholar, and above all a present-day philosopher, can be measured by his attitude to Nietzsche and Marx. Whoever does not admit that considerable parts of his own work could not have been carried out in the absence of the work of these two, only fools himself and others. The world in which we spiritually and intellectually live today is a world substantially shaped by Marx and Nietzsche." (Hennis 1988a:146, Baumgarten 1964:554-55).

That Weber had studied Marx and the Marxists very carefully is clear from his lectures in economics in the 1890s as well as from his notes during these years (e.g. GVAN). He saw Marx's ideas, as just mentioned, as formative for everybody trying to understand the modern world and also as fruitful with their focus on the economic dimension of things (e.g. MSS:68, Scaff 1989a:17). The *Communist Manifesto*, for example, he once characterized as "a scholarly achievement of the highest order" (PW:287; cf. MSS:68). He also felt that the economy was influenced by noneconomic factors, however, not just the other way around as Marx had argued (e.g. MSS:64-5).

Marxism was a whole system, Weber warned—"not a cab to be boarded at will" (PW:365). He was also very critical of Marx's tendency to speak in terms of laws, and suggested the alternative view of seeing Marxist laws as ideal types or propositions to be tested (e.g. CS:80, MSS:103). He strongly criticized the idea that "in the last analysis" it is economic factors that decide what happens in society (e.g. GASS:455–56).

It can be argued that Weber handled Marx in the same way as he handled other thinkers whose works impressed him. That is, he singled out certain parts of Marx's work as particularly useful, and then reworked these for his own purposes. As an example of this one can mention his use of "class," which he recast with the help of "status"; his preference for a plurality of "capitalisms," instead of a unique capitalism; and his reversal (in *The Protestant Ethic*) of the idea that it is always the economy that causes changes in the superstructure, and never the other way around.

Finally, it may be mentioned that Weber had a low view of Marx as an individual. In one of his lecture notes, Weber describes Marx as a "ruler by nature with unlimited personal ambition and without compassion. Belief in his mission for domination of minds. This, and not rule of the masses, was in fact his goal. *Contempt* for his associates and the masses" (Mommsen 1984:131 n. 163).

The secondary literature on the relationship between Marx and Weber is large. According to an often cited statement by Albert Salomon, Weber's sociology came into being as a result of a "dialogue with Marx's ghost" (Salomon 1945:596). Weber has also often been called "the bourgeois Marx." An early and still useful study in this context is *Max Weber and Karl Marx* by Karl Löwith ([1932] 1982). See also the discussion of "Weberian Marxism" in Maurice Merleau-Ponty, *Adventures of the Dialectic* (1973), which is followed up and added to in Michael Lowy, "Figures of Weberian Marxism" (1996).

For general overviews of the relationship between Marx and Weber, see e.g. Wolfgang Mommsen, "Capitalism and Socialism: Weber's Dialogue with Marx," pp. 53–73 in *The Political and Social Theory of Max Weber* (1989), Guenther Roth, "The Historical Relationship to Marxism," pp. 227–52 in Reinhard Bendix and Guenther Roth (eds.), *Scholarship and Partisanship* (1971), and Bryan Turner, "Marxism," pp. 3–105 in *For Weber* (1981). For general debates around various aspects of the Marx-Weber relationship, see e.g. Norbert Wiley (ed.), *The Marx-Weber Debate* (1987) and Robert Antonio and Ronald Glassman (eds.), *A Weber-Marx Dialogue* (1985).

For the reactions of Georg Lukács and Herbert Marcuse to Weber's work, see the former's *The Destruction of Reason* (1981) and the latter's "Industrialism and Capitalism in the Work of Max Weber" (1972). The reception of Weber's work among Marxists is otherwise presented and discussed in *Weber and the Marxist World* by Johannes Weiss. Bryan Turner relates Marx to the Frankfurt School and structural Marxism in

Chapters 2 and 3 of *For Weber*.
See also capitalism, class, materialism/idealism, socialism

mass religiosity *See* religion

mass-conditioned behavior (*massenbedingtes Sichverhalten*) This concept, which can be found in Weber's 1913 essay "Some Categories of Interpretive Sociology," is defined as "cases where the behavior of the individual is influenced by the *mere fact* that others participating in the situation also behave in a certain way" (SCIS:167). An example of this type of behavior would be a panic.

While Weber refers to mass behavior in *Economy and Society*, there is no equivalent term to "mass-conditioned behavior."
See also imitation

materialism/idealism Weber was neither a materialist nor an idealist, but rather attempted to go beyond this distinction in various ways. In the famous closing paragraph of *The Protestant Ethic*, for example, Weber states that it has not been his aim in this work "to substitute for a one-sided materialistic an equally one-sided spiritualistic causal interpretation of culture and of history" (PE:183; cf. PED:32, 83 n. 30). He vigorously defended himself against the accusation that his study was idealist (e.g. PED:32, 45). Weber also noted that just as it was possible to study the way that religious ideas influence interests (as in *The Protestant Ethic*), one could look at "the reverse causal relationship" (as in *The Economic Ethics of the World Religions*; cf. e.g. PE:27, PED:83 n. 30).

Talcott Parsons refers to "Weber's general theory of the relations between interests and ideas," and notes that this is particularly well developed in his sociology of religion (ES:211 n. 211). While ideas "define the situation," interests "motivate actors to implement implications of this definition of the situation" (Parsons 1975:668).

For Weber's relationship to the work of materialist Friedrich Albert Lange, see e.g. Björne Jacobsen, "Hiatus Irrationalis—Der Bruch zwischen Sein und Sollen" (2001).

matriarchy *See* women

Max Weber Gesamtausgabe *See* collected works

Max Weber Studies This biannual journal, which has been published since 2000, represents an important souce for analyses of Weber's work.

maxim (*Maxime*) Weber frequently uses the term "maxim" in his sociology, roughly in the sense of a rule—that is, as a statement of how an actor is to behave (*see* rule).

According to Weber's general sociology in Ch. 1 of *Economy and So-*

ciety, the meaning of a social relationship can be expressed in terms of maxims (ES:28, 31). Sometimes Weber uses the expression "maxims of conduct" (e.g. MSS:96, PE:51–2). An individual actor may have certain maxims for his or her behavior (MSS:125).

There can be legal, economic, ethical, and many other kinds of maxims (e.g. ES:866, PE:155, CS:98, 117). A legal maxim expresses how an actor *should* behave, according to the law; legal proverbs are also closely related to legal maxims (ES:775). In *The Protestant Ethic* Weber also cites several maxims from the work of Benjamin Franklin.

See also order, rule

meaning (*Sinn*)   The capacity to attach meaning to something is characteristic of human beings, according to Weber—and consequently also for the cultural sciences (including the social sciences), as opposed to the natural sciences. The concept of meaning is also at the very center of Weber's attempt to develop a new type of sociology in *Economy and Society*. According to the basic idea that underlies his so-called interpretive sociology, the meaning that an actor attaches to his or her action is central to the effort to explain it. To properly understand a meaning, however, typically also means that one has to see it as part of a larger context of meaning—what Weber calls complex of meaning (*Sinnzusammenhang*).

Weber defines sociology and its task in the important first paragraph in Ch. 1 of *Economy and Society*: "sociology . . . is a science concerning itself with the explanatory understanding of social action and thereby with a causal explanation of its course and consequences" (ES:4). Many of the twenty pages of explication that follow this paragraph are devoted to the concept of meaning and represent essential reading for an understanding of this concept (ES:4–24). Sociology, in all brevity, is "a science concerned with the subjective meaning of action" (ES:9).

All cultural sciences or "sciences of human action" (such as economics, history, political science, and sociology) deal with the meaning that human beings attach to their doings, and in this they differ from the natural sciences. This clearly adds to the difficulty of the analysis—but it also opens it up for questions that the natural sciences cannot address (ES:13, 15).

What Weber terms "behavior" becomes "action" (as in "social action") by having a meaning attributed to it by the actor. "Action," however, may also shade off into "behavior," when it is carried out without awareness, as in habitual, traditional, and sometimes affectual behavior. In cases like this, it may be difficult for sociologists to work with the actual meaning, and they may have to resort to what Weber terms "the intended meaning" (ES:9; *see* intention). Weber also addresses the situation when the "real" motive is more or less hidden to the actor (ES:9–10).

Statistical uniformities should only be treated as "actions," according to Weber, if there is an understandable meaning to them ("sociological statistics"; ES:12). If not (as with death rates), they instead fall into the category of actions and objects that are part of the scene where social action takes place. They become "conditions, stimuli, furthering or hindering circumstances of action," as he puts it (ES:13).

To get to the meaning of some behavior the sociologist needs to resort to the method of understanding (*Verstehen*), and this raises a series of problems. What kind of meanings can the sociologist access and how? For discussion of some of these questions, *see* understanding.

When meaning is used in an explanation the researcher has to be careful to present enough evidence, since only meanings that are clear and verifiable should be accepted (ES:5; cf. ES:58 n. 6). In some cases clarity and verifiability (*Evidenz*) may come from rational and logical insight (as in mathematics), in others from empathy (see *Evidenz*).

Meaning can be either empirical in nature (the factual meaning that an actor attributes to his or her behavior) or it can be hypothetical (the imagined meaning that is attributed to the behavior of a hypothetical actor; ES:4). Sociology uses both of these procedures, while economic theory exclusively draws on the latter.

Using the example of a woodcutter, Weber also makes a distinction between the observer's understanding of an action by simply looking at it, and the observer's understanding of the subjective intention that the actor puts into his or her action ("direct observational understanding" versus "explanatory understanding" or *aktuelles Verstehen* versus *erklärendes Verstehen*; ES:8–9). By simply looking at the woodcutter in action, we understand that the ax is brought down on the wood in order to chop it up ("direct observational understanding"). But by knowing the meaning that the woodcutter attaches to that action, however, we also know why the person in question is chopping wood—for exercise, to make a living or whatever the reason may be ("explanatory understanding").

Meaning, as Weber points out in his definition of sociology, is finally also crucial to sociology's task of *explaining social action*. "For a science which is concerned with the subjective meaning of action [as sociology is], explanation requires a grasp of the complex of meaning in which an actual course of understandable action thus interpreted belongs" (ES:9). In a word, Weber argues that if the actor's view of what he or she does is clear (including the complex of meaning), and if the actor adds the requisite action to that intention, the task of explaining the action in question is much facilitated (ES:10–12). It is indeed true that "subjective understanding is the specific characteristic of sociological knowledge"

(ES:15). Still, if you only look at the subjective meaning of the actor, but without reference to the action itself, all you have is a "hypothesis" in need of verification (ES:10).

According to Weber, the sociologist typically also has to go beyond the meaning ascribed by individual actors to understand what is meant by an action, and deal with the general complex of meaning (*Sinnzusammenhang*) that is constituted by such factors as a local context, a religion, a political ideology (ES:8–9).

More generally, sociology is not so much concerned with meanings as constructed by individuals (as history is) but with meanings as constructed by many people—with types of meaning and as a rule also with complexes of meaning.

Especially in his sociology of religion Weber addresses the issue of meaning in the sense of meaning of life. He argues that people have a metaphysical need for meaning, and that especially intellectuals focus on this issue. "The ultimate question of all metaphysics has always been something like this: if the world as a whole and life in particular were to have a meaning, what might it be, and how would the world have to look in order to correspond to it?" (ES:451; *see also* anthropology and philosophy). In modern times, in contrast to the days when religions predominated, the question of meaning has come to include many possible answers or meanings (see also on this point Weber's view of polytheism in e.g. GM:147–53).

For an introduction to Weber's use of the concept of meaning, see e.g. Martin Albrow, *Max Weber's Construction of Social Theory* (1990), pp. 208–18. According to Albrow, Weber dealt with many different aspects of meaning: "1. the actor's intended meaning; 2. meaning to the other person; 3. meaning on average; 4. meaning in terms of a dogmatic system; 5. meaning in ideal-typical terms; 6. meaning as discovered by the social scientist/historian; 7. meaning to self; 8. institutionalized meaning" (ibid., p. 211). Albrow also attempts to address the issue of how Weber viewed structures or systems of meaning, and argues that Weber used several different terms for these (from *Sinnzusammenhang* [*see* complex of meaning] to terms for large-scale systems of meaning such as *Gebilde* and *Struktur*). Arthur Stinchcombe argues that Weber's discussion of meaning has become "archaic": "the discussion of meaning in the beginning of the book [*Economy and Society*], for instance, would be written quite differently [today] by a modern scientist of Weber's quality, incorporating the recent advances in cognitive psychology and linguistics" (Stinchcombe 1986:282). Finally, Alfred Schutz's discussion of Weber's concept of meaning in *The Phenomenology of the Social World* ([1932] 1967), e.g. pp. 3–49, is in a class by itself (for a summary of Schutz on Weber, see e.g. Helmut Wagner, *Alfred Schutz: An Intellectual Biography* [1983], pp. 13–16, 122–25).

For the concept of meaning in Weber's early general sociology, see "Some Categories of Interpretive Action" (e.g. SCIS:151–53, 158, 179).

See also causality, comparative sociology, complex of meaning, *Evidenz*, explanation, intention, interpretive sociology, objectively correct rationality, social action, sociology, symbolism, traditional action, understanding; valuation, value-orientation and similar terms, values

meaning-context, meaning complex (*Sinnzusammenhang*)   *See* complex of meaning, meaning

means of administration (*Verwaltungsmittel*)   Weber, following Marx, emphasized the importance in capitalism of the workers being separated from the means of production. To this he added several other types of separation of persons from means—such as the separation of officials from the means of administration and the separation of soldiers from the means of war (e.g. GM:81–2, ES:218–19, 980–83). It is absolutely essential, for example, that there be a separation in modern bureaucracy between the official and the means of administration such as money and buildings.

"All states may be classified according to whether they rest on the principle that the staff of men themselves *own* the administrative means, or whether the staff is 'separated' from these means of administration" (GM:81). In feudalism, for example, the vassal pays for the administration of the area enfeoffed to him, something that deeply affects his relationship to the lord. When the administrative means are partly or totally controlled by the staff, political associations come into being that Weber calls "associations organized in 'estates'" (GM:81). The modern state has its beginning in the process whereby the prince started to take over the administration from various independent powers. "In the end, the modern state controls the total means of political organization, which actually come together under a single head" (GM:82).

See also administration, bureaucracy, means of production, means of war, organization or association

means of production (*Beschaffungsmittel, Produktionsmittel, Betriebsmittel*)   Weber speaks not only of the means of production but also of the means of administration, the means of war, and the like (GM:81–2, ES:980–83; for Weber's concept of production, see e.g. ES:71). The reasons that Weber gives for the expropriation of the workers from the means of production differ somewhat from those that can be found in the section on primitive accumulation in Marx's *Capital*. Weber, for example, mentions technical reasons—not just social; neither did he see the origin of modern capitalism as some early brutal act such as enclosures (ES:137–40).

See also expropriation, means of administration, means of war, workers

means of war (*Kriegsmittel*)   It is essential for modern rational capitalism that there exist a separation of the workers from the ownership of the means of production. A similar separation also exists in the administration of the modern state, including of soldiers from the means of war (e.g. GM:81, ES:980–82).

There are many examples in history where warriors themselves have owned their weapons and also provided for their own provision in war, such as the militias in the early medieval cities and the members of feudal hosts. For various social, political, and technical reasons, however, this type of self-equipment and self-provisioning in war has been replaced in the modern state by the bureaucratic army. "Only the bureaucratic army structure allows for the development of the professional standing armies which are necessary for the constant pacification of large territories as well as for warfare against distant enemies, especially enemies overseas" (ES:981). For patrimonial and other types of armies, see e.g. ES:1015–20, 1077–78. For the role of discipline in warfare, see ES:1150–55.

According to Talcott Parsons, "Weber was greatly interested in [military organization] to which he attributed great importance for social phenomena generally" (Weber 1947:336 n. 20). Weber planned to treat this topic systematically, Parsons adds, but never did.

See also means of administration, means of production

Meinen   *See* intention

Meitzen, August (1822–1910)   Agrarian historian and statistician who was the thesis adviser for Weber's *Habilitation* (Weber [1891] 1986). See e.g. August Skalweit, "Meitzen, August (1822–1910)" (1933).

Menger, Carl   *See* Battle of the Methods, economic theory

Menschentum, Menschentyp   *See* human beings, type of human beings

mentality (*Gesinnung*)   Weber uses the term *Gesinnung* in several different meanings, including ethos, spirit, mentality and intention (e.g. ES:325, 528, 1200–1201, RC:236–37).

Jean-Pierre Grossein, who translates *Gesinnung* into French as "disposition," argues that *Gesinnung* is closely related to such concepts as ethos (*Ethos*), spirit (*Geist*) and habitus in Weber's work ("Présentation" [1996], pp. 61 n. 1, 120).

He also points out that Weber draws on the notion of *Gesinnung* in his concept of ethics of ultimate ends (*Gesinnungsethik*). Keith Tribe describes the meaning of *Gesinnung* in Weber's work as follows: "an inner disposition, perhaps also a sentiment, a conscience, an ethos, an inner conviction; but in any case something which was cultivated in someone, and which as Hennis demonstrates [in *Max Weber's Science of Man* (2000)] was closely related to Weber's abiding interest in educational forms, both formal and informal" (Tribe 2000:210–11).

See also ethos, habitus, lifestyle, spirit of capitalism

mercantilism   *See* state

metaphysics   *See* philosophy

Methodenstreit   *See* Battle of the Methods

methodical   *See* asceticism, discipline

methodological individualism   It is clear that Weber is a methodological individualist in his formal statements about his sociology. A society or a group does not have an independent existence, according to Weber, only individuals do. According to the important paragraph 1 in Ch. 1 of *Economy and Society*, the basic unit of analysis in sociology is the individual, who orients his or her action to the behavior of others.

The "atom" of sociology, to cite an early text on general sociology by Weber, is "the individual and his action" (SCIS:158). "[Individuals] alone can be treated as agents in a course of subjective understandable action," he adds later in *Economy and Society* (ES:13; cf. his argument that sociology "must . . . adopt strictly individualistic methods" in a letter to Robert Liefmann dated March 9, 1920; cf. Mommsen 1965:44).

Sociology does not in principle use "collective concepts" as actors, Weber also notes, but can make use of this type of concepts for terminological reasons. While people may believe that states, organizations, and other collective actors do indeed exist and do indeed act, "for sociological purposes there is no such thing as a collective personality which acts" (ES:14).

Weber's version of methodological individualism differs from the one that is used in economic theory, which treats the individual as isolated from other actors. In Weber's sociology the actor is typically oriented to other actors, and some of these are also oriented to that actor—a type of methodological individualism not unlike the one used in game theory. There is also the fact that in his actual analyses, as opposed to his general statements about sociological methodology, Weber appears to treat social structures and groups as if they had an independent existence (see e.g. Bryan Turner, *For Weber* [1981], pp. 3–28—and for a counterargument e.g. Lawrence Scaff, "Weber before Weberian Sociology," pp. 15–41 in Keith Tribe, ed., *Reading Weber* [1989]).

Being in favor of methodological individualism, Weber stresses, does not mean being in favor of individualistic values (ES:18). Neither does it mean that the individual is an isolated atom; or, as Stephen Kalberg puts it, "Max Weber's methodological individualism implies that acting individuals and their 'action-orientations' are central" (Kalberg 1994a:579 n. 4). For a discussion of Weber's version of methodological individualism within the context of the history of that approach, see Lars Udehn, *Methodological Individualism* (2001).

See also functionalism, holism, individual and individualism, rational choice

methodology   By Weber's methodology is usually meant both his general sociological methodology (which can mainly be found in Ch. 1 of *Economy and Society*) and his more philosophical-methodological writings on the social sciences in general (what is usually referred to as his *Wissenschaftslehre*). To this may be added the actual methods that Weber used or advocated for data collection.

Weber's views on the general methodology of sociology, as expressed in Ch. 1 of *Economy and Society*, are formally part of his *Wissenschaftslehre*, so that the first section from this chapter has been included in *Gesammelte Aufsätze zur Wissenschaftslehre* (ES:3–38; see *Wissenschaftslehre*). For various reasons, however, one may want to distinguish Weber's views on the general methodology of sociology, in a stricter sense, from what he wrote on the methodology of the social sciences in general.

Weber's general sociological methodology is mainly to be found in the part of Ch. 1 of *Economy and Society* entitled "Methodological Foundations" (ES:4–22; cf. SCIS). It may be summarized as follows. Sociology studies primarily types of social actions, and in doing so it centers the analysis around the meaning that actors attach to their behavior and the context of meaning within which these actions take place. Causality involves a consideration of different courses of action on the sociologist's part, including comparisons with other actions that are objectively possible. It also demands that there has to be a certain correspondence between intended meaning and actual action. For more information on these aspects of Weber's sociological methodology, *see* causality, complex of meaning, *Evidenz*, meaning, social action, types.

Weber's writings on social science methodology in general are primarily to be found in a series of essays, some of which are known in English as *The Methodology of the Social Sciences* (MSS). This volume includes an essay on objectivity (1904), one on the cultural sciences (1906), and one on value-freedom (1917). The German original, *Gesammelte Aufsätze zur Wissenschaftslehre* (*Collected Essays in the Philosophy of Science*—GAW), contains several more essays, including "Roscher and Knies," "Critique of Stammler," and "Some Categories of Interpretive Sociology" (RK, CS, SCIS).

In these essays Weber discusses such topics as causality, the cultural sciences versus the natural sciences, the nature of history and economics, the role of probability, the ideal type, value-freedom, value-relevance, and the historical individual. For more information on these issues, *see* the entries for each of these topics.

In a letter of March 29, 1910 to Paul Siebeck, Weber wrote that "methodology is 'science about science'" (SCIS:145). He also notes in one of his methodological essays that one does not have to be an expert in methodology to be good at research. "Methodology . . . is no more the precondition of fruitful intellectual work than the knowledge of anatomy is the precondition for 'correct' walking" (MSS:115). Weber adds that being too much of an expert on methodology may well hinder the analysis (MSS:115). "Only by laying bare and solving substantive problems can sciences be established and their methods developed" (ibid.).

Some months before his death in 1920 Weber planned to put together his methodological essays in a separate volume. The essays he picked differed somewhat from those that Marianne Weber published in 1922 as *Gesammelte Aufsätze zur Wissenschaftslehre*.

Weber carried out a few surveys early on in his career but as his interests broadened to world-religions and universal history he increasingly had to rely on secondary sources. He nonetheless stated when he was in his fifties that "no sociologist . . . should think himself too good, even in his old age, to make tens of thousands of quite trivial computations in his head and perhaps for months at a time" (GM:135). For Weber's use of quantitative empirical data in his sociological analyses, see e.g. Paul Lazarsfeld and Anthony Oberschall, "Max Weber and Empirical Research" (1965) and Anthony Oberschall, *Empirical Social Research in Germany 1848–1914* (1965).

Weber himself, it should be emphasized, saw his methodological ideas as being at the very heart of his enterprise as a social scientist—something which has often been ignored. As an example of this, one can mention Reinhard Bendix's well-known study *Max Weber: An Intellectual Portrait* (1960), in which the author states that in his account of Weber's work he will ignore Weber's writings on methodology (ibid., p. xxiii).

For a brief introduction to Weber's essays in the philosophy of science, see e.g. Raymond Aron, "Max Weber" (1970), pp. 219–65, Dirk Käsler,

Max Weber (1988), pp. 174–96, and Talcott Parsons, *The Structure of Social Action* (1937), pp. 579–639. For fuller treatments, see e.g. Ola Agevall, *A Science of Unique Events: Max Weber's Methodology of the Cultural Sciences* (1999), H. H. Bruun, *Science, Values and Politics in Max Weber's Methodology* 1972, Sven Eliaeson, *Max Weber's Methodologies* (2002), Dieter Henrich, *Die Einheit der Wissenschaftslehre Max Webers* (1952), Alexander von Schelting, *Max Webers Wissenschaftslehre* (1934), and Gerhard Wagner and Heinz Zipprian (eds.), *Max Webers Wissenschaftslehre* (1994). The *Wissenschaftslehre* will appear as Vols. I/7 and I/12 in MWG.

Much more attention has been devoted to Weber's general methodology than to his sociological methodology, as this is to be found in Ch. 1 of *Economy and Society* and in his 1913 essay "Some Categories of Interpretive Sociology." It has also been suggested that Weber's ideas on sociological methodology differ from the methodology that is implicit in his sociological studies. For this argument, as well as the counter-argument that this is not the case, see e.g. Lawrence Scaff, "Weber before Weberian Sociology" (1989).

See also *Wissenschaftslehre*

Methodology of the Social Sciences, The   This work by Weber, which appeared in 1949, contains three of his methodological essays, translated and edited by Edward Shils and Henry Finch: "The Meaning of Ethical 'Neutrality' in Sociology and Economics," "'Objectivity' in Social Science and Social Policy," and "Critical Studies in the Logic of the Cultural Sciences." The translations are considered problematic.

See also *Gesammelte Aufsätze zur Wissenschaftslehre*, methodology, *Wissenschaftslehre*

Meyer, Eduard (1885–1930)   Historian who figures at the center of Weber's important essay "Critical Studies in the Logic of the Cultural Sciences" (MSS:113–88). See e.g. Friedrich Tenbruck, "Max Weber and Eduard Meyer" (1987).

Michels, Robert (1876–1936)   German-Italian political scientist and sociologist as well as a friend of Max Weber. See e.g. Wolfgang Mommsen, "Robert Michels and Weber: Moral Conviction versus the Politics of Responsibility" (1987).

monasticism   *See* asceticism

money (*Geld*)   Money is primarily discussed by Weber in his economic sociology. The role that the state plays in monetary matters and in the existence of money more generally is strongly emphasized. The evolution of money is mainly discussed in Weber's lectures on social and economic history (see especially GEH:236–53).

The following definition of money can be found in Ch. 2 on economic sociology in *Economy and Society*: "'money' we call a chartal means of payment which is also a means of exchange" (ES:76). The term "chartal" means that an authority has validated the material, which is used for money, by marking it. Or, as Weber describes "chartal money" at one point: i.e., "money that derives its character as means of payment from the marking of pieces rather than from their substantive content" (ES:336).

Weber states in his economic sociology that he will not develop a theory of money, but only look at the sociological consequences of its use. The most important of these is the way that money is used as a tool for economic calculation. "Money," according to Weber, "is the most abstract and 'impersonal' element that exists in human life" (GM:331). It is, however, neither neutral nor innocent, but a "weapon" in the "struggle of man against man" (ES:108). This last statement should not to be seen as a refutation of conventional monetary theory, but rather as an argument that when actual money prices are to be determined, interest and power struggles have to be taken into account.

Ch. 2 of *Economy and Society* contains a very long (and today partly outmoded) discussion of monetary policy that is deeply influenced by G. F. Knapp's *The State Theory of Money* (1905).

Little attention to Weber's ideas on money has been paid in the secondary literature. For one attempt at improving the situation, see Richard Swedberg, *Max Weber and the Idea of Economic Sociology* (1998), pp. 76–77.

See also lytric policy

monocracy (*Monokratie*) Monocracy means undivided rule by a single person. In a monocratic organization, for example, the chief holds supreme power and does not need to share it, as in a collegial situation (e.g. ES:220–26).

See also collegiality

monotheism/polytheism Weber charts the evolution from polytheism to monotheism in his sociology of religion in *Economy and Society* (e.g. ES:415–20). While Judaism and Islam are strictly monotheistic, Hinduism and Christianity conceal that they are not strictly monotheistic.

Weber was personally attracted to the position of polytheism, and his passages on this topic are of much importance for an understanding of his personal philosophy of life (e.g. GM:147–53, PW:78–9, Marianne Weber, *Max Weber* [(1926) 1975], p. 678).

For monotheism, see e.g. Stephen Kalberg, "Max Weber's Analysis of the Rise of Monotheism" (1994); and for polytheism, Wolfgang Schluchter, "The Battle of the Gods," pp. 265–78 in *Rationalism, Religion, and Domination* (1989) and Burkhard Gladigow, "Polytheismus" (2001).

See also value-spheres

motivation   *See* motive, economic motivation

motive (*Motiv*)   Weber's view of the role of motive in sociology follows closely from his theory of understanding. A motive is essentially what the actor himself or herself sees as the reason for his or her behavior (or, more precisely, as the observer perceives this). To this should be added that what actors want to accomplish with their acts and what actually happens are in many cases two very different things, as e.g. *The Protestant Ethic* reminds us. A motive is defined in Weber's general sociology in Ch. 1 of *Economy and Society* as "a complex of subjective meaning which seems to the actor himself or to the observer an adequate ground for the conduct in question" (ES:11).

When the sociologist attempts to establish an actor's motive, it also becomes important to establish the meaning that a person attaches to his or her behavior as well as the complex of meaning of which this meaning may be part (*Sinnzusammenhang*). For a discussion of issues related to motives, *see also* meaning, causality, explanation.

While there no doubt exists a link between Weber's notion of motive and his concept of interest, it is by no means obvious how this link is to be understood. According to Talcott Parsons, who explicitly addresses this issue, "action defining the situation . . . does not by itself motivate actors to attempt to implement implications of this definition of the situation"; and this is where interest comes into the picture (Parsons 1975:668). Parsons adds that when it comes to analyzing the link between motive and interest, *The Protestant Ethic* provides "an almost paradigmatic example of the necessary kind of analysis" (ibid.). Finally, Alfred Schutz marshals a number of severe criticisms of Weber's concept of motive in *The Phenomenology of the Social World* (Schutz [1932] 1967:86–91).

See also explanation, causality, intention, interest, psychology, unintended consequences.

music   *See* sociology of music

Musiksoziologie   *See* sociology of music

mutual responsibility (*Solidarität, Solidaritätsbeziehungen*) Weber draws on this concept in his general sociology and also refers to mutual responsibility elsewhere in his work.

In Weber's general sociology in Ch. 1 of *Economy and Society* the following definition can be found: "within a social relationship . . . certain kinds of action of *each* participant may be imputed to *all* others, in which case we speak of 'mutually responsible members'" (ES:46). One example of mutual responsibility is blood revenge. People may also be in a relationship of mutual responsibility to a god, as exemplified by the covenant of Israel with Yahweh. A mutual responsibility may be passive (something is imputed to you, which you have to endure) or active (you have to do something because of imputation).

In his discussion of the evolution of the modern firm, Weber often notes that an important step was taken when the actions of a firm became binding on its members (e.g. GEH:227). In his historical sociology Weber discusses mutual responsibility in connection with the financing of the patrimonial state (e.g. ES:1022–25).

The concept of mutual responsibility has not been much used by Weber's followers.

mystagogue (*Mystagoge*) The mystagogue is discussed in Weber's sociology of religion in *Economy and Society*; but he is much less central than the prophet, the priest and the magician. A mystagogue is primarily characterized by the fact that "he performs sacraments, i.e. magical actions that contain the boons of salvation" (ES:446–47). Dynasties of mystagogues have existed in history, and this represents an example of hereditary "sacramental charisma." As opposed to prophets, mystagogues have made a living through their practices.

Talcott Parsons describes Weber's concept of the mystagogue as "a concept apparently thought of as the religious counterpart of the demagogue" (Parsons 1963:xxxv). See also e.g. Volkhard Krech, "Mystik" (2001).

See also demagogue, mysticism

mystic *See* mysticism

mysticism (*Mystik*) Weber devotes much attention in his sociology of religion to mysticism and asceticism as contrasting ways of reaching salvation (e.g. GM:324–26, ES:541–56). While the mystic sees himself or herself as *a vessel* for the will of God, the ascetic sees himself or herself as *an instrument*. Through contemplation and similar means the mystic aims at achieving union with the divine. The insights of the mystic may be hard to communicate and they may therefore, from the viewpoint of the sociologist, border on knowledge devoid of meaning.

Weber notes that while asceticism means rejection of the world, mysticism means flight from the world (ES:544–45). Just as asceticism can be inner-worldly and other-worldly, so can mysticism. Other-worldly mysticism focuses squarely on non-action, while inner-worldly mysticism is less radical in this respect and therefore not only accessible to a minority.

For a discussion of mysticism, see e.g. Christopher Adair-Toteff, "Max Weber's Mysticism" (2002). For the view of mysticism among Weber's contemporaries, as well as the evolution of Weber's view, see Volkhard Krech, "Mystik" (2001).

See also ascetic Protestantism, asceticism, magician, mystagogue, priest, prophet

N*ahrungsspielraum* (scope of economic resources in relation to consumption needs)   *See* open and closed social relationships

nation (*Nation***)**   While Weber does not single out the concept of nation in his general sociology in Ch. 1 of *Economy and Society*, he devotes considerable space to it elsewhere in this work (e.g. ES:395–98, 921–26; cf. GASS:484–88).

The closest to a definition of "nation" that one can find in Weber's work may well be the following description in *Economy and Society*: "the concept of 'nation' . . . means, above all, that it is proper to expect from certain groups a specific sentiment of solidarity in face of other groups" (ES:922). "Thus, the concept belongs in the sphere of values" (ibid.).

According to Weber, the nation represents "one of the most vexing and emotionally charged concepts" (ES:395). In sociological terms, a national community is held together by a sense of belonging together, and thereby represents a communal relationship in Weber's terminology (ES:41). What creates this sense of belonging together may differ. It can be a language in common, a religion in common or notions of common descent (ES:922–23).

A nation is what Weber calls a political community and is also closely related to "'prestige' interests" (ES:925). These interests may take different forms. They may, for example, mean that a nation has a mission or that it is superior by virtue of its cultural values.

Weber sums up his analysis of the concept of the nation as follows: "the reasons for the belief that one represents a nation vary greatly, just as does the empirical conduct that actually results from affiliation or lack of it with a nation" (ES:924).

See in this context e.g. David Beetham, *Max Weber and the Theory of Modern Politics* (1985), pp. 119–50, Wolfgang Mommsen, "The Concept of Nation in Weber's Thought," pp. 48–60 in *Max Weber and German Politics 1890–1920* (1984), and Kari Palonen, "Was Max Weber a 'Nationalist'? A Study in the Rhetoric of Conceptual Change" (2001).

That Weber himself was a strong nationalist has often been noted; and the reader is again referred to Mommsen's *Max Weber and German Politics 1890–1920* (for a summary statement on Weber's nationalism, see pp. 63–7). More recently, Weber's cosmopolitanism has also been noted (e.g. Guenther Roth, "Between Cosmopolitanism and Ethnocentrism: Max Weber in the Nineties." [1993] and *Max Webers deutsch-englische Familiengeschichte 1800–1950* [2001]).

See also ethnic groups, political sociology, politics, power prestige, race

natural law   *See* rights

natural rights   *See* rights

natural sciences (Naturwissenschaften)   The natural sciences differ from the social sciences, according to Weber, in two very important ways: (1) they aim at formulating general and abstract laws; and (2) they make their observations from the outside, and are not concerned with the understanding of the objects that they study (ES:7, 15).

Weber's view of the very different nature of the natural and the social sciences was influenced by the discussion of this topic in Germany in his time. He was very familiar, for example, with philosopher Wilhelm Windelband's argument that the natural sciences deal with knowledge that can be formulated in the form of laws, while the social sciences only deal with what is individual and unique ("nomothetic sciences" vs. "ideographic sciences"). He also knew philosopher Wilhelm Dilthey's similar distinction between the natural sciences and the sciences which study inner experiences (*Naturwissenschaften* versus *Geisteswissenschaften*). Weber's own suggestions for how to deal with the difference between the natural and the social sciences differed, however, from the ideas of Windelband as well as Dilthey. Drawing primarily on the work on values of philosopher Heinrich Rickert and on the work on causality by physiologist and probability thinker Johannes von Kries, Weber fashioned his own distinct version of what constitutes a systematic and scientific social science.

Weber's views on the various points on which the natural and the social sciences differ can best be studied in his methodological essays (see especially MSS, CS, RK, SCIS). Since these are often difficult to penetrate (especially in translation), assistance from the secondary literature may be helpful. See e.g. Ola Agevall, *A Science of Unique Events: Max Weber's Methodology of the Cultural Sciences* (1999), Don Martindale, *The Nature and Types of Sociological Theory* (1960), pp. 377–83, and Talcott Parsons, *The Structure of Social Action* (1937), pp. 591–601.

See also causality, cultural sciences, economics, history, laws in the social sciences, natural sciences, psychology, social sciences, sociology

nature   *See* anthropology (for human nature), geography

Naumann, Friedrich (1860–1919)   Protestant theologian and religious activist and politician, who had friendly relations with Max Weber. See e.g. Peter Theiner, "Friedrich Naumann and Max Weber" (1987).

negatively privileged   *See* privileges

neighborhood (*Nachbarschaftsgemeinschaft*)   While this concept cannot be found in Weber's general sociology in Ch. 1 of *Economy and Society*, it plays an important role in his earlier drafts for *Economy and Society*.

A neighborhood is a universal type of group consisting of households that are situated next to each other and which tend to help each other in times of distress (ES:356, 360–63). This mutual aid follows the principle "do unto others as you would have them do unto you" (ES:361). A neighborhood constitutes a natural foundation for a local community (which consists of several neighborhoods—ES:363).

See also community

neo-Kantianism   This term is often used to describe a number of philosophical movements that emerged in Germany during the second half of the nineteenth century, inspired by the work of Immanuel Kant, and which came to an end with World War I. One of the key questions that these movements discussed had to do with the nature of scientific knowledge and methodology in the social versus the natural sciences; the role of culture was also at the center of neo-Kantianism. Weber drew heavily on neo-Kantianism to construct a social science that differed from the natural sciences. In doing so, he especially relied on the work of Heinrich Rickert.

The various schools of neo-Kantianism are mostly named after their geographical locations. The one that influenced Weber the most was the Baden or Southwestern School. The two key figures here are Wilhelm Windelband and Heinrich Rickert. Windelband (1848–1915) introduced the distinction between ideographic and nomothetic sciences, that is, sciences which try to describe and explain single events versus sciences which try to establish general laws. Heinrich Rickert (1863–1936), who was a disciple of Windelband, emphasized the infinite richness of reality, and the way in which scientists choose their topics because of their values (so-called value-relevance). Weber was inspired by many of Rickert's ideas—but, as usual, he added to them and changed them to suit his own thinking. It should finally also be noted that Weber was not 100 percent neo-Kantian, and that it is not known how much he knew of Kant's work.

For neo-Kantianism, see e.g. Guy Oakes, "Max Weber and the Southwest German School: The Genesis of the Historical Individual" (1987), Hans-Ludwig Ollig, "Neo-Kantianism" (1998), and Thomas Willey, *Back to Kant: The Revival of Kantianism in German Social and Historical Thought, 1860–1914* (1978). See also Heinrich Rickert, *The Limits of Concept Formation in Natural Science: A Logical Introduction to the Historical Sciences* ([1902] 1986) and Guy Oakes, *Weber and Rickert: Concept Formation in the Cultural Sciences* (1988).

See also interpretive sociology, philosophy; Rickert, Heinrich; value-freedom, value-relevance

neo-Weberianism This label is usually attached to a series of works in sociology—mainly in the Anglo-Saxon countries—that since the late 1970s have attempted to renew various fields of study with the help of Weber's ideas in an independent and undogmatic fashion. Some inspiration for a project such as neo-Weberianism may have come from neo-Marxism, and some neo-Weberians were once neo-Marxists.

Especially three areas have been at the center of neo-Weberian sociology: stratification, historical sociology and the sociology of the state. To this may be added organization theory—as well as a number of other topics such as education, religion, and health. Neo-Weberian approaches can also be found in anthropology and political science.

Two of the most important neo-Weberian studies are *Weberian Sociological Theory* (1986) by Randall Collins and *Marxism and Class Theory: A Bourgeois Critique* (1979) by Frank Parkin. Other influential contemporary sociologists whose work is often called neo-Weberian include Anthony Giddens, Michael Mann, and Theda Skocpol.

For a discussion of neo-Weberianism, see e.g. Stephen Sanderson, "The Neo-Weberian Revolution: A Theoretical Balance Sheet" (1988).

See also e.g. Jeff Manza, "Classes, Status Groups, and Social Closure: A Critique of Neo-Weberian Social Theory" (1992), Charles Perrow, "The Neo-Weberian Model," pp. 119–56 in *Complex Organizations* (1986), and Bryan Turner, "Max Weber's Historical Sociology: A Bibliographical Essay," pp. 22–37 in *Max Weber* (1992).

See also reception of Weber's work, secondary literature on Weber's work, Weber-inspired scholars and scholarship, Weber's work, Weberianism

Nietzsche, Friedrich   It is clear that Friedrich Nietzsche (1844–1900) influenced Weber, not least through *The Genealogy of Morals* and the concept of resentment (e.g. GM:270–71, 276–77). Weber is reported to have said: "The honesty of a present-day scholar, and above all a present-day philosopher, can be measured by his attitude to Nietzsche and Marx. Whoever does not admit that considerable parts of his own work could not have been carried out in the absence of the work of these two, only fools himself and others. The world in which we spiritually and intellectually live today is a world substantially shaped by Marx and Nietzsche." (Hennis 1988:146, Baumgarten 1964:554–55).

For Weber's relationship to Nietzsche's work, see e.g. Ralph Schroeder, "Nietzsche and Weber: Two 'Prophets' of the Modern World" (1987), Wilhelm Hennis, "The Traces of Nietzsche in the Work of Max Weber," pp. 146–62 in *Max Weber: Essays in Reconstruction* (1988), and Klaus Lichtblau, "Ressentiment, negative Priviligierung, Parias" (2001).

nomothetic sciences   *See* natural sciences, neo-Kantianism, value-freedom

norm (*Norm*)   Weber occasionally uses the term "norm" in his sociological writings. At one point in his sociology of law, for example, he notes that legal propositions, "as in the case of all norms," can be divided into "prescriptive, prohibitory, and permissive ones" (ES:667).

Weber's preferred term in his general sociology in Ch. 1 of *Economy and Society*, however, is not "norm" but *convention (Konvention)*. While the meaning of convention is more or less synonymous with the meaning of norm in contemporary sociology, in Weber's sociology it differs in that it is integrated (through the concept of "order" or *Ordnung*) with a series of other concepts, especially that of law.

See also convention, law, legal norm, organization

notables (*Honoratioren*, Lat. *honoratiores*)   Notables are persons whose economic situation is such that they can devote their full time to public matters and whose social standing is also such that people trust them. In some situations political power will tend to accumulate in the hands of the notables, especially if other people cannot afford to be involved in politics (e.g. ES:289–92, 948–52, 1009).

The following definition of notables can be found in Weber's sociology of domination in *Economy and Society*: "notables (*Honoratioren*) are persons (1) whose economic position permits them to hold continuous policy-making and administrative positions in an organization without (more than nominal) remuneration; (2) who enjoy social prestige of whatever derivation in such a manner that they are likely to hold office by virtue of the member's confidence, which at first is freely given and traditionally accorded" (ES:290; cf. ES:950).

Notables are in such a position that they can "live *for* politics, without living *from* politics" (ES:290). In this they differ, for example, from industrial workers and industrial entrepreneurs. Rule by notables, like direct democracy, is best suited to communities of a few thousand members. For administration by notables in England, see ES:1059–64.

According to Talcott Parsons, "there is no good English equivalent" for the term *Honoratioren*. Parsons' own definition reads as follows: "persons performing functions and exercising authority who do not depend on the position as a major source of income and generally enjoy an independent status in the social structure" (ibid.). In his comment on Weber's sociology of law Max Rheinstein notes that "in German the word *Honoratioren* is used, often with a slight implication of friendly ridicule, to mean the more respectable citizens of a town" (ES:664 n. 18).

See also legal *Honoratioren*, living for politics versus living off politics

O bedience (*Gehorsam*)   Weber defines obedience in the following manner in his sociology of domination in Ch. 3 of *Economy and Society*: "'obedience' will be taken to mean that the action of the person obeying follows in essentials such a course that the content of the command may be taken to have become the basis of action for its own sake" (ES:215). Weber adds that "furthermore, the fact that it is so taken is referable only to the formal obligation, without regard to the actor's own attitude to the value or lack of value of the content of the command as such" (ibid.).

See also discipline, domination, legitimacy

objektive Möglichkeit   *See* objective possibility

objective possibility (*objektive Möglichkeit*)   Even though history has a certain outcome, it makes sense under certain circumstances—and for methodological reasons—to assume that the outcome of some event could have been different; and this type of assumption plays an important role in understanding the causality involved, according to Weber. The term "counterfactual," as it is used today, is in many respects close to what Weber meant by objective possibility.

Weber's main discussion of objective possibility can be found in his methodological essays, especially in the second half of "Critical Studies in the Logic of the Cultural Sciences" (1906) which is entitled "Objective Possibility and Adequate Causation in Historical Explanation" (MSS: 164–88). Drawing on an example from Greek history taken from Eduard Meyer's work, Weber argues that the significance of the victory of the Greeks in the Battle of Marathon can only be properly understood if this outcome is contrasted to what would have happened if the Greeks had lost this battle or if there had not been any battle in the first place. If the Greeks had not won this battle (or if it had not taken place), one can assume that the Persians would have behaved as they used to do when they conquered a new territory. In this particular case, Greek culture would have become subordinate to Persian culture, and the course of Western history would have been different. By focusing on a single factor in this manner, Weber concludes, it is possible to better address the question of causality.

Weber also introduces the element of probability in his discussion of objective possibility, arguing that it is possible to calculate the degree to which something is objectively possible, even if it is not possible to supply an absolute number (MSS:183; the so-called loaded dice argument).

In Weber's general sociology in Ch. 1 of *Economy and Society* one can find a different approach to the issues raised through the concept of objective possibility. In order to explain social action, Weber here argues, it makes sense to start out from the assumption that an action is rational (ES:9–11). This way, for example, one can conceptualize what actually happened as deviations from a rational course of action. More generally, comparisons are needed to verify the impact of an action (ES:10). Again, in other words, Weber constructs alternative (and imaginary) routes of action, in order to better explain what actually happened.

According to Talcott Parsons, "the concept of 'objective possibility' (*objektive Möglichkeit*) plays an important technical role in Weber's methodological studies [and] according to his usage, a thing is 'objectively possible' if it 'makes sense' to conceive it as an empirically existing entity" (ES:61 n. 28). Parsons emphasizes that "the question whether a phenomenon which is in this sense 'objectively possible' will actually be found with any significant degree of probability or approximation, is a logically distinct question." According to Fritz Ringer, "Weber literally refers to objective 'possibility' in German; but 'probability' nevertheless seems the better translation" (Ringer 1997:67 n. 6).

For general discussions of the concept of objective possibility, see e.g. Fritz Ringer, *Max Weber's Methodology* (1997), pp. 63–73, Alexander von Schelting, *Max Webers Wissenschaftslehre* (1934), pp. 312–20, and Stephen Turner and Regis Factor, "Objective Possibility and Adequate Causation in Weber's Methodological Writings" (1981).

See also causality, comparative sociology, loaded dice argument, probability

objectively correct rationality (*Richtigkeitsrationalität*)   This term plays an important role in Weber's essay "Some Categories of Interpretive Sociology" (1913), which contains an early version of parts of Weber's general sociology in Ch. 1 of *Economy and Society*. Weber introduces the notion of objectively correct rationality in his presentation of his theory of causality (SCIS:154–57). Adequate causality demands in principle a correspondence between "expectations based on valid experience" (or objectively correct rationality) and what has been subjectively intended.

This correspondence, however, does not always exist, as the example of magic reminds us. While the use of magic may be subjectively rational and seem instrumental enough, it fails on the criterion of objectively correct rationality (SCIS:154–55). While the idea of objectively correct rationality is present in *Economy and Society*, the term is not.

See also causality

objectivity (*Objektivität*)   Weber attempted to develop a theory of objectivity that answers to the demands of cultural sciences (including the social sciences) and which consequently differs from the way that objectivity is perceived in the natural sciences. There are two parts to his argument: social scientists must realize (1) that science cannot be used to arbitrate between different values (value-freedom; *Wertfreiheit*), and (2) that their objects of study are intimately connected to the basic values of the society in which they live (value-relevance; *Wertbeziehung*). What is seen as important and relevant to study depends, in a word, on values.

Weber summarizes the first part of his doctrine of objectivity as follows: "an empirical science cannot tell anyone what he *should* do—but rather what he *can* do—and under certain circumstances—what he wishes to do" (MSS:54). In order to do this, it may be added, social scientists must also repress their personal values. The student who wants a sermon, Weber refers to a religious meeting; and the one who wants a vision, to the cinema (PE:29).

The second part of Weber's doctrine of objectivity is often forgotten, and it is sometimes argued that Weber has a superficial approach to ob-

jectivity and ignores the fact that any choice of study is infused with values. Through his concept of value-relevance, however, this is exactly the
kind of issue that Weber addresses. Every part of reality that seems deeply
meaningful to us, he argues, is deeply meaningful precisely because of its
relationship to values. The researcher, Weber says, has a cognitive or scientific interest in certain topics, and this is directly related to values. Another set of values that are involved in value-relevance are those that are
connected to science itself, such as truth.

In his inaugural speech in Freiburg Weber said of himself, "I am a
member of the bourgeois (*bürgerlich*) classes. I feel myself to be a bourgeois, and I have been brought up to share their views and ideals"
(PW:23; cf. Mommsen 1984:96 n. 26, 127). To this he added, "yet, it is
precisely the vocation of our science to say things people do not like to
hear . . . " (ibid.).

Weber discusses his ideas on objectivity primarily in "The Meaning of
'Ethical Neutrality' in Sociology and Economics" and also in "'Objectivity' in Social Science and Social Policy" and "Science as a Vocation"
(MSS:1–47, 49–112, GM:129–56; cf. Weber [1913] 1996 and the new
translation of the 1904 essay on objectivity by Keith Tribe in EW:359–
404).

Robert Merton succinctly summarizes Weber's concept of *Wertbeziehung* as "the fact that scientists commonly select for treatment problems, which are vitally linked with the dominant values and interests of
the day" (Merton [1938] 1970:54). Merton also notes that *Wertbeziehung* "suggests that differing social locations, with their distinctive
interests and values, will affect the selection of problems for investigation" (Merton 1996:248).

For Weber's ideas on objectivity, see especially Talcott Parsons,
"Value-freedom and Objectivity" (1971) as well as the discussion of this
essay in Otto Stammer (ed.), *Max Weber and Sociology Today* (1971),
pp. 27–82. See also H. H. Bruun, *Science, Values and Politics in Max Weber's Methodology* (1972), Alvin Gouldner, "Anti-Minotaur: The Myth
of Value-Free Sociology" (1962), and Fritz Ringer, *Max Weber's Methodology* (1997), pp. 122–49. For a comparison between Weber's ideas of
objectivity and those of Gunnar Myrdal, see Sven Eliaeson, *Max Weber's
Methodologies* (2002), pp. 118–22. For a critique of Weber's alleged
value-relativism, see Leo Strauss, *Natural Right and History* (1953), pp.
36–78; and for a response to Strauss, see Raymond Aron, "Max Weber
and Modern Social Science" (1985).

See cognitive interest, science, truth, value-freedom, value-relevance,
values

Occident   *See* West, the

occupation (*Beruf*)   In his economic sociology in Ch. 2 of *Economy and Society* Weber uses the famous term *Beruf* (which is usually translated as "vocation") in the sense of "occupation": "The term 'occupation' (*Beruf*) will be applied to the mode of specialization, specification and combination of the functions of an individual so far as it constitutes for him the basis of a continuous opportunity for income or earnings" (ES:140; cf. ES:140–44, Weber [1908] 1971).

Occupations may differ depending on a number of circumstances, such as their social structure, their economic structure, if they are free or unfree, permanent or sporadic, and so on (ES:140–44). For the historical evolution of various occupations, see *General Economic History* (especially GEH:115–91).

Gordon Wells, who has retranslated *The Protestant Ethic* together with Peter Baehr, notes that since the term *Beruf* has "both the mundane sense of occupation as well as being one to which the 'saints' are called we therefore normally translated it as calling but occasionally, when the focus is exclusively on the nature of work, as occupation" (Wells 2001:36). Keith Tribe points to the oddity that one word (*Beruf*) can be translated both as vocation and as occupation, and "that this paradox is of course one that lies at the heart of *Protestant Ethic*" (Tribe 2000:211). According to Talcott Parsons, Weber overly emphasized the role of the economic in his economic sociology, and as a result of this paid much too little attention to the concept of occupational role (and the concept of profession; Parsons, p. 54 in Weber 1947). He also notes that in an occupation that has become a vocation "the occupational role . . . embodies an especially strong element of ethical valuation" (ibid., p. 214 n. 46).

See also profession, vocation, work

office (*Amt*)   The term "office" roughly denotes the position or status that is associated with certain tasks assigned to an individual in an association or organization. No definition of the term appears to exist in Weber's work.

Weber primarily discusses two types of offices in his work: the bureaucratic office and the patrimonial office (e.g. ES:958–59, 1025–38). In the case of the former, work is a vocation. There is also specific training, a salary, and a sense of duty. The patrimonial official, in contrast, lacks the clear distinction between a public and a private sphere that is found in the office of a bureaucrat. He or she also views the office as something to be exploited for gain, in exchange for services.

Patrimonial offices, Weber notes, grew out of the prince's household in which a number of individuals worked (ES:1025–38). These officials were paid in different ways, through benefices, fees, and fiefs. It has also been common in history that offices have been sold—again something that is not the case with the typical bureaucratic office ("office-farming"; e.g. ES:965–67).

"The Roman Catholic church," Weber also notes, "rest[s] on the Roman concept of office" (AJ:5).

In his notes to one of Weber's texts on domination in *Economy and Society*, Talcott Parsons notes that the English word "office" covers three different terms in Weber's work: "'office' in the institutionalized status of a person" (*Amt*), "work premises" (*Büro*), and "organized work process of a group" (*Betrieb*; ES:303 n. 3). For the concept of office more generally, see Michael Walzer, "Office," pp. 129–64 in *Spheres of Justice* (1983).

See also administration, bureaucracy, charisma (for office charisma), means of administration, vocation

official   *See* bureaucracy, means of administration, office

oikos (Oikos)   An *oikos* can be described as the authoritarian household of a local or a central ruler that has want satisfaction as its primary task, as opposed to profit-making. This type of organization was common in antiquity as well as in the Middle Ages, and can also be found in many parts of the world, such as Egypt, Greece, and Germany. Weber often refers to the *oikos* in his economic history as well as in his sociology.

"The essence of the *oikos*," according to Weber, "is organized want satisfaction" (ES:381; cf. e.g. ES:348–49, GEH:58). While the *oikos* has developed out of the household, Weber says, it must not be seen simply as a large household producing its own goods. It is rather "the authoritarian household of a prince, manorial lord or patrician" (ibid.). Weber emphasizes that the household developed in two very different directions: that of the firm (and profit-making), and that of the *oikos* (and want satisfaction).

Karl Johann Rodbertus, who introduced the concept of *oikos* (the Greek word for "household"), had argued that the whole economy of antiquity should be seen as belonging to the stage of "the *oikos* economy." Weber's use of the term *oikos*, however, is considerably more restricted (ES:384 n. 5; cf. AA:42–6). For a discussion of Weber's use of *oikos* to analyze conditions in antiquity, see e.g. John Love, *Antiquity and Capitalism* (1991), pp. 59–109.

For Weber's role in the so-called *oikos* controversy, see e.g. Mohammad Nafassi, "On the Foundations of Athenian Democracy: Marx's

Paradox and Weber's Solution" (2000) and Johannes Winkelmann, *Wirtschaft und Gesellschaft: Erläuterungsband* (1976), pp. 40–41.

See also firm, household, profit-making

ökonomische Macht   *See* economic power

Oktroyierung   *See* imposition

open and closed relationships (*offene und geschlossene Beziehungen***)**   It is a fundamental quality of all social relationships, according to Weber, that participation or membership in them can be either open or closed to outsiders. In Weber's sociology, open and closed social relationships are also constitutive parts of other social formations, such as status groups and organizations. The idea of social closure also plays an important role in contemporary scholarship on stratification.

In Weber's general sociology, as presented in Ch. 1 of *Economy and Society*, open and closed social relationships are defined in the following way: "A social relationship . . . will be spoken of as 'open' to outsiders if and insofar as its system of order does not deny participation to anyone who wishes to join and is actually in a position to do so. A relationship will, on the other hand, be called 'closed' against outsiders so far as, according to its subjective meaning and its binding rules, participation of certain persons is excluded, limited, or subjected to conditions" (ES:43).

Certain relationships *within* a group may also be closed to those on the inside. When it is favorable to some actors' ideal or material interests to keep certain relationships open, they will typically be kept open; and when it is favorable that they be closed, they will typically be closed.

Economic relationships may similarly be open or closed, whether in markets, guilds, economic organizations, or many other economic settings (ES:341–43).

One reason for the closure of economic relationships may be that the number of competitors in relation to the possibilities for profit-making has increased. Weber calls this "scope of economic resources in relation to acquisition" (*Erwerbsspielraum*; there is also "scope of economic resources in relation to consumption needs" [*Nahrungsspielraum*]). When competition is curbed and some people excluded, a pretext for this is usually advanced; and this pretext can attach to anything, such as the religion, race, or language of those who are excluded. "It does not matter which characteristic is chosen in the individual case: whatever suggests itself most easily is seized upon" (ES:342).

When someone succeeds in excluding others from an opportunity, Weber speaks of appropriation. Property is consequently a form of appropriation.

A fairly large secondary literature deals with Weber's concept of closed social relationships or "closure." According to David Grusky, for example, there currently exists a "revised version" of Weber's analysis of class that relies on his concept of social closure (*Social Stratification* [2001], p. 18). For attempts to revive and improve upon Weber's ideas on social closure, see especially Frank Parkin, *Marxism and Class Theory* (1979). Parkin argues, for example, that the concept of social closure can help to explain the social structure of professions. He also notes a "serious flaw" in Weber's discussion of social closure, namely that the role of the state is neglected (*Max Weber* [1982], p. 102). See in this context also Raymond Murphy, *Social Closure* (1988) and Jeff Manza, "Classes, Status Groups, and Social Closure: A Critique of Neo-Weberian Social Theory" (1992).

See also appropriation, organization or association, property, status

opportunity (*Chance*) The German term *Chance* is used in two different meanings in *Economy and Society*: as "opportunity" (or "advantage") and as "probability" (*see* entry for this latter meaning). So far as *Chance* in the sense of opportunity is concerned, Weber refers to market opportunities, profit opportunities, opportunities for exchange, and many other types of opportunities.

"Economic opportunities" are defined in Weber's economic sociology in Ch. 2 of *Economy and Society* as follows: "the opportunities which are made available by custom, by the constellation of interest, or by a conventional or legal order for the purposes of an economic unit, will be called 'economic opportunities'" (ES:68–9; the translation has been changed).

In the section on open and closed social relationships there is a discussion of *Chance* in the sense of "advantage" (ES:43–6). A closed social relationship may, for example, have a monopoly on certain advantages. Weber also states that "appropriated advantages will be called 'rights'" (ES:44). The concept of property is also related to that of advantage.

There is a link between Weber's notion of *Chance* as opportunity and life chances (*Lebenschancen*), which is captured by Robert. K. Merton's concept of "opportunity structure." On this point, *see* life chances. In commenting on Weber's concept of *Chance* in his book *Life Chances*, Ralf Dahrendorf writes: "Weber clearly implies that economic chances are themselves scarce so that one has to compete for them. Weber is imaginative in finding names for such chances, and we have mentioned some of them already: market chances, chances of acquisition, exchange chances, price chances, interest chances, work utilization chances, capital formation chances." (Dahrendorf 1979:67–8).

See also interest, self-interest or self-interested kind of behavior

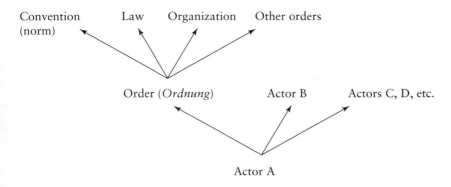

FIGURE 1. Different types of order to which action may be oriented, according to Weber.
SOURCE: Max Weber, *Economy and Society* ([1922] 1978), pp. 3–24, 33–6, 48–50.

order (*Ordnung*)   An order can roughly be defined as *prescriptions for how to act* that have acquired a certain independence in the minds of individual actors. While orders typically have a very high probability of being followed and reproduced, this probability, Weber often says, is never 100 percent. An order that is valid or legitimate is seen as *binding or exemplary* by the individual. The term "institution," as used in contemporary sociology, captures some of the meaning of "order." Weber, however, also uses the term "order" for organizations and conventions.

The concepts of social action and order are the two basic building blocks of Weber's sociology; and they are also directly related to each other. Social relationships can under certain circumstances become organizations or associations, and these constitute orders in Weber's sense. One may also speak of a more general order, such as the legal, social, and economic order of a community (*Rechtsordnung, soziale Ordnung,* and *Wirtschaftsordnung*; e.g. ES:312, 927). There is also the value-sphere (*Lebensordnung*). Finally, Weber uses the concept of order to characterize a convention and a law (ES:33–6). The concept of order, in brief, brings together phenomena on a micro-, meso-, and macro-level for Weber (see Figure 1).

In all of Weber's work, including Ch. 1 of *Economy and Society*, there are only a few brief statements about what constitutes an order. According to the most substantial of these, "only then will the content of a social relationship be called an order if the conduct is, approximately or on the average, oriented toward determinable 'maxims'" (ES:31). By the term "maxim" is meant "the meaning of a social relationship" (ES:28). Maxims can come into being in two ways. Either they emerge from a social relationship that remains relatively stable or they can be agreed upon and sealed by promise (ES:28).

That an order is legitimate or valid means that it is probable that it will be followed (ES:31). In this case the order is seen as "obligatory or exemplary" to the actor (*see* legitimation). An order's legitimacy may be guaranteed by external or internal means. An example of the former would be interests, and of the latter affectual, value-rational, or emotional means (ES:33). A legitimate order is called a *convention* if its order is guaranteed through disapproval (*see* convention); and it is called a *law* if a staff will ensure compliance with the help of coercion (*see* law).

Actors may orient their behavior to an order so as to evade it as well as to conform to it. A thief would be an example of the former, and a law-abiding citizen an example of the latter. Actors may orient their behavior to two orders simultaneously, say an economic order and a legal order (ES:33). The orders to which actors orient their behavior may also be in conflict with one another, as when dueling is prohibited by the state but encouraged by some other order, say the code of honor among officers (ES:32). The subtitle of *Economy and Society* was, according to a contract drawn up in December 1919 between Weber and his publisher, "The Social Orders and Powers" (Mommsen 2000:381). For Weber's somewhat different use of the term *Ordnung* in his 1913 essay, see "Some Categories of Interpretive Sociology" (SCIS:160–61).

It should finally be emphasized that like all key concepts in Weber's sociology, that of order, too, is closely related to the notion of meaning. A prescription for how to act, for example, only makes sense if it is understood. An order may either be part of what Weber calls a "complex of meaning" (*Sinnzusammenhang*) or constitute such a complex itself.

In modern sociology the concept of institution, as developed by Peter Berger and Thomas Luckmann, is close to the concept of order in Weber's work (*The Social Construction of Reality* [1967], pp. 53–67). According to Stefan Breuer's fine formulation, "Weber's sociology is both a sociology of action and a sociology of order" (Breuer 2001a:125).

See also complex of meaning, economic order, institution, law, legal order, legitimation, maxim, organization, orientation to others, value-sphere

Organisation   *See* organization or association

organization or association (Verband)   The core meaning of *Verband*—

which can be translated as "organization" as well as "association"—is that there is a staff that has as its task to carry out the rules of an order (*see* order). This concept is quite flexible and covers many different types of phenomena. In terms of Weber's general sociology, an organization or association then primarily consists of an order that is being carried out by a staff.

The exact definition of an organization or association, in Weber's general sociology in Ch. 1 of *Economy and Society*, is as follows: "a social relationship which is either closed or limits the admission of outsiders will be called an organization or association (*Verband*) when the content of its order (*Ordnung*) is guaranteed to be carried out by specific individuals: a chief and, possibly, an administrative staff which normally also has representative powers" (ES:48; my translation; cf. ES:264).

Weber adds that "whether or not an organization or association exists is entirely a matter of the presence of a person in authority, with or without an administrative staff" (ES:49; my translation). He is also careful to point out that an organization or association does not exist per se—just the probability that the social actions that constitute the organization or association will be taken.

By centering his concept of organization around the notion of order (*Ordnung*) Weber connects it to a number of other concepts in his general sociology, such as convention and law. Order itself is also closely linked to the notion of social action.

One reason for not translating *Verband* exclusively as organization (as in the current edition of *Economy and Society*), is that this concept not only covers the modern organization—that is, the consciously created organization—but also traditional and similar associations, including the household. The closest Weber comes to a term for the modern organization may well be what he terms "formal enterprise" (*Betriebsverband*; *see* enterprise).

Organizations or associations can be communal or associative in nature, that is, they can be centered around a subjective feeling of belonging together or around interests (*see* associative relationship, communal relationship). There exist economic, religious, and political associations or organizations. Action taken by the staff or on the orders of a staff is termed "organized action."

If the order of an organization or association has been created by its members, it is called *autonomous*; if it has been imposed by outsiders, it is termed *heteronomous*. If the chief and the staff are appointed through the autonomous order of the organization, the organization is called *autocephalous*; if not, it is called *heterocephalous*. There is *executive power* in an organization or association that can be appropriated by individuals.

Some individuals may also be appointed or assigned to handle this power. The order of an organization or association can be imposed or voluntarily agreed upon (ES:50–1). What Weber terms a ruling organization (*Herrschaftsverband*) exists if its members are dominated by virtue of the established order (ES:53). The probability that the rules of the leadership will be obeyed is called the "constitution" of the organization (ES:50).

There exist two types of rules in an organization or association: those that govern organized action (and make up the *administrative order* of the organization or association), and those that govern other kinds of social action (and make up its *regulative order*; ES:51–2). Both of these types of orders can typically be found in an organization or association.

Weber distinguishes between three types of organizations or associations: formal (or modern) organizations, voluntary organizations or associations, and compulsory organizations or associations. A modern firm would be an example of the first type; a sect of the second; and a church of the third.

The most celebrated part of Weber's "theory of organization" is his theory of bureaucracy (*see* that entry). Once a bureaucracy has come into being, it tends to take on a life of its own. Weber also points out that when one attempts to realize ideas, something else tends to happen. Weber refers to this phenomenon as "a universal 'Tragedy' . . . that dooms every attempt to realize ideas in reality" (Weber [1910] 2002:204). What this tragedy consists of is that an organization typically comes into being that has its own interests and is ruled by careerists.

A fairly long discussion of the concept of organization or association (including compulsory organization) can be found in "Some Categories of Interpretive Sociology" (SCIS:173–79). Weber here notes that "domination [is] the most significant foundation of nearly all organizational action" (SCIS:177). For the secondary literature on Weber's theory of bureaucracy and his theory of organization more generally, *see* bureaucracy.

By way of introducing the discussion of the different ways in which it is possible to translate Weber's term *Verband*, the following statement by one of Weber's translators on voluntary associations may be cited: "German is notoriously rich when it comes to associations or groups, and English pales in comparison. Following the German convention of his time, Weber used various words to note the fine conceptual differences. For example, *Verein, Anstalt, Verband, Genossenschaft, Gemeinschaft, Gesellschaft, Gemeinde, Einigung, Vereinigung, Vergesellschaftung, Gruppe,* and *Klub* are all in heavy use in this text" (Kim 2002:199). Kim also suggests that Weber's use of terms in this context may have been inspired by Otto von Gierke, since Gierke's work on groups and associations was very influential in Weber's day.

In Talcott Parsons' version of Ch. 1 of *Economy and Society Verband* is translated as "corporate group" (Weber 1947:145 n. 76). Guenther Roth changed this to "organization" in the current edition of *Economy and Society*, arguing that "corporate group" would lead to misunderstandings, among other reasons because *Verband* includes more than just economic or professional organizations (ES:61 n. 27). Roth adds that "the term 'organization' should be understood literally in the sense of a group with an 'organ', but not necessarily of a rationalized kind; the latter would make it an 'enterprise' or a 'formal organisation'" (ibid.). In the older parts of *Economy and Society*, Guenther Roth also notes, one may find Weber's earlier definition of "organization," for which he uses the German term *Organisation* (ES:301 n. 12, 952–54). Roth explains that the term *Organisation* refers to "the activities of a staff or apparatus," while *Verband* "is more broadly defined since the rules may be enforced by the head alone." Since a *Verband* usually has a staff, he adds, "the terminological difference between *Verband* and *Organisation* can be disregarded most of the time" (ibid.).

According to Stephen Kalberg, "Weber's notion of *Verband* (organisation) is a generic one" and Weber includes into it not only the family and the sib, but also states, churches, and voluntary organizations (Kalberg 1994b:58 n. 15). In his new translation of Ch. 1 of *Economy and Society* Keith Tribe translates *Verband* as "group body" and notes that it literally means "a banded-together group of people" (EW:350). Finally, *Verband* has also been translated exclusively as "association" or as "corps" (e.g. PW:380, Orihara 2002:9).

For a discussion of the somewhat different use of the term *Verband* in Ch. 1 of *Economy and Society* and in the 1913 article "Some Categories of Interpretive Sociology," see Orihara, "From 'a Torso with a Wrong Head' to 'Five Disjointed Pieces of Carcass'?" (2002), p. 9.

Finally, according to the editors of MWG, there was "a fifth planned chapter [in the last version of *Economy and Society*] on types of communities [*Gemeinschaften*] ('Forms of Associations' [*Verbände*])" (Baier, Lepsius, Mommsen, and Schluchter 2000:114; cf. Weber 1999d:xvii).

See also administration, bureaucracy, compulsory organization, economic organization, enterprise, firm, order, political organization, voluntary organization

organization theory and organizational sociology   Organization theory is an interdisciplinary enterprise, and Weber is one of the early and important figures in this field. The same can be said for organizational sociology, which falls more squarely within the field of sociology.

While both of these fields honor Weber, they also have a narrow view of his work. What Weber says about bureaucracy is essentially presented as his theory of organizations. There is no knowledge of Weber writings other than in *Economy and Society*. When it comes to *Economy and Society*, there is also little awareness of what Weber says about organizations in his general sociology in Ch. 1, as opposed to the parts that deal directly with bureaucracy.

For an introduction to the view of Weber in contemporary organization theory and organizational sociology, see e.g. the latest edition of Richard Scott, *Organizations* (2002). For a discussion of the extent to which Weber is and should be part of contemporary research in the field of organizations, see e.g. Stewart Clegg, "Max Weber and Contemporary Sociology of Organizations" (1994) and Marshall Meyer, "The Weberian Tradition in Organizational Studies" (1990). For a discussion whether contemporary organization theory ignores Weber's approach or not, see Robert Stern and Stephen Barley, "Organizations and Social Systems" (1996) versus Richard Scott, "The Mandate Is Still Being Honored: In Defense of Weber's Disciples" (1996). Drawing on a citation analysis of *Administrative Science Quarterly*, Michael Lounsbury and Ed Carberry argue that references to Weber have recently declined and become ritualistic ("From King to Court Jester: Weber's Fall from Grace in Organizational Theory" [2004]). Finally, that organization theory has misunderstood Weber's analysis of bureaucracy is the argument in Hans-Ulrich Derlien, "On the Selective Interpretation of Max Weber's Concept of Bureaucracy in Organization Theory and Administrative Science" (1999).

See also administration, bureaucracy, compulsory organization, enterprise, the firm, organization or association, political organization, voluntary organization

organizational sociology   *See* organization theory or organizational sociology

orientation to others   Sociology, according to Weber's definition in Ch. 1 of *Economy and Society*, deals with social action, and "action is social insofar as its subjective meaning takes account of the behavior of others and is thereby oriented (*orientiert*) in its course" (ES:4; cf. SCIS:152). Action can be oriented to the behavior of another individual or of several individuals, or to an order. It can also be oriented to the past, the present or the future.

The idea of orientation is consequently what ties individuals together for Weber, and also what connects them to an order. Examples of orders include conventions (norms), laws and organizations (Figure 2; *see* order).

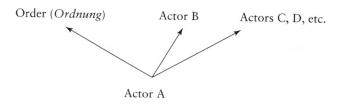

Order (*Ordnung*)   Actor B   Actors C, D, etc.

Actor A

FIGURE 2. What the actor may orient his or her action to, according to Weber.
SOURCE: Max Weber, *Economy and Society* ([1922] 1978), pp. 3–24.

According to Ch. 1 of *Economy and Society*, action can be oriented to several orders simultaneously; and these orders may also contradict each other. An example of this latter situation would be dueling. While one order, the code of honor among officers, may impose dueling as a duty, another, the legal order of the state, may forbid it (ES:33).

Action that is exclusively oriented to an object (say a machine) or to no object or human person (as in solitary prayer), does not qualify as "social" in this sense. The same is true for, say, two bicyclists who by accident collide with each other. Here as elsewhere, however, it should be kept in mind that according to Weber social action only constitutes the main focus of sociology, not its exclusive focus.

The discussion of orientation to others in "Some Categories of Interpretive Action" represents a useful complement to the text in Ch. 1 of *Economy and Society* (SCIS:153, 159–62). Weber here notes, for example, that action can be oriented to values. He also states that "an important (though not indispensable) normal component of social action is its meaningful orientation to the expectations of certain behavior on the part of others and, in accordance with that, orientation to the (subjectively) assessed probabilities (*Chancen*) for the success of one's action" (SCIS:159).

See also order, social action, sociology

other-worldly asceticism   *See* asceticism

outside interests (*betriebsfremde Interessen*)   In his discussion of the management of the modern capitalist firm Weber refers to the role of what he calls outside interests. The relevant passage in Weber's economic sociology in Ch. 2 of *Economy and Society* reads as follows: "we call 'outside interests' those which are not primarily oriented to the long-run profitability of the enterprise" (ES:139).

Outside interests are typically directed toward making a quick profit through speculation and therefore go counter to formal rationality.

See also firm

P

alyi, Melchior (1892–1970)   Hungarian-born economist who helped edit the original editions of *Economy and Society* and *General Economic History*. See "Palyi, Melchior," p. 885 in Part 2 of Vol. 2 of Hannah Caplan and Belinda Rosenblatt (eds.), *International Biographical Dictionary of Central European Emigrés* (1983).

paradoxical results of actions (*Paradoxie der Folgen*)   This expression refers to the fact that what people do may result in something totally different than what they had in mind. This is the case, Weber says, even with actions that have been thought through by the actor. Weber's most spectacular example of this is how certain religious ideas helped to develop a new stage of capitalism, as outlined in *The Protestant Ethic and the Spirit of Capitalism*.

In the section on the sociology of religion in *Economy and Society* Weber notes, for example, that "by a peculiar paradox, asceticism resulted in the contradictory situation already mentioned on several occasions, namely that it was precisely its rationally ascetic character that led to the accumulation of wealth" (ES:586; cf. e.g. PE:90). In *The Religion of China* Weber, after mentioning that Puritanism unintentionally led to a methodical way of life, refers to "the paradox of unintended consequences: i.e., the relation of man and fate, of what he intended by his acts and what actually came of them" (RC:238; cf. RC:245).

In "Politics as a Vocation" Weber notes that the end product of political action "regularly stands in completely inadequate and often even paradoxical relation to its original meaning" (GM:117). He also points out that anyone who wants to be involved with politics has to understand "ethical paradoxes," and that the person who fails to realize that good may come from evil, and that evil may come from good, is a "political infant" (GM:123).

Finally, Weber was well aware of the role that unintended and paradoxical results play in the economy, as famously described by Adam Smith, Mandeville, and others (e.g. RK:83).

For a discussion of the concept *Paradoxie der Folgen*, see Alexander von Schelting, *Max Webers Wissenschaftslehre* (1934), pp. 42–52 and Talcott Parsons, *The Structure of Social Action* (1937), p. 644.

See also ethic of ultimate values, intention, social mechanisms, unintended consequences

Paradoxie der Folgen   *See* paradoxical results of actions

pariah   *See* pariah capitalism, pariah people

pariah capitalism (*Paria-Kapitalismus*)   This type of capitalism is exemplified in Weber's work by the kind of capitalism created by the Jewish people (e.g. GEH:358–61, PE:271; cf. AJ:343–45). It includes profit-making activities based on money-lending and those of a political character—but not those of an industrial nature. The term "pariah" refers to the ritual segregation of the Jews and their negative status in the eyes of surrounding societies. The Jews did not invent rational, industrial capitalism, according to Weber, who on this point criticizes the argument in Werner Sombart's *The Jews and Modern Capitalism* ([1911] 1913; e.g. ES:611–15).

Weber's use of the term "pariah" in connection with the Jewish people has been criticized. For a discussion, see e.g. Gary Abraham, *Max Weber and the Jewish Question* (1992) Arnaldo Momigliano, "A Note on Max Weber's Definition of Judaism as a Pariah-Religion" (1980), and Freddy Raphaël, "Max Weber and Ancient Judaism" (1973).

See also capitalism, Judaism, pariah people

pariah people (*Pariavolk*)   Pariah people are characterized by being ritually separated from their surroundings and by being in an inferior position relative to the surrounding society. Examples include the Jews and some of the castes in India.

Weber defines a pariah people as follows in his sociology of religion in *Economy and Society*: "in our usage, 'pariah people' denotes a distinct hereditary social group lacking autonomous political organization and characterized by internal prohibitions against commensality and intermarriage originally founded upon magical, tabooistic, and ritual injunctions. Two additional traits of a pariah people are political and social disprivilege and a far-reaching distinctiveness in economic functioning" (ES:493; cf. AJ:3). See in this context also the chapter entitled "The Pariah Community" in *Ancient Judaism* (AJ:336–55).

After World War I Weber argued that "like the Jews we [Germans] have been turned into a people of pariahs" (Marianne Weber, *Max Weber* [(1926) 1975], p. 662).

According to Freddy Rafaël, "it should be pointed out that the terms

Pariavolk and *Herrenvolk* used by Weber are for him scientific concepts and in no way pejorative" (Rafaël 1973:55 n. 2). According to Talcott Parsons, "the term *Paria* is used by Weber in a technical sense to designate a group occupying the same territorial area as others, but separated from them by ritual barriers which severely limit social intercourse between the groups" (ES:209 n. 40). Parsons adds that it is common for people in groups of this type to have specialized occupations, "particularly occupations which are despised in the larger society." For further discussion of Weber's thesis of the Jews as a pariah people, see e.g. Gary Abraham, *Max Weber and the Jewish Question* (1992), Arnaldo Momigliano, "A Note on Max Weber's Definition of Judaism as a Pariah-Religion" (1980), and Freddy Raphaël, "Max Weber and Ancient Judaism" (1973).

See also caste, Judaism, pariah capitalism

party (*Partei*) Weber discusses political parties in his political writings as well as in his sociology. He was much concerned with the power position of the bureaucracy in modern political parties.

A party is defined as follows in Ch. 3 on domination in *Economy and Society*: "the term 'party' will be employed to designate associations, membership in which rests on formally free recruitment. The end to which its activity is devoted is to secure power within an organization for its leaders in order to attain ideal or material advantages for its active members" (ES:284; cf. ES:285–88, 938–39).

"'*Parties*'," Weber says, "reside in the sphere of power" (ES:938). He also distinguishes between a number of different types of parties, including "patronage parties," "ideological parties," and "charismatic parties" (ES:285–88). "Politics as a Vocation" contains a long section on political parties: their organization, historical evolution, and what characterizes parties in select countries (GM:99–113; cf. ES:1130–33). Finally, Weber was also disturbed by the emergence of party bureaucracy (e.g. Wolfgang Mommsen, *Max Weber and German Politics 1890–1920* [1984], pp. 109–11).

For a discussion of Max Weber's ideas on political parties, see Frank Parkin, *Max Weber* (1982), pp. 104–8; see also e.g. Rudolf Steininger, "Max Webers Parteienkonzept und die Parteienforschung" (1980).

See also *Herrenvolk*, politics

patriarchalism (*Patriarchalismus*) This concept plays a central role in Weber's sociology as well as in some of his studies in economic history.

Patriarchalism is defined in Ch. 3 of *Economy and Society* as "the situation where, within a group (household) which is usually organized on both an economic and a kinship basis, a particular individual governs who is designated by a definite rule of inheritance" (ES:231; cf. ES:1006–69).

Very important is also that those who hold power in patriarchal organizations are supposed to administer it in the service of the members.

Weber notes that "patriarchalism is by far the most important type of domination the legitimacy of which rests upon tradition" (GM:296). The typical patriarchal ruler is the father, the husband, and the master of a slave (GM:296; cf. e.g. GEH:47–8). Weber defines "pure patriarchalism" as patriarchal domination without any legal limits (ES:1009).

When domination is patriarchal (as well as when it is patrimonial), there exist certain norms that are seen as inviolable for the ruler but also an area where the ruler is free to do as he likes. Weber describes the latter as "a realm of free arbitrariness and favor of the lord" (GM:296).

Weber uses the term "primary patriarchalism" for the situation where the ruler (1) has no staff, and (2) rules a household through inheritance (ES:231).

For a presentation of Weber's views on patriarchalism, see e.g. Reinhard Bendix, *Max Weber: An Intellectual Portrait* (1960), pp. 330–33.

See also employment regime (*Arbeitsverfassung*), feminism, household, males, patrimonialism, traditional domination, women

patrimonialism (*Patrimonialismus*) Patrimonialism constitutes a special type of domination, which figures prominently in Weber's historical sociology.

Weber characterizes patrimonialism as a form of traditional domination in which (1) the administration as well as the military are seen by the ruler as his or her personal instruments, and (2) the ruler abides by tradition (ES:231–32; cf. ES:1006–10). Weber adds that in patrimonialism there is typically a "continuous struggle of the central power with various centrifugal powers" (ES:1055; cf. ES:1055–59).

At one point in *Economy and Society* Weber also describes patrimonialism as "a special case of patriarchal domination—domestic authority decentralized through assignment of land and sometimes equipment to sons of the house or other dependents" (ES:1011).

Patrimonialism, Weber argues, can grow out of charismatic domination as well as patriarchalism (e.g. GM:296, ES:1006, 1011). When domination is patrimonial (as well as when it is patriarchal), there exist certain norms that are seen as inviolable for the ruler as well as an area where the ruler is free to do as he wishes. Weber describes the latter as "a realm of free arbitrariness and favor of the lord" (GM:296). In patrimonial administration there is no sharp distinction between private and public as in a bureaucracy (ES:1028–31). Similarly, Weber notes in his sociology of law, there is in patrimonialism a tendency for public law and private law to become similar (ES:643–44).

There exist several different types of patrimonialism as well as of other forms of rule that are similar to this type of domination. What Weber calls "estate-type domination" represents, for example, a form of patrimonialism; more precisely it is characterized by the situation that the administrative staff has appropriated some power (ES:232). There is also prebendalism, which is a form of patrimonialism that is maintained through benefices, that is, through traditional allowances, incomes, and the like that cannot be inherited (ES:235). Finally, "sultanism" is characterized by Weber as a form of domination characterized by the ruler's personal autonomy (as in patrimonial domination), but where personal discretion is central (ES:232).

For a presentation of Weber's views on patrimonialism, see e.g. Reinhard Bendix, *Max Weber: An Intellectual Portrait* (1960), pp. 334–59. See also Guenther Roth, "Personal Rulership, Patrimonialism and Empire-Building in the New States" (1968). Elsewhere Roth refers to the fact that "the inherent instability of political patrimonialism, on account of its decentralization, is part of [Weber's] model" (Roth 1975:150). Finally, Weber's concept of patrimonialism has been widely used. See e.g. Gina Zabludovsky, "The Reception and Utility of Max Weber's Concept of Patrimonialism in Latin America" (1989).

See also state (for the patrimonial state); patriarchalism, traditional domination

personality (*Persönlichkeit*)   According to Weber, the individual may decide to take a personal stance on things; and this is where the Weberian concepts of "personality" and "inner distance" come in. In one of his writings, for example, Weber, refers to "the attempt to take the self by the forelock and pull it out of the mud, forming it into a 'personality'" (RI:342). "'*Personality*'," in brief, " . . . entails a constant and intrinsic relation to certain 'ultimate' values and 'meanings' of life" (RK:192; cf. MS:55).

In "The Life-Orders and Personality," an important lecture that Weber gave in the autumn of 1917, he is reported to have said that "only he who knows how to live up to the demands of the day has 'personality'" (Hennis 1988:70, cf. Weber 1984:703–4, 707; Marianne Weber, *Max Weber* [(1926) 1975], pp. 596–600).

See e.g. Harvey Goldman, *Max Weber and Thomas Mann* (1988), pp. 142–68, Wilhelm Hennis, "Max Weber's Theme: 'Personality and Life-Orders'," pp. 62–104 in *Max Weber: Essays in Reconstruction* (1988), and Ralph Schroeder, "'Personality' and 'Inner Distance': The Conception of the Individual in Max Weber's Sociology" (1991). While Jean-Pierre Grossein defines personality as something that structures the acts of the individual from the inside, Rogers Brubaker argues that personality is a philosophical, not a psychological concept (Grossein, "Présentation" [1996], p. 61 n. 2; Brubaker, *The Limits of Rationality* [1984], p. 95). See in this context also the discussion of the relationship between individuality and *Bildung* in Fritz Ringer, *Max Weber's Methodology* (1997), pp. 8–17. According to Leo Strauss, Weber argued that one could only become a "personality" through "absolute devotion to a cause" (*Natural Right and History* [1953], pp. 46–7).

See also depersonalization, individual and individualism, methodological individualism, valuation, value-orientation and similar terms, value-spheres

Pfründe (benefice)   *See* prebendalism

Pfründefeudalismus (prebendal feudalism)   *See* feudalism

philosophy   Though Weber worked as an economist, a professor of law, and a sociologist, he never taught philosophy or presented himself as a philosopher. Nonetheless, many aspects of his work are relevant to philosophy. And, as he once put it, "philosophy was my first love" (Honigsheim [1946–63] 2000:193).

In the section on the sociology of religion in *Economy and Society*, for example, Weber writes that "the ultimate question of all metaphysics has always been something like this: if the world as a whole and life in particular were to have a meaning, what might it be, and how would the world have to look in order to correspond to it?" (ES:451; cf. ES:499). Important existential questions are also raised in Weber's discussion of theodicy and in "Science as a Vocation" (e.g. GM:142–56). *The Protestant Ethic* refers repeatedly to the link between Puritanism and utilitarianism (e.g. PE:177, 183, 265 n. 33).

To Karl Jaspers, Weber was "an existential philosopher" (*On Max Weber* [1989], p. 9). To label Weber a philosopher, however, did not appeal to everybody; and Heinrich Rickert reputedly told Jaspers "that you turn Max Weber into a philosopher is your undisputable right. That you call him a philosopher is nonsense." Wolfgang Schluchter, who cites this statement, agrees with Rickert and argues that "Weber never claimed to be a philosopher in any technical sense of the word" (*Paradoxes of Modernity* [1996], p. 1). But Weber, Schluchter adds, was quite familiar with philosophy and took part in philosophical discussions; and there is definitely a philosophical dimension to his work (for a discussion of some aspects of this philosophical dimension, see e.g. ibid., pp. 1–101).

For Weber's relationship to individual philosophers, including Friedrich Nietzsche and Karl Jaspers, see e.g. Part 4 of Wolfgang Mommsen and Jürgen Osterhammel (eds.), *Max Weber and His Contemporaries* (1987). See also Karl Jaspers, "Max Weber as a Philosopher," pp. 103–35 in *On Max Weber*. For Weber's relationship to phenomenology, see e.g. Kenneth Muse, "Edmund Husserl's Impact on Max Weber" (1981); see also Alfred Schutz, *The Phenomenology of the Social World* ([1932] 1967). For Weber's philosophy of science, *see* methodology.

See also complex of meaning, meaning, neo-Kantianism, Nietzsche, rationalization (for philosophy of history), theodicy, values

philosophy of history   *See* rationalization

philosophy of science   *See* methodology

physiology   *See* psychophysics

planned economy (*Planwirtschaft*)   A planned economy is based on the satisfaction of wants as opposed to a market economy, which is based on profit-making.

According to the definition that Weber supplies in his economic sociology in Ch. 2 of *Economy and Society*, want satisfaction "results . . . from a 'planned economy' so far as economic action is oriented systematically to an established substantive order, whether agreed or imposed, which is valid within an organization" (ES:109).

Individual economic units in a planned economy are not independent; and calculations in kind are used as well as a budget. Weber's notion of a market economy is used as a contrast to that of a planned economy. In the former, economic action is oriented to exchange, individual units are independent, and money is used for calculation. The incentive to work in a market economy is in principle stronger than in a planned economy since the market is the ultimate judge. A key problem in a planned economy is how to formulate effective prices since market prices cannot be used.

See also budgetary management, calculation, market economy, socialism

plebiscitary domination and leadership (*plebiszitäre Herrschaft und Führerschaft*)   Weber paid a good deal of attention in his work to the role of plebiscitary leadership. One major reason for this was his own interest in having a political system in Germany in which a plebiscitary leader would play a key role.

Weber argues that charisma may be transformed in a democratic direction and the plebiscitary leader is a transitional figure in this process (ES:266–71).

A plebiscitary leader, more generally, is a leader who answers to the belief that there can be only one true leader who expresses the popular will. Examples include Napoleon I and Napoleon III.

In a plebiscitary democracy the charismatic authority of the leader is formally derived from the will of the governed. "It is characteristic of the *Führerdemokratie* that there should in general be a highly emotional type of devotion and trust in the leader" (ES:269). There are clear links between plebiscitary domination and Caesarism (*see* that entry).

In "Politics as a Vocation" Weber argues for having a political leader of the following kind: "a man must be a leader, and not only a leader but a hero as well, in a very sober sense of the word" (GM:128). According to Marianne Weber, "*the proper selection of leaders* was to Weber the most important problem of parliamentarianism and democratization" (Marianne Weber [1926] 1975:586).

Weber's ideas on the need for a plebiscitary leader are contested. See e.g. David Beetham, *Max Weber and the Theory of Modern Politics* (1975), pp. 215–49, Wolfgang Mommsen, *Max Weber and German Politics 1890–1920* (1984), pp. 184–89, 390–414, and Wolfgang Mommsen, "The Theory of the 'Three Types of Legitimate Domination' and the Concept of Plebiscitarian Democracy," pp. 72–94 in *The Age of Bureaucracy* (1974).

See also Caesarism, charisma, charismatic domination, demagogue, politics

political action   *See* politics

political capitalism (*politisch orientierter Kapitalismus*)   Weber distinguishes between a number of different types of capitalism in his writings, such as rational capitalism, pariah capitalism, and robber capitalism. Political capitalism is a type of capitalism where profit-making becomes possible via the state in some way—e.g. through contracts with the state or through contacts with people who are part of the state.

In his economic sociology in Ch. 2 of *Economy and Society* Weber states that some of the main forms of "capitalistic orientation of profit-making" have existed for thousands of years and that they can be found all over the world. These he calls "politically oriented capitalism" or "political capitalism" for short (*politisch orientierter Kapitalismus*; ES:164–66). They involve (1) opportunities for "predatory profit," such as financing of war; (2) opportunities created by the power of the state, e.g. for "colonial profits"; and (3) opportunities for "unusual transactions" with the state and state agencies.

Some types of domination go well with political capitalism (such as patrimonialism), while others do not (such as rational capitalism). Similarly, some forms of financing the state go well with this type of capitalism (such as tax farming), while others do not (such as compulsory service in kind).

Political capitalism existed in antiquity, according to Weber. In *The Agrarian Sociology of Ancient Civilizations*, where this topic is discussed, Weber notes that capital must not be exclusively associated with modern rational capitalism—"for the essence of capital is that it seeks profits in the place and manner in which they can be obtained most easily, and the easiest way to achieve profits in antiquity was not the creation of new methods to divide the production process in order to have larger, more disciplined, and better organized units of production" (ASAC:208–9).

In modern capitalism, the defense industry and the agricultural industry are often examples of political capitalism. The need for approval by state officials to land a contract would be another example.

For political capitalism in general, see e.g. Richard Swedberg, *Max Weber and the Idea of Economic Sociology* (1998), pp. 46–53. For an explication of the concept of political capitalism and its evolution in Weber's work, especially as he used it in his studies of antiquity, see John Love, *Antiquity and Capitalism* (1991), pp. 49–55, 224–45.

See also adventurers' capitalism, capitalism, economic superman

political community (*politische Gemeinschaft*)   As part of his political sociology Weber devotes considerable attention to political communities in *Economy and Society* (see especially ES:901–40). Examples of these include empires, nations, and states.

A political community is defined by Weber as "a community whose social action is aimed at subordinating to orderly domination by the participants a 'territory' and the conduct of the masses within it, through readiness to resort to physical force, including normally force of arms" (ES:901). Weber specifies that there exist three requirements for there to be a political community: (1) a territory; (2) physical force; and (3) social action that goes beyond economic action (ES:902). He adds that the individual is also expected to die for the community, and that this gives a "particular pathos" to the political community (ES:903). There is also a "community of memories" in this type of community (ibid.).

According to Guenther Roth (ES:939 n. 1), Weber's definition of political community as cited above represents "the early formulation of territorial political organization and of the state, which Weber later summarized in [Ch. 1 of Part 1 of *Economy and Society*; see especially ES:54–6]."

See also imperialism, nation, political organization, power prestige, state

political education   *See* education

political organization (*politischer Verband*)   What Weber terms political organization differs from the meaning that this term has in everyday language. A political organization is an organization that has an administrative staff that uses force within a given territory.

The exact definition of a political organization in Weber's general sociology in Ch. 1 of *Economy and Society* is as follows: "a 'ruling organization' will be called 'political' insofar as its existence and order is [sic] continuously safeguarded within a given *territorial* area by the threat and application of physical force on part of the administrative staff" (ES:54).

Examples of political organizations include village communities and workers' associations ("soviets"), when these use force and claim a territory. Groups that do not use force and try to influence politics do not constitute political organizations (ES:55). These latter also engage in political action as opposed to politically oriented action.

See also party, political community, political sociology, politics, state

political party   *See* party

political science   While Weber defined himself as an economist, sociologist, and jurist at various points of his career, he did not see himself as a political scientist. He nonetheless produced a political sociology of much interest to political science, as well as writings on various constitutional and political matters.

For a selection of Weber's articles on political topics, see his *Political Writings* (1994); and for an introduction to Weber for political scientists, see Lawrence Scaff, "Max Weber's Politics and Political Education" (1973). For Weber's political ideas, see Wolfgang Mommsen, *Max Weber and German Politics 1890–1920* (1984).

See also political sociology, politics

political sociology   Weber was passionately interested in politics and wrote a good deal on the topic. While he himself did not refer explicitly to his political sociology (as opposed to, say, his sociology of the state or of domination), one may nonetheless use this term to denote a number of his writings, such as "Politics as a Vocation," "Socialism," and his studies of domination.

Many of Weber's writings in political sociology have been collected by Peter Lassman and Ronald Speirs in the volume *Political Writings* (1994). Readers of German may consult the latest edition of Weber's *Gesammelte Politische Schriften* (1988), edited by Johannes Winkelmann, which includes a few additional texts. They may also consult relevant volumes in MWG.

The well-known "Parliament and Government in a Reconstructed Germany" can also be found in the current edition of *Economy and Society* (except for Section VI, which can be found in PW:233–71).

For a summary of Weber's political sociology, see e.g. Reinhard Bendix, *Max Weber: An Intellectual Portrait* (1960), pp. 285–494. For Johannes Winkelmann's attempt to reconstruct Weber's sociology of the state, see Max Weber, *Staatssoziologie* (1966; cf. WuG:815–68). For an introduction to Weber's political thought as well as his political sociology, see e.g. Ralph Schroeder, "From Weber's Political Sociology to Contemporary Liberal Democracy" (1998), David Beetham, *Max Weber and the Theory of Modern Politics* (1985), and Anthony Giddens, *Politics and Sociology in the Thought of Max Weber* (1984). See also in this context Peter Baehr, "The 'Masses' in Weber's Political Sociology" (1990). The standard work on Weber's personal views on politics is Wolfgang Mommsen, *Max Weber and German Politics 1890–1920* (1984).

See also citizenship, collegiality, demagogue, democracy, domination, imperialism, living for politics versus living off politics, nation, party, patrimonialism, plebiscitary domination and leadership, nation, political community, political organization, power, socialism, state

political sphere   *See* sphere

politics   What in everyday language is termed "politics" answers to two different kinds of social action, according to the terminology in Weber's general sociology in Ch. 1 of *Economy and Society*. There is first of all "politically oriented action" or attempts to influence or seize power. Then there is "political action" or the organized action of political groups.

The exact definition of politically oriented action is as follows: "social action, especially organized action, will be spoken of as 'politically oriented' if it aims at exerting influence on the government of a political organization; especially at the expropriation, redistribution or allocation of the powers of government" (ES:54). Political action is described in *Economy and Society* as "the actual organized action of political groups" (ES:55).

In his famous lecture "Politics as a Vocation," delivered on January 28, 1919, Weber explains what he means by "politics" in the following way: "'politics' for us means striving to share power or arriving to influence the distribution of power, either among states or among groups within a state" (GM:78, for the full text, see GM:77–128). "We wish to understand by politics only the leadership, or the influencing of the leadership, of a political association, hence today, of a state" (GM:77). Around the same time Weber also noted that "the essence of all politics . . . is conflict, the recruitment of allies and voluntary following"

(PW:173). Finally, Weber famously defines the work of the politician in "Politics as a Vocation" as "a strong and slow boring of hard boards" (GM:128).

Weber himself was intensely interested in politics, which he referred to as his "secret love" (in a letter of January 17, 1919 to Mina Tobler; cf. Weber 1988:19 n. 53). Nonetheless, he also had difficulties in translating his political interest into political action, and he once described himself as a "political 'loner'" (letter to Haussman of May 1, 1917; cf. Mommsen 1984:308).

In 1917 Weber stated in one of his public writings that "the author, who voted Conservative almost three decades ago and later voted Democratic, who then was given space in the [arch-conservative] *Kreuzzeitung* and now writes for liberal papers, is neither an active politician nor will he be one" (ES:1384). It can be added that while most of Weber's writings on politics are on the political situation in Germany, he was also interested in other countries, especially Russia (see e.g. PW, Weber 1995a).

Weber is generally considered to have been a fervent nationalist and a fervent liberal. In his liberalism he emphasized the need for separation of powers, a balance of power between capitalists and politicians, and a strong national leader; and in his nationalism he argued that Germany should have a colonial empire. He was very critical of Bismarck for having governed Germany in an authoritarian and pro-Junker manner, rather than letting the bourgeoisie develop its own political potential (see "Bismarck's Legacy," ES:1385–92). Weber believed in the freedom of the individual and also that Germany should be a leading nation in the world (a *Herrenvolk*, as he put it; *see* that entry).

Weber was a strong nationalist, and Karl Jaspers reports him as saying, "I thank God that I am a German" (Jaspers 1989:16). According to the same source, Weber was fearless as a political speaker and did not bend his opinions to the audience: "his courage to candidly speak what he saw and believed was equally great when he opposed the top powers of the old state or the workers" (ibid., p. 17).

When World War I broke out he proclaimed it "great and wonderful" (e.g. Käsler 1988:18). At the beginning of the war Weber administered some military hospitals with much skill. Toward the end of World War I and during its immediate aftermath, however, his political activities increased. Weber now, for example, helped to formulate the German response to the Versailles Treaty; he became deeply involved in the first draft of the constitution of the Weimar Republic; and for a while he was even thought of as a possible secretary of state for the interior (e.g. Wolfgang Mommsen, *Max Weber and German Politics 1890–1920* [1984], pp. 316–20, 332–89). According to Guenther Roth, recent information on Weber's political activities shows that they were "more extensive but also less influential than previously thought" (Roth 1989:138).

Modern rational capitalism needs a type of state that is predictable and also a predictable legal system (e.g. GEH:312–14; *see also* citizenship, the state). The administrators of this state should carry out their tasks in a rational and impartial manner (*homo politicus*; cf. GM:333–34).

For Weber's very special kind of liberalism, see e.g. Wolfgang Mommsen, "A Liberal in Despair," pp. 95–115 in *The Age of Bureaucracy* (1974). For more details, the reader is referred to Mommsen's important study, *Max Weber and German Politics 1890–1920*, pp. 390–414. See also David Beetham, "Max Weber and the Liberal Political Tradition" (1989). Weber's personal advocacy of a kind of democracy under charismatic leadership has been controversial. See in this context the discussion of Wolfgang Mommsen's famous assertion in 1959 (which he later modified), that Weber's ideas on this topic served "to make the German people inwardly willing to acclaim Adolf Hitler's leadership position" (cf. Mommsen 1984:410). For Weber's relationship to Carl Schmitt, see ibid., pp. 382–89.

A useful introduction to Weber's political thought can be found in David Beetham, *Max Weber and the Theory of Modern Politics* (1985). For a brief introduction to Weber's own political activities, see besides Mommsen's monograph e.g. Sven Eliaeson, "Constitutional Caesarism: Weber's Politics in Their German Contexts" (2000) and Guenther Roth, "Weber's Political Failure (Review of Max Weber, *Zur Neuordnung Deutschlands*, MWG 16)" (1989). For Weber's relationship to individual politicians, see e.g. Part 3 of Wolfgang Mommsen and Jürgen Osterhammel (eds.), *Max Weber and His Contemporaries* (1987). For Weber's relationship to anarchism, see Sam Whimster (ed.), *Max Weber and the Culture of Anarchy* (1999). Weber's political writings are in MWG, Vols. I/4 (1890s), I/15 (World War I), and I/16 (1918–20). His lectures on the state are in Vol. III/7, and a new edition of "Politics as a Vocation" can be found in Vol. I/17. For political science in nineteenth-century Germany, see e.g. the history of the so-called *Staatswissenschaften* (such as economics, politics, and statistics) in David Lindenfeld, *The Practical Imagination* (1997).

See also constitution, demagogue, domination, education (for political education), *Herrenvolk*, living off versus living for politics, legal domination, nation, party, plebiscitary domination and leadership, political community, power, state

"Politics as a Vocation"   *See* politics

polytheism   *See* monotheism/polytheism, value-spheres

population   While Weber did not devote any of his writings exclusively to population questions, he nonetheless touches on questions close to the concerns of demography in some of his writings.

Weber assigned, for example, a place to the study of population in relation to the economy in *The Handbook of Social Economics*. According to the plan of 1914, there was to be a section on "Economy and Population," which in its turn was to be divided into "The Theory of Population" and "Economy and Race" (see e.g. Johannes Winkelmann, *Max Webers hinterlassenes Hauptwerk* [1986], pp. 151, 168). Discussions of the role of population in the emergence of rational capitalism can also be found in the lecture course that Weber gave in 1919–20 and which has been reconstructed as *General Economic History* (e.g. GEH:352).

See also evolution, race, selection

positively privileged   *See* privileges

postmodernism   For parallels between Weber's work and those of Baudrillard, Foucault, and Lyotard, see Nicholas Gane, *Max Weber and Postmodern Theory* (2004).

power (*Macht*)   The core of Weber's famous definition of power is that you have power if you can enforce your own will even if another person tries to oppose you.

The exact definition of power, as this can be found in Weber's general sociology in Ch. 1 of *Economy and Society*, is "the probability that one actor within a social relationship will be in a position to carry out his own will despite resistance, regardless of the basis on which this probability rests" (ES:53; cf. the similar formulation in ES:926).

According to Weber's comment on this definition, the concept of power is "sociologically amorphous" (ES:53) in the sense that it covers a multitude of situations and qualities. The concept of domination, on the other hand, is more precise.

Power in the area of the economy differs from power more generally, Weber says in his analysis of domination (ES:214, 943–44; *see also* economic power, domination). For a full understanding of Weber's analysis of political power, the notion of power prestige is also important (*see* that entry).

Weber's famous definition of power in Ch. 1 of *Economy and Society* has been translated and summarized in a number of slightly different ways (for an enumeration of these, see e.g. Walliman, Rosenbaum, Tatsis, and Zito, "Misreading Weber: 'The Concept of *Macht*'" [1980]). In his recent translation of Ch. 1 of *Economy and Society* Keith Tribe offers the following version: "*Power (Macht)* can be defined as the chance, within a social relationship, of enforcing one's own will against resistance, whatever this chance might be based on" (EW:355).

See also collegiality, domination, economic power, power prestige, violence

power of control and disposal (*Verfügungsgewalt*)   *See* economic power

power prestige (*Machtprestige*)   In his discussion of political communities in *Economy and Society* Weber introduces the concept of power prestige, which is used to explain both the nature of nationalism and the reasons that political leaders of some political communities want these to expand (ES:910–12, 925).

Weber does not supply a definition of power prestige but simply notes that "the prestige of power means in practice glory over other communities" (ES:910–11). He adds that "this irrational element [can be found] in all political foreign relations"; and that power prestige lends a certain "dynamic" to political powers, especially the so-called great powers. Weber also argues that "the idea of the nation for its advocates stands in very intimate relation to 'prestige' interests" (ES:925).

See also power, nation

prebend   *See* prebendalism

prebendal feudalism   *See* feudalism

prebendalism (*Präbendalismus*)   Weber primarily discusses prebendalism in Ch. 3 on domination as well as in his historical sociology in *Economy and Society*. He describes it as a form of patrimonialism that is maintained through benefices, that is, through traditional allowances, incomes, and the like that cannot be inherited (for definitions of benefice, see ES:235, 1073; for a discussion of the concept of benefice; *see* that entry).

Weber notes in *Economy and Society* that "we shall speak of *prebends* and *prebendal* organization of offices in all cases of life-long assignment to officials of rent payments deriving from material goods, or of the essentially *economic* usufruct of land or other sources of rent, in compensation for the fulfillment of real or fictitious duties of office, for the economic support of which the goods in question have been *permanently* allocated by the lord" (ES:966–67).

For a discussion, see e.g. Bryan Turner, "Feudalism and Prebendalism," pp. 203–33 in *For Weber* (1981).

See also benefice, feudalism (for prebendal feudalism), patrimonialism, traditional domination

predestination (*Prädestination*)   Weber mainly discusses predestination in *The Protestant Ethic and the Spirit of Capitalism* and in his sociology of religion. It plays a key role in his argument that there exists a link between a certain type of religion and modern rational capitalism. The two main examples of predestination in Weber's work are Calvinism and Islam.

Predestination is central to Calvin's doctrine, according to *The Protestant Ethic* (PE:98–128). The fact that it was impossible for Calvin's followers to know if they belonged to the select few or not caused "religious anxiety" among them and was generally experienced as "intolerable" (PE:112, ES:1199). The response to this situation was an unrelenting attempt by the Calvinists to control their behavior as well as a search for "signs" that they were not among the damned (*"certitudio salutis"*). Success in business was interpreted as such a sign or as a "confirmation" (to use Weber's term; e.g. PE:172). "Inner-worldly asceticism and the disciplined quest for salvation in a vocation pleasing to God were the sources of the virtuosity in acquisitiveness characteristic of the Puritan" (ES:573–74).

In his sociology of religion Weber notes that one would expect predestination to lead to fatalism, but that it also may inspire the believer to great activity, in an attempt to realize God's design on earth (ES:572–76). While the element of predestination in Islam, for example, led the warrior to fight with complete abandon in battle, it did not produce the kind of methodical behavior and inner-worldly asceticism that one can find in Calvinism.

The reason for this, according to Weber, had to do with the fact that "the Mohammedan idea was that of predetermination, not predestination, and was applied to fate in this world, not in the next" (PE:227 n. 36; cf. 240 n. 106).

Finally, predestination constitutes one of the three consistent forms of theodicy (e.g. GM:358–59).

It is clear that predestination is at the very center of Weber's argument in *The Protestant Ethic*, and it is also clear that Weber presents no empirical evidence on how the believer's methodical behavior in religious matters spread to his or her behavior in economic matters. For a discussion of what this type of evidence might look like, and if it is realistic to think that it can ever be retrieved from historical sources, see Gordon Marshall, *In Search of the Spirit of Capitalism* (1982). See also in this context Kaspar von Greyerz, "Biographical Evidence on Predestination, Covenant, and Special Providence" (1993).

See also ascetic Protestantism, confirmation, Weber thesis, Protestantism

premium   *See* psychological or religious premium

press, the   Weber wanted the German Sociological Association to get involved in large-scale empirical research, and one of his suggestions was to investigate the press (for Weber's proposed survey, see Weber [1910] 1998).

prices   *See* market, the; self-interest or self-interested kind of behavior

priest (*Priester*)   Together with the magician and the prophet, the priest is one of the central figures in Weber's sociology of religion.

A priest is described in the section on religion in *Economy and Society*, as follows: "the term 'priest' may be applied to the functionaries of a regularly organized and permanent enterprise concerned with influencing the gods, in contrast with the individual and occasional efforts of magicians" (ES:425; cf. ES:424–27).

As opposed to the magician, the priest also draws on a doctrine or a system of religious concepts woven together into a consistent religious ethic (ibid.). A priesthood is based on a cult or a religious enterprise which has its own norms, special places, and relationships to various social groups (ES:426). A priest has a systematic education, as opposed to a magician, and is also paid, as opposed to a prophet.

For Weber's concept of the priest as well as its relationship to religious scholarship of the time, see Bernhard Lang, "Prophet, Priester, Virtuose" (2001).

See also magician, mysticism, prophet

primary patriarchalism   *See* patriarchalism

privileges (*Ermächtigungen, Priviligierungen*)   The English word "privileges" answers to two different terms in Weber's work: a special term in his sociology of law and a more general one in his description of social strata and classes. There are, to use an example of privileges in the latter meaning, social strata and classes that are either negatively or positively privileged. An example of a group that is negatively privileged would be slaves, while an example of a group that is positively privileged would be slave owners.

Modern law, Weber notes, is usually divided into prescriptive, prohibitory and permissive legal propositions (ES:667). The last of these he terms "privileges" in his sociology of law; the two former he calls "claims." Privileges are characterized by the fact that the law allows, and thereby increases, the likelihood that "one may . . . engage, or fail to engage, in certain conduct without interference from a third party" (ibid.).

Privileges fall into two main classes (ES:668). One consists of rights to freedom (*Freiheitsrechte*) that protect a person against the interference of a third party, especially the state. An example of this is freedom of conscience. The second class consists of privileges that give the individual autonomy to regulate his or her relationship to other people. Freedom of contract is an example of this.

See also claims, contract, rights, sociology of law, theodicy

probability (*Chance*)   The German term *Chance* is used in two different meanings in *Economy and Society*: as "probability" and as "opportunity" (*see* the separate entry for the latter meaning).

Weber also uses the notion of probability in different meanings in his work. For one thing, no social structure has a guaranteed existence, he argues in his general sociology in Ch. 1 of *Economy and Society*; there is only a probability that the social actions that make up the social structure will be repeated in the future as well. In the same chapter Weber also argues that sociology, like the other social sciences, cannot formulate laws, but only strong probabilities that something will happen. Finally, in his methodological writings Weber argues that the theory of causation, which fits the social sciences, contains an element of probability, in the sense that only if something is probable should it count as part of the causal chain.

As to the fact that no social structure exists per se, only a probability that the social actions that make up the structure will take place in the future as well as the past, Weber writes that "a 'state', for example, ceases to exist in a sociologically relevant sense whenever there is no longer any probability that certain kinds of meaningfully oriented social action will take place" (ES:27; cf. ES:28, 49).

The notion of probability also plays a role in Weber's argument that the social sciences cannot develop laws like those of the natural sciences. What the social sciences can do, however, Weber emphasizes, is to develop "typical probabilities confirmed by observation" (ES:18). As an example of this he mentions Gresham's Law.

Finally, probability is part of Weber's theory of causation ("adequate causation"). Drawing on ideas of the physiologist and probability thinker Johannes von Kries, Weber argues that social actions of a certain type qualify as a sufficient or adequate cause if there is a probability that they will affect the outcome. While statistics can work with objective probability, this is not the case in the cultural sciences (MSS:182–84). It is nonetheless possible to "estimate the relative 'degree' to which [some] outcome is 'favored'" by drawing on counterfactuals and what Weber terms objective possibility. This is the so-called loaded dice argument.

In commenting on Weber's statement in Ch. 1 of *Economy and Society* on the topic of probability, Talcott Parsons notes that since Weber uses *Chance* as interchangeable with *Wahrscheinlichkeit*, this term should be translated as "probability" (ES:59 n. 13). He adds that "As the term 'probability' is used in a technical mathematical and statistical sense . . . it implies the possibility of numerical statement. In most of the cases where Weber uses *Chance* this is out of the question. It is, however, possible to speak in terms of higher and lower degrees of probability. To avoid confusion with the technical mathematical concept, the term 'likelihood' will often be used in the translation [of *Economy and Society*]. It is by means of this concept that Weber, in a highly ingenious way, has bridged the gap between the interpretation of meaning and the inevitably more complex facts of overt action" (ibid.).

Parsons does not explicitly address the issue of whether the sociologist should also try to establish the probability involved, as seen from the perspective of the actor. In his 1913 essay on theoretical sociology, however, Weber makes clear that this is the case in his definition of social action: "an important (though not indispensable) normal component of social action (*Gemeinschaftshandeln*) is its meaningful orientation to the expectations of certain behavior on the part of others and, in accordance with that, orientation to the (subjectively) assessed probabilities for the success of one's action" (SCIS:159). Alfred Schutz argues that Weber, in discussing probability (*Chance*), mixes up the probability of the social scientist ("objective probability") with that of the actor ("subjective probability"; *The Phenomenology of the Social World* [(1932) 1967], pp. 152ff.; cf. pp. 237–39).

Various aspects of Weber's use of probability are also discussed in e.g. Ola Agevall, *A Science of Unique Events: Max Weber's Methodology of the Cultural Sciences* (1999) and Stephen Turner and Regis Factor, "Objective Possibility and Adequate Causation in Weber's Methodological Writings" (1981).

See also causality, loaded dice argument, opportunity, statistics

profession (*Beruf*)   The term *Beruf*, which is so central in Weber's work, can not only be translated as "vocation" and "occupation," but also as "profession."

In Weber's sociology of law, much attention is paid to the emergence of the legal profession (ES:784–808). The same is true for the profession of the priest in Weber's sociology of religion (e.g. ES:424–27). Weber's picture of the bureaucrat, who follows his duty and sticks to the rules, is also relevant for an understanding of his view of professions (e.g. ES:958–59). According to Weber, the monk was the first professional (ES:1172).

Talcott Parsons argues that Weber failed to develop an adequate analysis of the modern professions. His argument is that Weber's "emphasis on the economic rather than the occupational perhaps tends to account for one of Weber's conspicuous blind spots in this field, his failure to bring out the structural peculiarities of the modern professions and to differentiate between the organization of professional services and what may be called the 'administrative hierarchy' of occupational structure types" (p. 54 in Weber 1947).

Frank Parkin argues in *Marxism and Class Theory* (1979) that one can use Weber's notion of social closure in analyzing the professions.

See also occupation, open and closed social relations, vocation, work

profit-making (*Erwerben*)   Following the classical distinction of Aristotle and others between money-making and the management of a household, Weber contrasts what he calls profit-making to budgetary management. Capitalism is based on profit-making, and the planned economy on budgetary management.

According to Weber's economic sociology in Ch. 2 of *Economy and Society*, "'profit-making' is activity which is oriented to opportunities for seeking new powers of control over goods on a single occasion, repeatedly, or continuously" (ES:90).

"Capital" is related to profit-making, just as "wealth" is related to budgetary management. While profit-making aims at "profit," budgetary management aims at "rent." Calculations in profit-making are oriented to profitability, and to marginal utility in budgetary management. Rational profit-making entails capital accounting.

Profit-making is indifferent to substantive postulates. It is central to the concept of enterprise and it presupposes private property (and thereby also inheritance; *see* property).

Parsons notes apropos his translation of *Erwerben* as "profit-making" in Ch. 2 of *Economy and Society* that "in common usage the term *Erwerben* would perhaps best be translated as 'acquisition'" (ES:207 n. 16). He adds that he has not adopted this translation because "Weber is here using the term in a technical sense as the antithesis of *Haushalten* [budgetary management]" and that "'profit-making' brings out this specific meaning more clearly" (ibid.).

See also budgetary management, capital accounting, capitalism, property

property (*Eigentum*)   Property, from a sociological perspective, essentially consists of having access to something from which others are excluded. More precisely, Weber suggests that property consists of a form of monopolized and appropriated opportunity. The right to inheritance is also part of the concept of property.

Weber defines property in connection with his discussion of open and closed social relationships in his general sociology in Ch. 1 of *Economy and Society.* The exact definition reads as follows: "appropriated rights which are enjoyed by individuals through inheritance or by hereditary groups, whether communal or associative, will be called 'property' of the individual or of groups in question; and, insofar as they are alienable, 'free' property" (ES:44; cf. ES:343).

In his economic sociology Weber discusses a large number of different ways of appropriating the means of production (ES:130–40); and in his sociology of law Weber discusses legal aspects of property (e.g. ES:801). Property is also discussed in various parts of the *General Economic History* (e.g. GEH:26–50, 51–64).

Owning property is one thing, according to Weber, enjoying it is another. "The early Christian had his goods and women, 'as if he had them not'," we read in *The Religion of India* (RI:184). The prohibition against enjoying property naturally increased for the successful Puritan businessman (e.g. RC:245, PE:175–77).

See also appropriation, opportunity, open and closed social relations

prophecy   *See* prophet

prophet (*Prophet*)   Together with the magician and the priest, the prophet is one of the key figures in Weber's sociology of religion. The historical importance of the prophet is that he helped to challenge traditionalism, while he also invested the changes he made with a new legitimacy (e.g. ES:37). Finally, the prophet helped to break the power of magic and thereby furthered the process of rationalization (e.g. GEH:362).

A prophet is defined in the section on sociology of religion in *Economy and Society* as follows: "we shall understand 'prophet' to mean a purely individual bearer of charisma, who by virtue of his mission proclaims a religious doctrine or divine commandment" (ES:439).

The prophet differs from the priest in that he draws his authority from a personal call, not an office; and he differs from the magician (as well as the priest), in that he is not paid. The existing law is typically also set aside by the prophet and replaced with some reference to substantive justice ("It is written . . . but I say unto you . . . "—ES:242, 978, 1115). The prophet exemplifies what Weber calls charismatic leadership (GM:80).

Weber draws a distinction between what he calls "ethical prophecy" and "exemplary prophecy" (ES:447–50). In the former, the prophet is an instrument for the will of God and announces commands and norms that have to be followed, while in the latter it is his own personal behavior that becomes an example for others to follow. Muhammad was an ethical prophet and Buddha an exemplary prophet.

Weber discusses prophets from many different parts of the world and from various historical periods. In *Ancient Judaism* one can find a famous analysis of the old Hebrew prophets (see especially Ch. 11, "The Social Psychology of the Prophets," but also Chs. 4, 12). The Hebrew prophets tended to appear when Israel was threatened by the powers that surrounded it.

It is sometimes noted that Weber found elements in the prophets that he personally identified with. Marianne Weber, for example, comments on the parallels between Weber during World War I and Jeremiah, the prophet of doom (Marianne Weber, *Max Weber* [(1926) 1975], pp. 593–94). Talcott Parsons emphasizes the element of "breakthrough" in his comments on Weber's concept of the prophet as well as that of charisma. "The prophet," Parsons writes, "is above all the agent of the process of breakthrough to a higher, in the sense of more rationalized and systematized, cultural order" (Parsons 1963:xxxiii; cf. pp. xxxiii–xlix).

See e.g. Peter Berger, "Charisma and Religious Innovation: The Social Location of Israelite Prophecy" (1963). For a discussion of Weber's concept of the prophet as well as its relationship to religious scholarship of the time, see Bernhard Land, "Prophet, Priester, Virtuose" (2001) and Martin Riesebrodt, "Ethische und exemplarische Prophetie" (2001).

See also charisma, law prophet, magician, mysticism, priest

Protestant Ethic and the Spirit of Capitalism, The (*Die protestantische Ethik und der Geist des Kapitalismus*; **various translations**)   This famous study was originally published as two articles in 1904–5 in the *Archiv für Sozialwissenschaft und Sozialpolitik*. A second edition was published in 1920 as part of Weber's work *The Economic Ethics of the World Religions*.

Weber's argument in *The Protestant Ethic* is that Protestantism—and especially those forms of Protestantism that he terms ascetic Protestantism (Calvinism, Pietism, Methodism, and various sects growing out of the Baptist movement)—helped to end traditional capitalism and usher in a new type of capitalism, modern rational capitalism. It mainly accomplished this entrepreneurial feat by introducing a much more methodical attitude to work and profit-making. By being religious, ascetic Protestantism could also bypass the traditional resistance of religion to the positive evaluation of hard work and profit-making. A new type of entrepreneur and a new type of worker now emerged. Exactly how this argument is worked out in *The Protestant Ethic* is a much-debated question.

It is, however, generally agreed that the concept of calling (*Beruf*), which Luther introduced in his translation of the Bible, played a key role in this process, as well as religious asceticism. Working hard and re-investing the profit became part of the way of life of ascetic Protestants and "one particularly important component" of the spirit of capitalism, as Weber carefully phrases it (PED:95).

The link between religion and modern capitalism can, in other words, be found in the idea of vocation and in asceticism as a way of life more generally. Summing up his argument in *The Protestant Ethic*, Weber says that "religious forces have taken part in the qualitative formation and the quantitative expansion of that spirit [of modern rational capitalism] over the world" (PE:91). These religious forces, it may be added (to clarify Weber's argument), did not in any way help to create capitalist institutions since these were already in existence (but with a traditional spirit of capitalism) well before the advent of Protestantism (see GEH:352–69 for a fuller elaboration of Weber's argument on this point).

While Luther's view of vocation was deeply traditionalistic, this was not the case with Calvinism, owing to the latter's strong emphasis on the role of predestination. The gist of Weber's argument is that predestination made Calvinist believers feel extremely insecure; that this insecurity made them look for signs of not being damned; and that wealth was seen by some of Calvin's followers as such a sign (*certitudio salutis*; *see* Calvinism). Calvin himself, Weber carefully points out, did not view wealth in this manner.

Another important factor in heightening the idea of vocation and related notions was the sect, which is at the center of an article that complements *The Protestant Ethic*, entitled "The Protestant Sects and the Spirit of Capitalism" (GM:302–22; for earlier versions of this article, see Weber 1906a and [1906b] 1985 or [1906b] 2002).

In the last pages of *The Protestant Ethic* Weber sketches a program for future research, which he later would realize in the form of a series of studies of the relationship between economic ethics and religion (for the program, see PE:182–83; cf. PE:284 n. 119). The result of these efforts can be found in the three-volume *Collected Essays in the Sociology of Religion* (GAR; for translations of the main studies, see AJ, RI and RC).

The first and very influential translation of *The Protestant Ethic* (from the second German edition [1920]), by Talcott Parsons, was published in 1930. An often mentioned oddity with this translation is that Parsons inserted another text from Weber's sociology of religion at the very beginning ("Author's Introduction"), and that he did so in such a way that the reader is made to believe that it is part of *The Protestant Ethic*. A re-translation (also of the second German edition) was made by Stephen Kalberg in 2002 (Weber [1904–5] 2002b), and a translation of the first edition (1904–5) was made in 2002 by Peter Baehr and Gordon Wells (Weber [1904–5] 2002a). Another translation of the second edition, by

Peter Ghosh, is also on its way.

For summaries of *The Protestant Ethic*, see e.g. Reinhard Bendix, *Max Weber: An Intellectual Portrait* (1960), pp. 50–69 and Dirk Käsler, *Max Weber* (1988), pp. 74–94. A useful brief introduction can also be found in Gianfranco Poggi, *Calvinism and the Capitalist Spirit: Max Weber's Protestant Ethic* (1983).

Weber's own responses to the various critiques of *The Protestant Ethic* have recently been translated and published in David Chalcraft and Austin Harrington (eds.), *The Protestant Ethic Debate* (2001) as well as on pp. 221–339 in Peter Baehr's and Gordon Wells' translation of *The Protestant Ethic*. (For the debate inspired by *The Protestant Ethic*, see Weber thesis). For the full texts of the German-language critics, see Johannes Winkelmann (ed.), *Die Protestantische Ethik II: Kritiken und Antikritiken* (1978). In one of his answers to his critics Weber states that his study has its roots in lectures dating from 1897 and consequently predates Sombart's *Der moderne Kapitalismus*, published in 1902 (PED:62).

For a discussion of the translation of *The Protestant Ethic* and of Weber's contributions to the debate around this work, see the November 2001 issue of *Max Weber Studies*. For a critique of Parsons' translation, see Peter Ghosh, "Some Problems with Talcott Parsons' Version of 'The Protestant Ethic'" (1994). Cf. Weber [1904–5] 1993 for the two editions in German; *The Protestant Ethic* (in its two editions from 1904–5 and 1920) is due to appear as MWG, Vol. I/18.

See also *Ancient Judaism, Collected Essays in the Sociology of Religion, Economic Ethics of the World Religions, The*; Weber thesis, psychological and religious premium, *Religion of China, The*; *Religion of India, The*; social mechanisms

Protestant Ethic thesis   See *Protestant Ethic and the Spirit of Capitalism, The*; Weber thesis

"Protestant Sects and the Spirit of Capitalism, The"   See *Protestant Ethic and the Spirit of Capitalism, The*

Protestant work ethic   *See* work ethic

Protestantism   Weber assigns an important role to Protestantism in helping to create and spread the spirit of capitalism. This is especially the case with the part of Protestantism that Weber terms ascetic Protestantism and which is at the center of the argument in *The Protestant Ethic and the Spirit of Capitalism*. Inadvertently ascetic Protestantism made people turn to systematic profit-making and hard work—and thereby strengthened as well as gave these activities a religious legitimation.

Additional information on ascetic Protestantism, centered primarily on the role of sects in this religion, can also be found in Weber's article "The Protestant Sects and the Spirit of Capitalism" (GM:302–22; cf. "The Reformation and Its Impact on Economic Life" in ES:1196–1200).

While Lutheranism is similar to ascetic Protestantism when it comes to the idea that ordinary work should be carried out in the honor of God (vocation or *Beruf*), it lacks the reformist and activistic dimension of such religious movements as Calvinism and Methodism (e.g. ES:569–70, 1197–98, PE:112–13, 160). One reason for this is Lutheranism's emphasis on emotional unity with God; another its advocacy of obedience to earthly authorities. In brief, "Luther cannot be claimed for the spirit of capitalism" (PE:82).

While Protestantism at first found support in aristocratic circles, as time went on this tended to vanish and the middle classes became its main supporters (ES:1180–81).

Weber had ambivalent feelings toward Lutheranism and much preferred Puritanism. At one point he wrote that "Lutheranism . . . is the most terrible of terrors to me" (letter of February 5, 1906; cf. Mommsen 1984:167).

See e.g. Ernst Troeltsch, *Protestantism and Progress: A Historical Study of the Relation of Protestantism to the Modern World* (1912), Vol. 2 of *The Social Teachings of the Christian Churches* and Hartmut Lehmann and Guenther Roth (eds.), *Weber's Protestant Ethic* (1993).

See also ascetic Protestantism, Calvinism, Catholicism, Christianity, Weber thesis, religion (for Weber's personal relationship to Protestantism), Puritanism, vocation

psychic coercion   *See* coercion

psychological or religious premium (*Heilsprämie, psychologische Prämie*, and similar expressions)   This concept derives its importance from the role that it plays in Weber's explanation of why certain types of religion are effective in shaping the believer's personality while others are not. Setting a so-called psychological or religious premium on a certain type of behavior may considerably increase the likelihood that it will be practiced. Before the emergence of Protestantism there was, for example, no psychological premium in Christianity on work in one's secular profession (e.g. ES:1191; cf. e.g. RI:219, PED:108–9).

The concept of psychological premium is at the very center of the analysis in *The Protestant Ethic* (e.g. PE:97, 217, 234, 238). At one point Weber explains, for example, that the focus in the analysis is not on the impact of official statements or doctrine: "we are interested rather in something entirely different: the influence of those psychological sanctions which, originating in religious belief and the practice of religion, gave a direction to practical conduct and held the individual to it" (PE:97). Later Weber would summarize the same argument as follows: "it is not the ethical *doctrine* of a religion, but the form of ethical conduct on which *premiums* (*Prämien*) are placed that matter" (GM:321; cf. GM:459 n. 35, PED:108).

In his translation of *The Protestant Ethic* Parsons uses "sanction" for *Prämie*, which captures the negative side of what is involved but not the positive side (e.g. PE:97, 217, 238). The concept of psychological or religious premium, it may be added, is closely related to that of religious benefits (*Heilsgüter*). Parsons, finally, also translates *Antriebe* as "sanctions" in *The Protestant Ethic*, while a more literal translation might be "impulses" in the sense of "impulses that give a direction to practical conduct and hold the individual to it" (cf. PE:97).

See also confirmation, religious benefits, social mechanisms

psychologische Prämie   *See* psychological or religious premium

psychology   Weber was in general positive toward psychology and interested in its findings, including work in psychophysics and psychiatry. He was also of the opinion, however, that the psychology of his time had not developed so far that it could be used for the type of research that he himself was working on (e.g. PE:244 n. 114).

Weber states explicitly in *Economy and Society* that psychology does not constitute the foundation of interpretive sociology, and that the focus on meaning in this type of sociology does not somehow make it psychological (ES:17). Similarly, in his earlier research Weber notes that while psychology may be of help, "we will not . . . deduce institutions from psychological laws or explain them by elementary psychological phenomena" (MSS:89). Weber makes the same point in his reply to one of the critics of *The Protestant Ethic* (PED:35-7).

In addition, Weber points out in Ch. 1 of *Economy and Society*, some of the facts that psychology is interested in lack a distinct meaning, which means that they fall outside of Weber's definition of social action. "To still another category of facts devoid of meaning belong certain psychic or psychophysical phenomena such as fatigue, habituation, memory, etc.; also certain typical states of euphoria under some conditions of ascetic mortification; finally, typical variations in the reactions of individuals according to reaction-time, precision and other modes" (ES:7; cf. ES:13). The way to handle this type of phenomenon in Weber's sociology is as follows: "account must be taken of processes and stimuli which are devoid of subjective meaning, in the role of stimuli, results, favoring or hindering circumstances" (ibid.).

In his 1913 essay on interpretive sociology Weber is more blunt when it comes to the usefulness of psychology to his own brand of sociology: "interpretive sociology . . . is concerned neither with physiological phenomena which used to be called 'psychophysical' (pulse rates, for example, or changes in reaction time or the like) nor with strictly psychic conditions whereby the physiological phenomena may be characterized (for example, the combination of feelings of tension, pleasure, and aversion)" (SCIC:152). That Weber at this stage nonetheless wanted to clarify the relationship between interpretive sociology and psychology is clear from the fact that he devotes more than four pages in his 1913 article to this topic (SCIS:154–58).

For an argument that economic theory does not rest on psychology, see Weber's essay on marginal utility theory (ESS:249–60). For Weber's views on psychology, see Paul Honigsheim, *The Unknown Max Weber* ([1946–63] 2000), pp. 152–55; see also e.g. Sven Eliaeson, *Max Weber's Methodologies* (2002), pp. 44–6. For Weber's relationship to Freud, see e.g. Max Weber, "Freudianism" (Weber 1978:383–88), Tracy Strong, "Weber and Freud" (1987), and Howard Kaye, "Rationalization as Sublimation: On the Cultural Analyses of Weber and Freud" (1992). More generally, see Jörg Frommer, Sabine Frommer, and Michael Langenbach, "Max Weber's Influence on the Concept of Comprehension in Psychiatry" (2000).

See also acquisitive drive, marginal utility, motive, psychophysics

psychophysics   In Weber's time the term "psychophysics" was used to denote an area of physiological psychology which used experiments to explore topics such as fatigue at work and capacity to work. Weber was very interested in questions of this type and explored their potential for his own research on the role of work in capitalism. His two main writings on this topic consist of a huge survey article on psychophysics and his methodological introduction to a study of workers in large corporations (GASS:61–255; Weber [1908] 1980; cf. ES:1156). His conclusions, however, were mainly negative: the results of psychophysics, he came to believe, cannot be used in sociology.

This negative opinion is reflected in the following statement in Weber's general sociology in Ch. 1 of *Economy and Society*: "to still another category of facts devoid of meaning belong certain psychic or psychophysical phenomena such as fatigue, habituation, memory, etc." (ES:7; cf. ES:13). The way to handle phenomena of this type is as follows: "account must be taken of processes and stimuli which are devoid of subjective meaning, in the role of stimuli, results, favoring or hindering circumstances" (ibid.).

The same general conclusion can be found in Weber's essay on interpretive sociology from 1913: "interpretive sociology . . . is concerned neither with physiological phenomena which used to be called 'psychophysical' (pulse rates, for example, or changes in reaction time or the like) nor with strictly psychic conditions whereby the physiological phenomena may be characterized (for example, the combination of feelings of tension, pleasure, and aversion)" (SCIC:152).

See Dirk Käsler, *Max Weber* (1988) pp. 66–73 and Wolfgang Schluchter, "Psychophysics and Culture" (2000). See also the introduction by Wolfgang Schluchter and Sabine Frommer to Max Weber's writings on psychophysics in MWG, Vol. I/11.

See also psychology, industrial sociology

Puritanism   This type of religion is part of what Weber refers to as ascetic Protestantism in *The Protestant Ethic and the Spirit of Capitalism*. In this study Weber also notes: "when we use the expression [Puritanism] it is always in the sense which it took on in the popular speech of the seventeenth century, to mean the ascetically inclined religious movements in Holland and England without distinction of Church organization or dogma, thus including Independents, Congregationalists, Baptists, Mennonites, and Quakers" (PE:217 n. 2; cf. PE:96, RC:238). In the same study Weber also says that "Puritanism" is "a highly ambiguous word" and roughly refers to the "ascetic movement" within Protestantism (PE:96).

In *The Protestant Ethic and the Spirit of Capitalism* Weber uses Richard Baxter's work as an example of Puritan ethics. Baxter assigns a central place to wealth and its temptations, arguing that "you may labour to be rich for God but not for the flesh and the sin" (PE:162).

Weber's study *The Religion of China* ends with a famous chapter in which Confucianism and Puritanism are compared (RC:226–49). For a discussion, see e.g. Michael Walzer, "Puritanism as a Revolutionary Ideology" (1964).

See also ascetic Protestantism, Calvinism, Protestantism

Quote marks and italics in Weber's texts   The reader of Weber's work soon becomes aware that Weber was in the habit of liberally inserting quote marks around single concepts and expressions in his texts as well as italics (in the old-fashioned German form of extended spacing). In the title of the first edition of *The Protestant Ethic and the Spirit of Capitalism*, there are for example quote marks around "spirit," and similarly around "objectivity" and "value-freedom" in Weber's well-known essays on these topics from 1904 and 1917. By using quote marks and italics, one may say that Weber added a layer of meaning.

According to Hans Henrik Bruun, "Weber's quote marks and italics must be taken seriously" (Bruun 2004; cf. Bruun 1972:16 n. 2). Bruun notes that Weber typically used quote marks to distance or relativize some concept or expression (cf. Ghosh 1994:114–15, Roth in ES:cvii). It should finally be noted that translators of Weber's texts often fail to include Weber's quote marks and italics.

"**R**. Stammlers 'Überwindung' der materialistischen Geschichtsauffassung" See *Critique of Stammler*

race Weber argues in his sociology that a factor such as race should not be used as an explanation for two reasons. First, it falls outside the factors that interpretive sociology deals with since it has no inherent significance or meaning. Second, the current state of knowledge about race or any other inherited factors that supposedly lead to uniform behavior is very low. Weber was in general very critical of social science authors who used race as an explanation. This last statement does not, however, mean that one cannot find statements in Weber's work that today would be termed racist. This is especially the case with some of his early writings.

Weber writes in his general sociology in Ch. 1 of *Economy and Society* that if at some time in the future science will be able to link "non-interpretable uniformities" to differences in inherited characteristics, including race, these will have to be treated just like any other physiological data (ES:7–8; SCIS:153). This means that they should be treated as "stimuli which are devoid of subjective meaning . . . favoring or hindering circumstances" (ES:7; cf. ES:13). Weber also points out that belonging to the same (alleged) race does not imply some kind of communal relationship between its members; for this they have to mutually orient their actions to each other and develop a sense that they indeed belong together (ES:42; cf. ES:385).

In *Economy and Society* the concept of race is mainly discussed in the chapter on ethnic groups (ES:385–98). Weber here draws a sharp line between the question whether race really matters and people's belief that race matters. "Race" in the latter sense may be part of Weber's notion of ethnic group, defined as a group of people with the subjective belief that they have a common descent due to similarities in physical type and/or customs.

Once social action is inspired by a belief in "race," Weber also notes, it leaves reason behind: "Persons who are externally different are simply despised irrespective of what they accomplish or what they are or, conversely, viewed with superstitious awe" (ES:385).

In one of his writings from the mid-1910s Weber argues that assumptions about heredity should only be made as a last resort, after all social factors have been thoroughly explored (e.g. PE:30–1; cf. Weber [1908] 1980:126–32). Given the current stage of knowledge, this means that inheritance should be kept out of the picture ("with race theories you can prove and disprove anything you want"—ES:398 n. 1).

In his discussion of the theodicy of good fortune Weber touches on the issue of how "race" is used to legitimize power and domination. Just as successful individuals are not satisfied with their success, but also want to feel that they deserve it, so do certain groups: "every highly privileged group develops the myth (*Legende*) of its natural, especially its blood, superiority" (ES:953).

Weber had originally scheduled himself for writing a section on "Economy and Race" in the *Handbook of Social Economics* (*Grundriss der Sozialökonomik*). This section, however, was eventually given to Robert Michels.

While Weber in his major sociological works speaks in an objective tone and rarely refers to race in evaluative ways, this is less the case in some of his other work. In one of his most important early writings—the famous inaugural speech at the University of Freiburg of 1895—Weber speaks, for example, of "the German race," "the Slav race," "inferior races," and the like (e.g. PW:8, 12, 14; for Weber's attitude to the Poles, see e.g. Guenther Roth, "Between Cosmopolitanism and Ethnocentrism: Max Weber in the Nineties" [1993]). Similarly, a few years before his death—in the equally important "Parliament and Government in a Reconstructed Germany"—Weber refers to the fight of the German Army against "Africans, Gurkhas and all kinds of other barbarians" (ES:1382, cf. e.g. Mommsen 1984:191). While Weber, in brief, took a stance against racism, it is nonetheless common to find ethnic and racial slurs in his early social science writings, especially about the role of the Poles in Germany. There is much less of this type of material in Weber's later work.

According to Wolfgang Mommsen, Weber used Social Darwinist arguments in his early works, but "later rejected and fought all biological theories and concepts in the field of social science as unscientific" (Mommsen 1984:41).

For Weber's critical attitude to Alfred Ploetz, who in 1904 founded the German Society for Racial Hygiene, see Max Weber, "Max Weber on Race and Society" ([1910] 1971) and "Max Weber, Dr. Alfred Ploetz, and W. E. B Du Bois" (1973). Apropos Du Bois, Weber tried to arrange for a translation into German of *The Souls of Black Folk*—that "splendid work" (Scaff 1998:69).

See Karl-Ludwig Ay, "Max Weber und der Begriff der Rasse" (1993). There is currently not a single good article or book in English that summarizes and discusses Weber's views on race. For the moment, the reader is referred to Ernst Moritz Manasse, "Max Weber on Race" (1947). For the role of inheritance more generally in Weber's work, see e.g. Dirk Käsler, *Max Weber* (1988), pp. 66–73. For Weber and anti-Semitism as well as anti-Semitism in Germany in Weber's time, see e.g. Gary Abraham, *Max Weber and the Jewish Question* (1992).

See also ethnic groups, inheritance, Judaism, nation, selection

racism   *See* race

rational action   *See* rationality

Rational and Social Foundations of Music, The (Die rationalen und soziologischen Grundlagen der Musik, trans. 1958)   *See* sociology of music

rational capitalism   *See* capitalism

rational choice   Several advocates of rational choice sociology, which emerged in the 1990s, refer positively to various aspects of Weber's work in their writings (e.g. Edgar Kiser and Michael Hechter, "The Debate on Historical Sociology: Rational Choice Theory and Its Critics" [1998] and Raymond Boudon, "Beyond Rational Choice Theory" [2003]; for a summary statement and overview, see e.g. Zenonas Norkus, "Max Weber's Interpretive Sociology and Rational Choice Approach" [2000] and *Max Weber and Rational Choice* [2002]). The aspects that are singled out typically include Weber's adherence to methodological individualism and his ideas on rationality.

For an argument that Weber's sociology differs on crucial points from the rational choice paradigm, see e.g. Stephen Kalberg, *Max Weber's Comparative-Historical Sociology* (1994), pp. 62–8 and "On the Neglect of Weber's *Protestant Ethic* as a Theoretical Treatise" (1996). For an argument that Weber developed an interest-centered type of analysis which can be characterized as a social and flexible version of rational choice analysis, see Richard Swedberg, "The Changing Picture of Max Weber" (2003).

See also irrationality, marginal utility theory, methodological individualism, rationality

rational evident (providing a rational basis for certainty)   See *Evidenz*

rationalen und soziologischen Grundlagen der Musik, Die (The Rational and Social Foundations of Music)   *See* sociology of music

rationalism (*Rationalismus*)   Rationalism represents one of the great themes in Weber's work. While rationalism is traditionally defined as a reliance on reason as a guide for belief and action, Weber uses it in many different ways.

The term "rationalism" can often be found in the *Collected Essays in the Sociology of Religion* and also in *Economy and Society*. At one point Weber states that "rationalism is an historical concept which covers a whole world of different things" (PE:78). He also emphasizes that rationalism develops unevenly in different parts or spheres of society (e.g. PE:26, 77). While law can be highly rational in a society, for example, its economy can be primitive.

Sam Whimster defines rationalism, as used by Weber, as "an intellectual imposition of a coherent and ordered set of ideas upon the world" (EW:410). He also says that for Weber "rationalism is instanced in a wide variety of forms: ascetic rationalism, Confucian rationalism, legal rationalism, scientific rationalism, technological rationalism, economic rationalism, etc." Wolfgang Schluchter, who has devoted several major studies to the theme of rationalism in Weber's work, says that Weber uses the terms rationalism and rationalization "in a completely 'inflationary' manner" (Schluchter 1989:100; cf. Schluchter, 1981b, 1989).

See also rationalization, rationality

rationality (*Rationalität*)   The concept of rationality plays a central role in Weber's general sociology in Ch. 1 of *Economy and Society* and also in his sociology as a whole. The meaning of rationality is notoriously hard to define, not least since Weber typically differentiates between a formal concept of rationality and one that has to do with values.

In his general sociology in Ch. 1 of *Economy and Society* Weber discusses rationality in several different contexts: as part of his commentary on the definition of sociology in the first paragraph of *Economy and Society*, in his typology of different types of social action, and as part of many individual concepts.

For methodological convenience, Weber argues, sociology should start out by constructing what a rational action would look like—and then attempt to explain deviations from this.

Another important quality of using rational action is that it has the highest degree of verifiable certainty. Weber nonetheless emphasizes that the methodological use of rationality does not mean "a belief in the predominance of rational motives" or a positive attitude to "rationalism" (ES:18).

Social action, according to an important distinction in *Economy and Society* that involves rationality, can be either instrumentally rational or value-rational; affectual action, on the other hand, is usually irrational in nature. Weber furthermore draws on the concept of rational action to construct certain associations or organizations.

In Ch. 2 of *Economy and Society*, which is devoted to economic sociology, rationality similarly plays a key role. A distinction is drawn between "the formal rationality" and "the substantive rationality" of economic action (ES:85–6). Formal rationality in this context means quantitative calculation or accounting, while substantive rationality means the provisioning of groups of people in accordance with certain values. Money is central to formal rationality in economic affairs (ES:86–90).

In Ch. 3 of *Economy and Society*, which deals with domination, Weber defines legal domination in terms of the "rational grounds" on which it rests—that is, in terms of the belief in the legality of enacted rules (ES:215–26). Rationality also plays a role in Ch. 4 of *Economy and Society*, which is devoted to status groups and classes. While classes are connected to the market, where instrumental rationality is crucial, status groups rest on conventions and may develop irrational consumption patterns.

In Weber's sociology of law in *Economy and Society* a distinction is made between formal and substantive rationality when it comes to lawmaking and law-finding (ES:656–58). Formal rationality means that the intellect has control over the legal process, and substantive rationality means that decisions are made by referring to general norms and not just to the concrete details involved. Law has gone through various "stages of rationalization," Weber argues, from charismatic legal revelation to the systematization and administration of law by modern legal experts (e.g. ES:882).

Analysis in terms of rationality can also be found in Weber's sociology of religion, in *Economy and Society* as well as in *Collected Essays in the Sociology of Religion*. Asceticism has, for example, a rational element—and so do the systematization of religion, the elimination of magic, the decision to approach God in terms of law rather than, say, through one's emotions, and many other aspects of religious phenomena (e.g. AJ:396–97, 262–63, RC:226, 247, RI:119–21,148–49, ES:424, 426).

Weber also draws heavily on the concept of rationality in *The Protestant Ethic*. He notes, for example, that this concept may seem "superficially simple" but emphasizes that in reality it is characterized by "complexity" (PE:194 n. 9). He also notes that "a thing is never irrational in itself, but only from a particular rational point of view" (ibid.). For someone who does not believe in God, for example, the religious way of life is irrational. "What is rational from one point of view may well be irrational from another" (PE:26).

Friedrich Tenbruck argues that "the entirety of [Weber's] work, including his methodology, owes its existence to the question: what is rationality?" (1980:343). According to Rogers Brubaker, "rationality is an *idée-maîtresse* in Weber's work, one that links his empirical and methodological investigations with his political and moral reflections" (Brubaker 1984:1). He also notes that Weber uses the term rational in many contexts but perhaps most characteristically in connection with modern capitalism and ascetic Protestantism. Brubaker adds that "no fewer than sixteen apparent meanings of 'rational' can be culled from this highly schematic summary of Weber's characterization of modern capitalism and ascetic Protestantism: deliberate, systematic, calculable, impersonal, instrumental, exact, quantitative, rule-governed, predictable, methodical, purposeful, sober, scrupulous, efficacious, intelligible and consistent" (ibid., p. 2). Herbert Marcuse, finally, argues that Weber is only seemingly neutral in his use of rationality: "in Weber's sociology formal rationality turns without a break into capitalist rationality" (Marcuse 1972:133).

For an introduction to Weber's notion of rationality, see e.g. Martin Albrow, *Max Weber's Construction of Social Theory* (1990), pp. 114–34, Rogers Brubaker, *The Limits of Rationality* (1964), Stephen Kalberg, "Max Weber's Types of Rationality: Cornerstones for the Analysis of Rationalization Processes in History" (1980), and Wolfgang Schluchter, *The Rise of Western Rationalism* (1981).

See also instrumentally rational action, objectively correct rationality, rationalism, social action, value-rational action

rationalization (*Rationalisierung*)   This important term, which is not explicitly defined in Weber's work, refers to the growth of rationality—a process that is particularly typical of the West and which informs its economy, politics, and culture in a broad sense. Weber does not discuss this process very much in his general sociology in Ch. 1 of *Economy and Society*. It does, however, hold a central place in his *Collected Essays in the Sociology of Religion* and is also reflected in many parts of *Economy and Society*. The process of rationalization is also often seen as the core of Weber's philosophy of history.

In the introductory remarks to his *Collected Essays in the Sociology of Religion* Weber speaks of the "specific and peculiar rationalism of Western culture" (PE:26).

Weber typically uses the term rationalization in the sense of an increase in instrumentally rational action, but also points out that it can mean an increase in value-rational social action (ES:30). He notes that there are "many possible meanings of the concept of rationalization" (ibid.).

Rationalization covers many different phenomena, inside as well as outside the West. "There is, for example, rationalization of mystical contemplation . . . just as much as there are rationalizations of economic life, of technique, of scientific research, of military training, of law and administration. Furthermore, each one of these fields may be rationalized in terms of very different ultimate values and ends, and what is rational from one viewpoint may well be irrational from another. Hence rationalizations of the most varied character have existed in various departments of life and in all areas of culture."(PE:26).

Weber's analysis of the process of rationalization in the areas of religion and law can be studied in the sections devoted to sociology of religion and sociology of law in *Economy and Society* (ES:399–634, 641–900; cf. RSFM for the rationalization of music). Law, for example, has gone through various "stages of rationalization"—from charismatic legal revelation to the systematization and administration of law by modern legal experts (ES:882; cf. ES:776). "Religious rationalization," Weber notes, "has its own dynamics, which economic conditions merely channel; above all, it is linked to the emergence of priestly education" (ES:1179; cf. RC:226). Religion has replaced magic, and has over time become increasingly private and irrational in nature (e.g. ES:424).

It appears that it was around 1910 that Weber made the important discovery that rationality informs much of Western culture, as opposed to the cultures of other civilizations, and that this represented an important topic for him to study (Wolfgang Schluchter, *Rationalism, Religion, and Domination* [1989], p. 430; cf. Marianne Weber, *Max Weber* [(1926) 1975], p. 333).

Many commentators see the rationalization of the West as the central problem in Weber's work. According to Karl Mannheim, for example, "Max Weber's whole work is in the last analysis directed toward the problem: 'Which social factors have brought about the rationalization characteristic of Western civilization?'" (Karl Mannheim, *Man and Society in an Age of Reconstruction* [1940], p. 52).

More generally on the process of rationalization, see Rogers Brubaker, "The Specific and Peculiar Rationalism of Modern Western Civilization," pp. 8–48 in *The Limits of Rationality* (1984), Jürgen Habermas, "Max Weber's Theory of Rationalization," pp. 143–271 in Vol. 1 of *The Theory of Communicative Action* (1984), Benjamin Nelson, "Max Weber's

'Author's Introduction' (1920): A Master Clue to His Main Aims" (1974), and Wolfgang Schluchter, *The Rise of Western Rationalism* (1981). Finally, according to Wolfgang Schluchter, Weber uses the terms rationalization and rationalism "in a completely 'inflationary' manner" (Schluchter 1989:100).

See also disenchantment, irrationality, rationalism, rationality; West, the

Raubkapitalismus (robber capitalism)   *See* adventurers' capitalism

reception of Weber's work   One of the questions that is often discussed in the secondary literature on Weber has to do with the reception of his work in various countries, primarily in Germany but also in the United States, France, Japan, and elsewhere. Attention has furthermore been paid to the reception by certain groups, such as Marxists, economic historians, economists, and theologians.

The reception of Weber in Germany during his lifetime and for some time after World War II was unenthusiastic, as can be shown by the fact that less than two thousand copies of *Economy and Society* were sold during 1922–47 (Dirk Käsler, *Max Weber* [1988], p. 209). Since the mid-1960s, however, there has been a steady growth of interest in Weber in Germany. The current publication of the *Gesamtausgabe* has also led to an important advance in knowledge about Weber's work, including its reception in Germany. The current generation of Weber scholars includes Karl-Ludwig Ay, Stefan Breuer, Edith Hanke, Wilhelm Hennis, Dirk Käsler, Wolfgang Mommsen, Martin Riesebrodt, Wolfgang Schluchter, and many others.

The reception of Weber's work in the United States has been widespread, and has gone through several phases. Before the 1930s Weber was rarely referred to by sociologists. During the 1930s and 1940s a pioneering role was played by Talcott Parsons, through commentaries on Weber's texts as well as translations. Parsons translated not only *The Protestant Ethic and the Spirit of Capitalism* (1930) but also Part 1 or the first four chapters of *Economy and Society* (1947; for Chs. 1–2 he used a draft by economist A. M. Henderson). Other important early contributions and translations were made by Guenther Roth, Reinhard Bendix, Hans Gerth, and Don Martindale, among others. Guenther Roth and Claus Wittich jointly oversaw the putting together of *Economy and Society* (1968) into a single huge work of about fifteen hundred pages, a task that meant making new translations as well as checking existing ones.

Current Weber scholars in the United States and elsewhere in the English-speaking world include, among others, Stephen Kalberg, Guy

Oakes, Guenther Roth, Ralph Schroeder, Alan Sica, Keith Tribe, Bryan Turner, Stephen Turner, and Sam Whimster. The name of Weber, often in combination with a reference to *The Protestant Ethic*, can also now and then be found in the media, notably *Time*, *Newsweek*, and the *New York Times*.

In France, Raymond Aron has been the major figure, while Julien Freund and Pierre Bourdieu have been important as well. Many of Weber's writings have still not been translated into French, but important beginnings with the study and translation of Weber's work have been made by Jean-Pierre Grossein and Hinnerk Bruhns among others. Finally, Weber, like some other German scholars, has had a very strong reception in Japan.

For a general introduction to the reception of Weber's work, see Charles Turner, "Weberian Social Thought, History of" (2001). For the reception of Weber's work during his own lifetime, see Käsler, *Max Weber*, pp. 197–210; see also Arnold Zingerle, *Max Webers Historische Soziologie* (1981). For the reception of Weber in Japan, see Guenther Roth, "Max Weber at Home and in Japan: On the Troubled Genesis and Successful Reception of His Work" (1999); see also Wolfgang Schwentker, *Max Weber in Japan* (1998). For the United States, see e.g. Jere Cohen, Lawrence Hazelrigg and Whitney Pope, "De-Parsonizing Weber: A Critique of Parsons' Interpretation of Weber's Sociology" (1975), Guy Oakes, "Guenther Roth and Weberian Studies in America" (1997), and "Gerth, Mills, and Shils: The Origin of *From Max Weber*" (1999), and Richard Swedberg, "The Changing Picture of Max Weber" (2003).

For the reception of Weber in the media, see e.g. Alan Sica, "Weberian Theory Today"(2001). For France, see Monique Hirschhorn, *Max Weber et la sociologie française* (1988) and Philippe Steiner, "*L'Année Sociologique* et la reception de l'oeuvre de Max Weber" (1992). For Weber's lack of reference to the work of Durkheim and vice versa, see e.g. Edward Tiryakian, "A Problem for the Sociology of Knowledge: The Mutual Unawareness of Emile Durkheim and Max Weber" (1966) and Anthony Giddens, "Weber and Durkheim: Coincidence and Divergence" (1987). For Italy, see Giuseppe Antonio di Marco, "Max Weber in Italia: Linee di una interpretazione" (1983). For Mexico, see Rafael Farfan Hernandez, "La recepción actual de Weber" (1994). For Poland, see Jerzy Szacki, "Max Weber in Polish Sociology" (1982).

The reception of Weber in Marxist circles is discussed in Johannes Weiss, *Weber and the Marxist World* (1981).

See also neo-Weberianism, secondary literature on Weber's work, Weber, Max—Works, Weberianism, Weber-inspired scholars and scholarship

Rechtschöpfung (**lawmaking**)   *See* lawmaking and law-finding

Rechtsfindung   *See* lawmaking and law-finding

Rechtsformalismus (**legal formalism**)   *See* justice

Rechtshonoratioren   *See* legal *Honoratioren*

Rechtsstaat   *See* constitution

reflexivity   While the idea of objectivity is today accepted in social science, the notion of reflexivity—or that social scientists should be aware of the social forces that influence their thinking—is still somewhat controversial. Weber does not use the term "reflexivity," but covers much of the same ground through his notion of value-relevance, or the idea that researchers' studies are related to the values of their culture.
   See also objectivity, value-relevance

rejection of the world   *See* world-rejection

relationship   *See* social relationship

religion   Weber produced a general sociology of religion as well as a number of studies of the relationship between religion and the economy, centered around the thesis that ascetic Protestantism helped to create modern rational capitalism.
   For methodological reasons Weber states in the beginning of his sociology of religion in *Economy and Society* that a definition of religion cannot be given at the outset of the analysis, but only at its end (ES:399). However, he never supplied this definition since he never finished his sociology of religion. Weber also notes that "the essence of religion is not . . . our concern, as we make it our task to study the conditions and effects of a particular type of social action" (ES:399). To Weber, in brief, religion was primarily of interest to the sociologist as a kind of social action.
   For Weber's purposes in his studies, religion and magic primarily have to do with the ordering of the relations between gods, demons, and the like, on the one hand, and humans on the other. He also notes that in the early days of mankind, when religion was invented, the idea of being confronted with supernatural powers constituted a "new experience" for human beings (ES:403).
   The magical ethic was eventually replaced by a religious ethic (ES:437). In many religions, according to Weber, there exists a tension between ordinary reality and the realm of religion; and the way that this tension is handled has an important impact not only for the personality of the believer but also for society. While most religions, for example,

have had a conservative impact on economic life, ascetic Protestantism helped to spark the spirit of modern capitalism. In modern society religion is becoming more irrational in nature and also more private (e.g. ES:424).

People differ in their "religious capacities," according to Weber (e.g. ES:539, GM:287; cf. Krech 2001b). So-called religious virtuosi have a distinct religious status and are characterized by their capacity to work methodically on their salvation. Examples of religious virtuosi include the members of monastic orders and the ascetic sects in Protestantism. The opposite of virtuoso religiosity is what Weber calls mass religiosity. "By 'mass' we understand those who are religiously 'unmusical'" (GM:287).

While the privileged classes mainly have a need for religion to justify and legitimize their good fortune, it is different with the unprivileged. These need a release from their suffering; and to them religion is mainly an expression of their hope that they will one day receive a just compensation (e.g. ES:490–92).

A major theme in Weber's work on religion has to do with the relationship between religion and the economy, especially the role of religion in the emergence (or blocking) of modern rational capitalism. While most religions have blocked the emergence of this type of capitalism, ascetic Protestantism constitutes an important exception (*see* e.g. economic ethic, Weber thesis).

For Weber and religion, see e.g. Paul Honigsheim, *On Max Weber* (1968), pp. 90–109 and "Max Weber: His Religious and Ethical Background and Development," pp. 99–120 in *The Unknown Max Weber* ([1946–63] 2000). For Weber's participation in a Protestant group in the 1890s, see Rita Aldenhoff, "Max Weber and the Evangelical-Social Congress" (1987); and for his relationship to its leader, see Peter Theiner, "Friedrich Naumann and Max Weber: Aspects of a Political Partnership" (1987). From these and other sources it is clear that Weber was favorably disposed toward Protestantism, especially ascetic Protestantism, but was negative toward Catholicism.

Nonetheless, Weber considered himself as "totally 'unmusical'" in religious matters (letter to Ferdinand Tönnies, February 19, 1909; cf. Weber 1994a:65). In an often cited letter to Adolf von Harnack of February 5, 1906, Weber also states that "our nation has never in any way experienced the school of hard asceticism. . . . This is the source of all that I find contemptible in it (as in myself)" (Mommsen 1984:94; cf. Weber 1990:32–3). "He was . . . no Christian," as Karl Jaspers once described Weber's relationship to religion (Jaspers 1989:22).

See also the essays devoted to Weber's relationships to various theologians and historians of religion, including Ernst Troeltsch, in Part 2 of Wolfgang Mommsen and Jürgen Osterhammel (eds.), *Max Weber and His Contemporaries* (1987). For Weber from a theological viewpoint, see e.g. Thomas Ekstrand, *Max Weber in a Theological Perspective* (1999). A new edition of Weber's sociology of religion will appear as MWG, Vol. I/22-2. For an introduction to the key concepts in Weber's sociology of religion, see Hans Kippenberg and Martin Riesebrodt (eds.), *Max Webers "Religionssystematik"* (2001).

See also ascetic Protestantism, Buddhism, Calvinism, Catholicism, Christianity, church, *Collected Essays in the Sociology of Religion*, Confucianism, Hinduism, Islam, Judaism, monotheism/polytheism, priest, prophet, Protestantism, Puritanism, religious benefits, religious communities or groups, sacred law, salvation, sect, sociology of religion, world-religion

Religion of China, The (*Konfuzianismus und Taoismus*, trans. 1951) This study by Weber is part of his huge work *The Economic Ethics of the World Religions*. The key question raised in this work is: Why did rational capitalism not emerge by itself in China? Weber's answer is that several factors contributed to this, such as the power of the kin and the lack of a strong bourgeoisie.

The Religion of China first appeared in 1915 and was revised in 1920. The English translation was made by Hans Gerth and is based on the text in Vol. 1 of Weber's *Gesammelte Aufsätze zur Religionssoziologie*. A new edition of the German original has been published as MWG, Vol. I/19.

For a summary of the content of *The Religion of China*, see e.g. Reinhard Bendix, *Max Weber: An Intellectual Portrait* (1960), pp. 98–141, and Dirk Käsler, *Max Weber* (1988), pp. 97–111. For the early reception of this study, see again Käsler, *Max Weber*, pp. 205–6. See also Otto Van Der Sprenkel, "Max Weber on China" (1964).

See also Ancient Judaism, Collected Essays in the Sociology of Religion, Economic Ethics of the World Religions, The; Protestant Ethic and the Spirit of Capitalism, The; Religion of India, The

Religion of India, The (*Hinduismus und Buddhismus*, trans. 1958) This study by Weber is part of his huge work *The Economic Ethic of the World Religions*. The key question raised in this work is: Why did rational capitalism not emerge by itself in India? Weber's answer is that a series of factors contributed to this, not least the conservative power of Hinduism.

The Religion of India first appeared in 1916–17 but was later revised in 1920. The translation (which is considered problematic) was made by Hans Gerth and Don Martindale, and is based on the text in Vol. 2 of

Weber's *Gesammelte Aufsätze zur Religionssoziologie*. A new edition has been published as MWG, Vol. I/20.

For a summary of the content of *Ancient Judaism*, see e.g. Reinhard Bendix, *Max Weber: An Intellectual Portrait* (1960), pp. 142–200, and Dirk Käsler, *Max Weber* (1988), pp. 111–27. For its early reception or rather non-reception, see again Käsler, *Max Weber*, p. 206.

See also *Ancient Judaism, Collected Essays in the Sociology of Religion, Economic Ethics of the World Religions, The; Protestant Ethic and the Spirit of Capitalism, The; Religion of China, The*

religions of salvation (*Erlösungsreligionen*)   *See* salvation

religiöse Vergemeinschaftungen   *See* religious communities

religiosity   *See* religion

religious benefits (*Heilsgüter*)   This term is used by Weber to indicate what it is about religion that makes people want it and strongly hold on to it. It is related to a need in the believer for something that is considerably deeper than some doctrine or logical argument why God exists.

The term "religious benefits" can be found in Weber's general sociology in Ch. 1 of *Economy and Society*, where it is mentioned in the paragraph on political and hierocratic organizations (ES:54–6). A hierocratic organization, Weber explains, is a religious organization that uses religious benefits to coerce its members. This can be done either by distributing such religious benefits to the members or by denying them such benefits.

There does not seem to exist a definition of religious benefits in Weber's work. The reader, however, is told that religious benefits can be "worldly or other-worldly, material or spiritual" (ES:56). To this can be added that these benefits also have to constitute something of very high value to the believer.

In *The Protestant Ethic* Weber uses the term "psychological" or "religious premium," which is clearly related to the concept of religious benefits, in the sense that it represents a religious incentive for action (*see* psychological or religious premium). Another related term is "religious interests" (e.g. ES:517).

In the essay on the Protestant sects, Weber notes that sects assign religious benefits or premiums for proving oneself in front of the other members (GM:321).

According to Friedrich Wilhelm Graf, the term *Heilsgüter* was mainly used in Lutheran and Calvinist theology of the late sixteenth and seventeenth centuries. "I suspect," he adds in a letter to the author, "[that] Weber has taken the term from the works of Matthias Schneckenburger and

Karl Bernhard Hundeshagen which he had read very carefully for his work on the Protestant ethic" (Swedberg 1998:256; for Schneckenburger and Hundeshagen, see e.g. Friedrich Wilhelm Graf, "The German Theological Sources and Protestant Church Politics" [1993]).

"The German word [*Heilsgüter*] is a tricky compound noun," according to Sam Whimster (2002:96). "'Heil' means 'salvation' and 'Güter' has the double meaning of 'goods' (as in commodities) and 'goods' (as in virtue). 'Salvation goods' is exact but not terribly felicitous." An alternative would be "religious goods." It would also be possible to use "religious interests" (*see* the discussion of the expression "material and ideal interests" in the entry for interests).

See also interests, psychological or religious premium, social mechanisms

religious communities and groups The section on sociology of religion in *Economy and Society* is entitled "Religious Groups (The Sociology of Religion)" ("Religionssoziologie [Typen religiöser Vergemeinschaftung]"; ES:399–634). Weber here discusses several different types of religious communities or groups, of which the most famous are the church and the sect, but which also include the religious organization and various cults. Religious communities emerge when people orient themselves to each other with a sense of belonging together, in terms of some religion. Religious communities are organizations of domination (*Herrschaftsverbände*).

For an introduction, see Martin Riesebrodt, "Religiöse Vergemeinschaftungen" (2001).

See also church, congregation, hierocratic organization, religion, sect

religious ethic (*religiöse Ethik*) Weber discusses the concept of religious ethic as part of his sociology of religion in *Economy and Society* (ES:437–39). While the concept of magical ethic has to do with people's relationship to spirits, religious ethic has to do with their relationship to gods. At one point in time, "transgression against the will of god is an ethical sin which burdens the conscience, quite apart from its direct results" (ES:437). Religious ethics have developed throughout history and also been rationalized, through the efforts of prophets, priests, and laity.

In a letter to his publisher of December 30, 1913, Weber says that in his sociology of religion he discusses "the sociology of religious ethics" of "all religions" (Lang 2001:87).

"Religious Rejections of the World and Their Directions" *See* "Zwischenbetrachtung"

religious virtuoso (*religiöser Virtuose*) In his sociology of religion Weber notes (following Friedrich Schleiermacher) that people have different "religious capacities" and that only a small number of individuals have the capacity to work systematically toward their salvation (e.g. ES:538–41). Examples include the dervishes in Islam and the members of ascetic Protestant sects.

Guenther Roth notes that "'virtuosity' is one of Weber's many nominalist ironies" (Roth 1975:150). The reason for this has to do with the reference to virtue as well as technical skill in the word "virtuosity." "The 'virtuosi' are 'men of virtue', but they are so to speak highly accomplished technicians in matters moral." Roth also suggests "ideological virtuoso" as a terminological extension of Weber's concept of religious virtuoso (ibid.). For a discussion of Weber's concept of religious virtuoso as well as its relationship to religious literature of the time, see e.g. Bernhard Lang, "Prophet, Priester, Virtuose" (2001).

rent (*Rente*)   This concept is not formally defined in Weber's economic sociology in Ch. 2 of *Economy and Society*, but nonetheless plays an important role in his analysis of the economy. While profit is associated with capital and the enterprise, rent is associated with wealth and the budgetary unit (or the household).

Rent is "economically conservative," while profit is "economically revolutionary" (ES:205). In a society where the economy is centered on rent, there are property classes; while in a society centered on profit, there are commercial classes.

See also budgetary management

representation (*Vertretung, Vertretungsbeziehungen, Repräsentation*)   Representation is defined as follows in Weber's general sociology in Ch. 1 of *Economy and Society*: "within a social relationship . . . the action of certain members (the 'representatives') may be attributed to the others ('the represented')" (ES:46–7; cf. ES:292). Weber adds that the power of representation may be acquired in different ways. Representation is typically found in associations with specific purposes and in legally organized groups.

Weber also discusses representation in his sociology of domination (ES:292–99; cf. ES:1128–30). Weber notes that the power of representation may be acquired in different ways and suggests a typology for this. He also discusses interest groups.

See also interest groups

responsibility   *See* mutual responsibility

Richthofen, Else von (1874–1973)   Else was married to economist

Edgar Jaffé, a very close friend of the Webers, and was Max Weber's lover. See e.g. Martin Green, *The von Richthofen Sisters* (1974).

Richtigkeitsrationalität See objectively correct rationality

Rickert, Heinrich (1863–1936) Neo-Kantian philosopher and friend of Max Weber. Rickert had a profound impact on Weber's thought, especially in the philosophy of science. For the complex relationship between the ideas of Weber and Rickert, see e.g. H. H. Bruun, "Weber on Rickert" (2001) and Guy Oakes, *Weber and Rickert: Concept Formation in the Social Sciences* (1988).

See also historical individual, neo-Kantianism, science, value-relevance

rights (*Rechte*) Weber discusses different types of rights in his various studies. The term can be found in his general sociology as well as in his political sociology and his sociology of law. It also plays a certain role in Weber's political writings.

Rights are defined in Weber's general sociology in Ch. 1 of *Economy and Society* as "appropriated advantages [through a closed social relationship]" (ES:44).

The notion of rights (*Rechte*) also plays a key role in Weber's sociology of law, in which he notes that "we have previously defined the existence of a right as being no more than an increase of the probability that a certain expectation of the one to whom the law grants the right will not be disappointed" (ES:666–67). From a sociological perspective, Weber adds, there is a gradual transition from a right to a regulation.

One type of so-called privileges (that is, permissive legal norms) is constituted by rights to freedom (*Freiheitsrechte*; the term comes from Georg Jellinek; cf. ES:732 n. 3). These rights are what we today would call human rights.

Weber also touches on the issue of human rights in various places in his work (e.g. ES:871–72, 1209–10; cf. Weber's analysis of natural law: ES:865–80). He was thoroughly familiar with Georg Jellinek's *The Declaration of the Rights of Man and of Citizens* (1895), which was a major source of inspiration for *The Protestant Ethic*. Wolfgang Mommsen has criticized Weber's description, on the one hand, of natural law as a value-rational type of legitimation for the old-fashioned type of democracy and, on the other hand, of legitimacy based on (formal) legal domination as being characteristic for modern mass democracy (Mommsen, *Max Weber and German Politics 1890–1920* [1984], pp. 392–5, 448–53).

See also opportunity, appropriation, law, sociology of law

robber capitalism (*Raubkapitalismus*) *See* adventurers' capitalism

role   While Weber's sociology does not use the concept of role or some close equivalent, it nonetheless contains a number of stylized descriptions that may be useful in outlining, the role of, say, the bureaucrat or the charismatic leader.

Talcott Parsons argues that if Weber had paid more attention to the concept of role, he would have avoided overestimating the impact of economic factors (Parsons, p. 54 in Weber 1947).

Roscher, Wilhelm (1817–1894)   One of the leading members and founders of the German Historical School of economics. Roscher is at the center of Weber's *Roscher and Knies* (Weber [1903–6] 1975). See e.g. Bertram Schefold, "Roscher, Wilhelm Georg Friedrich (1817–1894)" (1987).

Roscher and Knies: The Logical Problems of Historical Economics (*Roscher und Knies und die logischen Probleme der historischen Nationalökonomie*, trans. 1975)   In this essay Weber addresses the status of "historical economics" as this can be found in the work of two prominent German economists, Wilhelm Roscher (1817–94) and Karl Knies (1821–98). More generally, Weber's study deals with the status of the cultural sciences.

Weber's essay was originally published in three parts from 1903 to 1906, and was also reprinted by Marianne Weber in *Gesammelte Aufsätze zur Wissenschaftslehre* (1922).

See Guy Oakes, "Introductory Essay," pp. 1–49 in Weber [1903–6] 1975; see also Wilhelm Hennis, "'A Science of Man': Max Weber and the Political Economy of the German Historical School" (1987).

See also economics

routinization (*Veralltäglichung*)   In order that charisma may find a permanent place in the world, Weber argues, it has to undergo a radical change—a process of adjustment to reality that in English is called routinization (ES:246–54, 1121–23).

See charisma, everyday life

rule   *See* domination, rules

rulership   *See* domination

rules (*Regeln*)   This concept, which is often used in contemporary sociology, is not part of Weber's general sociology, as outlined in Ch. 1 of *Economy and Society*.

In *Economy and Society*, however, Weber occasionally uses the word "rules" (see e.g. WuG:925). His essay "Critique of Stammler" also contains a famous section on the concept of a rule (CS:115–43). Weber here mainly attempts to draw a line between the approach of jurisprudence and that of social science. The former, he says, analyzes legal reality in a way that is similar to the way that card players look at the rules of the game they are playing. The key questions here are as follows: What are you allowed to do, and what are you not allowed to do according to the rules? Social science, in contrast, is interested in what actually happens in the card game. To what extent, more precisely, are the rules followed— why and by whom?

rural sociology Weber made important contributions to the field of rural sociology, which has declined in popularity in Anglo-Saxon sociology during the last few decades. Two of his most important contributions can be found in his study of agrarian workers east of the river Elbe and in his book on the social and economic history of antiquity (Weber [1892] 1984, [1909] 1976).

Special mention must also be made of a paper that Weber read before the Congress of Arts and Science held in 1904 in St. Louis as part of the Universal Exposition, entitled "Capitalism and Rural Society in Germany" (GM:363–85). There is finally Weber's course on universal economic and social history of 1919–20, known today in its reconstructed form as *General Economic History* (e.g. [1923] 1981:3–25, 65–111).

For a discussion of Weber's studies on agriculture, see e.g. Keith Tribe, "Prussian Agriculture—German Politics: Max Weber 1892–7" (1989) and Martin Riesebrodt, "From Patriarchalism to Capitalism: The Theoretical Context of Max Weber's Agrarian Studies (1892–3)" (1989). See also Lawrence Scaff, "The Typology of Agrarian Economies," pp. 49–59 in *Fleeing the Iron Cage* (1989), Paul Honigsheim, "Max Weber as Rural Sociologist," pp. 3–16 in *The Unknown Max Weber* ([1946–63] 2000), and Q. J. Munters, "Max Weber as Rural Sociologist" (1972).

See also employment regime (*Agrarverfassung*)

Russia Weber was interested in Russian politics as well as in Russian culture. He learned Russian to follow political events more closely, and he wrote articles on both the 1905 Revolution and the political situation in 1917. Weber had many Russian students and admired Russian culture.

For Weber's writings on Russia, see Weber 1995a. For a discussion of these writings as well as of Weber's political attitude to Russia more generally, see e.g. Richard Pipes, "Max Weber and Russia" (1955), Wolfgang Mommsen, "Max Weber and the Regeneration of Russia" (1997), and the introduction to Weber 1995a by Peter Baehr and Gordon Wells.

For Weber's personal attitude to Russians and Russian culture, see e.g. Marianne Weber, *Max Weber* ([1926] 1975), pp. 327–28 and Paul Honigsheim, *The Unknown Weber* ([1946–63] 2000), pp. 132, 135.

238 *The Max Weber Dictionary*

For Weber's relationship to some central figures in Russian culture, see e.g. Edith Hanke, "Max Weber, Leo Tolstoy and the Mountain of Truth" (1999) and Charles Turner, "Weber and Dostoyevsky on Church, Sect and Democracy" (1999).

See also socialism, Tolstoy's Question

Sacred law (*heiliges Recht*)   Weber discusses sacred law in his sociology of law, defining it as a legal code or system dominated by religious principles (ES:790). What Weber terms theocratic law represents one type of sacred law. The opposite of sacred law is secular law.

There exist many types of sacred law, such as Islamic law, Hindu law, and canon law. For a discussion of these, including the process of substantive rationalization of sacred law, see especially ES:809–38.

See also law, theocracy

sacrifice of the intellect   *See* intellectual sacrifice

salvation (*Erlösung*)   A major part of Weber's sociology of religion is devoted to the theme of salvation (see especially ES:500–76; cf. GM:323–59). Weber was especially interested in what causes the need for salvation; how people react to this need; and what impact people's efforts to achieve salvation have on themselves as well as on society, especially the economy. "Our concern is essentially with the quest for salvation, whatever its form, insofar as it produced certain consequences for practical behavior in the world" (ES:528).

Salvation is described by Weber as a liberation from suffering—and there can be economic and political salvation, just as religious salvation (e.g. ES:527). Religious salvation is an answer to suffering as well as to the tension between the world and religion. It can typically be reached if the believer behaves in a certain way or as a result of a decision by a god.

Depending on the religion, the means to salvation may include good works, ascetic behavior, ecstasy, and ritual. There is also salvation from the outside, including what Weber terms "institutional grace" or grace dispensed by an organization with divine credentials, such as the Catholic Church (e.g. ES:560). The individual may or may not be fundamentally changed by these efforts to reach salvation; similarly the effect of his or her actions may either change the world or strengthen its current features.

Religions of salvation (*Erlöslungsreligionen*) include, among others,

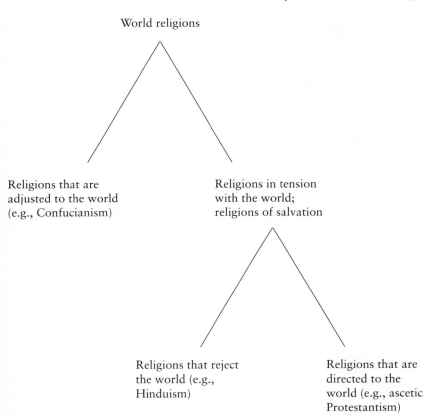

FIGURE 3. Religions of salvation and religions that are adjusted to the world.
SOURCE: Ole Riis, "Verdensreligionernes erhvervsethik" (2004).

Judaism, Christianity, Buddhism, Jainism, and Hinduism (see Figure 3). Weber's interest in salvation is directly related to his major research theme of how "the economic and social *singularity* of the Occident" is related to "the development of the religious ethos" (as Weber describes the purpose that underlies his studies in an advertisement for *Collected Essays in the Sociology of Religion*, reproduced in Wolfgang Schluchter, *Rationalism, Religion, and Domination* [1989], p. 425).

According to Parsons, Weber postulates that human beings have a need for salvation ("Introduction" [1963], pp. xlix–liv). Parsons also argues that Weber suggests four basic ways of reaching salvation, and that these can be established "by cross-tabulating the distinction between asceticism and mysticism with the distinction between other-worldly and inner-worldly positions" (ibid., p. li).

For a discussion of Weber's concept of religions of salvation, including the evolution of this concept in his work, see Edith Hanke, "Erlösungsreligionen" (2001).

See also meaning, philosophy, theodicy

Schmoller, Gustav (1838–1917)   The powerful leader of the German Historical School in Weber's day and the key opponent of Carl Menger in the Battle of the Methods. Weber and Schmoller knew each other but were not close. See e.g. Manfred Schön, "Gustav Schmoller and Max Weber" (1987).

See also Battle of the Methods, evolution, Historical School of economics

science (*Wissenschaft*)   Weber occasionally discusses science from a sociological and historical perspective in his sociological writings, and he also touches on it in his analysis of capitalism. It represents an important topic as well in his methodological writings. Weber's best-known work on science, "Science as a Vocation," contains a mixture of philosophical and sociological arguments (GM:129–56, Weber 1989).

In his theory of science, which is discussed in his methodological writings, Weber draws heavily on the work of philosopher Heinrich Rickert, who argues that science represents a construction of elements that the researcher selects from an infinite reality. According to Rickert, there exist two kinds of science. On the one hand, there are the natural sciences, where the researcher selects those parts of reality that lend themselves to being analyzed in terms of laws. On the other hand, there are the cultural sciences where the researcher selects topics according to their relationship to the values of society.

Weber also notes that "the belief in the value of scientific truth is the product of certain cultures and is not a product of man's original nature" (MSS:110; EW:402).

In his analysis in the *General Economic History* of what is distinctive about modern Western capitalism, Weber mentions "modern science" (GEH:312–14; cf. GEH:354, 276–77, ES:161–62). Elsewhere Weber also refers to "modern science" as "the technical basis of capitalism" (ES:1194). Weber emphasizes the close link between art and science during the Renaissance (e.g. GM:142). He also notes the relationship between Puritanism and science, and cites as an illustration the following statement by Dutch scientist Jan Swammerdam: "Here I bring you the proof of God's providence in the anatomy of a louse" (GM:142).

For the secondary literature on Weber's view of science from a sociological and historical perspective, see e.g. Ralph Schroeder, "Disenchantment and Its Discontents: Weberian Perspectives on Science and Technology" (1995); Ralph Schroeder and Richard Swedberg, "Weberian Perspectives on Science, Technology and the Economy" (2002).

For comments on "Science as a Vocation" as well as a new translation of this essay by Michael John, see Peter Lassman and Irving Velody (eds.), *Max Weber's "Science as a Vocation"* (1989). See also Wolfgang Schluchter, "Value-Neutrality and the Ethic of Responsibility," pp. 65–118 in Guenther Roth and Wolfgang Schluchter, *Max Weber's Vision of History* (1979).

For Weber's view of the relationship between science, capitalism, and religion, see especially Robert K. Merton, *Science, Technology and Society in Seventeenth-Century England* ([1938] 1970), and the discussion of Merton's thesis in Bernard Cohen (ed.), *Puritanism and the Rise of Science* (1990). See also Friedrich Tenbruck, "Max Weber and the Sociology of Science: A Case Reopened" (1974) and Bryan Turner, "Weber on Medicine and Religion," pp. 177–99 in *For Weber* (1981).

For Weber's relationship to Rickert, see e.g. Ola Agevall, *A Science of Unique Events: Max Weber's Methodology of the Cultural Sciences* (1999), pp. 109–47, Guy Oakes, *Weber and Rickert: Concept Formation in the Cultural Sciences* (1988), and Alexander von Schelting, *Max Webers Wissenschaftslehre* (1934).

Finally, a new edition of "Science as a Vocation" (which was originally delivered as a speech on November 7, 1917) can be found in MWG, Vol. I/17.

See also cultural sciences, knowledge (for cognitive or scientific interest), natural science, objectivity, science of reality, social science, technology, truth

"Science as a Vocation" *See* science

science of reality (*Wirklichkeitswisssenschaft*) This term, which Weber borrowed from philosopher Heinrich Rickert, is often misinterpreted to mean that the exclusive ambition of social science is to capture empirical reality. Instead it means that the social sciences constitute the kind of reality they study by relating it to values and the significance that people attach to these values in their concrete lives. Its opposite, in other words, is a science of laws of the type that can be found in the natural sciences.

The key passage in Weber's work regarding this term can be found in one of his methodological essays: "The type of social science in which we are interested is an empirical science of concrete reality (*Wirklichkeitswissenschaft*). Our aim is the understanding of the characteristic

242	The Max Weber Dictionary

uniqueness of the reality in which we move. We wish to understand on the one hand the relationships of the cultural significance of individual events in their contemporary manifestations and on the other the causes of their being historically so and not otherwise" (MSS:72).

Lawrence Scaff, who has retranslated this passage, prefers the term "science of actuality" (Scaff 1989a:83). Bruun comments that "Weber's sparing use of the term [*Wirklichkeitswissenschaft*] seems to indicate that he was less than enthusiastic about it; one reason for this may be that the word was a fertile source of misconceptions, particularly in discussions concerning the historicist belief in a science which is able to 'reproduce' reality" (Bruun 1972:102 n. 15).

See also social sciences

scope of economic resources in relation to consumption needs/acquisition (*Nahrungsspielraum/Erwerbsspielraum*)   *See* open and closed social relationships

secondary literature on Weber's work   The secondary literature on Weber's work is enormous, and there unfortunately does not exist one major bibliography which covers the bulk of this material.

A useful introductory guide to the material in English is nonetheless Peter Kivisto and William Swatos, *Max Weber: A Bio-Bibliography* (1988). The reader may also wish to consult the much fuller and later volume by Alan Sica, *Max Weber, A Comprehensive Bibliography* (2004). An early and still useful bibliography, which mainly contains material in German, is that of Constans Seyfarth and Gert Schmidt, *Max-Weber Bibliographie* (1977). For ongoing analysis of Weber's work, see especially *Max Weber Studies* (2000–).

sect (*Sekte*)   The concept of sect plays an important role in Weber's sociology of religion and has the church as its theoretical counterpart. While specific religious qualifications are needed to become a member of a sect, one typically becomes a member of a church through birth.

The number of members is not decisive for the existence of a sect, but rather the organizational structure and the self-image of the members as a religious elite. Weber also appears to have seen the sect as the archetype of organizations in modern society that wield strong influence over public opinion and cultural questions.

According to *The Religion of India*, "a 'sect' in the sociological sense of the word is an exclusive association of religious virtuosos or of especially qualified religious persons recruited through individual admission after establishment of qualification" (RI:6; cf. e.g. ES:56, ES:1204–10, GASS:463).

In *The Protestant Ethic and the Spirit of Capitalism* one important chapter is devoted to the sects that make up what Weber terms ascetic Protestantism (PE:95–154; the reader may note that Calvinism, according to Weber, is best characterized as a sect-like church).

Another important study in this context is "The Protestant Sects and the Spirit of Capitalism" (GM:302–22). Weber here states that "the 'church' [is] a compulsory association for the administration of grace, and the 'sect' [is] a voluntary association of religiously qualified persons" (GM:314). It is also in this study that one finds Weber's important addition to the argument in *The Protestant Ethic*, namely that the Puritan sects "bred . . . selected qualities" in their members (GM:320). They did so mainly by making their members "hold their own" under the watchful eyes of the other members (see also ES:1206).

While sects have played a key role in U.S. religious life, it is churches that have been predominant in Europe. In *Economy and Society* Weber also explores the relationship between sects and democracy, arguing that there exists "an elective affinity between the sect and political democracy" (ES:1208). The reason for this has to do with two structural features of the sect: its treatment of clerical officials as its servants, and its practice of direct democracy in its administration. More generally, "the consistent sect gives rise to an inalienable right of the governed against any power" (ES:1209).

But the sect also plays another role in modern society: "in an important sense, the *sect* represents for the nascent modern age the archetype of those social groupings (*Gruppenbildungen*) which today mould 'public opinion', 'cultural values' and individualities'" (PED:77).

"The Protestant Sects and the Spirit of Capitalism" was preceded by two shorter versions (Weber 1906a, 1906b; the latter has been translated as Weber [1906b] 1985 and Weber [1906b] 2002; see also the introduction to Weber [1906b] 1985 by Loader and Alexander). The link that exists between the sect and the voluntary organization, and which Weber discusses in this article, is also touched on in his 1910 talk on voluntary organizations at the German Sociological Society (Weber [1910] 2002). Many of Weber's examples in his articles come from the United States.

On Weber's thought concerning sects, see e.g. S. D. Berger, "The Sects and the Breakthrough into the Modern World: On the Centrality of the Sects in Weber's Protestant Ethic Thesis" (1971), Benton Johnson, "A Critical Appraisal of the Church-Sect Typology" (1957), and William Swatos, "Weber or Troeltsch? Methodology, Syndrome, and Development of Church-Sect Theory" (1976). There is also Martin Riesebrodt, "Religiöse Vergemeinschaftungen" (2001).

See also ascetic Protestantism, Calvinism, coercion, religious benefits, religious communities or groups, voluntary organization

selection (*Auslese*)   This concept is part of Weber's general sociology, as outlined in Ch. 1 of *Economy and Society*. The idea of selection also plays an important part in Weber's epistemology, in the sense that social science analysis always entails a selection of what is significant from an infinitely manifold empirical reality.

Selection is defined in Weber's general sociology in Ch. 1 of *Economy and Society* as follows: "the struggle, often latent, which takes place between human individuals or social types, for advantages and for survival, but without a meaningful orientation in terms of struggle, will be called 'selection'" (ES:38). Weber adds that if the selection has to do with individuals during their lifetime, it is a question of "social selection," and if it has to do with heredity, "biological selection" (ibid.).

Competition and conflict on a large scale lead, according to Weber, to the selection of certain qualities. Selection, more generally, is inevitable in human society because it cannot be eliminated. In his explication of the concept of selection Weber issues a warning against using terms such as "fitness to survive" or "the survival of the strongest" (ES:40). The use of these types of terms, he says, can lead to the introduction of "uncritical value-judgments into empirical investigation."

Weber was also very interested in the role the modern factory plays in the selection of workers ("every modern factory rests on the principles of selection"—PW:284). See in this context Weber's studies on the psychophysics of work as well as his methodological introduction to a planned study of the selection and adaptation of workers in large industries (GASS:61–255 and Weber [1908] 1980).

In Weber's political writings one can find a Social Darwinist terminology, but not an endorsement of Social Darwinism (e.g. PW:2, 14). For example, Weber uses expressions such as "a survival of the unfit" (PE:61). According to Wolfgang Mommsen, "Weber did not hesitate to employ the Darwinistic terminology of 'the struggle for existence' and the 'survival' of the fittest . . . although he later rejected and fought all biological theories and concepts in the field of social science as unscientific" (Mommsen 1984:41). To this should be added that Wilhelm Hennis has argued that Weber is not at all a Social Darwinist but rather is influenced by Nietzsche's idea of "moral breeding" (Hennis 1998a:34).

For an attempt to cast Weber as a modern evolutionary thinker, see W. G. Runciman, "Was Max Weber a Selectionist despite Himself?" (2001).

See also competition, conflict, race

self-interest, self-interested kind of behavior (*interessenbedingt, bedingt*

durch Interessenlage)   There exist three types of regular behavior, according to Weber: custom, usage, and what he calls the self-interested type of behavior.

The self-interested type of behavior is one of the "empirical uniformities" that Weber introduces in his general sociology in Ch. 1 of *Economy and Society*. His description is as follows: "a uniformity of orientation [toward social action] may be said to be 'determined by self-interest', if and insofar as the actors' conduct is instrumentally (*zweckrational*) oriented toward identical expectations" (ES:29).

The self-interested type of behavior represents a more stable form of behavior than behavior that is oriented to tradition or to norms. Action that is determined by self-interest is very common in the economy and helps to explain, for example, the stability of prices.

Talcott Parsons notes in a comment on his translation of Ch. 1 of *Economy and Society* that the term *Interessenlage* is difficult to translate into a single term since it "involves two components: the motivation in terms of self-interest and orientation to the opportunities presented by the situation" (ES:59–60 n. 16). In his new translation of Ch. 1 of *Economy and Society* Keith Tribe uses the term "conditioned by interests" for *bedingt durch Interessenlage* and *interessenbedingt* (EW:333).

See also consensual action, empirical uniformities, interest, legitimacy

separation of powers   *See* collegiality

sexuality   *See* body, the

shaman   *See* magician

sib (*Sippe*)   *See* kin group

Siebeck, Paul (1855–1920)   Owner of the publishing house J. C. B. Mohr (Paul Siebeck) and publisher of Weber's work. See e.g. Wolfgang Mommsen, "Die Siebecks und Max Weber" (1996).

Simmel, Georg (1858–1918)   Sociologist and philosopher as well as a friend of Max Weber. Simmel was married to Gertrud Simmel (1864–1938), who was also a friend of the Webers. For Weber on Simmel's work, see Weber 1972. See also e.g. David Frisby, "The Ambiguity of Modernity: Georg Simmel and Max Weber" (1987).

Sinn   *See* meaning

Sinnadäquanz (**causality on the level of meaning**)   *See* causality

Sinnzusammanhang   *See* complex of meaning

Sippe   *See* kin group

Sitte   *See* custom

social   Weber uses the term "social" in a very precise sense in his general sociology, as outlined in Ch. 1 of *Economy and Society*. The primary meaning of "social," as in such terms as "social action" and "social relationship," is "orientation to the behavior of others." As Weber states in his explication of his definition of sociology: "action is 'social' insofar as its subjective meaning takes account of the behavior of others and is thereby oriented in its course" (ES:4).

An action can be oriented in different ways, for example, to the behavior of others, to orders, or to the past or the present (*see* orientation to others for a discussion of this).

That orientation to others involves meaning is something that e.g. Martin Albrow has emphasized (*Max Weber's Construction of Social Theory* [1990], pp. 267–69).

See also orientation to others, social action, social relationship, society

social action (*soziales Handeln*)   Social action constitutes the "central subject matter" of Weber's sociology (ES:24). It can be briefly described as a type of behavior that is oriented to the behavior of another actor, and to which the actor attaches a meaning.

The importance of the concept of social action to Weber's sociology comes out very clearly from the prominent place that Weber assigns it in his well-known definition of sociology in paragraph 1 in Ch. 1 of *Economy and Society*: "sociology . . . is a science concerning itself with the interpretive understanding of social action and thereby with a causal explanation of its course and consequences" (ES:4). "Action" is here defined as behavior invested with meaning; and "social action" means action that is oriented to the behavior of another actor (for more details, *see* action, behavior, orientation to others).

In paragraph 2 of Ch. 1 of *Economy and Society* Weber presents his famous typology of sociologically important forms of social action: instrumentally rational action, value-rational action, affectual action, and traditional action (ES:24–5). Most concrete forms of social action contain a mixture of Weber's types.

While the concepts of affectual social action and traditional social action have presented little problems to students of Weber, this is not the case with rational action. There is, first of all, instrumentally rational action, which covers actions in which people and objects are treated as means to an end. Then there is value-rational social action, which is generally considered a difficult concept. It is worth emphasizing that it covers behavior that has to fulfill three conditions: (1) there has to be a conscious belief in a value; (2) there has to be planning for the realization of this value; and (3) the behavior must be carried out regardless of the prospect for success.

Weber also introduces other typologies of social action. Empirical uniformities of social action, for example, come in the form of usage, custom, or self-interest (ES:29–31; *see* those entries). Social actions may also take many other forms, as outlined in Ch. 1 of *Economy and Society*.

Finally, while social action constitutes the main focus of Weber's sociology, Weber is also careful to point out that it by no means represents its exclusive focus (ES:24; cf. SCIS:159). There are furthermore the facts that sociology deals with a number of facts without any intrinsic meaning, and also that all action is not social (ES:12–13, 22–23).

For introductions to Weber's concept of social action, see e.g. Martin Albrow, *Max Weber's Construction of Social Theory* (1990), pp. 140–49, Raymond Aron, "Max Weber" [1970], pp. 220–22, and Talcott Parsons, *The Structure of Social Action I* (1937), pp. 640–58. Alfred Schutz's analysis in *The Phenomenology of the Social World* ([1932] 1967) stands in a class by itself in its attempt to elucidate as well as go beyond Weber's concept of social action.

In his essay of 1913, "Some Categories of Interpretive Sociology," Weber used a different term for social action than in Ch. 1 of *Economy and Society* (*Gemeinschaftshandeln* versus *soziales Handeln*; cf. e.g. Mommsen 2000:366 and Hiroshi Orihara, "From 'a Torso with a Wrong Head' to 'Five Disjointed Pieces of Carcass'?" [2002], pp. 8–9). In the 1913 essay "social action" is defined as follows: "we shall speak of 'social action' (*Gemeinschaftshandeln*) wherever human action is subjectively related in *meaning* to the behavior of others" (SCIS:159). Hiroshi Orihara argues that *Gemeinschaftshandeln* (which he translates as "community action") means "action . . . subjectively connected to other's behavior," and that it subsumes societal action (*Gesellschaftshandeln*). The term *Gemeinschaftshandeln* is not used in Ch. 1, where it is replaced by *Vergemeinschaftung*, which is usually translated as "communal social relationship" and which Orihara translates as "community-formation" (ES:40; Orihara 2002:8–9; see Figure 4). See also in this context Guenther Roth and Claus Wittich who translate *Gemeinschaftshandeln* as "social action" (ES:1375).

See also affectual action, associational action, community action, expectations, imitation, instrumentally rational action, mass-conditioned behavior, orientation to others, paradoxical results of action, social mechanisms, "Some Categories of Interpretive Sociology," traditional action, unintended consequences, value-rational action

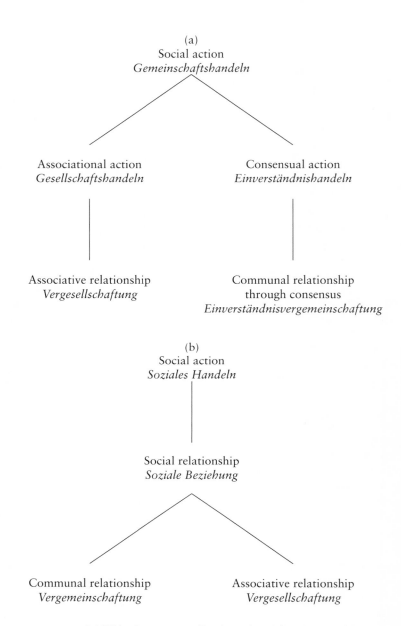

FIGURE 4. (a) Weber's conceptualization of social action in "Some Categories of Interpretive Sociology" (1913). (b) Weber's conceptualization of social action in *Economy and Society* (1920).
SOURCE: Jean-Pierre Grossein, "Présentation," p. 89, in Max Weber, *Sociologie des religions*. Copyright Editions Gallimard, Paris, 1996.

social carrier *See* carrier

social change This expression, which is often used in contemporary sociology, does not appear as an explicit term in Weber's work. Nonetheless, it can be said that Weber's sociology is deeply concerned with social change. In early society, for example, charisma represents a revolutionary force, breaking up traditionalism and leading to social change (e.g. ES:37, 245). In early society, Weber also notes, social changes were often presented as if they were the way things had always been (ES:37, 755).

The Protestant Ethic can be characterized as a study investigating one of the causes involved in the process of social change that helped to bring about modern rational capitalism. Similarly, many of Weber's other studies look at the conditions under which social change becomes possible as well as those under which it is blocked (e.g. RC, RI, ES). In modern society much change comes in the form of instrumentally rational action, that is, via organizations such as the firm and the state.

See also charisma, conflict, the firm, capitalism, prophet

social closure *See* open and closed social relationships

Social Darwinism *See* selection

social economics (*Sozialökonomik*) This term appears in several different places in Weber's work, most importantly in Weber's essay on objectivity of 1904 and in the title of the *Handbook of Economics* (*Grundriss der Sozialökonomik*). While the "social" in "social economics" indicates that we here have a type of economic analysis that indeed is "social," the meaning of the expression "social economics" is nonetheless not entirely clear. Among its possible meanings are the following: (1) economics in the sense in which this term was used in Germany around 1900; (2) economic sociology; (3) sociology; and (4) a broad type of economics that would include not only economics but also economic history and economic sociology (see e.g. Reinhard Bendix and Guenther Roth, *Scholarship and Partisanship: Essays on Max Weber* [1971], pp. 37–8, Roth in ES:lxiii, Heino Nau, *Eine "Wissenschaft von Menschen"* (1997), Richard Swedberg, *Max Weber and the Idea of Economic Sociology* (1998), pp. 4, 177–79).

According to a useful distinction that Weber introduces in his essay on objectivity of 1904, social economics does not only study "economic phenomena," but also "economically relevant phenomena" and "economically conditioned phenomena" (MSS:64–5). Economic phenomena include straightforward economic entities such as banks or modern corporations. Economically relevant phenomena are non-economic phenomena that influence economic ones. The impact of Protestantism on the economic mentality of the 1500s and 1600s, as analyzed in *The Protestant Ethic*, is an example of this. Economically conditioned phenomena are non-economic phenomena that are importantly influenced by economic ones, such as the impact of the work that some people do on their attitude to religion. Peasants, for example, tend to emphasize magical forces in their religion, due to their work with nature.

See also economics, economic theory, *Handbook of Social Economics*

social interaction   This concept is not part of Weber's general sociology in Ch. 1 of *Economy and Society*, where its closest equivalent is the social relationship. Weber sharply criticized Georg Simmel's key sociological concept of interaction (*Wechselwirkung*) on the ground that it was far too broad in nature to capture what is specific about sociology. He argued that practically everything in reality—not only social actions, in other words—involves reciprocal impact (see Weber 1972:162).

See also social action, social relationship

social mechanisms   Though Weber does not use this term (which is common in contemporary sociology), one may nonetheless argue that he lays bare a number of interesting social mechanisms in his work, not least in his sociology of religion.

Several mechanisms operate together, for example, in *The Protestant Ethic and the Spirit of Capitalism* to transform the element of vocation or calling in ascetic Protestantism into a specific component of the spirit of rational capitalism. One of these is asceticism; another is what Weber refers to as confirmation (*Bewährung*) or fact that the religious person regularly checks for signs that he or she has done the right thing (similarly for the charismatic leader; cf. ES:241). More generally, an interlocking chain of motivations is described in *The Protestant Ethic* (PED:70; *Motivationsverknüpfungen*, Johannes Winkelmann, ed., *Die Protestantische Ethik II: Kritiken und Antikritiken* [1978], p. 163). Because of the doctrine of predestination, the individual believer felt insecure; this insecurity led to a search for signs that one was not among the damned; and wealth was seen as one of these signs (*see* Calvinism).

There is also the sect, which can be described as a concatenation of several other mechanisms. One of these, ensuring that rules of behavior are followed, has to do with the fact that sect members want to be able to hold their own in front of the other members; another mechanism working to the same effect is that the individual member is always under the scrutiny of other members.

One mechanism that made Catholicism less effective in implementing its ideas on how to live as a true Christian among believers was its use of confession, according to Weber (e.g. PE:106, 250 n. 149, PED:108–9).

By confessing their sins, believers got relief from the knowledge of having sinned—but also lost an incentive to mend their ways.

For Weber's concept of confirmation, see e.g. Jean-Pierre Grossein, "Présentation" (1996), pp. 75, 120.

See also paradoxical results of actions, psychological or religious premium, unintended consequences, sect

social psychology   *See* psychology

"Social Psychology of the World Religions, The"   *See* "Einleitung"

social relationship (*soziale Beziehung*)   This concept plays a central role in Weber's sociology. Its core meaning is that two or more actors orient their action to one another.

The exact definition of a social relationship in Weber's general sociology in Ch. 1 of *Economy and Society* reads as follows: "the term 'social relationship' will be used to denote the behavior of a plurality of actors insofar as, in its meaningful content, the action of each takes account of that of the others and is oriented in these terms" (ES:26; see also ES:27–8 for an explication of this concept).

A social relationship consists, in other words, of two or more interconnected forms of social action, in Weber's terminology. If both of the actors attach the same meaning to their actions, the relationship is "objectively symmetrical," but if their meanings strongly diverge, it is "objectively asymmetrical."

See also associative relationship, communal relationship, conflict, competition, domination, open and closed social relationships, power, selection, social action

social sciences (*Sozialwissenschaften*)   The social sciences or "the sciences of human action" differ, according to Weber, from the natural sciences in two principal ways: (1) they are concerned with the perception of the action by the individuals themselves (not only with their outer behavior); and (2) they cannot formulate laws of the type that the natural sciences can (ES:7, 15). What Weber says in his various writings about the cultural sciences is also applicable to the social sciences.

In drawing such a sharp line between the social and cultural sciences, on the one hand, and the natural sciences, on the other, Weber was influenced by the debate on this issue that was going on in his days, and in which a number of philosophers and social scientists participated.

Weber's suggestion for how to deal with this question differed, however, from other proposals in that he strongly insisted on the systematic and scientific nature of the social and cultural sciences, including sociology. For example, he worked out a theory of causality for the social and cultural sciences in which counterfactuals, probability, and evidence all play important roles.

Weber's views on these topics are primarily to be found in his essays on methodology, in which they also were given their initial form (see especially MSS, CS, RK, SCIS). In his essay on objectivity Weber notes that "if one wishes to call those disciplines which treat the events of human life with respect to their cultural significance 'cultural sciences', then social science in our sense belongs in that category" (MSS:67). The concept of cultural sciences, as Weber uses it, appears in other words to be broader than that of the social sciences (which appears to include sociology, history, economics, and political science). This would mean that sciences that are neither social nor fall into the category of the natural sciences, such as psychology and jurisprudence, are part of the cultural sciences.

For guidance regarding the discussion of the differences between the natural and the social and cultural sciences, see e.g. Ola Agevall, *A Science of Unique Events: Max Weber's Methodology of the Cultural Sciences* (1999), Don Martindale, *The Nature and Types of Sociological Theory*, pp. 377–83, and Talcott Parsons, *The Structure of Social Action*, pp. 591–601.

See also causality, cultural sciences, economics, history, laws in the social sciences, natural sciences, psychology, sociology

social structure (*Struktur, soziale Struktur, Gebilde*)   As a sociologist Weber was deeply concerned with social action and social structure. However, he only sometimes uses the terms "structure" and "social structure" in his sociology; and these are not part of his general sociology as outlined in Ch. 1 of *Economy and Society*. Instead Weber speaks of different kinds of order (*Ordnung*) in his general sociology (for use of the terms structure and social structure, see e.g. ES:980–81, 1146).

In contemporary sociology the concept of social structure roughly refers to a set of positions or social interactions with a certain permanency, while Weber rather means by "valid order" prescriptions for how to act that are seen as obligatory or desirable by the actors, who also orient their actions to such an order. Major orders in society, such as the legal or political order, are typically also enforced with the help of the law.

It has been argued that Weber's type of sociology, which can be found in his studies of concrete topics in *Economy and Society* and elsewhere, differs from the type of interpretive sociology that he advocated in his chapter on general sociology in Ch. 1 of *Economy and Society*. While Weber emphasizes social structure in the former, he is mainly concerned with social action and meaning in the latter. For this argument, see e.g.

Bryan Turner, *For Weber* (1981), and for an answer, see e.g. Lawrence Scaff, "Weber before Weberian Sociology" (1989).

See also order

social types *See* types

socialism Socialism was a live issue in Weber's time, and Weber touches on it in several of his political writings as well as in his social science writings. His single most important work is an article of 1918 entitled "Socialism" (PW:272–303). Weber's death prevented him from carrying out a planned lecture series on socialism in the summer semester of 1920 (Wolfgang Mommsen, *Max Weber and German Politics 1890–1920* [1984], 103 n. 52).

While noting that the word "socialism" has many meanings, Weber primarily defines it by contrasting it to a privately owned economy (e.g. PW:281). Different types of socialism clearly exist (e.g. PW:286–87). Nonetheless, Weber felt that socialism would entail a universal bureaucratization and a stifling of freedom. He vehemently opposed it whenever he could.

In his economic sociology in Ch. 2 of *Economy and Society* Weber stresses that a capitalist economy constitutes the (formally) most efficient way of organizing an economy; and that a socialist organization of the economy would do away with much of what makes capitalism so efficient, such as the entrepreneur and the insecure social situation of the worker (e.g. ES:161–64). The problems of formulating effective prices are also formidable outside of a capitalist type of economy (ES:100–7). As a political ideology socialism is grounded in natural rights ideas (e.g. ES:871–74).

Weber argued that if socialism was fully implemented, it would lead to a disaster for mankind. In "Socialism" he argues that in a capitalist economy the state and the private economy balance each other, but in socialism there will just be one vast power elite that decides everything (e.g. PW:286; cf. PW:103–5). "State bureaucracy would rule alone if private capitalism were eliminated" (ES:1402). In socialism the workers would be worse off since they would face a united power elite. Instead of the dictatorship of the proletariat, there would be "the dictatorship of the official" (PW:292).

More generally, socialism would increase the already strong trend toward bureaucratization of the world ("universal bureaucratization"—e.g. PW:279). The world would revert to the kind of slavery and tyranny that characterized ancient Egypt (e.g. ASAC:365–66).

During the turbulent period after World War I Weber spoke out very strongly against revolutionary activities in Germany: "Liebknecht belongs in the madhouse and Rosa Luxemburg in the zoo" (Mommsen 1984:305). The revolution he termed a "carnival" (ibid., p. 301; see also, more generally, pp. 295–311).

For Weber and socialism, see e.g. David Beetham, *Max Weber and the Theory of Modern Politics* (1985), pp. 82–9 and Mommsen, *Max Weber and German Politics 1890–1920*, pp. 104–23, 277–80, 295–311. For Weber's view of the concept of communism as well as his view of the Soviet Union, see Stefan Breuer, "Soviet Communism and Weberian Sociology" (1998). For Weber's relationship to individual socialist politicians, see Part 3 of Wolfgang Mommsen and Jürgen Osterhammel (eds.), *Max Weber and His Contemporaries* (1987).

See also communism, political sociology, politics

sociation (*Vergesellschaftung*) *See* communal and associative social relationships

societal action *See* associational action

society (*Gesellschaft*) While Weber occasionally uses the term "society" in his sociological writings, it plays no role in his general sociology, and it is not part of his "Basic Sociological Terms" as outlined in Ch. 1 of *Economy and Society*. One reason for Weber's decision not to use "society" as a sociological concept has probably to do with his firm stance in favor of methodological individualism and his strong aversion to holism.

For a discussion of this issue, see e.g. the section on Weber in David Frisby and Derek Sayer, *Society* (1986), pp. 67–72. According to these two authors, "on one of the few occasions upon which Weber refers to society, he speaks of 'society' as 'the general structure of human groups'" (ibid., p. 69; the reference is to ES:356). They also note that "although one of his major works is entitled *Economy and Society*, it does not discuss 'the definition of the concept of society' but rather societal tendencies to action or sociation (*Vergesellschaftung*) which is contrasted with action motivated by a tendency toward solidarity and communality (*Vergemeinschaftung*)" (ibid., p. 68). Stephen Kalberg states that "it is noteworthy that Weber uses 'society' (*Gesellschaft*) only on two occasions in *Economy and Society*, both times in quotation marks [ES:306, 356]" (Kalberg 1985:63 n. 6). Weber's use of the terms "society" and "social" is also discussed in Martin Albrow, *Max Weber's Construction of Social Theory* (1990), pp. 267–69.

See also group, holism, methodological individualism

sociological theory While Weber himself saw the introductory chapter in *Economy and Society* as an exercise in sociological categories and not in sociological theory, it may nonetheless constitute what comes closest to what sociologists today tend to call "sociological theory" (for Talcott Parsons' translation, see ES:1–62, and for Keith Tribe's, see EW:311–58; see also SCIS). To this may be added Chs. 2–4 in *Economy and Society* as well as some passages in Weber's methodological writings (ES:63–307; e.g. MSS, CS, RK).

While Weber noted that facts are always infused with theory, he also argued that the general maxim in sociological research should be that "theory must follow the facts, not vice versa" (PED:36–7).

See also empiricism, general sociology, sociology, methodology

sociological types *See* types

sociology (*Soziologie*) Weber was trained in law, and he worked for most of his academic career as an economist. It was not until he was in his early forties that he turned much of his scholarly attention to sociology—a science that otherwise did not impress him. The type of sociology that Weber himself tried to develop falls squarely within the cultural sciences, as opposed to the natural sciences. It has social action as its "central subject" and is termed "interpretive sociology" (ES:24). The meaning that the individual attaches to his or her action is also of crucial importance to Weber's type of sociology: "Subjective understanding is the specific characteristic of sociological knowledge" (ES:15).

Weber summarizes his ideas on interpretive sociology in the important Ch. 1 of *Economy and Society*. This chapter exists today in two different translations—one by by Talcott Parsons (ES:1–62) and one by Keith Tribe (EW:311–58).

Weber drew heavily on historical material in his sociology but also made use of surveys. His two main works in sociology are *Economy and Society* and *Collected Essays in the Sociology of Religion*. His most famous work, *The Protestant Ethic and the Spirit of Capitalism*, is included in the latter of these two works, and so are a number of other studies of the relationship between the economy and religion (see the three volumes of GAR, available in English translation as PE, RC, RI, and a few additional essays). Weber, finally, made contributions to a number of subfields in sociology; *see* political sociology, sociology of law, sociology of religion, and similar entries.

Weber summarizes the nature and task of sociology in the important paragraph 1 in Ch. 1 of *Economy and Society*. This key passage has the following wording in the original:

Soziologie (im hier verstandenen Sinn dieses sehr vieldeutig gebrauchten Wortes) soll heissen: eine Wissenschaft, welche soziales Handeln deutend verstehen und dadurch in seinem Ablauf und seinen Wirkungen ursächlich erklären will. "Handeln" soll dabei ein menschliches Verhalten (einerlei ob äusseres oder innerliches

Tun, Unterlassen oder Dulden) heissen, wenn und insofern als der oder die Handelnden mit ihm einen subjectiven Sinn verbinden. "Soziales" Handeln aber soll ein solches Handeln heissen, welches seinem von dem oder den Handelnden gemeinten *Sinn* nach auf das Verhalten *anderer* bezogen wird und daran in seinem Ablauf orientiert ist. (WuG:1)

Talcott Parsons' translation reads as follows:

Sociology (in the sense in which this highly ambiguous word is used here) is a science concerning itself with the interpretive understanding of social action and thereby with a causal explanation of its course and consequences. We shall speak of "action" insofar as the acting individual attaches a subjective meaning to his behavior—be it overt or covert, omission or acquiescence. Action is "social" insofar as its subjective meaning takes account of the behavior of others and is thereby oriented in its course. (ES:4).

Tribe's version reads:

Sociology, a word often used in quite diverse ways, shall mean here: a science which seeks interpretative understanding (*deutend verstehen*) of social action, and thereby will causally explain its course and effects. By "action" is meant human behaviour linked to a subjective *meaning* (*Sinn*) on the part of the actor or actors concerned; such behaviour may be overt or occur inwardly—whether by positive action or by refraining from such action, or by acquiescence to some situation. Such behaviour is "social" action where the meaning intended by actor or actors is related to the behaviour of *others*, and conduct so oriented. (EW:312; for the translation of the same paragraph by Eric Matthews, see Weber 1978:7)

The paragraph raises a number of difficult questions—among them: What is meant by meaning? How does the sociologist get access to the meaning of an actor? What does an explanation look like in sociology? Weber devotes twenty pages of explication to answering such questions. From these pages it is clear that the main task of sociology is to produce types and to analyze uniformities in social behavior. A particularly useful tool in doing so, Weber argues, is the ideal type.

For a brief introduction to Weber's type of sociology, and what is distinctive about it, *see* meaning, causality, interpretive sociology, and methodological individualism.

Weber's general sociology in Ch. 1 of *Economy and Society* is written in a notoriously difficult way. "Arranged by numbers and letters," Marianne Weber writes, "sentence follows upon sentence, blow upon blow, as it were" ([1926] 1975:676). Weber himself feared that "people are going to shake their heads" when they tried to read this chapter (ibid.). His fears came true when he lectured on Ch. 1 some months before his death and the students soon petitioned him to lecture on a different topic.

Much of Weber's early work has a sociological flavor to it and can be read as sociology (e.g. Scaff 1989b). Nonetheless, it was first toward the end of his life that Weber decided to turn his full attention to sociology and to develop his own systematic version of it. One reason for this late interest may have been Weber's low opinion of sociology. According to Karl Jaspers, for example, "most of what goes by the name sociology appeared fraudulent to him" (Jaspers 1989:20). Similarly, according to Guenther Roth, "at the turn of the century, sociology meant for Weber an inflated approach, vainly claiming the status of a master science in pursuit of the empirical and normative laws of social life. . . . Yet by 1910 Weber accepted the term 'sociology' for his interpretive study of social action as well as his comparative approach" (Roth in Bendix and Roth 1971:37). According to Dirk Käsler, it was around 1908–9 "that Weber designated himself as a sociologist for the first time" (Käsler 1988:15).

There exist several useful introductions to Weber's sociology as well as to his work in general. These include Raymond Aron, "Max Weber" (1970), Reinhard Bendix, *Max Weber: An Intellectual Portrait* (1960), Dirk Käsler, *Max Weber: An Introduction to His Life and Work* (1988), and Frank Parkin, *Max Weber* (1982). For Weber's relationship to Georg Simmel, see e.g. David Frisby, "The Ambiguity of Modernity: Georg Simmel and Max Weber" (1987); see also Weber 1972. For Weber's relationship to Emile Durkheim, see e.g. Anthony Giddens, "Weber and Durkheim: Coincidence and Convergence" (1987).

See also *Deutsche Gesellschaft für Soziologie* (German Sociological Association), economic sociology, interpretive sociology, *Kategorienlehre*, methodology, interpretive sociology, orientation to others, political sociology, rural sociology, science (for the sociology of science), sociology of art, sociology of law, sociology of religion, type, understanding

sociology of art   Weber never developed a full-blown sociology of art, although he told his wife about his plans for "a sociology embracing all the arts" (Marianne Weber [1926] 1975:500; cf. Winkelmann 1986:36). Various scattered remarks on art can nonetheless be located in Weber's writings—plus a major study in the sociology of music (RSFM).

In his sociology of religion, for example, Weber discusses the birth of symbolism as well as the relationship to art of various religions (e.g. ES:404–5, 607–9, 619–20). In "Science as a Vocation" Weber mentions the tendency in the days of the Renaissance to see art as a science ("art was raised to the rank of a science"—GM:142; cf. RC:151). In the modern world, in contrast, "the esthetic sphere" and "the intellectual sphere" (of which science is a part) are separate (GM:340–43).

There is also a tendency in the modern world for art to become an alternative to religion. Or in Weber's words, art "provides a *salvation* from the routines of everyday life, and especially from the increasing pressures of theoretical and practical rationalism" (GM:342).

For Weber's personal interests in art, including music, see e.g. Paul Honigsheim, *The Unknown Max Weber* ([1946–63] 2000), pp. 200–15. For Weber's relationship to Max Klinger and German Expressionism, see Sam Whimster (ed.), *Max Weber and the Culture of Anarchy* (1999), pp. 196–231.

See also sociology of music, symbolism

sociology of domination   *See* domination

sociology of education   *See* education

sociology of law (*Rechtssoziologie*)   Weber is considered as one of the founders of the sociology of law. His major contribution to the field can be found in the book-length section devoted to this topic in *Economy and Society* (ES:641–900; cf. ES:33–6, 311–38). The focus in this section is on the different fields of substantive law, legal rights, legal norms, legal *Honoratioren*, and the rationalization of law (ES:641–900; cf. ES:33–6, 311–13). Weber's major writings on the sociology of law have been collected by Max Rheinstein in *On Law in Economy and Society* (Weber 1954).

Sociology of law and jurisprudence look at law from different perspectives, according to Weber. While the jurist primarily focuses on the internal logic of legal rules, the sociologist studies the impact of these rules on social behavior (ES:32–33, 311–12, CS:115–43, SCIS:158–59).

From a legal perspective, Weber says, modern law consists of legal propositions or norms which are either prescriptive, prohibitory, or permissive (ES:667). In sociological terms, the former two constitute "claims," and the latter "privilege." Claims essentially provide a higher degree of certainty that promises will be kept, while privileges make possible the creation of new law and are thereby enabling in nature (ibid.).

More generally, Weber defines law in his general sociology in Ch. 1 of *Economy and Society* as conventions enforced by a staff of people (ES:34). Lawmaking as well as law-finding can be either rational or irrational as well as substantive or formal (ES:656–57). According to a famous passage in Weber's sociology of law in *Economy and Society*, law has gone through the following stages: (1) charismatic legal revelation through "law prophets"; (2) the making and application of law by legal *Honoratioren*; (3) the imposition of law by secular or theocratic powers; and (4) the systematic elaboration and administration of law through people specially trained in law (ES:882; for the rationalization of law, see also ES:776).

Much of Weber's work on law is centered around the economy. At one point in his sociology of law, for example, Weber notes that the development of legal institutions is "indispensable for a modern capitalist society" (ES:682). While many general statements on the role of law in modern capitalism can be found in Weber's sociology of law, it does not contain a systematic discussion of these legal institutions. The main reason for this, it appears, is that Weber had assigned this topic to another author in the *Handbook of Social Economics* (ES:682).

For general introductions to Weber's sociology of law, see e.g. Max Rheinstein, "Introduction," pp. xvii–lxiv in Weber 1954, Sally Ewing, "Formal Justice and the Spirit of Capitalism: Max Weber's Sociology of Law" (1987), and Alan Hunt, "Max Weber's Sociology of Law" (1978). See also Anthony Kronman, *Max Weber* (1983), Wolfgang Schluchter, "Types of Law and Types of Domination," pp. 82–138 in *The Rise of Western Rationalism* (1981), Wolfgang Schluchter, "The Sociology of Law as an Empirical Theory of Validity" (2002), and Bryan Turner, "Weber and the Sociology of Law," pp. 318–51 in *For Weber* (1981). Volume I/22–3 of MWG will be devoted to Weber's sociology of law in *Economy and Society*.

According to some commentators, Weber's sociology of law is centered around the theme of law and economy (e.g. Kronman, *Max Weber*, p. 118 and Richard Swedberg, *Max Weber and the Idea of Economic Sociology* [1998], pp. 82–107). Talcott Parsons, on the other hand, has emphasized the centrality of Weber's sociology of law to his sociology as a whole: "in my opinion, the great extent to which the core of Weber's substantive sociological work, both theoretical and empirical, lay in the sociology of law has not been adequately appreciated" (Parsons 1975:174–75). For the reception of Weber's sociology of law in the United States, Germany, and some other countries, see Pierre Lascoumes (ed.), *Actualité de Max Weber pour la sociologie du droit* (1995).

See also claims, commercial legislation, contract, constitution, convention, education (for legal education), England Problem, firm (for legal personality), jurisprudence, justice, kadi justice, law, law prophet, law specialist, lawmaking and law-finding, legal *Honoratioren*, legal domination, legal norm, legal order, privileges, rights, sacred law

sociology of music Weber's study in the sociology of music has been translated as *The Rational and Social Foundations of Music*. The main emphasis in this study is on the rationalization of music (cf. PE:14–15).

According to Paul Honigsheim, "for Weber, music was almost a necessity of life" (Honigsheim 1968:83; more generally on Weber's relationship to music, see ibid., pp. 81–89).

The Rational and Social Foundations of Music was probably written in 1910–11 but was only published in 1921 (with an introduction by Theodore Kroyer). For information on this work, see e.g. Dirk Käsler, *Max Weber* (1988), pp. 168–71. For a discussion, see e.g. Don Martindale and Johannes Reidel, "Max Weber's Sociology of Music" (1963), Christoph Braun, "The 'Science of Reality' of Music History: On the Historical Background to Max Weber's Study of Music" (1999), and Alan Turley, "Max Weber and the Sociology of Music" (2001).

A new edition of Weber's study of music will be published as MWG, Vol. I/14.

See also *Rational and Social Foundations of Music, The*; rationalization, sociology of art

sociology of organizations   *See* organization theory or organizational sociology

sociology of politics   *See* political sociology

sociology of religion (*Religionssoziologie*)   Weber is considered as one of the founders of the sociology of religion. The task of this field, according to Weber, is not so much to inquire into the essence of religion as to study "the conditions and effects of a particular type of social action" (ES:399). It is also imperative to include "the viewpoint of the religious believer's 'meaning'" (ibid.).

Weber's main contribution to the sociology of religion can be found in *Economy and Society* (ES:399–634) and in the three volumes of the *Collected Essays in the Sociology of Religion* (which include *The Protestant Ethic and the Spirit of Capitalism*; see also GAR I–III, partly translated as AJ, RI, RC). In these works Weber presents a general sociological analysis of religious behavior as well as studies of the economic ethics of Hinduism, Buddhism, Taoism, Confucianism, Judaism, and certain aspects of Christianity and Islam.

One may also look at Weber's sociology of religion from another angle, namely his interest in ascetic Protestantism from *The Protestant Ethic* onwards. In the last lines of *The Protestant Ethic* Weber sketched a program for further study of the cultural significance of ascetic Protestantism (PE:182–83; see also PE:284 n. 119). This program, dating from 1905, was first laid aside but was revived around 1910, and the result was *The Economic Ethics of the World Religions*, published in the *Collected Essays in the Sociology of Religion*.

The various writings that make up *Collected Essays in the Sociology of Religion* were mainly produced in the 1910s. The section on the sociology of religion in *Economy and Society* was probably written in 1913–14, but not published until after Weber's death. The text, which is unfinished, is entitled "Religionssoziologie (Typen religiöser Vergemeinschaftung)," which is translated in the current edition of *Economy and Society* as "Religious Groups (The Sociology of Religion)." Weber's writings on the sociology of religion in the edition of *Economy and Society* that is planned for MGW will be published as Vol. I/22-2 under the title *Religiöse Gemeinschaften* (*Religious Communities*). While writing his sociology of religion for *Economy and Society*, Weber referred to it as his "systematization of religion" (*Religionssystematik*; cf. Hans Kippenberg and Martin Riesebrodt, *Max Webers "Religionssystematik"* [2001], p. 1).

For a summary of the content of Weber's sociology of religion, see e.g. Reinhard Bendix, *Max Weber: An Intellectual Portrait* (1960), pp. 285–429 and Dirk Käsler, *Max Weber* (1988), pp. 74–141. See also e.g. Pierre Bourdieu, "Legitimation and Structured Interests in Weber's Sociology of Religion" ([1971] 1987; cf. Bourdieu, "Mit Weber gegen Weber" [2000]) and Talcott Parsons' introduction to the section on religion in *Economy and Society*, published under the title *The Sociology of Religion* (Weber 1963). For complementary information about publication dates as well as Weber's designs for his sociology of religion, see Wolfgang Schluchter, "The Sociology of Religion: A Reconstruction of Its Development," pp. 411–32, 469–72 in *Rationalism, Religion and Domination* (1989).

A scholarly introduction to the key concepts in Weber's sociology of religion can be found in Kippenberg and Riesebrodt, *Max Webers "Religionssystematik."*

For comments on the individual studies that make up *Collected Essays in the Sociology of Religion*, see the volumes that Wolfgang Schluchter has edited (Schluchter 1981a, 1983, 1984, 1985, 1987; for some of Schluchter's ideas on these works in English, see *Rationalism, Religion, and Domination*). See also in this context S. N. Eisenstadt, "Some Reflections on the Significance of Max Weber's Sociology of Religions for the Analysis of Non-European Modernity" (1971).

For Weber's important plan for his *Collected Essays in the Sociology of Religion*, as advertised in 1919, see Schluchter, *Rationalism, Religion, and Domination*, p. 425. Weber's main concern in this work, according to this plan, was to address the following question: "What is the economic and social *singularity* of the Occident based upon, how did it arise and especially, how is it connected to the religious ethos?" (ibid.). He also states that these essays "were intended . . . to be published together with the treatise on *Economy and Society* . . . and to interpret and supplement the section on the sociology of religion" (GAR, I:237; cf. Reinhard Bendix and Guenther Roth, *Scholarship and Partisanship* [1971], pp. 113–14 n. 8).

See also ascetic Protestantism, asceticism, Buddhism, church, Catholicism, *Collected Essays in the Sociology of Religion*, Confucianism, congregation, Hinduism, Islam, Judaism, magician, monotheism/polytheism, mystagogue, prophet, priest, Weber thesis, Protestantism, religion, religious benefits, religious ethic, religious virtuoso, salvation, sect, symbolism, Taoism, tension, theodicy, world-religions

sociology of science   *See* science

Solidarität   *See* mutual responsibility

Solidaritätsbeziehungen   *See* mutual responsibility

Sombart, Werner (1863–1941)   German economist and economic historian as well as a colleague of Max Weber. See e.g. Bertram Schefold, "Sombart, Werner (1863–1941)" (1987).

"Some Categories of Interpretive Sociology" ("Über einige Kategorien der verstehenden Soziologie")   This article is of much importance in that it represents the first place in which Weber explicitly outlines and discusses many of the tasks of an *interpretive sociology*: what sets such a sociology apart from the other social sciences, what is the role of *Verstehen*, what constitutes social action, and so forth. The same set of questions is addressed more fully, and in somewhat different terms, in Ch. 1 of *Economy and Society*.

Weber's essay is about thirty pages long and makes difficult reading. It is divided into seven sections, the first of which is entitled "The Meaning of 'Interpretive' Sociology." Two sections are devoted to the relationship of this type of sociology to psychology and law. The remaining sections discuss specific concepts ("social action," "association and associational action," "consensus," and "institution and organization").

"Some Categories of Interpretive Sociology" was published in 1913 in *Logos*, a philosophical journal. According to one of its notes, the second part of the article was originally written for the *Handbook of Social Economics* (Weber [1913] 1981:179 n. 1). It is also clear that Weber's terminology had changed somewhat between the *Logos* essay (1913) and Ch. 1 of *Economy and Society* (1919–20). According to Weber himself, the main reason for these changes was simply to make his approach "more easily understandable" (ES:3; for a discussion of these changes, *see* social action). Reflecting when they were written, some texts in *Economy and Society* use the terminology from the *Logos* essay while others draw from the terminology in Ch. 1.

For a discussion, see e.g. Edith Graber, "Translator's Introduction to Max Weber's Essay on Some Categories of Interpretive Sociology"

(1981). For the argument that "Some Categories of Interpretive Sociology" constitutes the lead theoretical chapter in the early version of *Economy and Society*, see Hiroshi Orihara, "From 'A Torso with a Wrong Head' to 'Five Disjointed Body-Parts without a Head'" (2003). For a partial translation of "Some Categories," see ES:1375–80.

See also *Economy and Society*, interpretive sociology, social action

sorcery *See* magic

Sozialökonomik *See* social economics

Soziologie *See* sociology

soziologische Grundbegriffe *See* basic sociological terms

spheres *See* value-spheres

spirit of capitalism (*Geist des Kapitalismus*) This concept plays a key role in Weber's famous study *The Protestant Ethic and the Spirit of Capitalism* and is primarily used to denote the kind of methodical as well as entrepreneurial approach to work and profit-making which emerged in the West during the late sixteenth and the seventeenth centuries, largely though not exclusively under the impact of ascetic Protestantism. Weber says that his choice of the term "spirit of capitalism" was ad hoc.

Weber specifies in *The Protestant Ethic* that he is not interested in the spirit of capitalism in general, but primarily in "the spirit of modern [rational] capitalism" (PE:68). Religious forces helped to form and to diffuse this spirit—and thereby became one of its "driving forces" (*Triebkräfte*—GAR, I:53; cf. PE:68, 91).

Weber uses Benjamin Franklin and some of his sayings to illustrate what the spirit of modern capitalism is like. It is ethical in nature and part of a lifestyle (e.g. PE:58). The spirit of modern rational capitalism is contrasted to the "traditionalistic spirit" of capitalism that preceded it (PE:65).

Weber differentiates sharply between economic spirit (or economic mentality), on the one hand, and economic "form" (or economic organization), on the other (e.g. PE:64, 67). For example, the economic spirit may change while the economic form remains the same—and this is precisely what happened during the transitional period that Weber discusses in *The Protestant Ethic* (e.g. PED:75).

Even if the spirit of modern capitalism in the West is predominantly rational, it also has its charismatic-speculative elements. In *Economy and Society* Weber refers at one point to "the double nature of . . . the 'capitalist' spirit," and argues that "these two structural elements" are "everywhere intertwined" (ES:1118).

The last chapter in Weber's lecture course of 1919–20, which has been reconstructed under the title *General Economic History*, is entitled "The Evolution of the Capitalistic Spirit (*Gesinnung*)" (GEH:352–69). Here, in contrast to *The Protestant Ethic*, Weber starts the analysis of the growth of modern capitalism long *before* Protestantism, and he also addresses its development *after* the height of Protestantism.

In his response to one of his critics Weber refers to "what in an ad hoc way I christened the 'sprit of capitalism'," and adds that "as far as *terminology* is concerned, I would always be prepared to exchange this term for a more suitable one" (PED:31, 38). When Weber published the first edition of his study, he also set the word "spirit"(*Geist*) within quote marks, which presumably indicates a certain distance from it. To this may be added that the expression "spirit of capitalism" is also prominent in Werner Sombart's *Der moderne Kapitalismus* (1902), which was published a few years before *The Protestant Ethic* (1904–5). That Sombart's use of the expression predates Weber's study does not, however, mean that Sombart also suggested Weber's main thesis. In fact, Weber states that he lectured on the general thesis of *The Protestant Ethic* already in 1897 (PED:62).

According to Wilhelm Hennis, Weber would have avoided much confusion if he had used the term "habitus" rather than spirit (Hennis 1988a:31). According to Jean-Pierre Grossein, such terms as *Geist* (spirit), *Gesinnung* (mentality), and "habitus" all mean roughly the same thing (Grossein, "Présentation" [1996], p. 61 n. 1).

Frank Parkin has illustrated the relationship between the "form" and "spirit" of capitalism in *The Protestant Ethic* in the following manner:

	SPIRIT	FORM
(1)	–	–
(2)	–	+
(3)	+	–
(4)	+	+

SOURCE: Frank Parkin, *Max Weber* (1982), p. 42.

In Situation 1, neither the spirit of modern capitalism nor capitalist institutions are present. In Situation 2, which is characteristic of what Weber calls traditional capitalism in *The Protestant Ethic*, you find capitalist institutions but not the spirit of modern capitalism. In Situation 3, which existed in Massachusetts in the 1600s, according to Weber, you may find the spirit of modern capitalism but not capitalist institutions. When the spirit of modern capitalism and capitalist institutions are both present, the result is modern rational capitalism. (I have changed Parkin's term "substance" to "form," in order to make it more compatible with the terminology in *The Protestant Ethic*.)

See also capitalism, ethos, habitus, lifestyle, mentality, Weber thesis, vocation

sport   Weber touches on the topic of sport in *The Protestant Ethic*, where he analyzes "the Puritan aversion to sport" (PE:167; cf. 166). To the Americans, Weber notes in the same work, money-making has become a "sport" (PE:182).

Weber himself was not very good at sports as a child and does not appear to have had any favorite sport (or exercised much) as an adult (see e.g. Marianne Weber [1926] 1975:40, 68, 70–71).

stages in history (*Stufen der Geschichte*)   *See* evolution

Stammler, Rudolf (1856–1938)   Neo-Kantian philosopher of law and the target of Weber's attack in *Critique of Stammler* (Weber 1977; see also ES:4, 34, 325–33). See e.g. Guy Oakes, "Introduction" to *Critique of Stammler*.

Stand   *See* status

Ständestaat   *See* state

ständische Herrschaft (estate-type domination)   *See* patrimonialism

state (*Staat*)   One can find a comparative and historical analysis of the state in Weber's work. A state, according to his famous definition, is an organization that has a monopoly on the legitimate use of violence within a specific territory.

The exact definition of the state in Weber's general sociology in Ch. 1 of *Economy and Society*, reads as follows: "a compulsory political organization with continuous operations (*politischer Anstaltsbetrieb*) will be called a 'state' insofar as its administrative staff successfully upholds the claim to the monopoly of the legitimate use of physical force in the enforcement of its order" (ES:54; cf. similarly GM:78, 82, 336).

A compulsory political organization, in its turn, is defined as an organization whose "existence and order is continuously safeguarded within a given territorial area by the threat and application of physical force on part of the administrative staff" (ibid.).

A state cannot be defined by its goal, but only by its means, according to Weber. While the use of physical force may vary, it is nonetheless specific for the state and what it always will resort to in the last instance (ES:54–5). Since the state is "a relation of men dominating men" (GM:78–9), there is also the related issue of legitimation (charismatic, traditional, and legal domination; *see* legitimation).

A state needs a staff, and the character of this staff has changed over history, from the small circle of men around a traditional leader to the large bureaucracy of modern days. This staff has similarly been financed and rewarded in different ways (*see* administration). The state has also acquired its resources in different ways, with liturgies and taxes being the most common sources of income (Weber speaks of the liturgical state [*Liturgiestaat*] and the tax state [*Steuerstaat*]—e.g. GEH:95, AA:131, ES:350–53).

In terms of Weber's economic sociology, a state is an economically active organization, that is, an organization whose primary goal is not economic but which has secondary economic goals (ES:74). The state may also be seen as an "enterprise" (ES:1394).

What characterizes the modern state is primarily that it is rational (e.g. GEH:338–51). Its functions include legislative tasks, the defense of its territory, and various cultural tasks (ES:905). It also has a legal and administrative order to which the actions of the administrative staff are oriented (ES:56). This order fits rational capitalism because it is predictable (e.g. PW:148). The modern state and its political system also operate as a counterweight to the power of the economy (e.g. PW:103–5). The modern state has a monopoly on regulating the monetary system and on the creation of money (ES:166–67). It conducts a rational economic policy and has a rational taxation system (RC:41). Its staff is organized in the form of a bureaucracy, just as with large-scale capitalist enterprises (*see* bureaucracy). The legitimation of the modern state is typically legal in nature.

Finally, a state does not act; only individuals do (ES:13). Neither does it exist once and for all; all that exists is the *probability* that certain kinds of social actions that add up to "the state" will take place in the future as in the past (ES:27–8; cf. SCIS:159).

Different types of state exist; and "all states may be classified according to whether they rest on the principle that the staff of men themselves own the administrative means, or whether the staff is 'separated' from these means of administration" (GM:81). There are, for example, the clan state, the corvée state, the patrimonial state, the *Ständestaat*, or the feudal state (e.g. ES:197–98 [the corvée state], ES:1040–41 [the patrimonial state], ES:1085–88 and PW:100–10 [the *Ständestaat*], AA:77–8). The welfare state, in Weber's view, predates Bismarck's Germany by many centuries since it has not been uncommon throughout history for rulers to assume responsibility for their subjects' welfare (e.g. ES:1107, RI:142–43, 242, RC:73–74, 184, AJ:303; see e.g. PW:68 for the authoritarian potential of the welfare state).

For Weber's use of the concept of the *Rechtsstaat*, *see* constitution.

Weber discussed the economic as well as the social policy of the state in several of his writings. As to economic policy, Weber comments, for example, on mercantilism as well as imperialism (e.g. ES:913–21, GEH:343–51).

For Weber's view of social policy in Germany in his day, see Wolfgang Mommsen, *Max Weber and German Politics 1890–1920* (1984), pp. 101–23.

For a summary of Weber's view of the modern state, see e.g. Reinhard Bendix, *Max Weber: An Intellectual Portrait* (1960), pp. 417–56 and Mommsen, *Max Weber and German Politics 1890–1920* (1984), pp. 35–67, 390–414. See also Stefan Breuer, "Max Webers Staatssoziologie" (1993). For the argument that some of Weber's ideas in *The Protestant Ethic* may also help to explain the structure of the modern European state, see Phillip Gorski, *The Disciplinary Revolution: Calvinism and the Rise of the State in Early Modern Europe* (2003). For Johannes Winkelmann's attempt to reconstruct Weber's "sociology of the state," see his edition of Max Weber, *Staatssoziologie* as well as the current (fifth) edition of *Wirtschaft und Gesellschaft*, pp. 815–68. Weber's lectures of relevance to "the sociology of the state" are scheduled to appear as MWG, Vol. III/7.

See also coercion, constitution (also for *Rechtsstaat*), domination, legitimation, imperialism, means of administration, money, nation, political organization, violence

statistics   Weber was positive toward the use of statistics in sociology and social science (e.g. Paul Honigsheim, *On Max Weber* [1968], pp. 67, 143), and used some elementary forms of quantitative methods, especially in those of his studies that were based on surveys. In his interpretative sociology, as outlined in Ch. 1 of *Economy and Society*, Weber discusses which kinds of statistics can be used in analyzing social action and which kinds fit less well. The former are those that include in principle information about the actors' understanding of their actions, while the latter are those that do not.

In his general sociology in Ch. 1 of *Economy and Society* Weber states that "statistical uniformities" can only be treated as "actions" if there is an understandable meaning to them ("sociological statistics"; ES:12). Examples of this include statistics on prices and occupational distribution. If such an element of understanding, however, is not present (as is the case with statistics on death rates and the production rates of machines), you have "statistics of processes devoid of subjective meaning" (ibid.; cf. SCIC:153). This latter type of statistics falls into the category of actions and objects that are part of the scene where social action takes place, and which Weber describes as "conditions, stimuli, furthering or hindering

The Max Weber Dictionary

circumstances of action" (ES:13).

In *The Protestant Ethic* Weber refers to a well-known set of statistics by Martin Offenbacher which purported to show that German Protestants had higher education and more wealth than German Catholics at the end of the nineteenth century (PE:188–89). These statistics, however, are today known to be flawed, as was first pointed out by economic historian Kurt Samuelson (*Religion and Economic Action* [1961], pp. 2–3, 138–46; cf. George Becker, "Replication and Reanalysis of Offenbacher's School Enrollment Study: Implications for the Weber and Merton Theses" [1997]). Defenders of Weber's argument sometimes counter that this does not refute Weber's more general thesis about ascetic Protestantism and the spirit of capitalism (e.g. Seymour Lipset and Reinhard Bendix, *Social Mobility in Industrial Society* [1959], p. 55).

Weber carried out a few surveys in the early part of his career (and planned a few others that never materialized), but as his interests broadened to world-religions and universal history, he was increasingly forced to rely on secondary sources. When he was in his fifties, Weber stated that "no sociologist . . . should think himself too good, even in his old age, to make tens of thousands of quite trivial computations in his head and perhaps for months at a time" (GM:135).

For a presentation and discussion of Weber's use of various quantitative methods, see in particular Paul Lazarsfeld and Anthony Oberschall, "Max Weber and Empirical Research" (1965) and Anthony Oberschall, *Empirical Social Research in Germany 1848–1914* (1965). For Weber's use of Johannes von Kries' ideas on probability and causation, see e.g. Stephen Turner and Regis Factor, "Objective Possibility and Adequate Causation in Weber's Methodological Writings" (1981). For Weber's exchange with the leading statistician Ladislaus von Bortkiewics at the 1911 meeting of the German Sociological Association, see *Schriften des Vereins für Sozialpolitik* (1911):139ff. (cf. GASS:424–30, Lazarsfeld and Oberschall, "Objective Possibility and Adequate Causation in Weber's Methodological Writings," p. 189). Finally, mention should be made of Weber's comments on the limits of statistics in his presentation of religious activist Paul Göhre's book based on three months in a factory (Weber [1892] 1993).

See also causation, empiricism, probability

status (*Stand*) Weber introduced the notion of status in his sociology, among other reasons to complement class analysis which in his opinion could not account for all social stratification.

The closest to a formal definition of status that can be found in *Economy and Society* may well be the following: "'status' (*ständische Lage*) shall mean an effective claim to social esteem in terms of positive or negative privileges" (ES:305). Weber also supplies the following description of status in one of his works: "'status' . . . is a quality of social honor or a lack of it, and is in the main conditioned as well as expressed through a specific style of life" (RI:39).

A society, according to Weber, can be stratified according to class or according to status. As opposed to "class" and "class situations," "status" and "status situations" are based on lifestyle as well as esteem or honor. There are other differences as well: "in contrast to classes, *Stände* (status groups) are normally groups. They are, however, often of an amorphous kind" (ES:932). And as opposed to a class, a status group is typically related to consumption rather than to production. Its spirit is furthermore deeply antagonistic to the bargaining and the naked economic struggle of the market.

Property or lack of property does not translate into status or lack thereof in the short run, but tends to do so in the long run. Status groups also tend to be closed off and to create monopolies, special conventions, and their own "status-legends" (cf. ES:639, GM:276–77). There are "occupational status groups" as well as "hereditary status groups" and "political or hierocratic status groups" (ES:306).

Weber discusses the concept of status (and class) in two places in *Economy and Society*. The first is in the brief and unfinished Ch. 4, and the second is in a much fuller section known as "Class, Status, Party" in Ch. 9, written some years earlier (ES:302–7 and ES:926–40 respectively; for an alternative translation, see Weber 1978:57–61, 43–56). Many sociologists are familiar with "Class, Status, Party" because of its prominent place in the well-known anthology *From Max Weber*, edited by Hans Gerth and C. Wright Mills (GM); it is also reprinted in various anthologies on class and stratification. There are no major differences between Weber's analysis of status in these two texts. According to the editors of MWG, "the unfinished fourth chapter ['Status Groups and Classes'] is a new, terminologically sharpened version of the posthumous text ('Classes, Status Groups, Parties')" (Horst Baier, M. Rainer Lepsius, Wolfgang Mommsen, and Wolfgang Schluchter, "Overview of the Text of *Economy and Society* by the Editors of the Max Weber *Gesamtausgabe*" [2000], p. 113).

For an introduction to Weber's concept of status, see e.g. Frank Parkin, "Class, Status, and Party," pp. 90–108 in *Max Weber* (1982). It is often pointed out that it is very hard to translate the term *Stand* in Weber's work, and that its meaning ranges somewhere from "status group" to "estate" (e.g. Roth in ES:300 n. 4). Reinhard Bendix says, for example, that "I believe that 'status group' is an adequate translation of *Stand*.

In medieval society its original meaning was 'estate'" (Bendix 1960:85). Ralf Dahrendorf similarly notes that "in translating Weber's term *Stand*, most translators have used the word 'status'. This—though not false—is misleading in that it does not convey the double meaning of the German *Stand* as 'status' and 'estate'" (Dahrendorf 1959:7 n. 5).

Keith Tribe argues that "status groups" is "a clumsy term," and that "the *Stände* [in Weber's time] were 'occupational groups', self-regulating, hence called 'corporations' or guilds" (Tribe, "Translator's Appendix," p. 109 in Wilhelm Hennis, *Max Weber's Science of Man* [2000]). Talcott Parsons, finally, argues that "there is no English term which even approaches adequacy in rendering this term [*Stand*]," and that one therefore has to figure out its meaning depending on the context in which Weber uses it (Weber 1947:348 n. 27). For a general discussion of the multiple uses that Weber makes of the term *Stand* as well as a vigorous critique of the tendency to translate it as "status group," see Morton Wenger, "The Transmutation of Weber's *Stand* in American Sociology and Its Social Roots" (1980).

See also class, lifestyle

stratification   *See* class, status

structure   *See* social structure

struggle   *See* conflict

***Stufen* (stages)**   *See* evolution

subjectivity, subjectivistic, subjectivism   Through its focus on the meaning of the individual actor, Weber's sociology is often described using terms such as "subjectivity," "subjectivistic," and "subjectivism." These indeed capture one aspect of Weber's project of an interpretive sociology, namely that it does not look at the behavior of actors from the outside but always tries to include the meaning that they assign to their actions.

These terms, however, are also used in contemporary social science as synonymous with arbitrary, fleeting and impossible to use in real science; and these meanings do not at all capture what Weber's interpretive sociology is about. As the entries on empathy, *Evidenz*, meaning, and complex of meaning make clear, Weber was well aware of the many difficulties for the sociologist that come from assigning such a central role to the meaning of the individual actor. He also insisted very strongly that clarity and empirical proof are included in the process of understanding (*Verstehen*) that the researcher undertakes.

See also complex of meaning, empathy, *Evidenz*, interpretive sociology, meaning, methodological individualism, understanding

suffering   *See* theodicy

sultanism (*Sultanismus*)   Weber uses this term to denote a form of traditional domination in which (1) the administration as well as the military are seen by the ruler as his or her personal instruments; and (2) where the ruler rules by discretion (ES:231–32). If the ruler abides by tradition instead of just using discretion, there is patrimonialism (ibid.).
      See also patrimonialism, traditional domination

switchmen   Weber uses the metaphor of switchmen in the following well-known passage in his sociology of religion:

Not ideas, but material and ideal interests, directly govern men's conduct. Yet very frequently the "world images" that have been created by "ideas" have, like switchmen, determined the tracks along which action has been pushed by the dynamic of interest. (GM:280)

      For the context of this passage as well as various interpretations, *see* interest

symbolism   In his sociology of religion Weber argues that the birth of magic and religion also meant the birth of symbolism. The reason for this was that "a realm of souls, demons and god" was now added to the ordinary realm of life (ES:404). The existence of "magical symbolism" also meant that naturalism was displaced (ES:405).
      "Analogical thinking . . . originated in symbolistically rationalized magic" (ES:407). Art, too, is related to the kind of symbolism that grew out of the religious and magical realm.
      See also meaning, sociology of art, tension

Taoism   Weber discusses Taoism primarily in *The Religion of China* (*Konfuzianismus und Taoismus*). There are also some scattered remarks elsewhere (e.g. ES:431, 428–29, 629).
      Taoism is centered around the concept of Tao or the eternal order of the cosmos (RC:181). It is profoundly traditionalistic and magic plays a central role in it. At one point Weber refers to Taoism as "the magical garden of heterodox doctrine" (RC:227). He characterizes Taoism "a popular enterprise of practical magic" and contrasts it to the rational character of Confucianism and its anchoring in a small elite (ES:502).
      For a discussion of Taoism, see e.g. Wolfgang Schluchter, *Rationalism, Religion, and Domination* (1989), pp. 85–116, Wolfgang Schluchter

(ed.), *Max Webers Studie über Konfuzianismus und Taoismus* (1983), and the introductory and editorial material to *The Religion of China* in MWG, Vol. I/19.

See also *Economic Ethics of the World Religions, The*; *Religion of China, The*

tax state   *See* state

taxation   *See* state

teacher of ethics (*ethischer Lehrer*)   Weber discusses the teacher of ethics, such as the guru, in his sociology of religion. "Such a teacher," according to *Economy and Society*, "gathers disciples around him, counsels private persons, and advises princes in public affairs and possibly tries to make them establish a new ethical order" (ES:444).

technique   *See* technology

technology (*Technik*)   Weber pays much attention to the role of technology throughout history. It should also be noted that Weber does not restrict the term technology to machinery of the type that is used in the economy. It also refers to various techniques that are used in religion, for example by the ascetic.

Non-economic forms of technique or technology play an important role in Weber's sociology of religion; and Weber refers, for example, to "technologies of meditation," "salvation technologies," and the like (e.g. RI:163, 166).

In his economic sociology in Ch. 2 of *Economy and Society* Weber contrasts economic action to "technical action" in the following manner: "economic action is primarily oriented to the problem of choosing the end to which a thing should be applied; technology, to the problem, given the end, of choosing the appropriate means" (ES:5–6).

But even if Weber makes a sharp conceptual distinction between economic and technical action, in reality economic concerns are usually taken into account when technical problems are solved—such as whether or not to use platinum for the parts of a machine (ES:66).

Weber argues against the tendency to see human history or the economy as driven primarily by technology; and he similarly makes a sharp distinction between the origin of capitalism and the Industrial Revolution. The causality between technology and the economy, Weber repeatedly emphasizes, can go either way, and technology is as little the major force in history as any other single factor (e.g. GASS:456).

The *General Economic History* contains many examples of the role of technology in the evolution of the economy, from different types of plows to the first factory (see e.g. Ch. 27, "The Development of Industrial

Technique"). In an often cited passage Weber also refers to the machine as "congealed spirit" (PW:158). In his analysis in the *General Economic History* of what is distinctive about modern Western capitalism, Weber mentions "rational technology" (GEH:354, 276–77; cf. GEH:312–14, ES:161–62). Elsewhere Weber refers to "modern science" as "the technical basis of capitalism" (ES:1194).

According to Talcott Parsons, "the German word *Technik* which Weber uses . . . covers both the meanings of the English word 'technique' and of 'technology'" (ES:206 n. 4).

See in this context e.g. Randall Collins, "A Theory of Technology," pp. 77–116 in *Weberian Sociological Theory* (1986), Ralph Schroeder, "Disenchantment and Its Discontents: Weberian Perspectives on Science and Technology" (1995), and Ralph Schroeder and Richard Swedberg, "Weberian Perspectives on Science, Technology and the Economy" (2002).

See also enterprise, science

tension (*Spannung, Spannungsverhältnis,* and similar terms)   While Weber does not define the concept of tension or assign a place to it in his general sociology in Ch. 1 of *Economy and Society*, it nonetheless plays a key role in his sociology. It is central to Weber's sociology of religion, and is also present in other parts of his sociology.

There may exist a tension between the religious realm and the ordinary world, as well as between religion and the different value-spheres in society, according to Weber (e.g. ES:451, 590, GM:327–28, 331–33, 358). The Puritans, for example, lived in "a tremendous and grandiose tension toward the 'world'" (RC:227). In the Confucian ethic, on the other hand, there is no tension between "ethical demand and human shortcoming" (RC:235–36).

Various ways of seeking salvation as well as efforts to make sense of the world represent ways to respond to this tension. Another way of escaping the tension between religion and the world of economics is through mysticism. To the mystic, the economy means nothing. There is also the Puritan ethic of vocation. According to this ethic, you accept the economic world as it is and concentrate on your vocation (e.g. GM:333). In brief, the way that the tension with the world is handled will have important consequences for the personality of the believer as well as for society.

For a discussion of the role of tension in Weber's sociology of religion, see e.g. Talcott Parsons, "Introduction" (1963).

See also salvation, symbolism, theodicy

territory   *See* geography, state

theodicy (*Theodizee*)   Weber often refers to the concept of theodicy (a term that is usually traced back to Leibniz's essay on this topic of 1710), but gives it a social rather than a theological interpretation. The question of how to reconcile the existence of God with the existence of evil in the world is either seen from a social perspective or interpreted in social terms.

In *The Protestant Ethic* Weber refers to "the theodicy problem," which he describes as "all those questions about the meaning of the world and of life" (PE:109). To cite "Politics as a Vocation": "the age-old problem of theodicy consists of the very question of how it is that a power which is said to be at once omnipotent and kind could have created such an irrational world of undeserved suffering, unpunished injustice, and hopeless stupidity" (GM:122).

Ways of explaining the evils of human existence from a religious perspective include the idea that one suffers to expiate sins by oneself in an earlier life or by one's ancestors, or simply from living in an imperfect world (e.g. ES:518–29). The equivalent compensatory promises are that one will do better in a future life, that one's descendants will do better in the future, and that one will have a better existence in the afterlife. Dualism represents another way of dealing with the problem of theodicy. According to Weber, there exist three consistent forms of theodicy: dualism, predestination, and the doctrine of karma (e.g. GM:358–59).

Weber discusses the role of theodicy in various religions and also constructs his own types of theodicy. One of these is "the theodicy of good fortune" (*Theodizee des Glückes*), another "the theodicy of suffering" (*Theodizee des Leidens*). The latter refers to how religion has explained why people suffer, and also how it has held out related "compensatory promises" (GM:271). The theodicy of good fortune refers to non-religious situations and therefore qualifies as a "sociodicy." According to Weber, successful people are as a rule not satisfied with what they have; they also want to feel that they *deserve* to be fortunate. "Good fortune wants to be 'legitimate' fortune" (GM:271; cf. ES:491, 953).

Weber indicates that not only individuals but also groups have a need for a theodicy of this type. "Every highly privileged group develops the myth (*Legende*) of its natural, especially its blood, superiority" (ES:953).

For a discussion of the concept of theodicy as well as Weber's use of it, see e.g. Bryan Turner, "Theodicy, the Career of a Concept," pp. 142–76 in *For Weber* (1991). See also Edith Hanke, "Erlösungsreligionen" (2001), pp. 221–23.

See also ethics, legitimacy, meaning, salvation

theology   Statements such as "I am a layman in theology" and "I am not a theologian" can be found in Weber's work (e.g. PED:108, PE:284

n. 119 [my trans.]). Nonetheless, much of what Weber wrote in his sociology of religion may be of interest to theologians; *see* that and related entries.

Literature on Weber that may be of interest from a theological point of view includes Hans Kippenberg and Martin Riesebrodt (eds.), *Max Webers "Religionssystematik"* (2001) and Thomas Ekstrand, *Max Weber in a Theological Perspective* (1999). A number of theologians have also taken part in the debate around *The Protestant Ethic*. See also the information in the essays devoted to Weber's relationship to various theologians in Part 2 of Wolfgang Mommsen and Jürgen Osterhammel (eds.), *Max Weber and His Contemporaries* (1987).

See also Buddhism, Catholicism, Christianity, *Collected Essays in the Sociology of Religion*, Hinduism, Islam, Judaism, Weber thesis, Protestantism, religion, sociology of religion

theoretical sociology   *See* sociological theory

theory   *See* sociological theory

theory of knowledge   *See* knowledge, theory of

Tobler, Mina (1880–1967)   Swiss pianist, Max Weber's lover, and member of the Webers' closest circle of friends. See M. Rainer Lepsius, "Mina Tobler and Max Weber" (2004).

Tolstoy's Question   In "Science as a Vocation" Weber refers to Tolstoy's central question "What shall we do and how shall we live?" as an example of the importance for human beings of choosing which values to organize their lives around (GM:143, 152–53). Weber was deeply impressed by the uncompromising manner in which Tolstoy lived his life (e.g. Wolfgang Mommsen, *Max Weber and German Politics 1890–1920* [1984], pp. 47, 104).

For Weber's relationship to Tolstoy, see e.g. Edith Hanke, "Max Weber, Leo Tolstoy and the Mountain of Truth" (1999).

See also Russia

traditional action (*traditionales Handeln*)   This represents one of the four major types of social action, together with instrumentally rational action, value-rational action and affectual action (*see* those entries). It is a type of action that is caused by tradition.

What primarily characterizes traditional action, according to Weber's general sociology in Ch. 1 of *Economy and Society*, is that it is "determined through habituation" (ES:25). "The great bulk of all everyday action to which people have become habitually accustomed approaches this type" (ES:25; cf. ES:4–5). Traditional behavior is often on the verge of being non-social since the actor invests so little meaning in this type of action.

Traditional action was especially strong in early society, and charisma was one of the few forces that could successfully oppose it (e.g. ES:37).

See also affectual action, charisma, custom, instrumentally rational action, social action, traditional domination, traditionalism, value-rational action

traditional capitalism   *See* capitalism

traditional domination (*traditionale Herrschaft*)   Domination constitutes one of the major themes in Weber's sociology, and traditional domination—together with charismatic domination and legal domination-constitutes one of its three major forms (ES:226–41; cf. e.g. EES:101–4).

According to Weber's definition in Ch. 3 on domination in *Economy and Society*, traditional domination rests on "an established belief in the sanctity of immemorial traditions and the legitimacy of those elevated to authority under such rule to issue commands (traditional authority [*Herrschaft*])" (ES:215; cf. ES:226, GM:296). In a situation of traditional domination you obey a person, not an official, and you do it out of loyalty. The traditional ruler operates in two different spheres: one that is bound by tradition, and one in which there are no rules.

If there is no staff, traditional domination may take the form of "gerontocracy" or "primary patriarchalism." The first of these is defined as rule of elders; the latter as a form of domination in which one person has the hereditary right to rule a household (ES:231).

If the administration as well as the military are seen by the ruler as his or her personal instruments, there is either "patrimonialism" (if the ruler abides by tradition) or "sultanism" (if he rules by discretion; ES:231–32). "Estate-type domination" represents a form of patrimonialism, more precisely a situation in which the administrative staff has appropriated some power (ES:232).

"Prebendalism" is a form of patrimonialism that is maintained through benefices, that is, through traditional allowances, incomes, and the like that cannot be inherited (ES:235). Finally, traditional domination strengthens traditional attitudes toward the economy.

See also domination, traditional action, traditionalism

traditionalism   This topic constitutes a major theme in Weber's sociology—as a special type of social action, as a special form of domination, and, more generally, as the prevalent state of early human society.

One of Weber's four types of social action, as outlined in his general sociology in Ch. 1 of *Economy and Society*, is traditional action (ES:24–

5; cf. ES:4). A traditional social action is defined as one that is "determined through ingrained habituation" (ES:25). Weber adds that "the great bulk of all everyday action to which people have become habitually accustomed approaches this type" (ibid.).

Similarly, one of Weber's three types of domination (*Herrschaft*) is traditional domination (ES:226–41; cf. EES:101–4, GM:296). It is defined as follows: "authority (*Herrschaft*) will be called traditional if legitimacy is claimed for it and believed in by virtue of the sanctity of age-old rules and powers" (ES:226; *Herrschaft* can not only be translated as domination but also as authority).

Early society can according to Weber be characterized as basically traditional, with charisma as the main source of change (e.g. ES:37).

See also charisma, custom, domination, traditional action, traditional capitalism, traditional domination

translations of Weber's works   For many years an important discussion of the translation of Weber's work into English (as well as into other languages) has been under way.

It is often noted, for example, that the translations of *The Religion of India*, *The Methodology of the Social Sciences*, and *The City* are highly problematic. Before citing any of these translations, authors may want to check the passages concerned against the German originals (parts of MSS exist in a second translation [EW:359–404]; and for the first half of the essay on Eduard Meyer, see Weber 1978:111–31).

There also exists a lively discussion of Talcott Parsons' translation, made from the second edition (1920) of *The Protestant Ethic*. There is an alternative translation of the second edition by Stephen Kalberg and also a translation of the first edition (1904–5) by Peter Baehr and Gordon Wells (see Weber [1904–5] 2002a [1904–5] 2002b).

Some of Weber's works are now available in at least two English translations, such as *The Protestant Ethic* and Ch. 1 of *Economy and Society*. In many ways, if by no means all, the more recent translations are of better quality than the first ones.

Hostility to Parsons' translations of Weber has for a long time been very strong. This can be exemplified by the following quote from C. Wright Mills' correspondence with Dwight Macdonald in 1943 which summarizes Parsons' translation of *Economy and Society* as follows: "the son of a bitch translated it so as to take all the guts, the radical guts, out of it" (Mills cited in Tribe 2004:1). Mills, it can be added, did not read German himself but had probably formed his opinion based on conversations with his colleague and co-editor Hans Gerth. See e.g. Guenther Roth, "Interpreting and Translating Max Weber" (1992), Keith Tribe,

"Transformation and Translation: Max Weber in English" (2004), Peter Ghosh, "Some Problems with Talcott Parsons' Version of 'The Protestant Ethic'" (1994), and the symposium on translating Weber in a recent issue of *Max Weber Studies* (2 [2001], 1).

Triebfeder des Wirtschaftens   *See* economic motivation

Troeltsch, Ernst (1865–1923)   Theologian with an expertise in Protestantism and a friend of the Webers. Married to Marta Troeltsch (1874–1947). See e.g. Friedrich Wilhelm Graf, "Friendship between Experts: Notes on Weber and Troeltsch" (1987).

truth   The relationship of truth to science is discussed in "Science as a Vocation." In this essay it is argued that the pursuit of science is based on the value of truth and knowledge—something has to be judged as "worth being know" for there to be science in the first place (GM:143). The value of truth, on the other hand, cannot be proven with the help of science. Weber also notes that "the belief in the value of scientific truth is the product of certain cultures and is not a product of man's original nature" (MSS:110, EW:402).

According to Karl Jaspers, Weber had "a passion for truth" (Jaspers 1989:128). Among Weber's last words, as reported by his wife, were the following: "The true is the truth" ("Das Wahre ist die Wahrheit"—Marianne Weber [1926] 1975:698).

See also objectivity

types (*Typus*)   The use of types is characteristic for sociology and a necessary part of its mode of analysis, according to Weber. Churches and sects are two examples of sociological types.

According to Weber's general sociology, which can be found in Ch. 1 of *Economy and Society*, sociology "seeks to formulate type concepts and generalized uniformities of empirical process" (ES:19; see also ES:29). In this it differs from history which primarily looks at individual events of significance.

Weber also advocates the use of a special conceptual construction in social science, including sociology—the ideal type. This involves an analytical accentuation of certain elements, and it should not be confused with, say, an empirical or average type.

While sociology primarily deals with types of actions, it can also look at large individual events or structures of importance, as *The Protestant Ethic* illustrates. In this particular study Weber analyzes the (modern) capitalist spirit with the help of the concept of the historical individual.

Guenther Roth has argued that Weber's ideas on social types developed out of his attempt to find an alternative to the concern with social laws and various schemes of stages, which were common among social scientists in his day (see Reinhard Bendix and Guenther Roth, *Scholarship and Partisanship* [1971], pp. 253–65). For a discussion of Weber's way of handling typologies in empirical research, see Paul Lazarsfeld and Anthony Oberschall, "Max Weber and Empirical Social Research" (1965).

See also historical individual; history; human beings, types of human beings; ideal type

Ü̈ber einige Kategorien der verstehenden Soziologie See *Some Categories of Interpretive Sociology*

unanticipated consequences *See* unintended consequences

understanding (*Verstehen*) This concept stands at the very center of the type of sociology that Weber attempted to create and which he defines in the first paragraph in Ch. 1 of *Economy and Society*: "sociology . . . is a science concerning itself with the explanatory understanding (*deutend verstehen*) of social action and thereby with a causal explanation of its course and consequences" (ES:4; for an explication of this definition, including the concept of understanding, see ES:4–24). To properly understand the subjective dimension of an action, Weber also says, the meaning that an actor attaches to his or her behavior also needs to be set within a broader complex of meaning (*Sinnzusammenhang*).

Understanding aims simultaneously at (1) laying bare and (2) at grasping the meaning that actors attach to their actions. This naturally involves interpretation, and Weber therefore speaks of "interpretive understanding" (and calls his brand of sociology "interpretive sociology"). Weber also rejected the opposition between understanding and explanation, and argued that understanding constitutes an integral part of explanation.

The sociologist can in some cases reach an elementary understanding of an action simply by observing it ("direct observational understanding"; *aktuelles Verstehen*). For a fuller understanding, however, the meaning that an actor attaches to his or her action has to be accessed ("explanatory understanding"; *erklärendes Verstehen*—ES:8–9). By simply observing someone cutting wood—to use Weber's prime example—we understand that the ax is brought down on the wood in order to chop it up. But it is only by getting access to the meaning that the woodcutter attaches to his action that we can know if he is chopping wood for exercise, to make a living, or for some other reason (ES:8–9).

In discussing this last point Weber introduces the concept "complex of meaning" (*Sinnzusammenhang*), indicating that the subjective intention of the actor is part of a larger set of meanings which also need to be taken into account by the analyst.

Some meanings that actors attach to their actions are impossible or very hard for the sociologist to access. Others are easier for the observer to understand, and Weber cites the saying (supposedly originating with Simmel) that "one need not have been Caesar to understand Caesar" (ES:5; cf. Robert K. Merton, *The Sociology of Science* [1973], p. 123). In some cases, finally, the sociologist ascribes meaning to the actor.

For the sociologist, the meaning of an action must reach a certain degree of clarity and be verifiable (what Weber calls evident; see *Evidenz*). This verifiable certainty can come in two forms: through clarity of meaning or through empathy. In the former case the basis for the certainty is "rational," and in the latter "emotionally empathetic or artistically appreciative" (ES:5). An example of rationally based certainty would be the proposition that two plus two equals four; and of the emotionally empathetic when we try to understand Caesar by adopting the viewpoint of Caesar.

Weber also rejected the idea that understanding cannot be used to establish laws (or their equivalents) in the social sciences, but only individual events. As Parsons (1971:36) has put it, Weber was opposed to "the doctrine that the methodological dichotomy between nomothetic and ideographic orientations coincided with that between observation of 'external' realities in almost the physical sense and participation with the object of observation through *Verstehen*."

Sam Whimster has summarized the meaning of *Verstehen* as follows: "Very simply, it means to understand the actions and meanings of another person or cultural artifact, and it is enabled by our capacity to empathize with the motives, thinking, and expressions of another human being" (EW:412).

For an introduction to the concept of understanding, see e.g. Dirk Käsler, *Max Weber* (1988), pp. 175–80 and Guy Oakes, "The *Verstehen* Thesis and the Foundations of Max Weber's Methodology" (1977). For a presentation of the thinkers who influenced Weber's concept of understanding and also how the concept evolved, see e.g. Don Martindale, *The Nature and Types of Sociological Theory* (1966), pp. 377–81, Marianne Weber, *Max Weber* (1926 [1975]), pp. 312–13, and Wolfgang Schluchter, *Rationalism, Religion, and Domination* (1989), pp. 19, 485 n. 74. For an argument that Weber tried to unite interpretation and understanding, see

Fritz Ringer, *Max Weber's Methodology* (1997). See also the discussion of Weber's concept of meaning in e.g. Thomas Burger, *Max Weber's Theory of Concept Formation* (1987), pp. 102–15, Alexander von Schelting, *Max Webers Wissenschaftslehre* (1934), pp. 325–29, 361–403, and Talcott Parsons, *The Structure of Social Action* (1937), pp. 635–37 and "Value-freedom and Objectivity" (1971), pp. 36–9. Martin Albrow has also suggested that *aktuelles Verstehen* can be translated as "immediate understanding" rather than "direct observational understanding" (cf. ES:8–9), and *erklärendes Verstehen* as "motivational understanding" rather than "explanatory understanding" (see Albrow 1990:204). Alfred Schutz's *The Phenomenology of the Social World* ([1932] 1967) contains a critique of various aspects of Weber's theory of understanding that is in a class by itself for its depth and penetration.

Finally, it has been argued that Weber's structural type of sociology, which can be found in his studies of concrete topics in *Economy and Society* and elsewhere, differs from the type of interpretive sociology based on understanding that Weber advocates in his chapter on theoretical sociology in Ch. 1 of *Economy and Society* (for a discussion of this point, see e.g. Lawrence Scaff, "Weber before Weberian Sociology" [1989]).

See also causality, complex of meaning, culture, explanation

uniformities (*Regelmässigkeiten*)   There exist empirical uniformities in social life, Weber notes and these are important to sociology.

Very early in his chapter on general sociology in *Economy and Society* Weber identifies three major forms of such empirical uniformities: custom, self-interest, and usage (ES:29–31); *see* those entries. In his new translation of Ch. 1 of *Economy and Society* Keith Tribe translates *Regelmässigkeiten* as "actual regularities" (EW:333).

See also custom, self-interest or self-interested kind of behavior, usage

unintended consequences   Social actions have unintended as well as intended consequences. In instrumentally rational actions the actor takes secondary results (*Nebenfolgen*) into account, while this is not the case in value-rational actions. In certain situations, the results of some actions may be so different from the intentions of the actors that they seem paradoxical. The main example of this is the creation of a spirit of capitalism, which was partly the result of trying to behave according to certain religious guidelines.

See also ethic of ultimate values, intention, motive, paradoxical results of actions, social mechanisms

United States   The United States plays a prominent role in many of Weber's writings, such as *The Protestant Ethic*, "The Protestant Sects and the Spirit of Capitalism," and "Politics as a Vocation" (e.g. PE:47–78, GM:107–11, 302–13). Among the topics that Weber discusses are Benjamin Franklin as an example of the spirit of modern capitalism and the role in American life of sects, presidents, and political bosses. Weber and his wife visited the United States in September–December 1904, but their letters from this trip (amounting to some two hundred pages) have not yet been published.

For the classic account of Weber's trip to the United States, see Marianne Weber, *Max Weber* ([1926] 1975), pp. 279–304; see also e.g. Lawrence Scaff, "The 'Cool Objectivity of Sociation': Max Weber and Marianne Weber in America" (1998) and John Patrick Diggens, *Max Weber* (1996), pp. 1–44. For a critique of Weber's portrait of the economic history of colonial America, see Gabriel Kolko, "Max Weber on America: Theory and Evidence" (1961). For a discussion of Weber's references to America in World War I, see Wolfgang Mommsen, *Max Weber and German Politics 1890–1920* [1984]. See also e.g. Guenther Roth, "Marx and Weber on the United States—Today" (1985) and Wolfgang Mommsen, "Die Vereinigten Staaten von Amerika im politischen Denken Max Webers" (1971). It may finally be mentioned that several major studies based on the Webers' letters from their trip to the United States are under way.

universal history (*Universalgeschichte*)   Weber famously refers to "universal history" in his later work. There exists in particular a well-known reference to "the universal history of culture" as well as some pages outlining what such a history might look like, in the "Introduction" to Weber's *Collected Essays in the Sociology of Religion* (for a translation, see "Author's Introduction" in the standard edition of *The Protestant Ethic*; PE:13–31). In 1919–20 Weber also gave a course entitled "Outline of Universal Social and Economic History" (*Abriss der universalen Sozial- und Wirtschaftsgeschichte*).

Sometimes Weber uses the term "universal history" more or less in the sense of "civilization." For an example of this, see e.g. Max Weber (ed. Johannes Winkelmann), *Soziologie, Universalgeschichtliche Analysen, Politik* (1973).

Stephen Kalberg notes that "stemming originally from the German polymath Johann Gottfried von Herder (1744–1803), 'universal history' (*Universalgeschichte*) came to refer in the nineteenth century to a mode of German historiography that avoided specialist studies and instead attempted to offer a synthesizing portrait of an entire historical epoch or area of culture" (Kalberg in Weber [1904–5] 2002b:255 n. 1). According to Karl Jaspers, Weber's type of universal history differed from those of

Hegel, Ranke, and Burckhardt in two respects: it was sociological and it was centered around "human existence" (*On Max Weber* [1989], p. 84). For discussions of the role of universal history in Weber's work, see e.g. Wolfgang Mommsen, "Max Weber's Political Sociology and His Philosophy of World History" (1965) and "Max Webers Begriff der Universalgeschichte" (1986).

See also civilization, *General Economic History*, history, rationalization (for philosophy of history)

Universalgeschichte   *See* universal history

urban sociology   Most of what Weber wrote on urban sociology is to be found in his study "The City (Non-Legitimate Domination)" in *Economy and Society* (ES:1212–1372; published as a separate volume in English, translated by Don Martindale and Gertrud Neuwirth—Weber [1921] 1958a). Weber was mainly interested in the city, it seems, as part of his general research on what produced the rational type of capitalism and the uniqueness of the West. For this reason Weber also investigated the role of the city in the various studies that make up *The Economic Ethics of the World Religions* (e.g. RC:13–20, RI:89–91, 127–29).

As part of his lecture series of 1919–20, which has been reconstructed as *General Economic History*, Weber also addressed the role of the city in history (GEH:315–37). The city, Weber says, has made a number of crucial contributions to human culture, such as the political party, science in the modern sense, Judaism, early Christianity, and theology.

For a summary of the material in *The City*, see e.g. Reinhard Bendix, *Max Weber: An Intellectual Portrait* (1960), pp. 70–9 and Dirk Käsler, *Max Weber* (1988), pp. 42–8. For a critique of Weber's view of the city in antiquity, see M. I. Finley, "The Ancient City: From Fustel de Coulanges to Max Weber and Beyond" (1977). For the place of *The City* in urban theory, see e.g. Don Martindale, "Prefatory Remarks: The Theory of the City" (1958). For the early reception of Weber's views, see Käsler, *Max Weber*, p. 200. For a discussion, see also Hinnerk Bruhns and Wilfried Nippel (eds.), *Max Weber und die Stadt im Kulturvergleich* (2000) as well as the introductory material by Nippel in the new edition of *The City* (MWG, Vol. I/22–5).

See also citizenship, *City, The*; *Economic Ethics of the World Religions*

usage (*Brauch*)   "[I]f an orientation toward social action occurs regularly, it will be called 'usage' insofar as the probability of its existence within a group is based on nothing but actual practice" (ES:29). A usage differs from what Weber terms a "custom" by not being based on long duration.

Usage can lead to the formation of social groups and also facilitates the formation of ethnic identity (ES:320).

Talcott Parsons says in a comment to Ch. 1 of *Economy and Society* that "'usage' has seemed to be the most appropriate translation [of *Brauch*] since, according to Weber's own definition, the principled criterion is that 'it is done to conform with the pattern'" (ES:59 n. 16). Parsons also notes that the concept of usage has a "normative component" (Parsons 1975:667; cf. ES:59 n. 16). In his new translation of Ch. 1 of *Economy and Society* Keith Tribe translates *Brauch* as "practice" (EW:333).

See also custom, empirical uniformities, self-interest or self-interested kind of behavior

usury (*Wucher*)   Usury can be defined either as taking interest for a loan when this is forbidden, or as taking interest that is considered far too high. Weber assigned an important place in his work to this phenomenon.

Usury may, for example, be linked to a situation of double ethic, that is, to a situation in which members of one's own community are treated differently from strangers. According to the Bible, "you may exact interest on a loan to a foreigner but not on a loan to a fellow-countryman" (Deuteronomy 23:20; cf. AJ:70, 343).

For a critique of Weber's argument that usury was condoned in ancient Judaism, see Freddy Raphaël, "Max Weber and Ancient Judaism" (1973), p. 60. For a discussion of Weber's view on usury, see Lutz Kaelber, "Max Weber on Usury and Medieval Capitalism" (2004).

See also double ethic, economic ethic

utilitarianism   *See* philosophy

utility (*Nutzleistung*)   The concept of utility plays a central role in Weber's economic sociology, for he defines economic action as action that is concerned with utility. Weber, however, uses his own, rather special concept of utility. Utility does not so much indicate a given quality as an *opportunity* to realize a desire for this quality.

Weber starts out his economic sociology in Ch. 2 of *Economy and Society* by defining what constitutes economically oriented action: "action will be said to be 'economically oriented' so far as, according to its subjective meaning, it is concerned with the satisfaction of a desire for 'utilities'" (ES:63). (The reader should note that the phrase "economically oriented" is also used by Weber in a quite different sense in Ch. 2 of *Economy and Society*, namely as a type of economic action that uses violence to reach its goal or has a main goal that is not economic.)

Weber then argues that economic analysis should not start out with needs and their satisfaction since this would exclude profit-making; and he therefore emphasizes desire (*Begehren*) rather than need. He also notes that his definitions of economic action and economically oriented action not only encompass the element of desire but also the provision for satisfying this desire.

The concepts of goods and of services in Weber's economic sociology are both defined in relation to utility.

According to Raymond Aron, the German term for utilities—*Nutzleistungen*—means "enactments of utility" ("prestation d'utilité"). "*Leistung* comes from the verb *leisten*, which means to accomplish, to produce, and *Nutz* is the root of the word *utility*" (Aron 1970:282). The term *Nutzleistungen* can be found already in Weber's lectures on economics of the 1890s (GVAN:31). It is, however, less commonly used for utility in German economics than *Nutzen* or *Nützlichkeit*.

See also economic action, marginal utility

V

alidity (*Geltung*)   The term "validity" appears in two different contexts regarding Weber's work: it is used by Weber himself in his discussion of legitimacy, and it is often referred to in discussions of Weber's theory of values.

As to its first meaning, Weber argues that an order is considered valid only if there is a probability that actions complying with it will be guided by a belief in its legitimacy (ES:31). One may also ask to what extent the analysis of values and values themselves are scientifically valid. For the relationship of validity to values, see e.g. H. H. Bruun, *Science, Values and Politics in Weber's Methodology* (1972), pp. 160–61, 184–89 and Thomas Burger, *Max Weber's Theory of Concept Formation* (1987), pp. 87–93.

valuation, value-orientation and similar terms (*Werten, Orientierung an Werte*)   These terms cover complex as well as contested aspects of Weber's work. For example, individuals always orient their actions toward values when they invest their actions with meaning (ES:40). In taking a personal stand, they may also be actively orienting their behavior toward certain values (e.g. RK:192). See e.g. H. H. Bruun, "Weber on Rickert" (2003) and Rogers Brubaker, *The Limits of Rationality* (1984), pp. 5–6, 62–73.

value (as in economic value; *Wert*)   In his economic sociology in Ch. 2 of *Economy and Society* Weber states that he will not take up "the controversial issue of value" (ES:63). Value will, in other words, be left to the economists.

For the term "value" in its non-economic sense, *see* values

value-freedom (*Wertfreiheit*)   Social scientists should try to be objective in the sense of being value-free (that is, stay away from the argument that science can be used to choose between different values), even while they realize that their objects of study are connected to values in a number of ways (what Weber calls value-relevance or *Wertbeziehung*).

Weber argued forcefully against academic teachers engaging in political and other propaganda when they were lecturing: "the prophet and the demagogue do not belong on the academic platform" (GM:146). He also was against students introducing political action into the classroom (ibid., p. 145).

Weber discusses these issues primarily in "The Meaning of 'Ethical Neutrality' in Sociology and Economics," "'Objectivity' in Social Science and Social Policy," and "Science as a Vocation" (MSS:1–47, 49–112, GM:129–56; see also Weber [1913] 1996).

A value judgment (*Wertung*) is defined in the following way in Weber's methodological writings: "practical evaluations of the unsatisfactory or satisfactory character of phenomena subject to our influence" (MSS:1; for an alternative translation, see Hennis 1994:113).

For a general introduction to Weber's notion of value-neutrality, see e.g. Wilhelm Hennis, "The Meaning of '*Wertfreiheit*': On the Background of Max Weber's 'Postulate'" (1994). According to Talcott Parsons, while the concept of value-freedom (*Wertfreiheit*) refers to the "*in*dependence" of the role of the social scientist, that of value-relevance refers to its "*inter*dependence" with the other roles of the social scientist (Parsons 1971:34). Value-freedom, however, also means that the social scientist is free to follow the values of science (ibid., p. 33). See more generally along these lines Talcott Parsons, "Value-freedom and Objectivity" (1971) and the discussion of this essay in Otto Stammer, ed., *Max Weber and Sociology Today* (1972), pp. 27–82.

Weber took part in a major dispute in German-speaking social science over the role of values, the so-called *Werturteilsstreit*, that reached its peak during 1909–14. For an introduction to this debate, which is difficult to get a good grasp on, see e.g. Dirk Käsler, *Max Weber* (1988), pp. 184–96; and for some of the key documents, Heino Nau (ed.), *Der Werturteilsstreit* (1996). For Weber's failed attempt, as part of this debate, to turn the German Sociological Association into a value-free organization, see e.g. Reinhard Bendix and Guenther Roth, *Scholarship and Partisanship* (1971), pp. 40–42. Weber's writings and speeches in the *Werturteilsstreit* will be published in MWG, Vol. I/12.

According to Guenther Roth, *Wertfreiheit* is usually translated as "value-freedom" (Parsons, Bruun, Runciman), but other versions also exist such as "ethical neutrality" (Shils) and "value-neutrality" (Guenther Roth and Wolfgang Schluchter, *Max Weber's Vision of History, Ethics and Methods* [1979], pp. 65–6 n. 1).

See also objectivity, cognitive interest, value-relevance

value-idea (*Wert-Idee*) Weber uses this term in his methodological essays to indicate ideas which give significance or value to something, regardless of whether this significance is negative (as with prostitution) or positive (as with religion; MSS:81). People in society are often unaware of the ultimate value-ideas that constitute its culture. As reality moves on, new value-ideas emerge and old ones disappear; "the light of the great cultural problems moves on" (MSS:112).

See also culture, values

value judgment *See* value-freedom

value-neutrality *See* value-freedom

value-orientation See valuation, value-orientation and similar terms

value-rational action (social action that is *wertrational*) This represents one of the four major types of social action, together with affectual action, instrumentally rational action, and traditional action (*see* those entries). It is a type of action that is caused by the actor's conscious attempt to realize certain values, come what may.

What primarily characterizes value-rational action, according to Weber's general sociology in Ch. 1 of *Economy and Society*, is that it is "determined by a conscious belief in the value for its own sake of some ethical, aesthetic, religious, or other form of behavior, independently of its prospects or success" (ES:24–5).

Value-rational action is characterized by being conscious and involving planning. As opposed to instrumentally rational action, it is carried out for its own sake, regardless of the result and the cost to the actor. The action is undertaken because the actor feels forced or compelled to act in this manner.

One may choose between different possible ends in a value-rational manner, but still use instrumental rationality in deciding upon the means.

According to Raymond Aron, value-rational action is "rational action in relation to a value" (Aron 1970:220). Examples include a captain going down with his ship or Lassalle letting himself be killed in a duel. Rogers Brubaker notes that value-rational action is "directed toward the realization of some value believed to be *inherent* in a certain way of acting [while instrumentally rational action is directed] toward the achievement of some end or ends that are expected to *result from* a certain way of acting" (Brubaker 1984:51). See also Talcott Parsons, *The Structure of Social Action* (1937), Vol. 2, pp. 642–45, where the link between value-rational action and Weber's concept of ethic of ultimate ends is discussed. Weber's concept of value-rationality is also at the center of Raymond Boudon's attempt to construct a rational choice sociology; see e.g. Raymond Boudon, *The Origin of Values: Sociology and Philosophy of Beliefs* (2001).

See also ethic of ultimate ends, rationality, social action, values

value-relevance (*Wertbeziehung*)   The notion of value-relevance is part of Weber's methodology and raises many difficult questions. Value-relevance plays a role in the researcher's choice of subjects to study, in the construction of social science concepts, and in the doctrine of objectivity. In the social or cultural sciences the subjects to be studied are chosen, according to Weber, because of their relationship to values, that is, because of their value-relevance; and this also has consequences for the way that social science concepts are constructed. In trying to be objective, Weber argues as well, the researcher must not only be value-neutral but must also realize that the objects of his or her study are selected and constituted in relation to values.

When a topic is researched in the social or cultural sciences, it is selected because of its relationship to the values of the society in which the researcher lives—in brief, because of its cultural significance. In *The Protestant Ethic* Weber discusses this issue in terms of "historical individuals," and he stresses that a notion such as "the capitalist spirit" has to be carefully constructed to properly reflect the values that the researcher wants to study (PE:47–8). In Weber's general sociology, as this can be found in Ch. 1 of *Economy and Society*, this issue is discussed in relation to the concept of meaning.

Within the context of the doctrine of objectivity, value-relevance can be said to constitute the second half of Weber's theory of objectivity which is often neglected. Weber discusses value-relevance primarily in "The Meaning of 'Ethical Neutrality' in Sociology and Economics," "'Objectivity' in Social Science and Social Policy," and "Science as a Vocation" (MSS:1–47, 49–112, GM:129–56).

Weber borrowed the term value-relevance from the philosopher Heinrich Rickert, whose "principle of value-relevance" holds that the historian selects those parts of infinite reality that embody the general cultural values that are held by people in the society in which the historian lives. For the relationship between Rickert's and Weber's ideas on this particular point, see e.g. H. H. Bruun, *Science, Values and Politics in Max Weber's Methodology* (1972), pp. 78–144, Thomas Burger, *Max Weber's Theory of Concept Formation* (1987), pp. 39–43, and Guy Oakes, *Weber and Rickert* (1988), pp. 78–90.

According to Talcott Parsons, while value-freedom (*Wertfreiheit*) is connected to the "*in*dependence" of the role of the social scientist, value-relevance is connected to its "*inter*dependence" with the other roles of the social scientist (Parsons 1971:34). Value-freedom, however, also means that the social scientist is free to follow the values of science (ibid., p. 33). See more generally Parsons, "Value-freedom and Objectivity" and the discussion of this essay in Otto Stammer, ed., *Max Weber and Sociology Today* (1971), pp. 27–82.

See also cultural problems of the time, cultural sciences, historical individual, knowledge (for cognitive and scientific interest), objectivity, value-freedom

values (*Werte*)   Values play an absolutely key role in Weber's methodology as well as in his sociology. In his methodological writings Weber argues that values are constitutive for the cultural sciences in the sense that these sciences study phenomena that are related to values, that is, phenomena that are significant to people.

In his sociology Weber also often analyzes various types of ethics, such as the economic ethics of the world-religions. These ethics are typically practical ethics, that is, ethics that grow out of practical actions and concerns rather than from philosophical or theological discussions.

Weber's writings on methodology are difficult to penetrate, and this applies particularly to what they say about values (see MSS, CS, RK, SCIS). The cultural sciences are concerned with phenomena that differ from those that are studied in the natural sciences in that they are not only observed from the outside but also seen as significant by people. This latter means that they are related to values or are value-relevant in Weber's terminology (*see* that entry). Via the notion of significance, values also enter in complex ways into the construction of social science concepts, according to Weber, as well into the theory of causation.

In the empirical world values can not only be studied in the form of various types of ethics and religions, but also as they exist in the different value-spheres of society. The disenchantment of the world means, for example, a shift from one type of values to another; and different values are also involved in, say, value-rational action and instrumentally rational action.

According to Leo Strauss, "Weber never explained what he understood by 'values'" (Strauss 1953:39). For secondary literature on Weber and values, see e.g. Martin Albrow, *Max Weber's Construction of Social Theory* (1990), pp. 227–46 and H. H. Bruun, *Science, Values and Politics in Max Weber's Methodology* (1972). For Rickert on values, see e.g. Ola Agevall, *A Science of Unique Events: Max Weber's Methodology of the Cultural Sciences* (1999), pp. 139–43.

See also ethics, value (economic value), value-freedom, value-ideas; valuation, value-orientation and similar terms; value-spheres, meaning

value-spheres (*Lebensordnungen, Wertsphären*)　　There exist several value-spheres or life-orders, according to Weber, and the individual has to decide for himself or herself which values to follow in each of these. Since these values often are in conflict with each other, this is not an easy task.

The spheres that Weber famously mentions in the "Intermediate Reflections" (*Zwischenbetrachtung*) in his *Collected Essays in the Sociology of Religion* are as follows: the economic sphere, the political sphere, the esthetic sphere, the erotic sphere, and the intellectual sphere (GM:323–57, EW:220–41). As history has evolved, the value-spheres have become increasingly distinct from one another. Weber's ideas on value-spheres are, in other words, an integral part of his analysis of modernity.

Each of the spheres, Weber emphasizes, has a limited autonomy as well as an inner logic (*Eigengesetzlichkeit*). Their values also clash: "the various value spheres stand in irreconcilable conflict with each other" (GM:147). There is, for example, a typical tension between economic and religious values. The struggle between different spheres is also referred to by Weber in terms of polytheism and gods struggling with each other. In the modern world, he adds, this struggle is quite obvious.

The sociological status of the concept of value-spheres is unclear. A value-sphere should not, for example, be equated with an institution. It does, on the other hand, show some similarities with what Weber calls an order (*Ordnung*), in the sense that it consists of various prescriptions (maxims) for how to behave. The notion of value-spheres can be found in Weber's early methodological essays and plays a key role in his later sociology of religion (see especially GM:323–59). It is not, however, part of Ch. 1 of *Economy and Society*.

According to Ralph Schroeder, "in the German original, Weber interchangeably uses both the term '*Lebensordnungen*'—or life-orders—and

'*Wertsphären*'—or value-spheres. . . . Here we will use 'spheres of life' to capture the meaning of both German terms" (Schroeder 1992:31–2). Schroeder also emphasizes the element of inner logic in each sphere, noting that this has to do with the pattern that is peculiar to the sphere (2003).

The German term for the limited and internal autonomy of the value-spheres is, to repeat, *Eigengesetzlichkeit*—a term, Guenther Roth says, which "literally [means] 'autonomy', but the noun gets adequate meaning only as part of a theory of social development and modernity, indicating the emergence of separate value and institutional spheres" (Roth 1992:457). Jean-Pierre Grossein suggests that *Eigengesetzlichkeit* is better translated as "intrinsic logic" (Grossein, "Présentation" [1996], p. 122).

For discussions of value-spheres, see e.g. Rogers Brubaker, *The Limits of Rationality* (1984), pp. 82–7, Lawrence Scaff, *Fleeing the Iron Cage* (1989), pp. 93–7, and Ralph Schroeder, *Max Weber and the Sociology of Culture* (1992), pp. 23–5.

It may finally be mentioned that according to some authors there exists a distinct affinity between Weber's concept of value-sphere and that of field in modern sociological theory (e.g. John Levi Martin, "What Is Field Theory?" [2003], pp. 20, 23).

See also ideas, monotheism/polytheism, order, values; valuation, value-orientation and similar terms; *Zwischenbetrachtung*

Veralltäglichung   *See* routinization

Verantwortungsethik   *See* ethics of responsibility

Verband   *See* organization or association

Verein   *See* voluntary organization

Verein für Sozialpolitik (Association for Social Policy)   The Verein—of which Weber was an active member for most of his academic career—was founded in 1872 as an association for reform-minded scientists, journalists, and industrialists. It was dominated by the economists, most of whom were members of the Historical School.

What united the members of the Verein was a belief that reforms were urgently needed in Germany. Foremost among its concerns was the so-called social question (*Arbeiterfrage*), and the Verein initiated, financed and carried out a huge number of empirical investigations of this topic. This academic approach to the issue of social problems earned the members of the Verein the nickname "socialists of the chair" (*Kathedersozialisten*).

Max Weber and his brother Alfred both participated vigorously in many of the activities of the Verein, not least its meetings. One of Max Weber's first studies was carried out under the auspices of the Verein, namely his study of rural workers east of the river Elbe (Weber [1892] 1984; cf. [1894] 1989). His writings on objectivity are closely connected to his activities in the Verein, and so are his writings on the psychophysics of labor (Weber [1917] 1949, [1908–9] 1988).

For the history of the Verein, see e.g. Dieter Lindenlaub, *Richtungskämpfe im Verein für Sozialpolitik* (1967). See also e.g. Abraham Asher, "Professors as Propagandists: The Politics of the *Kathedersozialisten*" (1963). For Weber's participation in the Verein, see several of the essays in Part 1 of Wolfgang Mommsen and Jürgen Osterhammel (eds.), *Max Weber and His Contemporaries* (1987).

Verfassung   *See* constitution

Verfügungsgewalt   *See* economic power

Vergemeinschaftung   *See* communal relationship

Vergesellschaftung   *See* associative relationship

verification   To verify something roughly means to provide evidence that a statement is true. Since sociology, as Weber saw it, is characterized by its concern with subjective understanding, the process of verification has to provide evidence for both the subjective understanding and the corresponding action. If you only look at the subjective intention of the actor without reference to the action itself, for example, all you have is a "hypothesis" in need of verification (ES:10).

See also *Evidenz* (for Weber's concept of verifiable certainty), meaning, validity

Vermögen (**wealth**)   *See* budgetary management

Verständnis (**understanding**)   *See* meaning

Verstehen   *See* understanding

verstehende Soziologie   *See* interpretive sociology

Vertretung   *See* representation

Vertretungsbeziehungen   *See* representation

Verwaltung   *See* administration

Verwaltungsverband (**administrative organization**)   *See* administration

violence (***Gewalt***)   Violence plays a crucial role in Weber's work, not least in his analysis of the state. Even if Weber assigns a central role to ideas, values, and legitimation in his sociology, violence is the ultimate arbitrator. This is true not only for the state that mainly draws on, say, charismatic or traditional legitimation but also for the modern democratic state that draws on legal-rational legitimation.

The concept of violence sometimes tends to disappear in Weber's writings. It is, for example, subsumed under his category of coercion (*Zwang*); and coercion can be either physical or psychological.

See also coercion, domination, *Gewalt* (for other meanings than violence), legitimacy, means of war, power, state

virtuoso *See* religious virtuoso

vocation (*Beruf*) The term "vocation" or "calling" holds a central role in Weber's work, especially in *The Protestant Ethic and the Spirit of Capitalism*. An individual can be described as having a vocation when that individual attaches a very strong sense of purpose to his or her work. The central argument in *The Protestant Ethic* is that the notion of vocation was first developed in Protestantism and then became part of the capitalist spirit. It first had a religious meaning, in other words, which was later lost.

In *The Protestant Ethic* Weber points out that according to the Protestants, a vocation represents "a task set by God" which has to be fulfilled (PE:79). There also exists a clear link between charisma and vocation, according to Weber (GM:79). When *Beruf* later became secular it was perceived as "an obligation which the individual is supposed to feel and does feel toward the content of his professional activity, no matter in what it consists, in particular no matter whether it appears on the surface as a utilization of his personal powers, or only of his material possessions" (PE:54). Weber argues that the sense of "one's duty in a calling, is what is most characteristic of the social ethic of capitalistic culture, and is in a sense the fundamental basis of it" (ibid.).

In *The Protestant Ethic* Weber also discusses how the notion of "calling" or "vocation" emerged in Protestantism, and how it came to mean the ethical duty to perform one's work well and in a methodical manner (see especially PE:79–81, 204–11). By seeing their work as a vocation, religious believers helped to spark modern capitalism by creating a lifestyle that embodied a new capitalist spirit. This was as true for workers as for capitalists.

The concept of *Beruf* has its origin in religious tasks set by God, and was extended by Luther, through his translation of the Bible, to secular work, according to Weber (see especially Sirach 11:20–1, PE:79, 204 n. 1, 207 n. 3). While Luther saw vocation as ascribing value to one's traditional work, ascetic Protestants extended it to whatever task best served God (PE:160). "The notion of 'calling'," Weber sums up, "derives in all Protestant countries from the Bible translations, and among the Calvinists it explicitly includes the legal profit from capitalist enterprises" (ES:1199).

Weber argues in *The Protestant Ethic* that working hard and constantly re-investing the profit became part of the way of life of the ascetic Protestants, and also "*one* particularly important *component*" of the spirit of capitalism (PED:95).

Working hard and looking at work as the major task in life eventually became the norm in modern capitalism. "The Puritan wanted to work in a calling; we are forced to do so," to cite one of the most famous sentences in Weber's study (PE:181; for a more general analysis of the relationship of religion to work, see e.g. ES:1187).

In Weber's economic sociology in Ch. 2 of *Economy and Society* the term *Beruf* is also used in the sense of "profession" and "occupation." "The term 'occupation' (*Beruf*) will be applied to the mode of specialization, specification and combination of the functions of an individual so far as it constitutes for him the basis of a continuous opportunity for income or earnings" (ES:140).

The concept of vocational ethic refers to the general ethic of work in such social formations as a society or a community and so on. Buddhism, for example, lacks a full-scale secular vocational ethic since it is a monastic religion (ES:1191). For the concept of work ethic, *see* that entry.

Weber terms a person who wants to work in her vocation, a *Berufsmensch*. Keith Tribe describes *Berufsmensch* as "that entirely mundane phenomenon, a person entirely identified with their occupation, lacking a sense of life beyond its immediate horizon" (Hennis 2000a:211).

According to Peter Ghosh, Weber uses the term *Beruf* in the sense of both "vocation" and "profession," because there is a direct link between the Reformation sects and modern professional life ("Some Problems with Talcott Parsons' Version of 'The Protestant Ethic'" [1994], pp. 109–10). Gordon Wells notes that since the term *Beruf* has "both the mundane sense of occupation as well as being one to which the 'saints' are called we therefore normally translated it as *calling* but occasionally, when the focus is exclusively on the nature of work, as *occupation*" (Wells 2001:36).

According to Keith Tribe, "'vocation' involves a decision on the part of individuals about the way in which they wish to lead their lives; it is linked to *Lebensführung*, as is the idea of 'calling' in the existing translation of *Protestant Ethic*" (Hennis 200a:211).

Stephen Kalberg, in his new translation of the 1920 edition of *The*

Protestant Ethic, gives "calling" as his first choice in translating *Beruf*, which he defines as "a task given by God" (Kalberg 2002:lxxvii).

Finally, according to Harvey Goldman, while *Beruf* used to mean "calling" or "vocation," today it means "occupation" or "profession" (*Max Weber and Thomas Mann* [1988], p. 3).

For the concept of calling, see e.g. Arnold Eisen, "Called to Order: The Role of the Puritan *Berufsmensch* in Weberian Sociology" (1979) and Harvey Goldman, "Weber and the Puritan Calling," pp. 18–51 in *Max Weber and Thomas Mann*. See also Werner Conze, "Beruf," in Otto Brunner et al. (eds.), *Geschichtliche Grundbegriffe* (1972). For an attempt to scrutinize and question Weber's sources for his assertion that Luther introduced the concept of *Beruf* through his translation of the Bible, see Tatsuro Hanyu, "Max Webers Quellenbehandlung in der 'Protestantischen Ethik': Der 'Berufs'-Begriff" (1994).

See also lifestyle, occupation, politics (for "Politics as a Vocation"), *Protestant Ethic and Spirit of Capitalism, The*; Weber thesis, profession, science (for "Science as a Vocation"), work, work ethic

voluntary association   *See* voluntary organization

voluntary organization (*Verein*)   The definition of such an organization in Weber's general sociology in Ch. 1 of *Economy and Society* reads as follows: "an organization (*Verband*) which claims authority only over voluntary members will be called a *voluntary organization*" (ES:52).

A voluntary organization, Weber specifies, always has rationally established rules. Just as the sect is the polar opposite of the church, the voluntary organization is the polar opposite of the compulsory organization. Nonetheless, "every voluntary association . . . represents a relation of domination between people," and a small group of people is typically in charge (Weber [1910] 2002:203).

In 1910 Weber gave a speech at the German Sociological Association which dealt among other things with voluntary organizations (Weber [1910] 2002). He here said that America is "the land of associations par excellence" (ibid., pp. 200–1). For an analysis of voluntary organizations in the United States based on Weber's visit to this country, see especially "The Protestant Sects and the Spirit of Capitalism" (GM:302–22, ES:1207). According to Weber, the sect was "the prototype" for the various clubs and secular organizations that so many Americans belonged to (GM:311; cf. Weber [1910] 2002:201). For Weber's discussion of the voluntary organization (*Zweckverein*) in his early theoretical sociology, see "Some Categories of Interpretive Sociology" (SCIS:163–65). For Weber's view of civil society, including voluntary associations, see e.g. Sung Ho Kim, "Max Weber and Civil Society: An Introduction to Max Weber on

Voluntary Associational Life" (2002).
    See also compulsory organization, organization or association, sect

"Vorbemerkung"   *See* "Author's Introduction"

W

ahlverwandtschaften   See elective affinities

war   *See* coercion, means of war

water and bureaucracy   *See* geography

wealth   *See* profit-making

Weber, Alfred (1868–1958)   Brother of Max Weber and economist as well as sociologist. See e.g. Eberhard Demm, "Max and Alfred Weber and the Verein für Sozialpolitik" (1987) Wolfgang Schluchter, "Max und Alfred Weber—zwei ungleiche Brüder" (1994).
    See Weber, Max—Life

Weber, Marianne (1870–1954)   An intellectual as well as a fighter for women's rights, Marianne Weber (born Schnitger) was also Max Weber's wife from 1893 onward (for Marianne Weber's ancestry, see Figure 5). Her biography *Max Weber* is still unsurpassed in its genre. For Marianne Weber and also some of her writings in translation, see e.g. Patricia Madoo Lengermann and Jill Niebrugge-Brantley, Ch. 6 ("Marianne Weber [1870–1954]—A Woman-Centered Sociology") in *The Woman Founders: Sociology and Social Theory, 1830–1930* (1998) and their "Commentary" (2003). See also e.g. Guenther Roth, "Introduction to the New Edition," pp. xv–lx in Marianne Weber, *Max Weber* ([1926] 1975) and Christa Krüger, *Max und Marianne*

Weber, Max—Life   Karl Emil Maximilian Weber was born on April 21, 1864, in Erfurt, Germany. His father Max Sr. (1836–1897) was a magistrate and his mother Helene (born Fallenstein; 1844–1919) a deeply religious person of Huguenot ancestry. Both parents came from wealthy and well-connected families. Weber had several brothers and sisters, including Alfred Weber (1868–1958) who became a well-known social scientist in his own right (see Figure 5). The Weber family moved to Berlin in 1869, where Weber's father got involved in a parliamentary career as a liberal and pragmatic politician. As a child Weber was bored at school but early displayed a precocious intelligence. He graduated from the *Gymnasium* or humanistic high school (received the *Abitur*) in 1882.

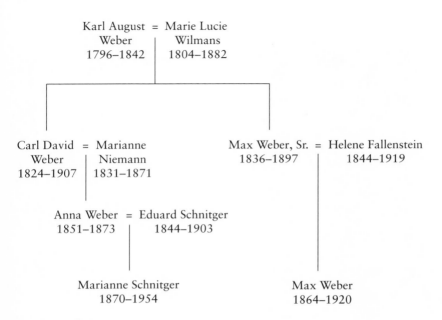

FIGURE 5. The relationship between the families of Max Weber and Marianne Schnitger.

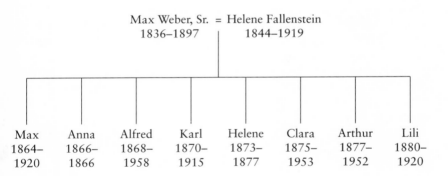

FIGURE 6. Max Weber, his sisters and brothers.

During 1882–95 Weber studied law and several other subjects, first ; the University of Heidelberg and then at the University of Berlin. He als did his military service during this time. His main specialty was historic; jurisprudence, and he received his doctorate in 1889 and his universit teaching qualification (*Habilitation*) in 1891. In the late 1880s Webe also worked as a law clerk (*Referendar*) and became active in the *Verei für Sozialpolitik*, a professional association for political economists.

After his *Habilitation* Weber taught law at the University of Berlin. I 1893 he was offered a chair in political economy at the University c Freiburg; he also married Marianne Schnitger (1870–1954), a distant re ative (see Figure 6). The marriage remained unconsummated and Webe would many years later have erotic relationships with the pianist Min Tobler and Else Jaffé (born von Richthofen), both friends of the famil'.

In 1896 Weber accepted a prominent position as professor of politic; economy at the University of Heidelberg. In 1897 he had a destructiv quarrel with his father—who died later that year without being recor ciled with his son. Weber soon began to experience nervous and ment; difficulties of various kinds, which tormented him for several years an finally made him resign from his academic position in 1903. From th; time till the late 1910s Weber did not teach but lived as a private schol; on family money.

In 1904 Weber and his wife visited the United States. The same year h also became co-editor of the *Archiv für Sozialwissenschaft und Sozia politik*, which soon developed into Germany's foremost social scienc journal. In 1909 Weber helped found the German Sociological Associ; tion (*Deutsche Gesellschaft für Soziologie*), and in 1909–14 he partic pated in a fierce academic debate about the role of value judgments in s cial science (the *Werturteilsstreit*).

During the early period of World War I Weber organized and manage a number of military hospitals. During the rest of the war Weber partic pated in the debate about Germany's role in the war. After the war h worked on the constitution of the Weimar Republic. In 1918 Weber a cepted a chair in political economy at the University of Vienna on a tri; basis. In 1919 he moved to the University of Munich, where he taugh courses in sociology, political science, and economic history. He died c pneumonia on June 14, 1920.

Weber made a deep impression on his contemporaries, through h; knowledge as well as his character. He had a deep sense of justice as we as a volcanic temperament. Karl Jaspers, for example, describes him ; follows: "he shouted everyone down, monopolized entire conversation; and was arrogant and radical" (Jaspers 1989:12).

For an introduction to Weber's life, see e.g. Dirk Käsler, *Max Webe*

(1988), pp. 1–23. There does not exist a standard biography of Weber (cf. Dirk Käsler, "Der retuschierte Klassiker: Zum gegenwärtigen Forschungsstand der Biographie Max Webers" [1989]). In the meantime, see especially Marianne Weber's biography of her husband, *Max Weber* ([1926] 1975). For a psychoanalytic study of Weber, see Arthur Mitzman, *The Iron Cage* (1985).

For Weber's family and ancestry, see Guenther Roth, *Max Webers deutsch-englische Familiengeschichte 1800–1950* (2001), and for a sample in English from this massive volume, see "Weber the Would-Be Englishman: Anglophilia and Family History" (1993).

For Weber's illness, see (beside the account in Marianne Weber's biography) Jorg Frommer and Sabine Frommer, "Max Webers Krankkeit-soziologische Aspekte der depressiven Struktur" (1993). For the trip of Max and Marianne Weber to the United States, see e.g. Lawrence Scaff, "The 'Cool Objectivity of Sociation': Max Weber and Marianne Weber in America" (1998).

For Max and Marianne Weber, *see* Weber, Marianne. For Weber's relationship to his brother Alfred, see e.g. Eberhard Demm, "Max and Alfred Weber and the Verein für Sozialpolitik" (1987) and Wolfgang Schluchter, "Max und Alfred Weber—zwei ungleiche Brüder" (1994). For Weber's relationship to Mina Tobler, see M. Rainer Lepsius, "Mina Tobler and Max Weber" (2004). It may finally be mentioned that there only exist a small number of photographs of Max Weber; and that many of these are reproduced in Hans Norbert Fügen, *Max Weber* (1985).

See also politics, reception of Weber's work, Weber, Max—Works

Weber, Max—Works Weber's first writings may well be the essays in history that he wrote as a teenager and which Marianne Weber describes in her biography (Marianne Weber, *Max Weber* [(1926) 1975], pp. 46–7). Weber's first public writing is otherwise his dissertation, which consists of a chapter from a book-length study, known in translation as *The History of Commercial Partnerships in the Middle Ages* (Weber [1889] 2003:85–125). Weber's second dissertation, his so-called *Habilitationsarbeit*, was published in 1891 under the title *Roman Agrarian History in Its Bearing on Public and Civil Law* (no translation exists; Weber [1891] 1986).

An important role in Weber's early production is also played by a study that Weber wrote for the *Verein für Sozialpolitik*, entitled *The Conditions of the Agrarian Workers in the Areas East of Elbe* (Weber [1892] 1984). No translation of this work exists, but for a summary, see e.g. Weber's famous inaugural lecture as a professor of economics at the University of Freiburg, "The National State and Economic Policy" (Weber [1895] 1980).

While working as an economist in the 1890s, Weber also thought of publishing a textbook in economics; he published a memorable essay on the decline of Rome; and he wrote early and short versions of what some years later would become *The Agrarian Sociology of Ancient Civilizations* (Weber [1898] 1990, [1896] 1999, [1909] 1976). Weber also wrote much about the stock exchange, mainly as part of the political debate that surrounded this institution in the 1890s (e.g. Weber [1894, 1896] 2000, 1999a; for an introduction, see Knut Borchardt, "Max Weber's Writings on the Bourse: Puzzling Out a Forgotten Corpus" [2002]).

In the early 1900s Weber produced some important methodological essays as well as the study that was to make him internationally known: *The Protestant Ethic and the Spirit of Capitalism* (Weber [1904–5] 1930, 1949). The research program sketched toward the end of *The Protestant Ethic* would later inspire a series of studies entitled *The Economic Ethics of the World Religions* (Weber [1920] 1951, [1921] 1958a, [1921] 1958b). This work falls primarily in the sociology of religion (and is part of his *Collected Essays in the Sociology of Religion*) but also complements, Weber says, *Economy and Society*. This latter work, which was never completed, contains a general sociology centered around the concept of meaning (interpretive sociology; Ch. 1), an economic sociology (Ch. 2), and a sociology of domination (Ch. 3). The reader will also find book-length sections in historical sociology, urban sociology (*The City*), the sociology of law, and the sociology of religion as well as (in some editions) a study of the rationalization of music (Weber [1922] 1978, 1958). After Weber's death a volume of economic history was produced on the basis of notes that students had taken during a course given in 1919–20, the *General Economic History* (Weber [1923] 1981).

In "Science as a Vocation" Weber writes: "in science each of us knows that what he has accomplished will be antiquated in ten, twenty, fifty years. That is the fate to which science is subjected; it is the very *meaning* of scientific work" (GM:138; cf. EW:273). To this Weber adds that "scientific works can surely last as 'gratifications' because of their artistic quality, or they may remain important as a means of training. Yet they will be surpassed scientifically."

During his lifetime Weber also wrote on various political topics, and some of these writings have been gathered together in a volume entitled *Political Writings* (Weber 1994b). This volume contains the famous essay "Politics as a Vocation," which is often mentioned together with "Science as a Vocation" (PW:309–69, GM:77–128, 129–56). It also contains an analysis of the political situation in Germany in Weber's days, "Parliament and Government in a Reconstructed Germany" (ES:1382–1469; note that Section VI of this article can only be found in PW:233–71).

Weber's style is often commented on, usually in a disparaging manner.

It is especially the two first chapters in *Economy and Society* that have attracted such negative comments. According to Marianne Weber, "sentence follows upon sentence, blow upon blow [in Ch. 1 of *Economy and
Society*]" (Marianne Weber 1926 [1975]:676). Guenther Roth notes that
"Weber uses a profusion of quotation marks as an alienating device to indicate that he uses familiar terms with reservations, with a new meaning,
or in an ironic sense" (ES:cvii). According to an often cited statement by
Karl Jaspers, "indifference toward the work in its linguistic form, composition, extent, and proportions harmonizes [in Weber's work] with his
forcefulness of thought, precision in forming concepts, and accuracy in
developing his thought" (Jaspers 1989:123). Finally, one reason for the
small amount of footnotes and references in *Economy and Society* is that
Weber wrote it straight from memory (*"aus dem Kopf"*—Marianne Weber [1926] 1975:676).

For general introductions to Weber's work, the reader is especially referred to the section on Weber in Vol. 2 of Raymond Aron's *Main Currents in Sociological Thought* (1970) and to Dirk Käsler, *Max Weber*
(1988). Other useful introductions include Reinhard Bendix, *Max Weber:
An Intellectual Portrait* (1960) and Frank Parkin, *Max Weber* (1982).

Weber's collected works are gradually being published in Germany as
Max Weber Gesamtausgabe, see collected works. A CD-ROM is also
available which contains the great majority of Weber's works in their pre-
collected works version (Weber 1999b). The CD-ROM can be used to
look up specific words, establish their frequency, and the like. The full
text of many of Weber's works—in German as well as in English—is
available on the Internet. One Web site to start from is: http://www.ne.jp/
asahi/moriyuki/abukuma/index.htm.

Most of Weber's works are also available in German in moderately
priced paperbacks. This is less the case with Weber's works in English,
though a number of central texts are available in various monographs, anthologies, and the like—such as *The Agrarian Sociology of Ancient Civilizations, Ancient Judaism, Critique of Stammler, Economy and Society*;
Gerth and Mills (eds.), *From Max Weber*; *The Methodology of the Social
Sciences, Political Writings, The Protestant Ethic and the Spirit of Capitalism, The Religion of China, The Religion of India,* and *Roscher and Knies.*

The most authoritative bibliography of Weber's work may well be the
one that can be found on the home page of the publisher of Weber's collected works (http://www.mohr.de/mw/mwg.htm; cf. *Prospektus der
Max Weber Gesamtausgabe* 1981). There is, finally, also a useful bibliography in Käsler, *Max Weber*, pp. 243–74. A list of all translations of Weber's work into English can be found in Alan Sica, *Max Weber: A Comprehensive Bibliography* (2004), pp. 9–16.

For a long time *Economy and Society* was seen as Weber's major work, but this opinion has lately been challenged (e.g. Friedrich Tenbruck, "The Problem of Thematic Unity in the Works of Max Weber" [1980]; for a critique of Tenbruck, see e.g. Martin Riesebrodt, "Ideen, Interessen, Rationalisierung: Kritische Anmerkungen zu F. H. Tenbrucks Interpretation des Werkes Max Webers" [1980] and John Love, "Developmentalism in Max Weber's Sociology of Religion: A Critique of F. H. Tenbruck" [1993]). Alternative candidates include *The Economic Ethics of the World Religions*, Weber's theory of rationalization, and his sociology of religion in combination with *Economy and Society* (e.g. Stephen Kalberg, "The Search for Thematic Orientations in a Fragmented Oeuvre: The Discussion of Max Weber in Recent German Sociological Literature" [1979], Hennis 1988a).

See also *Ancient Judaism, Collected Essays in the Sociology of Religion, Collected Works, Economy and Society, General Economic History, Handbook of Social Economics*, letters, *Methodology of the Social Sciences, The; Protestant Ethic and the Spirit of Capitalism, The*; Weber thesis, reception of Weber's work, *Religion of China, The; Religion of India, The*; secondary literature on Weber's work, translations of Weber's works, Weber, Max—Life

Weber thesis   As soon as Weber had published the two articles that constitute the first edition of *The Protestant Ethic and the Spirit of Capitalism* in the *Archiv für Sozialwissenschaft und Sozialpolitik* in 1904–5, the discussion of his thesis started—and it has continued till today. At the heart of this debate is Weber's central claim: did religion, in the form of ascetic Protestantism, indeed play a key role in the emergence of modern Western capitalism?

The literature that addresses Weber's thesis is enormous and spans many languages. What makes this literature, as well as Weber's original argument, so difficult to handle, however, is not only the sheer amount of material, but also the fact that Weber's argument raises some very hard questions in several different disciplines. Economic historians, for example, may know the history of capitalism very well but rarely the history of Christianity, and vice versa for historians of religion. To this can be added that Weber's argument is difficult to penetrate since it draws on his own, rather special methodology based on adequate causation and other concepts.

In Weber's own time, it should be noted, it was not uncommon to argue that a distinct relationship existed between capitalism and Protestantism. This fact also influenced the debate. Käsler, for example, notes that "Weber's position, generally speaking, found wide agreement among contemporary theologians, but among historians and national economists, by contrast, it was overwhelmingly criticized" (Käsler 1988:202).

Weber's answers to his critics have recently been published in a volume edited by David Chalcraft and Austin Harrington, *The Protestant Ethic Debate* (2001) as well as in Peter Baehr's and Gordon Wells' translation of the first edition of *The Protestant Ethic* (Weber [1904–5] 2002a:221–339).

Some of the better-known (and later) critiques of the Weber thesis include Kurt Samuelson's *Religion and Economic Action* (1961), R. H. Tawney's *Religion and the Rise of Capitalism* (1954), and H. M. Robertson's *Aspects of the Rise of Economic Individualism* (1935).

From Kurt Samuelson's and many other scholars' criticisms of Weber's thesis it is obvious that a number of elementary misunderstandings have plagued (and continue to plague) the debate over the Weber thesis. Weber did not, for example, argue that Protestantism had somehow created capitalism—but that ascetic Protestantism had been of substantive help in creating and diffusing the new and entrepreneurial spirit (or mentality) of modern capitalism. What was at issue, according to the key formulation in *The Protestant Ethic*, was whether "religious forces have taken part in the qualitative formation and the quantitative expansion of that spirit [of modern capitalism] over the world" (PE:91).

It is also incorrect to argue, as many critics of Weber have done, that capitalist institutions existed before Luther, and that Weber somehow missed this fact. Weber makes a clear distinction between capitalist institutions ("forms") and their mentality ("spirit"), and argues that the former existed well in advance of the advent of Protestantism (cf. GEH:302–22 for an elaboration of this point).

Finally, in looking at ascetic Protestantism and other religions Weber was primarily interested in what had helped to spark modern capitalism—not (as many critics have tried to argue) in claiming that Confucian and certain religious beliefs cannot harmoniously co-exist with and encourage modern capitalist activities, once these have been introduced from the outside (a point that Weber himself made about Japan—e.g. RI:275).

In discussing the series of misunderstandings that have plagued the discussion of the Weber thesis it should also be noted that few authors have taken the time to penetrate the methodology and terminology underlying *The Protestant Ethic*—for example, what Weber means when he calls the spirit of capitalism a "historical individual," or how his theory of "adequate causation" is used to link ascetic Protestantism and the spirit of capitalism.

One of the less disputable errors that can be found in *The Protestant Ethic* has to do with the statistics that Weber presents in Ch. 1 and its footnotes. More precisely, Weber here draws on a set of well-known statistics by Martin Offenbacher that purportedly show that German Protestants were more successful in education and had more wealth than German Catholics at the end of the nineteenth century (PE:188–89). These statistics, however, have been found to be based on serious errors, as pointed out by economic historian Kurt Samuelson (who in his turn made a mistake in his recalculations; cf. Samuelson, *Religion and Economic Action*, pp. 2–3, 138–46, Richard Hamilton, *The Social Misconstruction of Reality* [1996], p. 38, George Becker, "Replication and Reanalysis of Offenbacher's School Enrollment Study" [1997]).

Arguing that Samuelson's study does not necessarily refute Weber's more general thesis about ascetic Protestantism and the spirit of capitalism, Seymour Martin Lipset and Reinhard Bendix point out that according to Weber the link between religion and the spirit of capitalism had already been broken by the end of the nineteenth century (*Social Mobility in Industrial Society* [1959]. p. 55; cf. PE:181–82).

For a discussion of how Weber's methodological stance informs *The Protestant Ethic*, see Ola Agevall, *A Science of Unique Events: Max Weber's Methodology of the Cultural Sciences* (1999), pp. 231–54. As another example of relevant criticism one can mention Gordon Marshall's observation that many parts of Weber's argument, as it currently stands, are not accompanied by empirical evidence, and that the information that would be necessary to confirm or disconfirm Weber's argument is not available (*In Search of the Spirit of Capitalism* [1982]). He also adds that it would be extremely hard to find relevant empirical data.

Marshall has furthermore suggested that it may be helpful to separate "the economic part" of Weber's argument from its "religious part." The former is centered around the issue whether a new type of entrepreneur emerged and if there also was a significant increase in methodical capitalist activities from the 1500s onwards; and the latter revolves around the issue of the relationship between ascetic Protestantism and a certain type of economic behavior.

There is also discussion of the extension, so to speak, of Weber's thesis, namely to what extent it is also correct for areas outside of the West. For an introduction to this question, see e.g. S. N. Eisenstadt (ed.), *The Protestant Ethic and Modernization* (1968) and Robert Bellah, *Tokugawa Religion* (2957). For further references, see *Economic Ethics of the World Religions, Religion of China, The*; and *Religion of India, The*.

There is no good guide to the current state of the discussion of Weber's thesis. Many of the relevant items in English are, however, cited in Richard Hamilton's *The Social Misconstruction of Reality*.

Good general introductions to the debate can nonetheless be found in

Gordon Marshall's *In Search of the Spirit of Capitalism* (1982) and in the anthology *Weber's Protestant Ethic* (1993), edited by Hartmut Lehmann and Guenther Roth. Some of the older collections of contributions to the debate are also still useful, such as Robert Green (ed.), *The Weber Thesis Controversy* (1973), and Philippe Besnard (ed.), *Protestantisme et capitalisme* (1970). That Weber's argument only covers one phase of the slow evolution of Western capitalism comes out very clearly in the course that Weber gave in 1919–20 on economic history and which has been reconstructed and published as *General Economic History* (see especially pp. 352–69). This very point about the slow evolution of Western capitalism has also been made by Randall Collins in "Weber's Last Theory of Capitalism" (1980). A neglected aspect of Weber's argument, it may be added, has to do with his theory of "a new entrepreneur" emerging as a result of Protestantism (PE:69, 75).

Weber's studies of the religions of China, India, and ancient Judaism were part of an attempt to broaden as well as follow up on the initial thesis in *The Protestant Ethic*. Each of these studies has been made the subject of an edited volume by Wolfgang Schluchter (see Schluchter 1981a, 1983, 1984, 1985, 1987, 1988).

In discussing Weber's thesis in *The Protestant Ethic*, it is common to cite studies that argue in favor of Weber as well as studies that argue against him. To this may be added studies that have been inspired by Weber but go in their own direction. Attempts have been made, for example by Robert K. Merton, to study the relationship between Protestantism and modern science; by Michael Walzer to study the relationship between Protestantism and modern radical politics; and by Phillip Gorski to study the relationship between Calvinism and the modern European state. See Robert K. Merton, *Science, Technology and Society in Seventeenth Century England* ([1938] 1970), Michael Walzer, *The Revolution of the Saints* (1966), and Phillip Gorski, *The Disciplinary Revolution: Calvinism and the Rise of the State in Early Modern Europe* (2003). Colin Campbell also draws heavily on Weber in explaining the birth of modern consumer behavior in *The Romantic Ethic and the Spirit of Modern Consumption* (1987).

See also *Protestant Ethic and the Spirit of Capitalism, The*; paradoxical results of people's actions, unintended consequences, vocation (for *Beruf*), Weber thesis

Weberianism There exists no real equivalent in Weber scholarship to Marxism, that is, there exists no distinct school of people who see it as their main task to work within the Weberian paradigm and further develop it. "There has never been a Weberian school of sociology" (Turner

2001:164–71). There does, on the other hand, exist a number of social scientists who use bits and pieces of Weber's work in their own analyses. There also exists a seemingly endless explication of what Weber really "meant" as well as a concern with intricate details of his work and life—what may be called Weberology.

See also neo-Weberianism, reception of Weber's work, secondary literature on Weber's work, Weber-inspired scholars and scholarship

Weber-inspired scholars and scholarship   Due to his personality as well as his status as a private scholar for much of his career, Weber had very few doctoral students and at his death there was no Weberian school of sociology. Indeed, it would take mainstream sociology in Germany (and in other countries) many decades to start to appreciate Weber's work.

Nonetheless, several major intellectuals in German-speaking countries have been inspired by Weber in some important manner, including Norbert Elias, Karl Jaspers, Karl Mannheim, and Alfred Schutz. Many people in Weber's direct milieu also developed their own ideas under a certain influence from Weber—just as he developed his own ideas under a certain impact from them. These include scholars such as Georg Simmel, Georg Lukács, Otto Hintze, and Ernst Troeltsch. In today's Germany there are a number of prominent scholars who devote much of their energies to Weber's work, including Wilhelm Hennis, Wolfgang Mommsen, and Wolfgang Schluchter. The publication of Max Weber's collected works since the mid-1980s has done much to create what may be termed Weberology or a close scrutiny of his texts as well as his life.

In the United States, there is a long list of major sociologists who have been deeply influenced by some aspect of Weber's work—including Reinhard Bendix, Peter Berger, Peter Blau, Randall Collins, Everett C. Hughes, Seymour Martin Lipset, Robert K. Merton, Talcott Parsons, Edward Shils, Theda Skocpol, and Arthur Stinchcombe. Other Anglo-Saxon sociologists who have been inspired by Weber include Anthony Giddens, Michael Mann, and Frank Parkin. Among French intellectuals, Weber has had a certain impact especially on Raymond Aron, Raymond Boudon, and Pierre Bourdieu. There is also the Israeli scholar S. N. Eisenstadt.

Since the late 1970s there has been a revival of interest in Weber's work, known as neo-Weberianism. Some of the people just mentioned belong here, such as Randall Collins, Frank Parkin, and Michael Mann (*see* neo-Weberianism).

Weber's influence on modern sociology more generally is considered very important. When classical sociological theory is taught, Weber, Marx, and Durkheim are usually at the center (while Simmel is more marginal). Concepts such as charisma, status and authority, and domination (*Herrschaft*) are today part of the general terminology of sociology. Weber's impact on organization theory through his ideas on bureaucracy, stratification, status, and social closure, has also been important.

See e.g. Charles Turner, "Weberian Social Thought, History of" (2001).

See also neo-Weberianism, secondary literature on Weber's work, Weber, Max—Works, Weberianism

Weberology   *See* Weberianism

welfare state   *See* state

Wertbeziehung   *See* value-relevance

Wertfreiheit   *See* value-neutrality

Wert-Idee   *See* value-idea

Werturteilsstreit   *See* value-freedom

West, the   Weber saw the West as unique in many of its social, economic and cultural features; and much of his research was devoted to finding out why just the West, and not the rest of the world, had made such progress. Why had only the West developed a civilization which could be seen as having a universal significance? And how should this civilization be characterized?

One of the answers that he gave to the question of the special development of the West can be found in *The Protestant Ethic*, namely that the West had developed a unique type of economic system—rational capitalism—under the impact of a very special type of religion—ascetic Protestantism. Elsewhere in his work Weber investigates the relationship of other religions to the rise of rational capitalism—as well as the role of different types of states, legal systems, and other factors (see especially ES, RC, RI). Furthermore, only the West, according to Weber, had developed such features as human rights, modern science, the modern rational state, and individualism. A unifying theme in Western civilization, is its emphasis on *rationalization*.

A useful introduction to what characterizes Western society and culture can be found in Weber's introduction to his collected essays in the sociology of religion (PE:13–31; see also e.g. ES:1192–93). What is characteristic of the "cultural phenomena" of "Western civilization," Weber here says, is that they have "*universal* significance and value" (PE:13). More precisely, there is "a specific and peculiar rationalism of Western culture" which needs to become the object of study (PE:26).

In late 1919 Weber wrote to his publisher that his analyses aimed at laying bare "the foundations of the special development (*Sonderentwick-lung*) of the West" (Grossein 2003:lvii). When, shortly before his death, Weber wrote an advertisement for his forthcoming *Collected Essays in the Sociology of Religion*, he similarly stated that his object of study was "the economic and social *singularity* of the Occident" (Schluchter 1989:425; *see* the entry for *Collected Essays in the Sociology of Religion*). As part of this work Weber also planned "a sketch devoted to the rise of the social singularity of the Occident, i.e., an essay on the development of the European bourgeoisie in antiquity and the Middle Ages" (ibid.).

Weber's switch from a focus on economy, society, and religion to a broader focus on the West and its uniqueness in relation to other civilizations has been dated to around 1910 (Wolfgang Schluchter, *Rationalism, Religion, and Domination* [1989], p. 430; cf. Marianne Weber, *Max Weber* [(1926) 1975], p. 333). For a discussion of Weber's notion of the West and its culture, see e.g. Benjamin Nelson, "On Orient and Occident in Max Weber" (1976) and Wolfgang Schluchter, *The Rise of Western Rationalism* (1981).

Wirklichkeitswisssenschaft   *See* science of reality

Wirtschaft und Gesellschaft   *See Economy and Society*

Wirtschaftsethik der Weltreligionen   See *Economic Ethics of the World Religions.*

Wirtschaftsgeschichte   This is the title under which one of Weber's lecture courses of 1919–20 was reconstructed and published in 1923.
   See *General Economic History*

Wissenschaftslehre   By this term (which Weber himself did not use, and which has its origin in the work of the philosopher Heinrich Rickert) is meant Weber's views on the methodology of the social sciences, including sociology. His most important writings on this topic can be found in a volume of essays put together after his death under the title of *Gesammelte Aufsätze zur Wissenschaftslehre* (1922; for a slightly different version, see the 1988 edition). In these essays Weber addresses such issues as causality, objectivity, what differentiates the social and cultural sciences from the natural sciences, and how to construct so-called ideal types (*see* causality, cultural sciences, ideal type, objectivity).

According to Talcott Parsons, "the general purport of these critical essays [that is, the *Wissenschaftslehre*] was Weber's insistence that in studies of society, as much as in the natural sciences, causal explanation depends upon the employment of analytical theory" (Parsons 1963:xxii–xxiii).

A couple of the most important of the essays in the *Wissenschaftslehre* have been translated as *The Methodology of the Social Sciences*—including Weber's essays on objectivity (1904), cultural science (1906), and value-freedom (1917). Other important essays have been published separately in English, in particular *Critique of Stammler, Roscher and Knies* and "Some Categories of Interpretive Sociology."

Weber's views on the methodology of sociology, as this can be found in Ch. 1 of *Economy and Society*, is formally part of his *Wissenschaftslehre*, in the sense that the first section of this chapter has been included in *Gesammelte Aufsätze zur Wissenschaftslehre* (ES:3–38). For a brief discussion of these views, *see* methodology (with references to other relevant entries).

In a letter to his publisher just before his death Weber expressed interest in putting together a volume of his methodological essays (Weber to Paul Siebeck in November 1919; cf. Ola Agevall, *A Science of Unique Events: Max Weber's Methodology of the Cultural Sciences* [1999], p. 3). This work did not materialize, but in 1922 Marianne Weber edited a volume of this type, entitled *Gesammelte Aufsätze zur Wissenschaftslehre* (1922; GAW). Her choice of essays differed slightly from that of her husband.

There exists a huge literature on Weber's methodology of the social sciences. For brief introductions, see e.g. Raymond Aron, *Main Currents in Sociological Thought* (1970), Vol. 2, pp. 219–65, Dirk Käsler, *Max Weber* (1988), pp. 174–96, and Talcott Parsons, *The Structure of Social Action* (1937), pp. 579–639. For fuller treatments, see e.g. Agevall, *A Science of Unique Events*, H. H. Bruun, *Science, Values and Politics in Max Weber's Methodology* (1972), Sven Eliaeson, *Max Weber's Methodologies* (2002), Dieter Henrich, *Die Einheit der Wissenschaftslehre Max Webers* (1952), Alexander von Schelting, *Max Webers Wissenschaftslehre* (1934), and Gerhard Wagner and Heinz Zipprian (eds.), *Max Webers Wissenschaftslehre* (1994). The *Wissenschaftslehre* will appear as MWG, Vols. I/7 and I/12.

See also causation, explanation, ideal type, meaning

women   Weber never wrote exclusively on women, but he occasionally refers to them in his work. It is, for example, common to find references to women in Weber's economic sociology and economic history when the household is discussed (e.g. GEH:47–8, ES:362–65, 370–75, 1009). In *The Protestant Ethic* Weber discusses the work habits of female workers (PE:62–3; cf. PED:81 n. xli). In Weber's sociology of religion, some attention is also paid to the role of women (e.g. ES:488–89, RI:151, 171–72).

At one point in his sociology of law, Weber notes that male jurors in

Germany "practically never" find a male guilty in cases of rape unless the victim is considered "chaste" (ES:893). And in his historical sociology he refers to "the normal superiority of the physical and intellectual energies of the male" (ES:1007).

The role of matriarchy is discussed by Weber in connection with the household (e.g. ES:368–69).

See also body, feminism, household, males, patriarchalism

work (*Arbeit*)   Work plays an important role in Weber's studies, especially in his economic sociology but also in his sociology of religion. In *The Protestant Ethic*, for example, one can find Weber's famous analysis of vocation (*Beruf*; PE:79–92). He also traces the relationship of various religions to work (e.g. ES:1187).

Before Protestantism, Weber argues in *The Protestant Ethic*, work had no specific religious value in Christianity. Luther invested it with such a value in the 1500s, but only spoke of traditional work. The Puritans added an activistic element to this religious valuation of work. Some time later, however, the religious meaning of work was lost in the West—but not the idea that work has a value in itself and represents an extremely important goal for the individual.

In his economic sociology Weber draws a distinction between managerial work and other kinds of work (ES:115). He also presents a typology of work throughout history and discusses motivation to work (ES:125–28, 202–8).

In the *General Economic History* Weber discusses the evolution of human work from agriculture by way of handicraft work to factory work (see e.g. GEH:115–94, 302–15).

See also division of labor, economic ethic, economic motivation, employment regime (*Agrarverfassung*), industrial sociology, occupation, profession, psychophysics, vocation, work ethic, workers

work ethic   This concept, which has become part of everyday language and is often used as a synonym of "Protestant work ethic," has its roots in Weber's study *The Protestant Ethic and the Spirit of Capitalism*. The *Oxford English Dictionary* describes the term "work ethic" as follows: "work seen as virtuous in itself, a term usually connected with Protestant attitudes and deriving from Max Weber's thesis on the origins of capitalism." One may also say that work ethic means an inner compulsion to work.

While the concept of work ethic originally had strong religious connotations, these have faded with time. During the twentieth century a number of studies were carried out which attempted to measure the work ethic of various groups in society. For some of these studies as well as a discussion of whether modern work ethic is weakening or not, see e.g. Seymour Martin Lipset, "The Work Ethic, Then and Now" (1992) and Adrian Furnham, *The Protestant Work Ethic: The Psychology of Work Related Beliefs and Behaviours* (1990).

workers   Weber touches on the role of the workers in many of his social science writings and sometimes also in his political speeches. He made, for example, a major study of agricultural workers in the 1890s and later carried out a study of workers in a textile factory (Weber [1892] 1984; for a summary in English, see e.g. [1895] 1980, [1908–9] 1988).

The Protestant Ethic also contains an important discussion in which workers with and without a vocation are contrasted (PE:59–63; cf. 77–78, 282 n. 108).

In his economic sociology in Ch. 2 of *Economy and Society* Weber notes that the highest degree of (formal) efficiency is reached if the workers do not own the means of production, if the owners and the management are free to choose workers as they see fit, and if there are no regulations on consumption, production, and prices (e.g. ES:161–64). This implies, among other things, freedom of contract in the labor contract— a freedom that Weber argued was illusory from a substantive point of view (ES:729–31).

Weber also came into contact with workers through his various political activities. According to Karl Jaspers, "his courage to candidly speak what he saw and believed was equally great when he opposed the top powers of the old state or the workers" (Jaspers 1989:17). For a brief summary of Weber's studies in the 1890s of agrarian workers, see e.g. Reinhard Bendix, *Max Weber: An Intellectual Portrait* (1960), pp. 14–23 and Dirk Käsler, *Max Weber* (1988), pp. 51–63; see also e.g. Weber, "The Nation State and Economic Policy" (PW:1–28). For Weber on industrial workers, see e.g. Käsler, *Max Weber*, pp. 14, 66–73. See also Weber's studies of the psychophysics of work as well as his methodological introduction to a planned study of the selection and adaptation of workers in large industries (GASS:61–255 and Weber [1908] 1980). Finally, see also Peter Baehr, "The 'Masses' in Weber's Political Sociology" (1990).

Weber's lectures on workers and the labor movement are scheduled to appear as MWG, Vol. III/4.

See also coercion, depersonalization, discipline, employment regime (*Agrarverfassung*), exploitation, expropriation, Marxism, means of production, politics, privileges, psychophysics, socialism, work

works of Weber   *See* Weber, Max—Works

world-rejection (*Weltablehnung*)   The religious believer may attempt to control the world—or to reject it. If the latter alternative is chosen, this will have consequences both for the believer and for society.

The concept of world-rejection plays a prominent role in Weber's sociology of religion. It is, for example, at the center of his famous "Intermediate Reflections" (*Zwischenbetrachtung*), which are known to English readers as "Religious Rejections of the World and Their Directions" (GM:323–59). According to Weber, the two prime examples of world-rejecting religions are ancient Buddhism and early Christianity (ES:627–30). In the former, the goal of individuals was to withdraw from anything tying them to life on earth and to ultimately enter nirvana. Early Christians were uninterested in life on earth and had their eyes set on the next world.

For the concept of world-rejection and its evolution in Weber's work, see e.g. Stefan Breuer, "Weltablehnung" (2001).

See also sociology of religion, *Zwischenbetrachtung*

world-religions (*Weltreligionen*)   In the introduction to his *Collected Essays in the Sociology of Religion* (*Gesammelte Aufsätze zur Religionssoziologie*), Weber writes that "by 'world religion', we understand the five religions or religiously determined systems of life-regulation which have known how to gather multitudes of confessors around them" (GM:267). These five world-religions are Confucianism, Hinduism, Buddhism, Christianity, and Islam. Weber regarded Judaism as a sixth world-religion (Dirk Käsler, *Max Weber* [1988], p. 95).

In Weber's time the term "world-religion" (*Weltreligion*) was used by some scholars as the opposite of "local" or "popular" religion (*Volksreligion*; cf. Weber 1996:4).

See also religion

Z

auberer   *See* magician

Zur Geschichte der Handelsgesellschaften im Mittelalter   *See History of Commercial Partnerships in the Middle Ages*

Zurechnung (imputation)   *See* mutual responsibility

Zweckrationalität   *See* instrumentally rational action

"Zwischenbetrachtung"   This is the title of an essay in Weber's *Collected Essays in the Sociology of Religion* (*Gesammelte Aufsätze zur Religionssoziologie*), which is known to most English readers as "Religious

Rejections of the World and Their Directions" (GM:323–59)—even though a new translation by Sam Whimster has just appeared ("Intermediate Reflection on the Economic Ethics of the World Religions"; EW:215–44). The title of the German original is "Zwischenbetrachtung: Theorie der Stufen und Richtungen religiöser Weltablehnung"; the term *Zwischenbetrachtung* ("intermediate reflection") refers to the placement of this essay in Weber's work between *The Religion of China* and *The Religion of India* (GAR, I:537–73).

The "Intermediate Reflection" is one of Weber's most important and spectacular essays. It contains important passages on theodicy, asceticism, and mysticism. First and foremost, however, it contains a long and detailed exposition of the different value-spheres in life—economic, political, esthetic, erotic, and intellectual.

Weber's essay was originally published in the *Archiv für Sozialwissenschaft und Sozialpolitik* in 1915 and revised for republication in 1920.

See also *Collected Essays in the Sociology of Religion*, value-spheres

References

Abel, Thomas, and William Cockerham. 1993. "Life Style or *Lebensfuehrung?* Critical Remarks on the Mistranslation of Weber's 'Class, Status, Party'." *Sociological Quarterly* 34, 3:551–56.

Abraham, Gary. 1992. *Max Weber and the Jewish Question: A Study of the Social Outlook of His Sociology.* Urbana, IL: University of Illinois Press.

Adair-Toteff, Christopher. 2002. "Max Weber's Mysticism." *Archives Européennes de Sociologie* 43:339–53.

Agevall, Ola. 1999. *A Science of Unique Events: Max Weber's Methodology of the Cultural Sciences.* Ph.D. diss. Uppsala: Uppsala University.

———. Forthcoming. "Science, Values, and the Empirical Argument in Max Weber's *Freiburger Antrittsrede.*" *Max Weber Studies.*

Ahonen, Pertti. 1999. "'Wirtschaft' in Max Weber." Pp. 133–70 in Pertti Ahonen and Kari Palonen (eds.), *Dis-Embalming Max Weber.* Jyväskylä, Finland: Sophi/ Jyväskylä University.

Albrow, Martin. 1970. *On Bureaucracy.* London: Macmillan.

———. 1990. *Max Weber's Construction of Social Theory.* London: Macmillan.

Aldenhoff, Rita. 1987. "Max Weber and the Evangelical-Social Congress." Pp. 193–202 in Wolfgang Mommsen and Jürgen Osterhammel (eds.), *Max Weber and His Contemporaries.* London: Unwin.

Alexander, Jeffrey. 1983. *The Classical Attempt at Theoretical Synthesis: Max Weber.* Vol. 3 of *Theoretical Logic in Sociology.* Berkeley, CA: University of California Press.

Antoni, Carlo. 1959. *From History to Sociology: The Transition in German Historical Thinking.* Detroit: Wayne State University Press.

Aron, Raymond. 1964. *German Sociology.* New York: Free Press.

———. 1970. "Max Weber." Pp. 219–317 in Vol. 2 of *Main Currents in Sociological Thought.* Garden City, NY: Anchor Books.

———. 1985. "Max Weber and Modern Social Science." Pp. 335–73 in *History, Truth, Liberty: Selected Writings of Raymond Aron.* Chicago: University of Chicago Press.

———. 1990. *Memoirs: Fifty Years of Political Reflection.* New York: Holmes & Meier.

Asher, Abraham. 1963. "Professors as Propagandists: The Politics of the *Kathedersozialisten.*" *Journal of Central European Affairs* 23:282–302.

Ay, Karl-Dieter. 1993. "Max Weber und der Begriff der Rasse." *Aschkenas: Zeitschrift für Geschichte und Kultur der Juden* 1:189–218.

Bachofen, Johann Jakob. [1861] 2003. *Mutterrecht: English Selections.* Lewistown, NY: Edward Mellen Press.

Baehr, Peter. 1988. "Max Weber as a Critic of Bismarck." *Archives Européennes de Sociologie* 29:149–64.

———. 1990. "The 'Masses' in Weber's Political Sociology." *Economy and Society* 19, 2:242–65.

———. 2000. "The 'Iron Cage' and the 'Shell as Hard as Steel': Parsons, Weber, and the *stahlhartes Gehäuse* Metaphor in *The Protestant Ethic and the Spirit of Capitalism.*" *History and Theory* 40 (May):153–69.

Baehr, Peter, and Gordon Wells. 2002. "The Protestant Ethic and the 'Spirit' of Capitalism: Editors' Introduction." Pp. ix–lxiii in Max Weber, *The Protestant Ethic and the "Spirit" of Capitalism and Other Writings.* New York: Penguin Books.

Baier, Horst, M. Rainer Lepsius, Wolfgang Mommsen, and Wolfgang Schluchter. 2000. "Overview of the Text of *Economy and Society* by the Editors of the Max Weber *Gesamtausgabe.*" *Max Weber Studies* 1:104–14.

Barbalet, J. M. 2000. "*Beruf,* Rationality and Emotion in Max Weber's Sociology." *Archives Européennes de Sociologie* 41, 2:329–51.

Baumgarten, Eduard (ed.). 1964. *Max Weber: Werk und Person. Dokumente.* Tübingen: J. C. B. Mohr.

Becker, George. 1997. "Replication and Reanalysis of Offenbacher's School Enrollment Study: Implications for the Weber and Merton Theses." *Journal of the Scientific Study of Religion* 36, 4:483–96.

Beetham, David. 1985. *Max Weber and the Theory of Modern Politics.* 2nd ed. Cambridge, UK: Polity Press.

———. 1989. "Max Weber and the Liberal Political Tradition." *Archives Européennes de Sociologie* 30:311–23.

Bellah, Robert. 1957. *Tokugawa Religion: The Values of Pre-Industrial Japan.* Glencoe, IL: Free Press.

Bendix, Reinhard. 1960. *Max Weber: An Intellectual Portrait.* Garden City, NY: Doubleday.

———. 1968. "Bureaucracy." Pp. 206–19 in Vol. 2 of David Sills (ed.), *International Encyclopaedia of the Social Sciences.* New York: Macmillan and Free Press.

Bendix, Reinhard, and Guenther Roth. 1971. *Scholarship and Partisanship: Essays on Max Weber.* Berkeley: University of California Press.

Berger, Peter. 1963. "Charisma and Religious Innovation: The Social Location of Israelite Prophecy." *American Sociological Review* 28:940–50.

Berger, Peter, and Thomas Luckmann. 1967. *The Social Construction of Reality.* New York: Doubleday.

Berger, S. D. 1971. "The Sects and the Breakthrough into the Modern World: On the Centrality of the Sects in Weber's Protestant Ethic Thesis." *Sociological*

Quarterly 12:486–99.

Berman, Harold, and Charles Reid. 2000. "Max Weber as Legal Historian." Pp. 223–39 in Stephen Turner (ed.), *The Cambridge Companion to Weber*. Cambridge, UK: Cambridge University Press.

Besnard, Philippe (ed.). 1970. *Protestantisme et capitalisme: La controverse post-weberienne*. Paris: Armand Colin.

Bologh, Roslyn Wallach. 1987. "Marx, Weber, and Masculine Theorizing: A Feminist Analysis." Pp. 145–68 in Norbert Wiley (ed.), *The Marx-Weber Debate*. London: SAGE.

———. 1990. *Love or Greatness: Max Weber and Masculine Thinking—A Feminist Inquiry*. London: Unwin Hyman.

Borchardt, Knut. 2002. "Max Weber's Writings on the Bourse: Puzzling Out a Forgotten Corpus." *Max Weber Studies* 2, 2:139–62.

Borchardt, Knut, and Cornelia Meyer-Stoll. 1999. "Einleitung." Pp. 1–111 in Max Weber, *Börsenwesen. Schriften und Reden 1893–1898. Max Weber Gesamtausgabe I/5*. 2 vols. Tübingen: J. C. B. Mohr.

Boudon, Raymond. 1996. "The 'Cognitivist Model': A Generalized Rational-Choice Model." *Rationality and Society* 8, 2:123–50.

———. 1997. "The Present Relevance of Max Weber's *Wertrationalität* (Value Rationality)." Pp. 4–29 in Peter Koslowski (ed.), *Methodology of the Social Sciences, Ethics, and Economics in the Newer Historical School*. New York: Springer Verlag.

———. 2001. *The Origin of Values: Sociology and Philosophy of Beliefs*. New Brunswick, NJ: Transaction.

———. 2003. "Beyond Rational Choice Theory." *Annual Review of Sociology* 29:1–21.

Bourdieu, Pierre. [1971] 1987. "Legitimation and Structured Interests in Weber's Sociology of Religion." Pp. 119–36 in Scott Lash and Sam Whimster (eds.), *Max Weber, Rationality and Modernity*. London: Allen & Unwin.

———. 2000. "Mit Weber gegen Weber." Pp. 111–29 in Pierre Bourdieu, *Das religiöse Feld. Texte zur Ökonomie des Heilgeschehens*. Konstanz: UVK Universitätsverlag.

Braun, Christoph. 1999. "The 'Science of Reality' of Music History: On the Historical Background to Max Weber's Study of Music." Pp. 176–95 in Sam Whimster (ed.), *Max Weber and the Culture of Anarchism*. London: Macmillan.

Breuer, Stefan. 1985. "Stromuferkultur und Küstenkultur. Geographische und ökologische Faktoren in Max Webers 'ökonomischer Theorie der antiken Staatenwelt'." Pp. 111–50 in Wolfgang Schluchter (ed.), *Max Webers Sicht des antiken Christentums: Interpretation und Kritik*. Frankfurt am Main: Suhrkamp.

———. 1988. "Der okzidentale Feudalismus in Max Webers Gesellschaftsgeschichte." Pp. 437–75 in Wolfgang Schluchter (ed.), *Max Webers Sicht des okzidentalen Christentums. Interpretation und Kritik*. Frankfurt am Main: Suhrkamp.

———. 1991. *Max Webers Herrschaftssoziologie*. Frankfurt: Campus Verlag.

———. 1993. "Max Webers Staatssoziologie." *Kölner Zeitschrift für Soziologie und Sozialpsychologie* 45, 2:199–219.

————. 1998a. "The Concept of Democracy in Weber's Political Sociology." Pp. 1–13 in Ralph Schroeder (ed.), *Max Weber, Democracy and Modernization.* London: Macmillan.

————. 1998b. "Soviet Communism and Weberian Sociology." Pp. 145–65 in Ralph Schroeder (ed.), *Max Weber, Democracy and Modernization.* London: Macmillan.

————. 1999. *Georg Jellinek und Max Weber.* Baden-Baden: Nomos Verlag.

————. 2001a. "Magie, Zauber, Entzauberung." Pp. 119–30 in Hans Kippenberg and Martin Riesebrodt (eds.), *Max Webers "Religionssystematik."* Tübingen: J. C. B. Mohr.

————. 2001b. "Weltablehnung." Pp. 227–40 in Hans Kippenberg and Martin Riesebrodt (eds.), *Max Webers "Religionssystematik."* Tübingen: J. C. B. Mohr.

Brubaker, Rogers. 1984. *The Limits of Rationality: An Essay on the Social and Moral Thought of Max Weber.* London: George Allen & Unwin.

Bruhns, Hinnerk. 1996. "Max Weber, l'économie et l'histoire." *Annales. Histoire Sciences Sociales* 51:1259–87.

————. 1998. "À propos de l'histoire ancienne et de l'économie politique chez Max Weber." Pp. 9–59 in Max Weber, *Économie et Société dans l'Antiquité.* Paris: La Découverte.

Bruhns, Hinnerk, and Wilfried Nippel (eds.). 2000. *Max Weber und die Stadt im Kulturvergleich.* Göttingen: Vandenhoeck & Ruprecht.

Bruun, H. H. 1972. *Science, Values and Politics in Max Weber's Methodology.* Copenhagen: Munksgaard.

————. 2001. "Weber on Rickert: From Value Relations to Ideal Type." *Max Weber Studies,* 1, 2:138–60.

————. 2004. Conversation with the author, March 22, in Copenhagen.

Burger, Thomas. 1987. *Max Weber's Theory of Concept Formation: History, Laws, and Ideal Types.* Durham, NC: Duke University Press.

Burkgard, Gladigow. 2001. "Polytheismus." Pp. 131–50 in Hans Kippenberg and Martin Riesebrodt (eds.), *Max Webers "Religionssystematik."* Tübingen: J. C. B. Mohr.

Camic, Charles. 1986. "The Matter of Habit." *American Journal of Sociology* 91:1039–87.

Campbell, Colin. 1987. *The Romantic Ethic and the Spirit of Modern Consumerism.* Cambridge, UK: Blackwell.

Caplan, Hannan, and Belinda Rosenblatt (eds.). 1983. *International Biographical Dictionary of Central European Emigrés.* New York: K. G. Saur.

Carruthers, Bruce, and Wendy Nelson Espeland. 1991. "Accounting for Rationality: Double-Entry Bookkeeping and the Rhetoric of Economic Rationality." *American Journal of Sociology* 97:31–69.

Chalcraft, David. 1994. "Bringing the Text Back In: On Ways of Rendering the Iron Cage Metaphor in the Two Editions of 'The Protestant Ethic'." Pp. 16–45 in Larry Ray and Michael Reed (eds.), *Organizing Modernity: New Weberian Perspectives on Work, Organization and Society.* London: Routledge.

———. 1999. "Love and Death. Weber, Wagner and Klinger." Pp. 196–213 in Sam Whimster (ed.), *Max Weber and the Culture of Anarchy*. London: Macmillan.

Chalcraft, David, and Austin Harrington (eds.). 2001. *The Protestant Ethic Debate: Max Weber's Replies to His Critics, 1907–1910*. Liverpool: Liverpool University Press.

Clarke, Simon. 1982. *Marx, Marginalism and Modern Sociology: From Adam Smith to Max Weber*. London: Macmillan.

Clegg, Stewart. 1994. "Max Weber and Contemporary Sociology of Organizations." Pp. 46–80 in Larry Ray and Michael Reed (eds.), *Organizing Modernity: New Weberian Perspectives on Work, Organization and Society*. London: Routledge.

Cohen, Bernard (ed.). 1990. *Puritanism and the Rise of Science: The Merton Thesis*. New Brunswick, NJ: Rutgers University Press.

Cohen, Jere, Lawrence Hazelrigg, and Whitney Pope. 1975. "De-Parsonizing Weber: A Critique of Parsons' Interpretation of Weber's Sociology." *American Sociological Review* 40:229–41.

Collins, Randall. 1980. "Weber's Last Theory of Capitalism." *American Sociological Review* 45:925–42.

———. 1986a. *Max Weber: A Skeletal Key*. London: SAGE.

———. 1986b. *Weberian Sociological Theory*. Cambridge, UK: Cambridge University Press.

———. 1998. "Democratization in World-Historical Perspective." Pp. 14–31 in Ralph Schroeder (ed.), *Max Weber, Democracy and Modernization*. London: Macmillan Press.

Conze, Werner. 1972. "Beruf." Pp. 154–215 in Vol. 1 of Otto Brunner et al. (eds.), *Geschichtliche Grundbegriffe*. Stuttgart: Klett-Cotta.

Dahrendorf, Ralf. 1956. *Industrie- und Betriebssoziologie*. Berlin: Walter de Gruyter.

———. 1959. *Class and Class Conflict in Industrial Society*. London: Routledge & Kegan Paul.

———. 1987. "Max Weber and Modern Social Science." Pp. 574–80 in Wolfgang Mommsen and Jürgen Osterhammel (eds.), *Max Weber and His Contemporaries*. London: Unwin.

———. 1979. *Life Chances: Approaches to Social and Political Theory*. Chicago: University of Chicago Press.

Demm, Eberhard. 1987. "Max and Alfred Weber and the Verein für Sozialpolitik." Pp. 88–98 in Wolfgang Mommsen and Jürgen Osterhammel (eds.), *Max Weber and His Contemporaries*. London: Unwin.

Derlien, Hans-Ulrich. 1999. "On the Selective Interpretation of Max Weber's Concept of Bureaucracy in Organization Theory and Administrative Science." Pp. 56–70 in Pertti Ahonen and Kari Palonen (eds.), *Dis-Embalming Max Weber*. Jyväskylä, Finland: Sophi/ Jyväskylä University.

Diggens, John Patrick. 1996. *Max Weber: Politics and the Spirit of Tragedy*. New York: Basic Books.

di Marco, Giuseppe Antonio. 1983. "Max Weber in Italia: Linee di una interpretazione." *Annali della Facoltà di Lettere e Filosofia dell'Università di Napoli* 23:245–370.

Eisen, Arnold. 1979. "Called to Order: The Role of the Puritan *Berufsmensch* in Weberian Sociology." *Sociology* 13:203–18.

Eisenstadt, S. N. 1968a. "Introduction: Charisma and Institution Building: Max Weber and Modern Sociology." Pp. ix–lvi in Max Weber, *On Charisma and Institution Building*. Chicago: University of Chicago Press.

——— (ed.) 1968b. *The Protestant Ethic and Modernization: A Comparative Approach*. New York: Basic Books.

———. 1971. "Some Reflections on the Significance of Max Weber's Sociology of Religions for the Analysis of Non-European Modernity." *Archives de Sociologie des Religions* 32:29–52.

———. 1989. "Max Weber on Western Christianity and the Weberian Approach to Civilizational Dynamics." *Canadian Journal of Sociology* 14, 2:203–23.

Ekstrand, Thomas. 1999. *Max Weber in a Theological Perspective*. Ph.D. diss. Uppsala: Uppsala University, Department of Theology.

Eliaeson, Sven. 1982. *Bilden av Max Weber: En Studie i Samhällsvetenskapens Sekularisering* [The Picture of Max Weber: A Study in the Secularization of Social Science]. Stockholm: Nordstedt.

———. 2000. "Constitutional Caesarism: Weber's Politics in Their German Context." Pp. 131–48 in Stephen Turner (ed.), *The Cambridge Companion to Weber*. Cambridge, UK: Cambridge University Press.

———. 2002. *Max Weber's Methodologies: Interpretation and Critique*. Cambridge, UK: Polity Press.

Elias, Norbert. 1996. *The Germans: Power Struggles and the Development of Habitus in the Nineteenth and Twentieth Centuries*. Cambridge, UK: Polity Press.

Elster, Jon. 1979. "Some Unresolved Problems in the Theory of Rational Behavior." Pp. 65–85 in Louis Levy-Garboa (ed.), *Sociological Economics*. London: SAGE.

———. 2000. "Rationality, Economy and Society." Pp. 21–41 in Stephen Turner (ed.), *The Cambridge Companion to Weber*. Cambridge, UK: Cambridge University Press.

Emerich, Francis. 1966. "Kultur und Gesellschaft in der Soziologie Max Webers." Pp. 89–114 in Karl Engish et al. (eds.), *Max Weber. Gedächtnisschrif der Ludwig-Maximilians-Universität München zur 100. Wiederkehr seine: Geburtstages 1964*. Berlin: Duncker & Humblot.

Emirbayer, Mustafa. Forthcoming. "Beyond Action Theory." In Charles Camic Philip Gorski, and David Trubek (eds.), *Max Weber at the Millennium: Econ omy and Society for the 21st Century*. Stanford, CA: Stanford University Press

Engerman, Stanley. 2000. "Max Weber as Economist and Economic Historian." Pp. 256–71 in Stephen Turner (ed.), *The Cambridge Companion to Weber* Cambridge, UK: Cambridge University Press.

Evans, Peter, and James Rauch. 1999. "Bureaucracy and Growth: A Cross-Na tional Analysis of the Effects of 'Weberian' State Structures on Economi

Growth." *American Sociological Review* 64:748–65.

Ewing, Sally. 1987. "Formal Justice and the Spirit of Capitalism: Max Weber's Sociology of Law." *Law & Society Review* 21, 3:487–512.

Factor, Regis. 1988. *Guide to the Archiv für Sozialwissenschaft und Sozialpolitik Group 1904–1933: A Comprehensive Bibliography.* New York: Greenwood Press.

Fahey, Tony. 1982. "Max Weber's *Ancient Judaism.*" *American Journal of Sociology* 88:62–87.

Farfan Hernandez, Rafael. 1994. "La recepción actual de Weber." *Sociologica* 9, 24:199–206.

Finley, M. I. 1977. "The Ancient City: From Fustel de Coulanges to Max Weber and Beyond." *Comparative Studies in Society and History* 19, 3:305–27.

Frisby, David. 1987. "The Ambiguity of Modernity: Georg Simmel and Max Weber." Pp. 422–33 in Wolfgang Mommsen and Jürgen Osterhammel (eds.), *Max Weber and His Contemporaries.* London: Unwin.

Frisby, David, and Derek Sayer. 1986. *Society.* London: Tavistock.

Frommer, Jorg, and Sabine Frommer. 1993. "Max Webers Krankheit—soziologische Aspekte der depressiven Struktur." *Fortschritte der Neurologie: Psychiatrie,* 61:161–71.

Frommer, Jörg, Sabine Frommer, and Michael Langenbach. 2000. "Max Weber's Influence on the Concept of Comprehension in Psychiatry." *History of Psychiatry* 11:345–54.

Fügen, Hans Norbert. 1985. *Max Weber.* Hamburg: Rowohlt.

Furnham, Adrian. 1990. *The Protestant Work Ethic: The Psychology of Work Related Beliefs and Behaviours.* London: Routledge.

Gane, Nicholas. 2004. *Max Weber and Postmodern Theory: Rationalization versus Re-enchantment.* New York: Palgrave.

Gerth, Hans, and C. Wright Mills (eds.). 1946. *From Max Weber.* New York: Oxford University Press.

Ghosh, Peter. 1994. "Some Problems with Talcott Parsons' Version of 'The Protestant Ethic'." *Archives Européennes de Sociologie* 35:104–23.

Giddens, Anthony. 1971. *Capitalism and Modern Social Theory: An Analysis of the Writings of Marx, Durkheim and Max Weber.* Cambridge, UK: Cambridge University Press.

———. 1972. *Politics and Sociology in the Thought of Max Weber.* London: Macmillan.

———. 1987. "Weber and Durkheim: Coincidence and Divergence." Pp. 182–89 in Wolfgang Mommsen and Jürgen Osterhammel (eds.), *Max Weber and His Contemporaries.* London: Unwin.

Glassman, Ronald, and Vatro Murvar (eds.). 1984. *Max Weber's Political Sociology: A Pessimistic Vision of a Rationalized World.* Westport, CT: Greenwood.

Goertz, Gary, and Harvey Starr (eds.). 2003. *Necessary Conditions: Theory, Methodology, and Applications.* London: Rowman & Littlefield.

Goldman, Harvey. 1988. *Max Weber and Thomas Mann: Calling and the Shaping of the Self.* Berkeley: University of California Press.

Gorski, Phillip. 2003. *The Disciplinary Revolution: Calvinism and the Rise of the*

Early European State. Cambridge, UK: Cambridge University Press.

Gouldner, Alvin. 1962. "Anti-Minotaur: The Myth of Value-Free Sociology." *Social Problems* 9, 3:199–213.

Graber, Edith. 1981. "Translator's Introduction to Max Weber's Essay on Some Categories of Interpretive Sociology." *Sociological Quarterly* 22 (Spring):1145–50.

Graf, Friedrich Wilhelm. 1987. "Friendship between Experts: Notes on Weber and Troeltsch." Pp. 215–33 in Wolfgang Mommsen and Jürgen Osterhammel (eds.), *Max Weber and His Contemporaries*. London: Unwin.

———. 1993. "The German Theological Sources and Protestant Church Politics." Pp. 27–49 in Hartmut Lehmann and Guenther Roth (eds.), *Weber's Protestant Ethic*. Cambridge, UK: Cambridge University Press.

Green, Martin. 1974. *The von Richthofen Sisters: The Triumphant and the Tragic Modes of Love*. New York: Basic Books.

Green, Robert (ed.). 1973. *The Weber Thesis Controversy*. 2nd ed. Lexington, MA: D. C. Heath.

Greyerz, Kaspar von. 1993. "Biographical Evidence on Predestination, Covenant, and Special Providence." Pp. 273–84 in Hartmut Lehmann and Guenther Roth (eds.), *Weber's Protestant Ethic*. Cambridge, UK: Cambridge University Press.

Grossein, Jean-Pierre. 1996. "Présentation." Pp. 51–129 in Max Weber, *Sociologie des Religions*. Paris: Gallimard.

———. 2003. "Présentation." Pp. vii–lviii in Max Weber, *L'éthique protestante et l'esprit du capitalisme*. Paris: Gallimard.

Grusky, David (ed.). 2001. *Social Stratification: Class, Race, and Gender in Sociological Perspective*. 2nd ed. Boulder, CO: Westview.

Habermas, Jürgen. 1972. "Comment on Talcott Parsons, 'Value-freedom and Objectivity'." Pp. 59–66 in Otto Stammer (ed.), *Max Weber and Sociology Today*. New York: Harper.

———. 1975. "Max Weber's Concept of Legitimation." Pp. 97–102 in *Legitimation Crisis*. Boston: Beacon Press.

———. 1984. *The Theory of Communicative Action*. Cambridge: Polity Press.

Hamilton, Gary, and Cheng-Shu Kao. 1987. "Max Weber and the Analysis of East Asian Industrialization." *International Sociology* 2, 3:289–300.

Hamilton, Richard. 1996. *The Social Misconstruction of Reality*. New Haven, CT.: Yale University Press.

Hanke, Edith. 1999. "Max Weber, Leo Tolstoy and the Mountain of Truth." Pp. 144–61 in Sam Whimster (ed.), *Max Weber and the Culture of Anarchy*. London: Macmillan.

———. 2001. "Erlösungsreligionen." Pp. 209–26 in Hans Kippenberg and Martin Riesebrodt (eds.), *Max Webers "Religionssystematik."* Tübingen: J. C. B. Mohr.

Hanke, Edith, and Wolfgang Mommsen (eds.). 2001. *Max Weber. Herrschaftssoziologie*. Tübingen: J. C. B. Mohr.

Hanyu, Tatsuru. 1994. "Max Webers Quellenbehandlung in der 'Protestantischen Ethik': Der 'Berufs'-Begriff." *Archives Européennes de Sociologie* 35

1:72–103.

Hartmann, Tyrell. 2001. "Antagonismus der Werte." Pp. 315–34 in Hans Kippenberg and Martin Riesebrodt (eds.), *Max Webers "Religionssystematik."* Tübingen: J. C. B. Mohr.

Heesterman, Jan. 1984. "Kaste und Karma: Max Webers Analyse der indischen Sozialstruktur." Pp. 72–86 in Wolfgang Schluchter, *Max Webers Studie über Hinduismus und Buddhismus: Interpretation und Kritik*. Frankfurt am Main: Suhrkamp.

Hennis, Wilhelm. 1987. "A Science of Man: Max Weber and the Political Economy of the German Historical School." Pp. 25–58 in Wolfgang Mommsen and Jürgen Osterhammel (eds.), *Max Weber and His Contemporaries*. London: Unwin.

———. 1988a. *Max Weber: Essays in Reconstruction*. Trans. Keith Tribe. London: Allen & Unwin.

———. 1988b. "Max Weber's 'Central Question'." Pp. 21–62 in *Max Weber: Essays in Reconstruction*. London: Allen & Unwin.

———. 1988c. "Max Weber's Theme: 'Personality and Life-Orders'." Pp. 62–104 in *Max Weber: Essays in Reconstruction*. London: Allen & Unwin.

———. 1994. "The Meaning of '*Wertfreiheit*': On the Background of Max Weber's 'Postulate'." *Sociological Theory* 12, 2:113–25.

———. 2000a. *Max Weber's Science of Man*. Trans. Keith Tribe. Newbury, UK: Threshold Press.

———. 2000b. "The Pitiless 'Sobriety of Judgment': Max Weber between Carl Menger and Gustav von Schmoller. The Academic Politics of Value Freedom." Pp. 105–38 in *Max Weber's Science of Man*. Newbury, UK: Threshold Press.

———. 2000c. "Max Weber as Teacher." Pp. 85–104 in *Max Weber's Science of Man*. Newbury, UK: Threshold Press.

Henrich, Dieter. 1952. *Die Einheit der Wissenschaftslehre Max Webers*. Tübingen: J. C. B. Mohr.

———. 1987. "Karl Jaspers: Thinking with Weber in Mind." Pp. 528–44 in Wolfgang Mommsen and Jürgen Osterhammel (eds.), *Max Weber and His Contemporaries*. London: Unwin.

Heymann, Ernst. 1931. "Goldschmidt, Levin (1829–1997)." Pp. 694–95 in Vol. 6 of Edwin R. A. Seligman and Alvin Johnson (eds.), *Encyclopaedia of the Social Sciences*. New York: Macmillan.

Hintze, Otto. [1926] 1964. "Max Webers Soziologie." Pp. 135–47 in *Soziologie und Geschichte*. Göttingen: Vandenhoeck & Ruprecht.

Hirschhorn, Monique. 1988. *Max Weber et la sociologie française*. Paris: Editions L'Harmattan.

Hollerbach, Alexander. 1968. "Jellinek, Georg." Pp. 252–54 in Vol. 8 of David Sills (ed.), *International Encyclopaedia of the Social Sciences*. London and New York: Macmillan and The Free Press.

Holton, Robert, and Bryan Turner. 1989. *Max Weber on Economy and Society*. New York: Routledge.

Honigsheim Paul. [1946–63] 2000. *The Unknown Max Weber*. Ed. Alan Sica.

New Brunswick, NJ: Transaction Publishers.

———. 1948. "Max Weber as Applied Anthropologist." *Applied Anthropology* 7:27–35.

———. 1968. *On Max Weber*. New York: Free Press.

Howe, Richard Herbert. 1978. "Max Weber's Elective Affinities: Sociology within the Bounds of Pure Reason." *American Journal of Sociology* 84:366–85.

Hübinger, Gangolf. 2001. "Intellektuelle, Intellektualismus." Pp. 297–313 in Hans Kippenberg and Martin Riesebrodt (eds.), *Max Webers "Religionssystematik."* Tübingen: J. C. B. Mohr.

Huff, Toby, and Wolfgang Schluchter (eds.). 1999. *Max Weber and Islam*. New Brunswick, NJ: Transaction Press.

Hunt, Alan. 1978. "Max Weber's Sociology of Law." Pp. 93–133 in *The Sociological Movement in Law*. London: Macmillan.

Jackson, Maurice. 1983. "An Analysis of Max Weber's Theory of Ethnicity." *Humboldt Journal of Social Relations* 10, 1:4–18.

Jacobsen, Björne. 2001. "Hiatus Irrationalis—Der Bruch zwischen Sein und Sollen." Pp. 31–50 in Hans Kippenberg and Martin Riesebrodt (eds.), *Max Webers "Religionssystematik."* Tübingen: J. C. B. Mohr.

Jagd, Søren. 2002. "Max Weber's Last Theory of the Modern Business Enterprise." *Max Weber Studies* 2, 2:211–38.

Jaspers, Karl. 1989. *On Max Weber*. New York: Paragon House.

Jellinek, Georg. [1895] 1901. *The Declaration of the Rights of Man and of Citizens: A Contribution to Modern Constitutional History*. New York: Holt.

John, Michael. 1985. "The Politics of Legal Unity in Germany, 1870–1896." *Historical Journal* 28, 2:341–55.

Johnson, Benton. 1957. "A Critical Appraisal of the Church-Sect Typology." *American Sociological Review* 22:88–92.

Kaelber, Lutz. 1998. *Schools of Asceticism: Ideology and Organization in Medieval Religious Communities*. University Park: Pennsylvania State University Press.

———. 2004. "Max Weber on Ususry and Medieval Capitalism," *Max Weber Studies* 4, 1:51–75.

Kalberg, Stephen. 1979. "The Search for Thematic Orientations in a Fragmented Oeuvre: The Discussion of Max Weber in Recent German Sociological Literature." *Sociology* 13:127–39.

———. 1980. "Max Weber's Types of Rationality: Cornerstones for the Analysis of Rationalization Processes in History." *American Journal of Sociology* 85:1145–79.

———. 1985. "The Role of Ideal Interests in Max Weber's Comparative Historical Sociology." Pp. 46–67 in Robert Antonio and Ronald Glassman (eds.), *A Weber-Marx Dialogue*. Lawrence: University Press of Kansas.

———. 1994a. "Max Weber's Analysis of the Rise of Monotheism." *British Journal of Sociology* 45:563–83.

———. 1994b. *Max Weber's Comparative Historical Sociology*. Chicago: Uni versity of Chicago Press.

———. 1996. "On the Neglect of Weber's *Protestant Ethic* as a Theoretical Treatise: Demarcating the Parameters of Postwar American Sociological Theory." *Sociological Theory* 14, 1:49–70.

———. 1998. "Tocqueville and Weber on the Sociological Origins of Citizenship: The Political Culture of American Democracy." Pp. 93–112 in Ralph Schroeder (ed.), *Max Weber, Democracy and Modernization*. London: Macmillan.

———. 1999. "Max Weber's Critique of Recent Comparative-Historical Sociology and a Reconstruction of His Analysis of the Rise of Confucianism in China." *Current Perspectives in Social Theory* 19:207–46.

———. 2001a. "Should the 'Dynamic Autonomy' of Ideas Matter to Sociologists?" *Journal of Classical Sociology* 1, 3:291–328.

———. 2001b. "The *Spirit of Capitalism* Revisited: On the New Translation of Weber's *Protestant Ethic* (1920)." *Max Weber Studies* 2, 1:41–58.

———. 2002. "Glossary." Pp. lxxvii–lxxxi in Max Weber, *The Protestant Ethic and the Spirit of Capitalism*, trans. Stephen Kalberg. Los Angeles, CA: Roxbury.

———. Forthcoming. *Max Weber's Sociology of Civilizations*.

Käsler, Dirk. 1984. *Die frühe deutsche Soziologie 1909 bis 1934 und ihre Entstehungs-Milieus: Eine wissenschaftssoziologische Untersuchung*. Opladen: Westdeutscher Verlag.

———. 1988. *Max Weber: An Introduction to His Life and Work*. Trans. Philippa Hurd. Cambridge, UK: Polity Press.

———. 1989. "Der retuschierte Klassiker: Zum gegenwärtigen Forschungsstand der Biographie Max Webers." Pp. 29–54 in Johannes Weiss (ed.), *Max Weber Heute*. Frankfurt am Main: Suhrkamp.

Kaye, Howard. 1992. "Rationalization as Sublimation: On the Cultural Analyses of Weber and Freud." *Theory, Culture & Society* 9:45–74.

Kellenbenz, H. 1965. "Wirtschaftsstufen." Pp. 260–69 in Vol. 12 of *Handwörterbuch der Sozialwissenschaften*. Stuttgart: G. Fischer.

Kim, Sung Ho. 2002. "Max Weber and Civil Society: An Introduction to Max Weber on Voluntary Associational Life." *Max Weber Studies* 2, 2:186–98.

Kippenberg, Hans. 2001a. "Meine Religionssystematik." Pp. 13–30 in Hans Kippenberg and Martin Riesebrodt (eds.), *Max Webers "Religionssystematik."* Tübingen: J. C. B. Mohr.

———. 2001b. "Religionsentwicklung." Pp. 77–100 in Hans Kippenberg and Martin Riesebrodt (eds.), *Max Webers "Religionssystematik."* Tübingen: J. C. B. Mohr.

Kippenberg, Hans, and Martin Riesebrodt (eds.). 2001. *Max Webers "Religionssystematik."* Tübingen: J. C. B. Mohr.

Kiser, Edgar, and Michael Hechter. 1998. "The Debate on Historical Sociology: Rational Choice Theory and Its Critics." *American Journal of Sociology* 104 (1998):785–816.

Kivisto, Peter, and William Swatos. 1988. *Max Weber: A Bio-Bibliography*. New

York: Greenwood Press.

Kocka, Jürgen. 1980. "The Rise of the Modern Industrial Enterprise in Germany." Pp. 77–116 in Alfred Chandler and Herman Daems (eds.), *Managerial Hierarchies*. Cambridge, MA: Harvard University Press.

———(ed.). 1986. *Max Weber, der Historiker*. Göttingen: Vandenhoeck & Ruprecht.

———. 1987. "Otto Hintze and Max Weber: Attempts at a Comparison." Pp. 284–95 in Wolfgang Mommsen and Jürgen Osterhammel (eds.), *Max Weber and His Contemporaries*. London: Unwin.

Kolko, Gabriel. 1959. "A Critique of Max Weber's Philosophy of History." *Ethics* 70:21–36.

———. 1961. "Max Weber on America: Theory and Evidence." *History and Theory* 1:243–60.

Krech, Volkhard. 2001a. "Mystik." Pp. 241–62 in Hans Kippenberg and Martin Riesebrodt (eds.), *Max Webers "Religionssystematik."* Tübingen: J. C. B. Mohr.

———. 2001b. "Religiosität." Pp. 51–76 in Hans Kippenberg and Martin Riesebrodt (eds.), *Max Webers "Religionssystematik."* Tübingen: J. C. B. Mohr.

Kries, Johannes von. 1888. "Ueber den Begriff der objektiven Möglichkeit und einige Anwendungen desselben." *Vierteljahrsschrift für wissenschaftliche Philosophie* 12, 1, 2, 3.

Kronman, Anthony. 1983. *Max Weber*. Stanford, CA: Stanford University Press.

Krüger, Christa. 2001. *Max und Marianne Weber. Tag- und Nachtansichten einer Ehe*. Munich: Pendo Verlag.

Lachmann, L. M. 1970. *The Legacy of Max Weber: Three Essays*. London: Heinemann.

Lang, Bernhard. 2001. "Prophet, Priester, Virtuose." Pp. 167–92 in Hans Kippenberg and Martin Riesebrodt (eds.), *Max Webers "Religionssystematik."* Tübingen: J. C. B. Mohr.

Lascoumes, Pierre (ed.). 1995. *Actualité de Max Weber pour la sociologie du droit*. Paris: Librairie Générale de Droit et de Jurisprudence.

Lassman, Peter, and Irving Velody (eds.). 1989. *Max Weber's "Science as a Vocation."* London: Unwin.

Lazarsfeld, Paul, and Anthony Oberschall. 1965. "Max Weber and Empirical Research." *American Sociological Review* 30:185–99.

Lehmann, Hartmut. 1988. "Asketischer Protestantismus und ökonomischer Rationalismus: Die Weber-These nach zwei Generationen." Pp. 529–53 in Wolfgang Schluchter (ed.), *Max Webers Sicht des okzidentalen Christentums. Interpretation und Kritik*. Frankfurt am Main: Suhrkamp.

Lehmann, Hartmut, and Guenther Roth (eds.). 1993. *Weber's Protestant Ethic: Origin, Evidence, Contexts*. Cambridge, UK: Cambridge University Press.

Lengermann, Patricia Madoo, and Jill Niebrugge-Brantley. 1998. *The Woman Founders: Sociology and Social Theory, 1830–1930*. New York: McGraw-Hill.

———. 2003. "Commentary on Craig R. Bermingham's 'Translation with Introduction and Commentary' of Marianne Weber's 'Authority and Autonomy in Marriage'." *Sociological Theory* 21:424–27.

Lepsius, M. Rainer. 2004. "Mina Tobler and Max Weber: Passion Confined." *Max Weber Studies* 4, 1:9–21.

Lestition, Steven. 2000. "Historical Preface to Max Weber, 'Stock and Commodity Exchanges'." *Theory and Society* 29:289–304.

Lichtblau, Klaus. 2001. "Ressentiment, negative Priviligierung, Parias." Pp. 279–96 in Hans Kippenberg and Martin Riesebrodt (eds.), *Max Webers "Religionssystematik."* Tübingen: J. C. B. Mohr.

Lindenfeld, David. 1997. *The Practical Imagination: The German Sciences of State in the Nineteenth Century.* Chicago: University of Chicago Press.

Lindenlaub, Dieter. 1967. *Richtungskämpfe im Verein für Sozialpolitik.* Wiesbaden: Steiner Verlag.

Lindholm, Charles. 1990. *Charisma.* Cambridge, UK: Basil Blackwell.

Lipset, Seymour Martin. 1992. "The Work Ethic, Then and Now." *Journal of Labor Research* 18, 1 (Winter):45–54.

———. 1963. *The First New Nation: The United States in Historical and Comparative Perspective.* New York: Basic Books.

Lipset, Seymour Martin, and Reinhard Bendix. 1959. *Social Mobility in Industrial Society.* Berkeley: University of California Press.

Little, David. 1974. "Max Weber and the Comparative Study of Religious Ethics." *Journal of Religious Ethics* 2:5–40.

Loader, Colin, and Jeffrey Alexander. 1985. "Max Weber, 'Churches and Sects in North America': An Alternative Path to Rationalization." *Sociological Theory* 3, 1:1–6.

Lounsbury, Michael, and Ed Carberry. 2004. "From King to Court Jester: Weber's Fall from Grace in Organizational Theory." Working Paper, Center for the Study of Economy and Society, Cornell University, Ithaca, NY.

Love, John. 1991. *Antiquity and Capitalism: Max Weber and the Sociological Foundations of Roman Civilization.* London: Routledge.

———. 1993. "Developmentalism in Max Weber's Sociology of Religion: A Critique of F. H. Tenbruck." *Archives Européennes de Sociologie* 34, 2:339–63.

———. 2000. "Max Weber's *Ancient Judaism.*" Pp. 200–20 in Stephen Turner (ed.), *The Cambridge Companion to Weber.* Cambridge, UK: Cambridge University Press.

Löwith, Karl. [1932] 1982. *Max Weber and Karl Marx.* London: George Allen & Unwin.

Lowy, Michael. 1996. "Figures of Weberian Marxism." *Theory and Society* 25:431–46.

Lukács, Georg. 1981. *The Destruction of Reason.* Atlantic Highlands, NJ: Humanities Press.

Lüthy, Herbert. 1968. "Once Again: Calvinism and Capitalism." Pp. 87–108 in S. N. Eisenstadt (ed.), *The Protestant Ethic and Modernization: A Comparative Approach.* New York: Basic Books.

Maine, Henry Sumner. [1861] 2001. *Ancient Law.* New Brunswick, NJ: Transaction Publishers.

Manza, Jeff. 1992. "Classes, Status Groups, and Social Closure: A Critique of

Neo-Weberian Social Theory." *Current Perspectives in Social Theory* 12:275–302.

MacKinnon, Malcolm. 1989. "Calvinism and the Infallible Assurance of Grace" *British Journal of Sociology* 39:143–210.

Manasse, Ernst Moritz. 1947. "Max Weber on Race." *Social Research* 14:191–221.

Mannheim, Karl. 1940. *Man and Society in an Age of Reconstruction*. London: Routledge & Kegan Paul.

Marcuse, Herbert. 1972. "Industrialization and Capitalism." Pp. 133–51 in Otto Stammer (ed.), *Max Weber and Sociology Today*. New York: Harper. See also the discussion of Marcuse's article by Bendix and others on pp. 152–86.

Marshall, Gordon. 1982. *In Search of the Spirit of Capitalism: An Essay on Max Weber's Protestant Ethic Thesis*. London: Hutchinson.

Martel, Gordon. 1992. *Modern Germany Reconsidered, 1870–1945*. London: Routledge.

Martin, John Levi. 2003. "What Is Field Theory?" *American Journal of Sociology* 109:1–49.

Martindale, Don. 1958. "Prefatory Remarks: The Theory of the City." Pp. 9–67 in Max Weber, *The City*. Trans. and ed. Don Martindale and Gertrud Neuwirth. New York: Free Press.

———. 1960. *The Nature and Types of Sociological Theory*. Boston: Houghton Mifflin.

Martindale, Don, and Johannes Reidel. 1963. "Max Weber's Sociology of Music." Pp. 365–93 in Don Martindale, *Community, Character, and Civilization*. New York: Free Press.

Max Weber Gesamtausgabe (Max Weber's *Collected Works*). 1984–Tübingen: J. C. B. Mohr.

Merleau-Ponty, Maurice. 1973. *Adventures of the Dialectic*. Evanston, IL: Northwestern University Press.

Merton, Robert K. [1938] 1970. *Science, Technology and Society in Seventeenth-Century England*. New York: Harper & Row.

———. 1968. *Social Theory and Social Structure*. Enlarged ed. New York: Free Press.

———. 1973. *The Sociology of Science: Theoretical and Empirical Investigations*. Ed. Norman Storer. Chicago: University of Chicago Press.

———. 1995. "Opportunity Structure." Pp. 3–78 in Freda Adler and William Laufer (eds.), *The Legacy of Anomie Theory*. New Brunswick, NJ: Transaction Publishers.

———. 1996. *On Social Structure and Science*. Ed. Piotr Sztompka. Chicago: University of Chicago Press.

Meyer, Marshall. 1990. "The Weberian Tradition in Organizational Studies." Pp. 191–215 in Craig Calhoun et al. (eds.), *Structures of Power and Constraint*. Cambridge, UK: Cambridge University Press.

Mitzman, Arthur. 1985. *The Iron Cage: An Historical Interpretation of Max Weber*. New Brunswick, NJ: Transaction Books.

———. 1987. "Personal Conflict and Ideological Options in Sombart and Weber." Pp. 99–105 in Wolfgang Mommsen and Jürgen Osterhammel (eds.), *Max Weber and His Contemporaries*. London: Unwin.

Momigliano, Arnaldo. 1977. "The Instruments of Decline." *Times Literary Supplement* 3917 (April 8):435–36.

———. 1980. "A Note on Max Weber's Definition of Judaism as a Pariah-Religion." *History and Theory* 19:313–18.

Mommsen, Wolfgang. 1965. "Max Weber's Political Sociology and His Philosophy of World History." *International Social Science Journal* 17:23–45.

———. 1971. "Die Vereinigten Staaten von Amerika im politischen Denken Max Webers." *Historische Zeitschrift* 213:358–81.

———. 1974. *The Age of Bureaucracy: Perspectives on the Political Sociology of Max Weber*. New York: Harper & Row.

———. 1980. *Theories of Imperialism*. New York: Random House.

———. 1984. *Max Weber and German Politics 1890–1920*. Chicago: University of Chicago Press.

———. 1986 "Max Webers Begriff der Universalgeschichte." Pp. 51–72 in Jürgen Kocka (ed.), *Max Weber, der Historiker*. Göttingen: Vandenhoeck & Ruprecht.

———. 1987. "Robert Michels and Weber: Moral Conviction versus the Politics of Responsibility." Pp. 121–38 in Wolfgang Mommsen and Jürgen Osterhammel (eds.), *Max Weber and His Contemporaries*. London: Unwin.

———. 1989. *The Political and Social Theory of Max Weber*. Cambridge, UK: Polity Press.

———. 1996. "Die Siebecks und Max Weber." *Geschichte und Gesellschaft* 22:19–30.

———. 1997. "Max Weber and the Regeneration of Russia." *Journal of Modern History* 69:1–17.

———. 2000. "Max Weber's 'Grand Sociology': The Origins and Composition of *Wirtschaft und Gesellschaft: Soziologie*." *History and Theory* 39:364–83.

Mommsen, Wolfgang, and Jürgen Osterhammel (eds.). 1987. *Max Weber and His Contemporaries*. London: Unwin.

Morgan, Lewis Henry. [1877] 2000. *Ancient Society*. New Brunswick, NJ: Transaction Publishers.

Munch, Peter. 1975. "'Sense' and 'Intention' in Max Weber's Theory of Social Action." *Sociological Inquiry* 45:59–65.

Munters, Q. J. 1972. "Max Weber as Rural Sociologist." *Sociologia Ruralis* 12, 2:129–76.

Murphy, Raymond. 1988. *Social Closure: The Theory of Monopolization and Exclusion*. Oxford: Clarendon Press.

Murvar, Vatro. 1967. "Max Weber's Concept of Hierocracy: A Study in the Typology of Church-State Relationships." *Sociological Analysis* 28, 2:69–84.

Muse, Kenneth. 1981. "Edmund Husserl's Impact on Max Weber." *Sociological Inquiry* 51, 2:99–104.

Nafassi, Mohammad. 2000. "On the Foundations of Athenian Democracy: Marx's Paradox and Weber's Solution." *Max Weber Studies* 1, 1:56–83.

Nau, Heino (ed.). 1996. *Der Werturteilsstreit: Die Äusserungen zur Werturteils-diskussion im Ausschuss des Vereins für Sozialpolitik (1913)*. Marburg: Metropolis-Verlag.

———. 1997. *Eine "Wissenschaft von Menschen": Max Weber und die Begründung der Sozialökonomik in der deutschsprachigen Ökonomie*. Berlin: Duncker & Humblot.

———. Forthcoming. *Max Weber als Ökonom*.

Nelson, Benjamin. 1974. "Max Weber's 'Author's Introduction' (1920): A Master Clue to His Main Aims." *Sociological Inquiry* 44, 4:269–78.

———. 1976. "On Orient and Occident in Max Weber." *Social Research* 43:114–29,

Nippel, Wilfried. 2000. "From Agrarian History to Cross-Cultural Comparisons: Weber on Greco-Roman Antiquity." Pp. 240–55 in Stephen Turner (ed.), *The Cambridge Companion to Weber*. Cambridge, UK: Cambridge University Press.

Norkus, Zenonas. 2000. "Max Weber's Interpretive Sociology and Rational Choice Approach." *Rationality and Society* 12:259–82.

———. 2001. *Max Weber und Rational Choice*. Marburg: Metropolis-Verlag.

———. 2002. *Max Weber and Rational Choice*. Vilnius: Institute of Social Research.

Oakes, Guy. 1977. "The *Verstehen* Thesis and the Foundations of Max Weber's Methodology." *History and Theory* 16, 1:11–29.

———. 1987. "Weber and the Southwest German School: The Genesis of the Concept of the Historical Individual." Pp. 434–46 in Wolfgang Mommsen and Jürgen Osterhammel (eds.), *Max Weber and His Contemporaries*. London: Unwin Hyman.

———. 1988. *Weber and Rickert: Concept Formation in the Cultural Sciences*. Cambridge, MA: MIT Press.

———. 1997. "Guenther Roth and Weberian Studies in America." *International Journal of Politics, Culture and Sociology* 11, 1:175–79.

———. 1999. "Gerth, Mills, and Shils: The Origin of *From Max Weber*." *International Journal of Politics, Culture and Sociology* 12, 3:399–433.

Oberschall, Anthony. 1965. *Empirical Social Research in Germany 1848–1914*. The Hague: Mouton.

Ollig, Hans-Ludwig. 1998. "Neo-Kantianism." Pp. 776–92 in Vol. 6 of Edward Craig (ed.), *Routledge Encyclopaedia of Philosophy*. London: Routledge.

Orihara, Hiroshi. 1999. "Max Webers Beitrag zum 'Grundriss der Sozialökonomik'. Das Vorkriegsmanuskript als ein integriertes Ganzes." *Kölner Zeitschrift für Soziologie und Sozialpsychologie* 51, 4:724–34.

———. 2002. "From 'a Torso with a Wrong Head' to 'Five Disjointed Pieces of Carcass'?: Problems of the Editorial Policies for the *Max Weber Gesamtausgabe* I/22 (Old Manuscript Known as 'Part II' of the *Economy and Society*)." Working Paper Series, Sugiyama Jogakuen University, Aichi-ken, Japan. See also the similar Orihara 2003.

———. 2003. "From 'a Torso with a Wrong Head' to 'Five Disjointed Body-Parts without a Head': A Critique of the Editorial Policy for *Max Weber*

Gesamtausgabe I/22." *Max Weber Studies* 3, 2:133–68. See also the similar Orihara 2002.

Osterhammel, Jürgen. 1987. "Varieties of Social Economics: Joseph A. Schumpeter and Max Weber." Pp. 106–20 in Wolfgang Mommsen and Jürgen Osterhammel (eds.), *Max Weber and His Contemporaries*. London: Unwin.

Palonen, Kari. 2001. "Was Max Weber a 'Nationalist'? A Study in the Rhetoric of Conceptual Change." *Max Weber Studies* 1, 2:196–214.

Parkin, Frank. 1979. *Marxism and Class Theory: A Bourgeois Critique*. London: Tavistock.

——. 1982. *Max Weber*. London: Routledge.

Parsons, Talcott. 1937. *The Structure of Social Action*. New York: McGraw-Hill.

——. 1963. "Introduction." Pp. xix–lxvii in Max Weber, *The Sociology of Religion*. Boston: Beacon Press.

——. 1971. "Value-freedom and Objectivity." Pp. 27–50 in Otto Stammer (ed.), *Max Weber and Sociology Today*. New York: Harper Torchback. See also the discussion of Parsons' paper by Max Horkheimer and others on pp. 51–82.

——. 1975. "On 'De-Parsonizing Weber'." *American Sociological Review* 40:666–70.

Peillon, Michel. 1990. *The Concept of Interest in Social Theory*. Lewiston, NY: Edwin Mellen Press.

Perrow, Charles. 1986. *Complex Organizations: A Critical Essay*. 3rd ed. New York: Random House.

Pipes, Richard. 1955. "Max Weber and Russia." *World Politics* 7:371–401.

Poggi, Gianfranco. 1983. *Calvinism and the Capitalist Spirit: Max Weber's Protestant Ethic*. Amherst, MA: University of Massachusetts Press.

——. 1986. "Max Weber: A Monumental Edition in the Making." *British Journal of Sociology* 37, 2:297–303.

——. 1988. "Max Weber's Conceptual Portrait of Feudalism." *British Journal of Sociology* 39:211–27.

Posner, Richard. 1998. "Weber, Max (1864–1920)." Pp. 684–86 in Vol. 3 of Peter Newman (ed.), *The New Palgrave Dictionary of Economics and the Law*. London: Macmillan.

Prospektus der Max Weber Gesamtausgabe. 1981. Tübingen: J. C. B. Mohr.

Raphaël, Freddy. 1973. "Max Weber and Ancient Judaism." *Leo Baeck Institute Year Book* 18:41–62.

Rathenow, Hans-Inge. 1976. *Die 'Deutsche Gesellschaft für Soziologie' 1900– 1933: Dokumentationsanalytische und wissenschaftsgeschichtliche Studie*. Ph.D. diss. Akademie der Wissenschaften der DDR, Berlin.

Raum, Johannes. 1995. "Reflections on Max Weber's Thoughts Concerning Ethnic Groups." *Zeitschrift für Ethnologie* 120:73–87.

Richter, Melvin. 1995. *The History of Political and Social Concepts: A Critical Introduction*. New York: Oxford University Press.

Rickert, Heinrich. [1902] 1986. *The Limits of Concept Formation in Natural Science: A Logical Introduction to the Historical Sciences*. Trans. Guy Oakes. Cambridge, UK: Cambridge University Press.

Riesebrodt, Martin. 1980. "Ideen, Interessen, Rationalisierung: Kritische Anmerkungen zu F. H. Tenbrucks Interpretation des Werkes Max Webers." *Kölner Zeitschrift für Soziologie und Sozialpsychologie* 32:111–29.

———. 1989. "From Patriarchalism to Capitalism: The Theoretical Context of Max Weber's Agrarian Studies (1892–3)." Pp. 131–57 in Keith Tribe (ed.), *Reading Weber*. London: Routledge.

———. 2001a. "Charisma." Pp. 151–66 in Hans Kippenberg and Martin Riesebrodt (eds.), *Max Webers "Religionssystematik."* Tübingen: J. C. B. Mohr.

———. 2001b. "Ethische und exemplarische Prophetie." Pp. 193–208 in Hans Kippenberg and Martin Riesebrodt (eds.), *Max Webers "Religionssystematik."* Tübingen: J. C. B. Mohr.

———. 2001c "Religiöse Vergemeinschaftungen." Pp. 101–18 in Hans Kippenberg and Martin Riesebrodt (eds.), *Max Webers "Religionssystematik."* Tübingen: J. C. B. Mohr.

Riis, Ole. 2004. "Verdensreligionernes erhvervsethik" [The Economic Ethics of the World Religions]. Conference on Max Weber, Copenhagen, March 22–23.

Ringer, Fritz. 1969. *The Decline of the German Mandarins: The German Academic Community, 1890–1933*. Cambridge, MA: Harvard University Press.

———. 1997. *Max Weber's Methodology: The Unification of the Cultural and the Social Sciences*. Cambridge, MA: Harvard University Press.

Robertson, H. M. 1935. *Aspects of the Rise of Economic Individualism: A Criticism of Max Weber and His School*. Cambridge, UK: Cambridge University Press.

Roth, Guenther. 1968. "Personal Rulership, Patrimonialism and Empire-Building in the New States." *World Politics* 20:194–206.

———. 1975. "Socio-Historical Model and Developmental Theory: Charismatic Community, Charisma of Reason and the Counterculture." *American Sociological Review* 40:148–57.

———. 1976. "History and Sociology in the Work of Max Weber." *British Journal of Sociology* 27, 3:306–18.

———. 1985. "Marx and Weber on the United States—Today." Pp. 215–33 in Robert Antonio and Ronald Glassman (eds.), *A Weber-Marx Dialogue*. Lawrence: University Press of Kansas.

———. 1988. "Introduction to the New Edition." Pp. xv–lx in Marianne Weber, *Max Weber: A Biography*. Brunswick, NJ: Transaction Books.

———. 1989. "Weber's Political Failure" (Review of Max Weber, *Zur Neuordnung Deutschlands*, MWG I/16). *Telos* 78:136–49.

———. 1992. "Interpreting and Translating Max Weber." *International Sociology* 7, 4:449–59.

———. 1993a. "Between Cosmopolitanism and Ethnocentrism: Max Weber in the Nineties." *Telos* 96:148–62.

———. 1993b. "Weber the Would-Be Englishman: Anglophilia and Family History." Pp. 83–121 in Hartmut Lehmann and Guenther Roth (eds.), *Weber's Protestant Ethic*, Cambridge, UK: Cambridge University Press.

———. 1996. "The Complete Edition of Weber's Work: An Update." *Contemporary Sociology* 25, 4:464–67.

———. 1997. "The Young Max Weber: Anglo-American Religious Influences and Protestant Social Reform in Germany." *International Journal of Politics, Culture and Sociology* 10:659–71.

———. 1999. "Max Weber at Home and in Japan: On the Troubled Genesis and Successful Reception of His Work." *International Journal of Politics, Culture and Sociology.* 12:515–25.

———. 2000. "Global Capitalism and Multi-Ethnicity: Max Weber Then and Now." Pp. 117–39 in Stephen Turner (ed.), *The Cambridge Companion to Weber.* Cambridge: Cambridge University Press.

———. 2001. *Max Webers deutsch-englische Familiengeschichte 1800–1950.* Tübingen: J. C. B. Mohr.

———. 2002a. "Max Weber: Family History, Economic Policy, Exchange Reform." *International Journal of Politics, Culture and Sociology* 15:509–20.

———. 2002b. "Max Weber's Views on Jewish Integration and Zionism: Some American, English and German Contexts." *Max Weber Studies* 3, 1:56–73.

Roth, Guenther, and Wolfgang Schluchter. 1979. *Max Weber's Vision of History, Ethics and Methods.* Berkeley: University of California Press.

Runciman, W. G. 2001. "Was Max Weber a Selectionist despite Himself?" *Journal of Classical Sociology* 1, 1:13–32.

Sacks, Harvey. 1999. "Max Weber's *Ancient Judaism*." *Theory, Culture & Society* 16, 1:31–9.

Sadri, Ahmad. 1992. *Max Weber's Sociology of Intellectuals.* New York: Oxford University Press.

Salomon, Albert. 1945. "German Sociology." Pp. 586–614 in Georges Gurvitch and Wilbert E. Moore (eds.), *Twentieth Century Sociology.* New York: Philosophical Library.

Samuelson, Kurt. 1961. *Religion and Economic Action.* London: Heinemann.

Sanderson, Stephen. 1988. "The Neo-Weberian Revolution: A Theoretical Balance Sheet." *Sociological Forum* 3, 2:307–14.

Scaff, Lawrence. 1973. "Max Weber's Politics and Political Education." *American Political Science* 57:128–41.

———. 1989a. *Fleeing the Iron Cage: Culture, Politics, and Modernity in the Thought of Max Weber.* Berkeley: University of California Press.

———. 1989b. "Weber before Weberian Sociology." Pp. 15–41 in Keith Tribe (ed.), *Reading Weber.* London: Routledge.

———. 1991. "Culture and Significance: Toward a Weberian Cultural Science." *Current Perspectives in Social Theory* 11:97–116.

———. 1994. "Max Webers Begriff der Kultur." Pp. 678–99 in Gerhard Wagner and Heinz Zipprian (eds.), *Max Webers Wissenschaftslehre.* Frankfurt am Main: Suhrkamp.

———. 1998. "The 'Cool Objectivity of Sociation': Max Weber and Marianne Weber in America." *History of the Human Sciences* 11, 2:61–82.

———. 2000. "Rationalization and Culture." Pp. 42–58 in Stephen Turner (ed.), *The Cambridge Companion to Weber.* Cambridge, UK: Cambridge University Press.

Schefold, Bertram. 1987a. "Brentano, Lujo (Ludwig Josef) (1844–1931)." Pp. 275–76 in Vol. 1 of John Eatwell et al. (eds.), *The New Palgrave: A Dictionary*

of Economics. London: Macmillan.

———. 1987b. "Knies, Karl Gustav Adolf (1821–1898)." P. 55 in Vol. 3 of John Eatwell et al. (eds.), *The New Palgrave: A Dictionary of Economics*. London: Macmillan.

———. 1987c. "Roscher, Wilhelm Georg Friedrich (1817–1894)." P. 221 in Vol. 4 of John Eatwell et al. (eds.), *The New Palgrave: A Dictionary of Economics*. London: Macmillan.

———. 1987d. "Sombart, Werner (1863–1941)." Pp. 422–23 in Vol. 4 of John Eatwell et al. (eds.), *The New Palgrave: A Dictionary of Economics*. London: Macmillan.

Schelting, Alexander von. 1934. *Max Webers Wissenschaftslehre*. Tübingen: J. C. B. Mohr.

Schluchter, Wolfgang (ed.). 1981a. *Max Webers Studie über das antike Judentum: Interpretation und Kritik*. Frankfurt am Main: Suhrkamp.

———. 1981b. *The Rise of Western Rationalism: Max Weber's Developmental History*. Berkeley: University of California Press.

——— (ed.). 1983. *Max Webers Studie über Konfuzianismus und Taoismus: Interpretation und Kritik*. Frankfurt am Main: Suhrkamp.

——— (ed.). 1984. *Max Webers Studie über Hinduismus und Buddhismus: Interpretation und Kritik*. Frankfurt am Main: Suhrkamp.

——— (ed.). 1985. *Max Webers Sicht des antiken Christentums: Interpretation und Kritik*. Frankfurt am Main: Suhrkamp.

——— (ed.). 1987. *Max Webers Sicht des Islams: Interpretation und Kritik*. Frankfurt am Main: Suhrkamp.

——— (ed.). 1988. *Max Webers Sicht des okzidentalen Christentums: Interpretation und Kritik*. Frankfurt am Main: Suhrkamp.

———. 1989. *Rationalism, Religion, and Domination: A Weberian Perspective*. Trans. Neil Salomon. Berkeley: University of California Press.

———. 1994. "Max und Alfred Weber—zwei ungleiche Brüder." *Ruperto-Carola (Ruprecht-Karls-Universität Heidelberg)* 46:29–35.

———. 1996. *Paradoxes of Modernity: Culture and Conduct in the Theory of Max Weber*. Stanford, CA: Stanford University Press.

———. 2000a. "Handlungs-und Strukturtheorie nach Max Weber." *Berliner Journal für Soziologie* 10:125–36.

———. 2000b. "Psychophysics and Culture." Pp. 59–80 in Stephen Turner (ed.), *The Cambridge Companion to Weber*. Cambridge, UK: Cambridge University Press.

———. 2002. "The Sociology of Law as an Empirical Theory of Society." *Journal of Classical Sociology* 2, 3:257–80.

Schmidt, Gert. 1976. "Max Weber and Modern Industrial Sociology: A Comment on Some Recent Anglo-Saxon Interpretations." *Social Analysis and Theory* 6:47–73.

Schön, Manfred. 1987. "Gustav Schmoller and Max Weber." Pp. 59–70 in Wolfgang Mommsen and Jürgen Osterhammel (eds.), *Max Weber and His Contemporaries*. London: Unwin.

Schroeder, Ralph. 1987. "Nietzsche and Weber: Two 'Prophets' of the Modern

World." Pp. 207–21 in Sam Whimster and Scott Lash (eds.), *Max Weber, Rationality and Modernity*. London: Allen & Unwin.

———. 1991. "'Personality' and 'Inner Distance': The Conception of the Individual in Max Weber's Sociology." *History of the Human Sciences* 4, 1:61–78.

———. 1992. *Max Weber and the Sociology of Culture*. London: SAGE.

———. 1995. "Disenchantment and Its Discontents: Weberian Perspectives on Science and Technology." *Sociological Review* 43:227–50.

———. 1998a. "From Weber's Political Sociology to Contemporary Liberal Democracy." Pp. 79–92 in Ralph Schroeder (ed.), *Max Weber, Democracy and Modernization*. London: Macmillan.

——— (ed.). 1998b. *Max Weber, Democracy and Modernization*. London: Macmillan.

———. 2003. Communication with the author.

Schroeder, Ralph, and Richard Swedberg. 2002. "Weberian Perspectives on Science, Technology and the Economy." *British Journal of Sociology* 53:383–401.

Schön, Manfred. 1987. "Gustav Schmoller and Max Weber." Pp. 59–70 in Wolfgang Mommsen and Jürgen Osterhammel (eds.), *Max Weber and His Contemporaries*. London: Unwin.

Schumpeter, Joseph. 1942. *Capitalism, Socialism, and Democracy*. New York: Harper.

———. 1954. *History of Economic Analysis*. London: George Allen & Unwin.

Schutz, Alfred. [1932] 1967. *The Phenomenology of the Social World*. Evanston, IL: Northwestern University Press.

Schwentker, Wolfgang. 1998. *Max Weber in Japan: Eine Untersuchung zur Wirkungsgeschichte 1905–1995*. Tübingen: J. C. B. Mohr.

Scott, Richard. 1996. "The Mandate Is Still Being Honored: In Defense of Weber's Disciples." *Administrative Science Quarterly* 41:163–71.

———. 2002. *Organizations: Rational, Natural, and Open Systems*. 5th ed. Englewood Cliffs, NJ: Prentice Hall.

Seyfarth, Constans, and Gert Schmidt. 1977. *Max-Weber Bibliographie: Eine Dokumentation der Sekundärliteratur*. Stuttgart: Enke.

Shils, Edward. 1965. "Charisma, Order and Status." *American Sociological Review* 30:199–213.

Sica, Alan. 1992. *Weber, Irrationality and Social Order*. Berkeley: University of California Press.

———. 2001. "Weberian Theory Today." Pp. 487–507 in Jonathan Turner (ed.), *Handbook of Sociological Theory*. New York: Kluwer.

———. 2004. *Max Weber: A Comprehensive Bibliography*. New Brunswick, NJ: Transaction Publishers.

Skalweit, August. 1933. "Meitzen, August (1822–1910)" P. 302 in Vol. 9 of Edwin R. A Seligman and Alvin Johnson (eds.), *Encyclopaedia of the Social Sciences*. New York: Macmillan.

Sombart, Werner. 1902. *Der moderne Kapitalismus*. Leipzig: Duncker & Humblot.

———. [1911] 1913. *The Jews and Modern Capitalism*. New York: Burt Franklin.

Stammer, Otto (ed.). 1971. *Max Weber and Sociology Today*. New York: Harper Torchback.

Stark, Werner. 1968. "The Place of Catholicism in Max Weber's Sociology of Religion." *Sociological Analysis* 29:202–10.

Steiner, Philippe. 1992. "*L'Année Sociologique* et la reception de l'oeuvre de Max Weber." *Archives Européennes de Sociologie* 33:329–49.

Steininger, Rudolf. 1980. "Max Webers Parteienkonzept und die Parteienforschung." *Kölner Zeitschrift für Soziologie und Sozialpsychologie* 32:54–75.

Stern, Robert, and Stephen Barley. 1996. "Organizations and Social Systems: Organization Theory's Neglected Mandate." *Administrative Science Quarterly* 41:146–62.

Stinchcombe, Arthur. 1986. "Max Weber's *Economy and Society*." Pp. 282–89 in *Stratification and Organization*. Cambridge, UK: Cambridge University Press.

Strauss, Leo. 1953. *Natural Right and History*. Chicago: University of Chicago Press.

Strong, Tracy. 1987. "Weber and Freud." Pp. 468–82 in Wolfgang Mommsen and Jürgen Osterhammel (eds.), *Max Weber and His Contemporaries*. London: Unwin.

Swatos, William. 1976. "Weber or Troeltsch? Methodology, Syndrome, and Development of Church-Sect Theory." *Journal for the Scientific Study of Religion* 15:129–44.

Swedberg, Richard. 1991. *Joseph A. Schumpeter: His Life and Work*. Princeton, NJ: Princeton University Press.

———. 1998. *Max Weber and the Idea of Economic Sociology*. Princeton: Princeton University Press.

———. 2000. "Afterword: The Role of Markets in Max Weber's Work." *Theory and Society* 29:373–84.

———. 2002. "The Economic Sociology of Capitalism: Weber and Schumpeter." *Journal of Classical Sociology* 2:227–55.

———. 2003a. "The Changing Picture of Max Weber." *Annual Review of Sociology* 29:283–306.

———. 2003b. *Principles of Economic Sociology*. Princeton, NJ: Princeton University Press.

Szacki, Jerzy. 1982. "Max Weber in Polish Sociology." *Polish Sociological Bulletin* 1–4:25–31.

Tawney, R. H. [1926] 1954. *Religion and the Rise of Capitalism*. New York: New American Library.

Tenbruck, Friedrich. 1974. "Max Weber and the Sociology of Science: A Case Reopened." *Zeitschrift für Soziologie* 3, 3:312–21.

———. 1980. "The Problem of Thematic Unity in the Works of Max Weber." *British Journal of Sociology* 31:316–51.

———. 1987. "Max Weber and Eduard Meyer." Pp. 234–67 in Wolfgang Mommsen and Jürgen Osterhammel (eds.), *Max Weber and His Contempo-*

raries. London: Unwin.

Theiner, Peter. 1987. "Friedrich Naumann and Max Weber: Aspects of a Political Partnership." Pp. 299–310 in Wolfgang Mommsen and Jürgen Osterhammel (eds.), *Max Weber and His Contemporaries*. London: Unwin.

Tiryakian, Edward. 1966. "A Problem for the Sociology of Knowledge: The Mutual Unawareness of Emile Durkheim and Max Weber." *Archives Européennes de Sociologie* 7:330–36.

Tribe, Keith. 1989a. "Prussian Agriculture—German Politics: Max Weber 1892–7." Pp. 85–130 in Keith Tribe (ed.), *Reading Weber*. London: Routledge.

——— (ed.). 1989b. *Reading Weber*. London: Routledge.

———. 1995. *Strategies of Economic Order: German Economic Discourse, 1750–1950*. Cambridge: Cambridge University Press.

———. 2000. "Translator's Appendix." Pp. 205–16 in Wilhelm Hennis, *Max Weber's Science of Man*. Newbury, UK: Threshold Press.

Tribe, Keith. 2004. "Transformation and Translation: Max Weber in English." Unpublished paper, Maison des Sciences de l'Homme, Paris.

Troeltsch, Ernst. 1912. *Protestantism and Progress: A Historical Study of the Relation of Protestantism to the Modern World*. London: Williams and Norgate.

———. 1960. *The Social Teachings of the Christian Churches*. 2 vols. New York: Harper & Brothers.

Trubek, David. 1972 "Max Weber on Law and the Rise of Capitalism." *Wisconsin Law Review* 1972:720–53.

Turley, Alan. 2001. "Max Weber and the Sociology of Music." *Sociological Forum* 16, 4:633–53.

Turner, Bryan. 1974a. "Islam, Capitalism and the Weber Thesis." *British Journal of Sociology* 25, 2:230–43.

———. 1974b. *Weber and Islam*. London: Routledge & Kegan Paul.

———. 1981. *For Weber: Essays on the Sociology of Fate*. London: Routledge.

———. 1992. *Max Weber: From History to Modernity*. London: Routledge.

Turner, Charles. 1999. "Weber and Dostoyevsky on Church, Sect and Democracy." Pp. 162–75 in Sam Whimster (ed.), *Max Weber and the Culture of Anarchy*. London: Macmillan Press.

———. 2001. "Weberian Social Thought, History of." Pp. 16407–12 in Vol. 24 of Neil Smelser and Paul Baltes (eds.), *International Encyclopaedia of the Social and Behavioral Sciences*. Amsterdam: Elsevier.

Turner, Stephen. 1983. "Weber on Action." *American Sociological Review* 48:506–19.

——— (ed.). 2000. *The Cambridge Companion to Weber*. Cambridge, UK: Cambridge University Press.

———. 2003. E-mail to Richard Swedberg on Weber's theory of causality.

Turner, Stephen, and Regis Factor. 1981. "Objective Possibility and Adequate Causation in Weber's Methodological Writings." *Sociological Review* 29:5–29.

———. 1994. *Max Weber: The Lawyer as Social Thinker*. London: Routledge.

Udehn, Lars. 2001. *Methodological Individualism: Background, History and Meaning*. London: Routledge.

Van Der Sprenkel, Otto. 1964. "Max Weber on China." *History and Theory* 3, 3:348–70.

Verein für Sozialpolitik. 1911. *Schriften des Vereins für Sozialpolitik*. Vol. 138. Berlin: Duncker & Humblot.

Wagner, Gerhard, and Heinz Zipprian (eds.). 1994. *Max Webers Wissenschaftslehre*. Frankfurt am Main: Suhrkamp.

Wagner, Helmut. 1983. *Alfred Schutz: An Intellectual Biography*. Chicago: University of Chicago Press.

Walliman, Isidor, Howard Rosenbaum, Nicholas Tatsis, and George Zito. 1980. "Misreading Weber: 'The Concept of *Macht*'." *Sociology* 14:261–75.

Walzer, Michael. 1964. "Puritanism as a Revolutionary Ideology." *History and Theory* 3:62–90.

———. 1966. *The Revolution of the Saints: A Study in the Origins of Radical Politics*. London: Weidenfeld and Nicolson.

———. 1983. *Spheres of Justice*. New York: Basic Books.

Waters, Malcolm. 1989. "Collegiality, Bureaucratization, and Professionalization: A Weberian Analysis." *American Journal of Sociology* 94:945–72.

Weber, Marianne. [1926] 1975. *Max Weber: A Biography*. Trans. Harry Zohn. New York: Wiley.

Weber, Max. [1889] 1988. "Zur Geschichte der Handelsgesellschaften im Mittelalter." Pp. 312–443 in *Gesammelte Aufsätze zur Sozial-und Wirtschaftsgeschichte*. Tübingen: J. C. B. Mohr.

———. [1889] 2003. *The History of Commercial Partnerships in the Middle Ages*. Trans. Lutz Kaelber. New York: Rowman & Littlefield.

———. [1891] 1986. *Die römische Agrargeschichte in ihrer Bedeutung für das Staatsrecht und Privatrecht. Max Weber Gesamtausgabe I/2*. Tübingen: J. C. B. Mohr.

———. [1892] 1984. *Die Lage der Landarbeiter im ostelbischen Deutschland. 1892. Max Weber Gesamtausgabe I/3*. 2 vols. Tübingen: J. C. B. Mohr.

———. [1892] 1993. "Zur Rechtfertigung Paul Göhres." Pp. 108–19 in Vol. 1 of *Landarbeiterfrage, Nationalstaat und Volkswirtschaftspolitik: Schriften und Reden 1892–1899. Max Weber Gesamtausgabe I/4*. Tübingen: J. C. B. Mohr.

———. [1892–99] 1993. *Landarbeiterfrage, Nationalstaat und Volkswirtschaftspolitik. Max Weber Gesamtausgabe I/4*. 2 vols. Tübingen: J. C. B. Mohr.

———. [1894] 1989. "Developmental Tendencies in the Situation of East Elbian Rural Labourers." Trans. Keith Tribe. Pp. 158–87 in Keith Tribe (ed.), *Reading Weber*. London: Routledge.

———. [1894, 1896] 2000. "Stock and Commodity Exchanges [*Die Börse* (1894)], Commerce on the Stock and Commodity Exchanges [*Die Börsenverkehr*]." Trans. Steven Lestition. *Theory and Society* 29:305–38, 339–71.

———. [1895] 1980. "The National State and Economic Policy (Inaugural Lecture)." Pp. 1–28 in *Political Writings*. Trans. Peter Lassman and Ronald Speirs. Cambridge, UK: Cambridge University Press.

———. [1895] 1985. "'Roman' and 'Germanic' Law." Trans. Piers Beirne. *International Journal of the Sociology of Law* 13, 3:237–46.

————. [1896] 1999. "The Social Causes of the Decay of Ancient Civilization." Trans. Christian Mackauer. Pp. 138–53 in Max Weber (ed. Richard Swedberg), *Essays in Economic Sociology*. Princeton, NJ: Princeton University Press.

————. 1897. "Agrarverhältnisse im Altertum." Pp. 1–18 in 2nd supplementary vol. of J. Conrad et al. (eds.), *Handwörterbuch der Staatswissenschaften*. Jena: Gustav Fischer.

————. 1898. "Agrarverhältnisse im Altertum." Pp. 57–85 in Vol. 1 of J. Conrad et al. (eds.), *Handwörterbuch der Staatswissenschaften*. 2nd ed. Jena: Gustav Fischer.

————. [1898] 1990. *Grundriss zu den Vorlesungen über Allgemeine ("theoretische") Nationalökonomie*. Tübingen: J. C. B. Mohr.

————. [1903–6] 1975. *Roscher and Knies: The Logical Problems of Historical Economics*. Trans. Guy Oakes. New York: Free Press.

————. [1904–5] 1930. *The Protestant Ethic and the Spirit of Capitalism*. Trans. Talcott Parsons. London: G. Allen & Unwin. This is a translation of the 2nd ed. of 1920.

————. [1904–5] 1993. *Die protestantische Ethik und der "Geist" des Kapitalismus*. Bodenheim: Neue Wissenschaftliche Bibliothek Athenäum. This work is based on the 1904–5 edition but also indicates what changes were made in the second edition of 1920.

————. [1904–5] 2002a. *The Protestant Ethic and the "Spirit" of Capitalism and Other Writings*. Trans. Peter Baehr and Gordon Wells. London: Penguin Books. This is a translation of the first edition of 1904–5.

————. [1904–5] 2002b. *The Protestant Ethic and the Spirit of Capitalism*. Trans. Stephen Kalberg. Los Angeles, CA: Roxbury Publishing Company. This is a translation of the second edition of 1920.

————. 1906a. "'Kirchen' und 'Sekten'." *Frankfurter Zeitung* 102 (April 13).

————. 1906b. "'Kirchen' und 'Sekten' in Nordamerika: Eine kirchen-und sozialpolitische Skizze." *Die Christliche Welt* 20, 24:558–62; 20, 25:577–83.

————. [1906b] 1985. "'Churches' and 'Sects' in North America: An Ecclesiastical and Socio-Political Sketch." Trans. Colin Loader. *Sociological Theory* 3:1–13.

————. [1906b] 2002. "'Churches' and 'Sects' in North America: An Ecclesiastical and Sociopolitical Sketch." Pp. 203–20 in Max Weber, *The Protestant Ethic and the Spirit of Capitalism*, trans. Peter Baehr and Gordon Wells. London: Penguin Books.

————. [1907] 1977. *Critique of Stammler*. Trans. Guy Oakes. New York: Free Press.

————. [1908] 1980. "A Research Strategy for the Study of Occupational Careers and Mobility Patterns: Methodological Introduction for the Survey of the Society for Social Action Concerning Selection and Adaptation (Choice and Course of Occupation) for the Workers of Major Industrial Enterprises (1908)." Trans. D. Hÿtch. Pp. 103–55 in Max Weber (ed. J. E. T. Eldridge), *The Interpretation of Social Reality*. New York: Schocken.

————. [1908] 1999. "Marginal Utility Analysis and 'The Fundamental Law of

Psychophysics'." Trans. Louis Schneider. Pp. 249–60 in Max Weber (ed. Richard Swedberg), *Essays in Economic Sociology*. Princeton, NJ: Princeton University Press.

———. [1908–9] 1988. "Zur Psychophysik der industriellen Arbeit." Pp. 61–255 in *Gesammelte Aufsätze zur Soziologie und Sozialpolitik*. Tübingen: J. C. B. Mohr.

———. 1909. Review of Franz Eulenberg, *Die Entwicklung der Universität Leipzig in den letzten hundert Jahren*. *Archiv für Sozialforschung und Sozialpolitik* 29:672–75.

———. [1909] 1976. *The Agrarian Sociology of Ancient Civilizations*. Trans. R. I. Frank. London: New Left Books.

———. [1909] 1984. "'Energetic' Theories of Culture." Trans. Jon Mark Mikkelsen. *Mid-American Review of Sociology* 9, 2:27–58.

———. [1910] 1971. "Max Weber on Race and Society." Trans. Jerome Gittleman. *Social Research* 38, 1:30–41. See Weber 1973a for "Max Weber on Race and Society, II."

———. [1910] 1973. "Max Weber on Church, Sect, and Mysticism." Trans. Jerome Gittleman. *Sociological Analysis* 34:140–49.

———. [1910] 1998. "Preliminary Report on a Proposed Survey for a Sociology of the Press." Trans. Keith Tribe. *History of the Human Sciences* 11, 2:111–20.

———. [1910] 2002. "Voluntary Associational Life (*Vereinswesen*)." Trans. Sung Ho Kim. *Max Weber Studies* 2, 2:199–209.

———. [1913] 1996. "Die Äusserungen zur Werturteilsdiskussion im Ausschuss des Vereins für Sozialpolitik (1913): Max Weber." Pp. 147–86 in Heino Nau (ed.), *Der Werturteilsstreit*. Marburg: Metropolis-Verlag.

———. [1913] 1981. "Some Categories of Interpretive Sociology." *Sociological Quarterly* 22 (Spring):151–80. Trans. Edith Graber. See also Graber 1981. For a translation of some of the key passages in this article by Guenther Roth and Claus Wittich, see also Weber [1922] 1978:1375–80.

———. [1915] 1946a. "Religious Rejections of the World and Their Directions." Trans. Hans Gerth and C. Wright Mills. Pp. 323–59 in Max Weber (eds. Hans Gerth and C. Wright Mills), *From Max Weber*. New York: Oxford University Press.

———. [1915] 1946b. "The Social Psychology of the World Religions." Trans. Hans Gerth and C. Wright Mills. Pp. 267–301 in Max Weber (eds. Hans Gerth and C. Wright Mills), *From Max Weber*. New York: Oxford University Press.

———. [1916] 1994b. "Between Two Laws." Trans. Peter Lassman and Ronald Speirs. Pp. 75–79 in Max Weber (eds. Peter Lassmann and Ronald Speirs), *Political Writings*. Cambridge, UK: Cambridge University Press.

———. 1917. "Ein Vortrag Max Webers über die Probleme der Staatssoziologie [25. Oktober 25, Wien]." *Neue Freie Presse* (Vienna), No. 19102, October 26:10.

———. [1917] 1949. "The Meaning of 'Ethical Neutrality' in Sociology and Economics." Trans. Edward A. Shils and Henry A. Finch. Pp. 1–47 in Max Weber (eds. Edward A. Shils and Henry A. Finch), *Essays in The Methodology of the Social Sciences*. New York: The Free Press.

———. [1918] 1994. "Socialism." Trans. Peter Lassman and Ronald Speirs. Pp. 272–303 in Max Weber (eds. Peter Lassman and Ronald Speirs), *Political Writings*. Cambridge, UK: Cambridge University Press.

———. [1919] 1946. "Science as a Vocation." Trans. Hans Gerth and C. Wright Mills. Pp. 129–56 in Max Weber (eds. Hans Gerth and C. Wright Mills), *From Max Weber*. New York: Oxford University Press.

———. [1919] 1994. "The Profession and Vocation of Politics." Trans. Peter Lassman and Ronald Speirs. Pp. 309–69 in Max Weber (eds. Peter Lassmann and Ronald Speirs), *Political Writings*. Cambridge, UK: Cambridge University Press.

———. [1920] 1946a. "Author's Introduction." Trans. Talcott Parsons. Pp. 13–31 in *The Protestant Ethic and the Spirit of Capitalism*. New York: Scribner.

———. [1920] 1946b. "The Protestant Sects and the Spirit of Capitalism." Trans. Hans Gerth and C. Wright Mills. Pp. 302–22 in Max Weber (eds. Hans Gerth and C. Wright Mills), *From Max Weber*. New York: Oxford University Press.

———. [1920] 1951. *The Religion of China: Confucianism and Taoism*. Trans. Hans Gerth. New York: Free Press.

———. [1920–21] 1988. *Gesammelte Aufätze zur Religionssoziologie*. 3 vols. Tübingen: J. C. B. Mohr.

———. 1921. *Gesammelte Politische Schriften*. Ed. Marianne Weber. Tübingen: J. C. B. Mohr.

———. [1921] 1952. *Ancient Judaism*. Trans. Hans H. Gerth and Don Martindale. New York: Free Press.

———. [1921] 1958a. *The City*. Trans. Don Martindale and Gertrud Neuwirth. Glencoe, IL: Free Press.

———. [1921] 1958b. *The Religion of India*. Trans. Hans Gerth and Don Martindale New York: Free Press.

———. [1922] 1972. *Wirtschaft und Gesellschaft. Grundriss der verstehenden Soziologie*. Ed. Johannes Winkelmann. 5th ed. Tübingen: J. C. B. Mohr.

———. [1922] 1978. *Economy and Society: An Outline of Interpretive Sociology*. Trans. Ephraim Fischoff et al. 2 vols. Berkeley: University of California Press.

———. [1922] 1988. *Gesammelte Aufsätze zur Wissenschaftslehre*. Ed. Marianne Weber. Tübingen: J. C. B. Mohr.

———. [1922] 1999. "The Three Types of Legitimate Domination." Trans. Hans Gerth. Pp. 99–108 in Max Weber (ed. Richard Swedberg), *Essays in Economic Sociology*. Princeton, NJ: Princeton University Press.

———. 1923. *Wirtschaftsgeschichte*. Munich: Duncker & Humblot.

———. [1923] 1981. *General Economic History*. Trans. Frank Knight. New Brunswick, NJ: Transaction Books.

———. [1924] 1988a. *Gesammelte Aufsätze zur Sozial-und Wirtschaftsgeschichte*. Ed. Marianne Weber. Tübingen: J. C. B. Mohr.

————. [1924] 1988b. *Gesammelte Aufsätze zur Soziologie und Sozialpolitik.* Ed. Marianne Weber. Tübingen: J. C. B. Mohr.

————. 1927. *General Economic History.* Trans. Frank Knight. New York: Greenberg.

————. 1936. *Jugendbriefe.* Ed. Marianne Weber. Tübingen: J. C. B. Mohr.

————. 1946. *From Max Weber.* Ed. and trans. Hans Gerth and C. Wright Mills. New York: Oxford University Press.

————. 1947. *The Theory of Social and Economic Organization.* Trans. A. M. Henderson and Talcott Parsons. New York: Oxford University Press.

————. 1949. *Methodology of the Social Sciences.* Ed. and trans. Edward A. Shils and Henry A. Finch. New York: Free Press.

————. 1954. *On Law in Economy and Society.* Ed. Max Rheinstein, trans. Edward Shils and Max Rheinstein. Cambridge, MA: Harvard University Press.

————. 1958. *The Rational and Social Foundations of Music.* Ed. and trans. Don Martindale, Johannes Riedel, and Gertrude Neuwirth. Carbondale, IL: Southern Illinois University Press.

————. 1963. *The Sociology of Religion.* Trans. Ephraim Fischoff. Boston, MA: Beacon Press.

————. 1966. *Staatssoziologie.* Ed. Johannes Winkelmann. 2nd ed. Berlin: Duncker & Humblot.

————. 1972. "Georg Simmel as Sociologist." Trans. Donald Levine. *Social Research* 39:155–63.

————. 1973a. "Max Weber, Dr. Alfred Ploetz, and W. E. B. Du Bois: Max Weber on Race and Society, II." Trans. Jerome Gittleman. *Sociological Analysis* 34, 4:308–12. See Weber [1910] 1971 for Part I of "Max Weber on Race and Society."

————. 1973b. *Soziologie, Universalgeschichtliche Analysen, Politik.* Ed. Johannes Winkelmann. Stuttgart: Alfred Kröner Verlag.

————. 1974. *On Universities: The Power of the State and the Dignity of the Academic Calling in Imperial Germany.* Trans. Edward Shils. Chicago: University of Chicago Press.

————. 1978. *Selections in Translation.* Ed. W. G. Runciman, trans. Eric Matthews. Cambridge, UK: Cambridge University Press.

————. 1984. *Zur Politik im Weltkrieg: Schriften und Reden 1914–1918. Max Weber Gesamtausgabe I/15.* Tübingen: J. C. B. Mohr.

————. 1988a. *Gesammelte Politische Schriften.* Ed. Johannes Winkelmann. 5th ed. Tübingen: J. C. B. Mohr.

————. 1988b. *Zur Neuordnung Deutschlands: Schriften und Reden 1918–1920. Max Weber Gesamtausgabe I/16.* Tübingen: J. C. B. Mohr.

————. 1989. "Science as a Vocation." Trans. Michael John. Pp. 3–31 in Peter Lassman and Irving Velody (eds.), *Max Weber's "Science as a Vocation."* London: Unwin.

————. 1990. *Briefe 1906–1908. Max Weber Gesamtausgabe II/5.* Tübingen: J. C. B. Mohr.

————. 1994a. *Briefe 1909–1910. Max Weber Gesamtausgabe II/6.* Tübingen: J. C. B. Mohr.

————. 1994b. *Political Writings*. Ed. and trans. Peter Lassman and Ronald Speirs. Cambridge, UK: Cambridge University Press.

————. 1995a. *The Russian Revolutions*. Trans. Gordon Wells and Peter Baehr. London: Polity Press.

————. 1995b. *Zur Psychophysik der industriellen Arbeit. Weber Gesamtausgabe I/11*. Tübingen: J. C. B. Mohr.

————. 1996. *Die Wirtschaftsethik der Weltreligionen: Hinduismus und Buddhismus. Max Weber Gesamtausgabe I/20*. Tübingen: J. C. B. Mohr.

————. 1999a. *Börsenwesen: Schriften und Reden 1893–1898. Max Weber Gesamtausgabe I/5*. 2 vols. Tübingen: J. C. B. Mohr.

————. 1999b. *Max Weber im Kontext: Gesammelte Schriften, Aufsätze und Vorträge*. CD-ROM. Berlin: Karsten Worm, InsoSoftWare.

————. 1999c. *Essays in Economic Sociology*. Ed. Richard Swedberg ed. Princeton, NJ: Princeton University Press.

————. 1999d. *Wirtschaft und Gesellschaft, Teilband 5: Die Stadt. Max Weber Gesamtausgabe I/22–5*. Tübingen: J. C. B. Mohr.

————. 2001a. *Wirtschaft und Gesellschaft, Teilband 1: Gemeinschaften. Max Weber Gesamtausgabe I/22–1*. Tübingen: J. C. B. Mohr.

————. 2001b. *Wirtschaft und Gesellschaft, Teilband 2: Religiöse Gemeinschaften. Max Weber Gesamtausgabe I/22–2*. Tübingen: J. C. B. Mohr.

———— 2004. *The Essential Weber: A Reader*. Ed. Sam Whimster. London: Routledge.

Wehler, Hans-Ulrich. 1985. *The German Empire, 1871–1918*. Dover, NH: Berg Publishers.

Weiss, Johannes. 1981. *Weber and the Marxist World*. London: Routledge & Kegan Paul.

Wells, Gordon. 2001. "Issues of Language and Translation in Max Weber's Protestant Ethic Writings." *Max Weber Studies* 2, 1:33–40.

Wenger, Morton, 1980. "The Transmutation of Weber's *Stand* in American Sociology and Its Social Roots." *Current Perspectives in Social Theory* 1:357–78.

Weyhe, Lothar. 1996. *Levin Goldschmidt: Ein Gelehrterleben in Deutschland*. Berlin: Duncker und Humblot.

Whimster, Sam. 1995. "Max Weber on the Erotic and Some Comparisons with the Work of Foucault." *International Sociology* 10, 4:447–62.

———— (ed.). 1999. *Max Weber and the Culture of Anarchy*. London: Macmillan.

————. 2002. "Notes and Queries: Translator's Note on Weber's 'Introduction to the Economic Ethics of the World Religions'." *Max Weber Studies* 3, 1:74–98.

Willey, Thomas. 1978. *Back to Kant: The Revival of Kantianism in German Social and Historical Thought, 1860–1914*. Detroit: Wayne State University Press.

Winkelmann, Johannes. 1952. *Max Webers Herrschaftssoziologie*. Tübingen: J. C. B. Mohr.

————. 1976. *Wirtschaft und Gesellschaft: Erläuterungsband*. Tübingen: J. C. B. Mohr.

———— (ed.). 1978. *Die Protestantische Ethik II: Kritiken und Antikritiken*. Gütersloh: Gütersloher Verlagshaus Gerd Mohn.

————. 1980. "Die Herkunft von Max Webers 'Entzauberungs'-Konzeption." *Kölner Zeitschrift für Soziologie und Sozialpsychologie* 32:12–53.

————. 1986. *Max Webers hinterlassenes Hauptwerk: Die Wirtschaft und die gesellschaftlichen Ordnungen und Mächte*. Tübingen: J. C. B. Mohr.

Wittfogel, Karl A. 1957. *Oriental Despotism*. New Haven, CT: Yale University Press.

Wright, Eric Olin. 2002. "The Shadow of Exploitation in Weber's Class Analysis." *American Sociological Review* 67 (2002):832–53.

Zabludovsky, Gina. 1989. "The Reception and Utility of Max Weber's Concept of Patrimonialism in Latin America." *International Sociology* 4, 1:51–66.

Zingerle, Arnold. 1981. *Max Webers Historische Soziologie*. Darmstadt: Wissenschaftliche Buchgesellschaft.